FROM SIMON TO]

FROM THE LIBRARY OF

NOREEN BURT.

OCTOBER. 1986.

FROM SIMON TO PETER

J. Glyn Owen

 EVANGELICAL PRESS

EVANGELICAL PRESS
16/18 High Street, Welwyn, Herts, AL6 9EQ, England.

© Evangelical Press 1985

First published 1985

ISBN 0 85234 195 4

Typeset by Inset, Chappel, Essex.
Cover photograph reproduced by kind permission
of Mr Yassimides.
Printed in Great Britain by The Pitman Press, Bath.

Contents

Preface

The substance of this volume was originally delivered in sermon form, and it is inevitable that some traces of that distinctive style will become evident to the reader.

Since the series was not initially planned with a view to publication, the author deeply regrets his inability to make adequate acknowledgements of the innumerable sources to which he is indebted in one way or another. References to quotations were largely discarded before the decision to go into print was made, and it has been impossible to recover them. The fact that the series had actually evolved over a number of years aggravated the problem of recognizing what may have reflected the influence of another, let alone trace it to its source. Regretfully, therefore, a general acknowledgement of indebtedness to authors ancient and contemporary is the most that can be offered, with only a few exceptions.

The author expresses his profound gratitude to those who have been involved with him in transcribing the tape recordings of the original sermons and preparing them for publication. The entire typing and retyping of corrected manuscripts was done by his secretary, Doris Grierson. Joan Eichner and Debbie Bowen rendered invaluable editorial assistance at different stages of the project, the former in the early stages, as well as in reading the final proofs,and the latter in preparing the manuscript for publication. Without their contribution the task would have been impracticable. Also, thanks are due to Reima Robertson for reading through the series before finally submitting the manuscript for publication.

It is the author's ardent prayer that the reader will not only find this record of Simon's life to be spiritually

1

enriching, but that the series will serve to magnify the sovereign and sufficient grace of God in Jesus Christ. The grace that transformed Simon into Peter is more than adequate for any contemporary wanderer who, hearing the call of the living Christ, turns from a life of sin to follow in his steps.

Introduction

At their first meeting, our Lord Jesus Christ looked into the eyes of quick, impetuous Simon and said to him, *"You are Simon son of John [or Jona]. You will be called Cephas"* *(which, when translated, is, Peter) (John 1:42).*

This renaming of a man must be understood against its biblical background. In ancient times a person's name signified his whole personality; it embodied his whole being, so to speak. Renaming, therefore, was a very solemn act. When such renaming was done by a man, it betokened his authority over the person renamed (2 Kings 23:34; 24:17). If someone bought a slave, for example, and added him to his household, he might very well want to give him quite a different name. The fact that he could do so meant that he had authority over him.

When such renaming was done by God, however, it did not simply mean that God had authority over the renamed man: he has authority over all of us, for we are in his hands. God's renaming also meant that God intended to transform the renamed man so that he would assume an altogether new character — a character that was in some way symbolized by the new name given him.

Simon, as he first appears before our Lord Jesus Christ, is very much the son of Jona. Jona means 'dove', and there is good reason to believe that our Lord plays upon that meaning.

Jesus is saying to Simon, 'So you are Simon the son of Jona — a young dove, fluttering around from place to place without a clear purpose, flying about in circles, high and low, here and there, at the whim of a fancy? I'll make you a different man. You shall be called Peter, which means "rock".' Jesus is casting his sovereign arm around Simon, claiming him as his own and promising to bring about a total change in him.

That is a wonderful promise. But more wonderful still, as far as we are concerned, is the actual transformation that took place in Simon, making him into Peter, the man of stability and decisiveness, the man of rock, whom we find in the book of Acts and in the two epistles which bear his name. Simon Peter was not only saved by the grace of God but ultimately, to use his fellow apostle's language, he was also 'made holy, useful to the Master and prepared to do any good work' (2 Timothy 2:21), so that, as God would have him labour here or there, the man was ready, and was willing to be made willing if he were not already willing. He became, ultimately, one of the most mature and stable and stalwart souls of the New Testament and apostolic age — Peter, the rock!

I believe that the story of this transformation is one of the great epics of history. It is a remarkable story made all the more remarkable because Simon represents all of us. Impetuous, impulsive, unstable, he is so human and so obviously made of the same stuff as we are that his character symbolizes ours. We all see ourselves in him at some point. For this very reason we cannot help but take courage as we see how the Lord teaches and transforms Simon. We learn what the grace of God can do for us, too.

It is as inspiring as it is revealing, then, to meditate upon the spiritual pilgrimage of Simon the son of Jona, following his many ups and downs until we see him standing transformed before us as Peter, the apostle of solid character and sterling worth, evangelist, pastor and servant of Jesus Christ. I propose to look in some detail at the record of that amazing change — a task which could result in such a transformation to ourselves that the prospect is as exciting as the discipline may prove exacting. Come, then, and behold the Lord at work in the remaking of Simon into Peter. And let us pray that we, too, shall know the same transforming grace.

1.
Preparation by John the Baptizer

John influenced Simon

The divine Potter always prepares his clay with meticulous care. Becoming personally and directly involved in the work that was to change Simon into Peter, Jesus first arranged that Simon should come under the influence of John the Baptizer. God often arranges things this way: when he is about to do something big, he will cause a man to be influenced by someone with a preparatory ministry. We begin our study at this point, namely, with the preparation of Simon by John the Baptizer.

Now there is some legitimate room for doubt as to whether Simon was actually a disciple of John, and so I do not dogmatize here. But whether or not he was directly a disciple, Simon at least must have been acquainted with the message of John the Baptizer. John's ministry had a widespread impact on the nation as a whole. We read that 'all the people of Jerusalem' (Mark 1:5) and 'all Judea and the whole region of the Jordan' (Matthew 3:5) went out after John to be baptized by him. We also read that Andrew, Simon Peter's brother, was a disciple of John the Baptizer (John 1:40). Knowing Andrew, the way he shared things with Peter and the way he ultimately persuaded him to come to the Messiah, we cannot imagine that Simon could have failed to be aware of John's message.

But in all probability Simon actually was a disciple of John the Baptizer. Listen to his words at the time when the eleven remaining disciples of Jesus were seeking a successor to Judas: 'It is necessary to choose one of the men who have been with us the whole time the Lord Jesus went in and out among us, beginning from John's baptism

5

to the time when Jesus was taken up from us. For one of
these must become a witness with us of his resurrection'
(Acts 1:21, 22). That implies that Simon was present on
the occasion of our Lord's baptism by John. Why was he
there? The most natural explanation would be that he was
there, just like his brother, as one of John's followers. Simon
was probably one of the serious young men who had
gathered around to learn from this authentic man of God,
this voice from above, who, in those days when the Word
of the Lord was scarce, knew his God.

In either case, whether directly or indirectly, the ministry
of John had an impact on Simon Peter, preparing the way
for what was to come. But in what sense? How would the
ministry of John prepare Simon to become Peter? What
were the distinctive characteristics of John's ministry?

John insisted on reformation

John's message was 'The kingdom of heaven is near.' The
Old Testament had promised a kingdom that would belong
to the Son of man and would outlast every other kingdom.
John was now saying, 'This kingdom of heaven is coming
now in the person of the King. He brings to this world all
the powers of the next world, and he is at hand!'

That was a startling message, but equally startling was
John's understanding of the nature of the kingdom. Simon
and all others like him versed in the Old Testament were
certainly waiting for the kingdom. But in the absence of an
evidently authentic prophet since Malachi, men had busily
woven their own ideas about what the promised reign of God
would be like. By John's time, such speculation had led the
nation to expect a powerful monarch to appear from the
skies and address himself immediately to the plight of the
Jews under Roman domination. He would lead them into
political liberty and material prosperity. This concept of the
expected kingdom was predominantly nationalistic and
materialistic.

Repentance
John the Baptizer knew differently. In the solitude of the

desert he had learned that God's promised reign would be *spiritual* before all else. Therefore John was not called to involve himself in political manoeuvring. Nor was he called to verse people in the tenets of some philosophical creed. Rather, he was called to summon men to repentance – to a change of mind, of heart and of life. Preparation for citizenship in a moral and spiritual kingdom must be correspondingly moral and spiritual. In preaching repentance, John urged men to make a moral verdict. He urged them to choose to be morally and spiritually different. Repentance would radically change their thinking and their living, their beliefs and their behaviour, he taught. And Simon heard that teaching.

The moral transformation which John sought included the end of national bigotry and of self-righteousness that boasted in mere physical descent. This was one of the damning features of the life of the Jews in our Lord's day and John's words were cutting and daring: 'Produce fruit in keeping with repentance. And do not think you can say to yourselves, "We have Abraham as our father." I tell you that out of these stones God can raise up children for Abraham' (Matthew 3:8, 9).

To the Jew there could be no word more devastating. Merely to be a physical descendant of Abraham does not save a man; in and of itself, it does not entail greatness or goodness; as such, it is no qualification for entrance into God's kingdom. As Jesus later told Nicodemus, a member of the Sanhedrin, a ruler of the Jews, 'I tell you the truth, unless a man is born again, he cannot see the kingdom of God' (John 3:3). No one, not even a child of Abraham, can even *see* the kingdom of God, let alone enter it, without a change of mind and heart, without repentance and renewal.

The fruit of repentance

John taught further that where genuine repentance is present there must be 'fruit in keeping with repentance'. You cannot be a penitent sinner and not show it. It will emerge in your attitude and your actions. Repentance is such a radical change of mind concerning oneself and concerning God and his glory that it compels one to ask, along with the multitudes who asked John the Baptizer: 'How do we express repentance? What should we do?'

John answers: ' "The man with two tunics should share with him who has none, and the one who has food should do the same." Tax collectors also came to be baptized. "Teacher," they asked, "what should we do?" "Don't collect any more than you are required to," he told them. Then some soldiers asked him, "And what should we do?" He replied, "Don't extort money and don't accuse people falsely — be content with your pay" ' (Luke 3:11—14).

In each reply, John speaks of a practical expression of moral and spiritual change. And in each reply he deals with the particular sin of each sector of society that comes to him. People of the first group are materialistic: they love to hoard food and clothing; self is in the centre. Then, says John, the practical token of repentance is to share what you have. This will show that you have turned away from the view that you yourself are the centre of the universe, to accept the view that other people should have a share in God's good things. This is repentance and its practical expression. And so he goes down the list.

The point is, of course, that we all have our own peculiar sin. It may not be quite the same sin or sins with all of us. Our most vulnerable points may vary. But we are all guilty of transgressing God's law and we generally have our own very personal points of weakness. And we must repent. Let none of us feel that the message of repentance is one which applies to everybody but ourselves. In the name of God, don't let yourself be bulldozed by the devil into a corner where you will perish! Repentance is a word for you and for me, for all of us.

John also taught that genuine repentance needs to be expressed symbolically as well as practically. Following the inward confessing and forsaking of sin came an outward symbolic affirmation before men: 'People went out to him from Jerusalem and all Judea and the whole region of the Jordan. Confessing their sins, they were baptized by him in the Jordan river' (Matthew 3:5,6).

What was the significance of John's baptism? Through his preaching the Spirit of God convicted individual hearts of particular, specific sins. What had previously seemed right was now seen as wrong in God's eyes, and therefore evil. This painful realization of offence against God and man cried out for relief, and John's baptism provided this relief. It offered cleansing from sin and freeing from guilt. As each person publicly confessed his sins, he was washed in spirit as he was washed in body. He was freed to live a changed life, freed ultimately to receive the baptism of the Holy Spirit that, as John prophesied, Jesus would later provide. John's baptism symbolized the inner cleansing which resulted from personal acknowledgement of wrongdoing and a change of mind relating to it.

Only on that score, let us note, was John's baptism 'for the forgiveness of sins' (Luke 3:3). Geldenhuys explains: 'This means that [John] called the people to repentance and then baptized those who confessed their sins and gave indications that they desired to live a different and better life, in the assurance that God grants pardon to those who sincerely repent.'[1] It is God who forgives. And when God forgives he forgets. This is another lesson for us to learn, and for us to follow. Some of us have memories that are longer than that of the Almighty! But forgiving and forgetting are basic to Christian fellowship. A man who is truly penitent is so aware of his own sin that he does not dwell upon the iniquities of others. Such was the radical transformation that John required, and it is radical still.

John instructed the Jews

The next main thing to notice is that John's ministry provided authoritative instruction. This has been assumed in what we have already discussed, but it needs to be made explicit here. From the very outset, John announced that God's kingdom was at hand and it was embodied in the person of the King. But what the nation did not know about the King who was coming was that his sovereignty was to be primarily *spiritual.* In what sense? What would his reign entail?

Sacrifice

John stressed that the sovereignty of the King is that of a

lamb rather than that of a lion. It is the sovereignty of a
sacrificial lamb that carries away the curse of sinners, rather
than the sovereignty of a lion that crushes a nation's external
foes. The King deals first and foremost with man's spiritual
slavery and moral tragedy: 'Look, the Lamb of God, who
takes away the sin of the world!' (John 1:29.) For if he could
not do that, there would be very little point in breaking the
dominion of Rome. If the King cannot transform human
nature, there is very little else he can accomplish. The King
is going to deal with basic issues. He is not coming clothed
in the panoply of war, ready to strike at Rome; he is coming
as the Lamb of God. Thus John points his sin-
acknowledging penitents to the sin-bearing Lamb of God,
and bids them see that which barred their access to God
now forever removed. Sin is borne away.

Renewal

John taught further that the sovereignty of the King extends
as surely to the renewal of human nature as to the removal
of sin. The King not only removes the objective condemnation that naturally shuts men out of the kingdom;
he also renews the subjective nature so as to qualify the
penitent for citizenship. John says, 'I baptize you with water.
But one more powerful than I will come, the thongs of
whose sandals I am not worthy to untie. He will baptize
you with the Holy Spirit and with fire' (Luke 3:16).

John knew the limitations of both his own ministry
and the symbol of water. He was only the preparer of the
way, the forerunner of the King, and his task was to prepare
a highway through desert places and over high mountains
on which the King might travel to the distant recesses of his
realm (Isaiah 40). 'But,' says John, 'I want you to know that
I am as conscious of the limitations of my ministry as I am
of the limitations of water. Water can do very little. In and
of itself it is impotent. But, whereas I baptize men with
water, one will come after me who is more powerful than
I, and he will baptize you with the Holy Spirit and with
fire.' The Holy Spirit and fire are not impotent: they change
a person's whole being!

Now the King's baptism is not the mere symbol of
renewal; it is the reality. It does not point to a power beyond

itself; it *is* the power. This is the actual power of God come down among men! The King breaks the grip of death upon the human heart. He changes the man from the inside. He purges him of evil. He regenerates his whole personality. When the Spirit of God comes upon a man he is never the same again! Hence the use of similar language by Luke with reference to the disciples' enduement of power on the Day of Pentecost (cf. Acts 1:5,8). Simon needed to learn this. The kingdom to which he was being called is not a kingdom you enter just because you are a Jew. You must be changed radically in heart to come in. The curse of sin must be removed and inwardly the power of sin must be dealt with in such a way that the man is made anew, transformed, redeemed, regenerated. The King who breaks the bonds of death is also the author of life. John's teaching told Simon that.

Judgement

John's instruction included at least one other vital point concerning the King in whose very person the promised kingdom comes. He who bears away sin and baptizes with the Holy Spirit also burns the chaff with unquenchable fire. This is a solemn note, unpalatable in the twentieth century as it was in the first: 'His winnowing fork is in his hand, and he will clear his threshing floor, gathering wheat into his barn and burning up the chaff with unquenchable fire' (Matthew 3:12).

Yes, Rome does come under his sway. All men and nations do. There is a finality about this King in whose person the kingdom is imminent. He is Lord of all. He is sovereign. He separates the sheep from the goats and the wheat from the chaff. And having gathered the wheat into his barn he will burn the chaff! And Simon heard this. I am not suggesting that he understood everything he heard, but I am suggesting that he must have been challenged and startled by this truly prophetic teaching of John. The Lord arranged it so.

John introduced Jesus

Let us notice that John specifically identified Jesus as the
one in whom all the kingly functions were embodied. Seeing
Jesus, he said to his followers, 'Look, the Lamb of God, who
takes away the sin of the world! This is the one I meant
when I said, "A man who comes after me has surpassed me
because he was before me." I myself did not know him but
the reason I came baptizing with water was that he might
be revealed to Israel . . . I have seen and I testify that this
is the Son of God' (John 1:29—34).

John is saying, in effect, 'The one I have been talking
about, the sin-bearing, Spirit-baptizing, chaff-burning King
has arrived! There he is!' John introduced the King, knowing
that his own day would soon recede into the past, that
Jesus would increasingly assume his appointed role, and that
the beginnings of the new order would soon emerge. Peter
was to become a key member of the church. Meantime,
Simon's preparation for life with Christ took place under
the ministry of John the Baptizer who, as we have seen,
summoned men to a reformation of life, gave them such
information as was needed to act decisively and introduced
to them the one in whom God's kingdom was embodied.
This preparation was arranged by divine appointment.
John's ministry was vital.

And it still is. In applying this, I would offer two
challenges. Firstly, has God sent a John the Baptizer along
your way? He may very well be the person you dislike most,
for he has exposed your weaknesses and sins; he has put his
finger on the raw spot that must be dealt with. But this is
a necessary preparation for the Christian life. There is no
healing until the wound is opened up, and John does that.
Just as the law precedes grace, so John is still the forerunner
of Jesus. John's ministry is absolutely fundamental.

Secondly, we need to understand that the man who
refuses to listen to John will not be able to hear Jesus.
Herod learned that in its literal sense (Luke 23:7—9).
Intrigued by reports about Jesus, Herod wanted him to
dance to his tune and work a miracle to prove who he was.
But Jesus would not speak to Herod. Here was the
opportunity, surely, for the Son of God to avoid his cross;

here was Herod asking for a sign! But Jesus said and did nothing. Have you ever tried to fathom the wonder of Jesus' silence before Herod? There is only one answer. Herod had killed John the Baptizer. And you cannot deal disparagingly with John and expect responsiveness from Jesus; you cannot dishonour John's person and expect Jesus to honour yours.

Jesus brings grace only to the one who has let his heart be furrowed, broken and searched under the ministry of the great forerunner. Those who are prepared humbly to walk in the ways mapped out by John's teaching will experience the glory of their sin taken away, their spirit renewed and their hope revived. When Simon and his friends heeded John's words, they entered on a life-transforming pilgrimage which ultimately brought them to the full knowledge of God's saving grace and eternal life in Jesus Christ his Son. May God lead us in that same pilgrimage!

Reference
1. Norval Geldenhuys, *Commentary on the Gospel of Luke*, (Marshall, Morgan & Scott, London, 1950), p. 136.

2.
The role of Andrew

It is God who makes a saint out of a sinner. The transformation of Simon into Peter is essentially his work. But God, in his infinite condescension, uses feeble, frail human beings to fulfil his purposes of grace. We have seen how he used John the Baptizer as his first instrument to prepare Simon for the great turning-point in his life. Now we come to the complementary ministry of Andrew, Simon's brother. Just as God used the illustrious John, that majestic solemn figure who continued the line of the prophets to its close, so also God uses the apparently less significant Andrew, who soon fades out of the biblical narrative altogether, but not before he has performed such a mighty task in the purpose of God as will make the whole body of God's church in human history indebted to him. Let us turn, then, to Andrew.

'Andrew, Simon Peter's brother, was one of the two who heard what John had said and who had followed Jesus. The first thing Andrew did was to find his brother Simon and tell him, "We have found the Messiah" (that is, the Christ). Then he brought Simon to Jesus' (John 1:40–42).

Andrew sought out his brother, Simon. The value of a brother's intervention in the life of another member of his family depends, of course, upon the quality of their relationship with each other. If it is no more than a blood relationship and not a personal one, then perhaps a brother should be silent about his faith. And this is very sad. If, however, the relationship is what it ought to be and there is a heart-to-heart brotherliness and real comradeship, if the brothers are brothers in deed and not simply in name, then a brother has a key that no one else really has — a key to the heart, mind, conscience and soul of his brother.

This immediately raises a most challenging issue, before we really get into our study: it is the issue of our relationship as Christian people with other members of our families who are as yet outside of Christ. This is a tender point in many of our lives. And there are difficulties and problems; God knows the difficulties and problems. But it is crucially important that on your part and mine the door should be kept open. If God shuts it, all right. If my brother or my sister shuts it, let me try to open it again. But it should not be shut *by me!* It is part of God's plan that where we are in our particular circumstances in life, we should be able to speak to those who are receptive. Is this true of us, or do we ourselves come between our words and our brothers and sisters in the home? Our oddities, our selfishness, our pride, our unfriendliness and much else — let us be honest before God — can so close the door between us and those who live with us that what we say conveys nothing of God at all, that though we come out from the presence of the living Lord and eagerly speak of him, our families will not listen. On the other hand, where we have earned their confidence, we have a key to their hearts.

We owe more than we realize to the fact that Andrew was so close to Simon as to gain his ear. I am personally very much impressed by Andrew's acceptability with Simon at this point, and this is the reason. Having delved for some time into the record of Simon Peter's life, I am convinced that he was not altogether the easiest person to live with, especially in his early days. Quick-tempered, impulsive, impetuous, arrogant at times, Simon must repeatedly have acted and spoken out of turn. In fact, apart from God's grace, one could well imagine a great rift developing between him and Andrew. Deep alienation could have resulted from Simon's being so difficult.

But Andrew seems to have taken in his stride all the outbursts and hurts, becoming as emotionally steady as Simon was volatile. He seems never to have retaliated so as to close the door between himself and Simon or to lose Simon's affection and confidence. In fact, Andrew emerged from

the difficult school of the home (which is *the* important
school of sanctification, isn't it?) with particularly great
skill in human relations. It was he, for instance, who later
(John 6:9) managed to strike up conversation with a lone
boy in a crowd of many thousands, and even to discover
what he had in his lunch pack! Those five small loaves and
two fish turned out to be objects of the Lord's greatest
blessing that day. You see, in the school where he had
such a tumultuous brother, Andrew learned how to be
gracious and amiable and approachable. He learned how
to act and react constructively.

And so, coming back to the issue of our relationship as
Christian people with members of our families who are as
yet outside of Christ, are we like Andrew, accepting and
acceptable, and thereby potentially helpful in bringing our
brothers to Christ? Or do we hinder them? Where we are
conscious of fault and know ourselves to hinder others, we
need to repent before God, seeking his forgiveness and the
grace to be different, so that we may be enabled to say at
least something meaningful and acceptable about him whom
we know as our Saviour. Not that all men will believe even
then, but the door will not have been closed by us.

Now let us come to the heart of our study, looking first
at the record itself, then at the divine strategy revealed in it.

Two 'findings'

*'The next day John was there again with two of
his disciples. When he saw Jesus passing by, he said,
"Look, the Lamb of God!" When the two disciples
heard him say this, they followed Jesus. Turning
around, Jesus saw them following and asked,
"What do you want?" They said, "Rabbi" (which
means Teacher), "where are you staying?"
"Come," he replied, "and you will see." So they
went and saw where he was staying, and spent that
day with him. It was about the tenth hour.
Andrew, Simon Peter's brother, was one of the
two who heard what John had said and who had
followed Jesus. The first thing Andrew did was*

> to find his brother Simon and tell him, "We have
> found the Messiah" (that is, the Christ). Then he
> brought Simon to Jesus' (John 1:35–42).

This record really centres round the two occurrences of
the verb 'find'. There are two 'findings' here: Andrew's
finding of the Messiah, then his finding of Simon.

'We have found the Messiah'
We can imagine the excitement in the air as Andrew comes
bounding in to Simon and announces, 'We have *found* the
Messiah!' There is a clear note of certainty here. Andrew
is not referring simply to John the Baptizer's identification
of Jesus and his introduction of him. Nor is Andrew referring
simply to the fact that he and a companion have found out
where Jesus lives and have spent some time with him there
that day. Over and above these things, Andrew is asserting
that he and his friend have found out for themselves the
truth of John's message. 'Listen to the wonder of it,' he
implies. 'As we looked into his face and heard his words,
we became overpoweringly convinced that this Jesus of
Nazareth is the sin-bearing, Spirit-baptizing, chaff-burning
King, the Christ of the Scriptures! We know him. We've
found him, Simon. The Messiah has arrived!' For Andrew
and his friend this conviction had dawned like a morning
without a cloud.
  Notice that Andrew's certainty is accompanied by a due
humility: '*We* have found the Messiah.' This is a simple
point, but, I think, a very important one. There is nothing
in his announcement that implies superiority on Andrew's
part. His certainty is personal but it is not exclusive — his
companion shares it. The plural 'we' both expresses that
truth and avoids offence. When we talk to our brothers
in the flesh there is often an old competitiveness present:
one brother hates to feel that another brother is somewhat
superior or has something which he does not have. So if
you go to your brother and boast, ('Look at *me*! Look
what *I've* found!'), you have lost before you have started.
Andrew avoids that trap. '*We* have found the Messiah.'
'I'm not alone,' he implies, 'but I'm in it.' Humility and
tact.

There is, too, a joyful solemnity in Andrew's announcement: 'We have found the *Messiah*.' The Messiah? Yes, the Anointed One of God, promised in the ancient Scriptures, the one to whom all the prophets looked forward, the one who holds the key of destiny for Old Testament and New Testament times, God's anointed Deliverer — Prophet, Priest and King! The joy of this discovery is coloured by the solemnity of the realization that Jehovah, the God of Abraham and the Lord of all creation, is fulfilling his ancient promises right here and now in their midst! Andrew and his companion have seen God's fulfilment of his promises right before their eyes in flesh and blood, in Jesus Christ. They have found the Messiah. There is something awesomely solemn about this first 'finding'.

'The first thing Andrew did was to find his brother Simon'
The narrative tells us of a second 'finding': Andrew finds Simon. Finding implies seeking, of course, at least in this context. I don't mean to say that Andrew had difficulty locating Simon. The point I am concerned to stress is that he deliberately looked for him. As he came out from the presence of the Lord that day with his unnamed friend, full of the excitement of his discovery that Jesus was the Messiah, Andrew immediately thought of Simon and deliberately sought him out. It wasn't that Simon just crossed his path; Andrew went to find him to share the good news. You see, Andrew did not allow himself to be so absorbed by the glory and the wonder of the presence of the Lord that he kept it all for himself. No, his thought and his heart went out to Simon.

Like the good shepherd in the parable of the lost sheep (Luke 15:3—7), Andrew sought Simon until he found him. For the spirit of that good shepherd who went into the wilderness was already in Andrew. He cared so much about the sheep that was bleating out there in his arrogance and his ignorance and his prejudice that, without fear or a second thought, he went after him until he found him. He must get him to Jesus.

Then, having found Simon, Andrew did for him the most that any man can do for another: 'He brought Simon to Jesus.' Literally, physically, he brought him to Jesus. Was there an argument? Did Simon resist? I cannot say because Scripture does not say. But one thing I do know: Andrew brought Simon to the place where Jesus was. It was as simple as that, and as sublime as that!

The underlying strategy of God

We dare not be blind to the fact that behind the ostensibly simple historical events we have been considering there was a supernatural hand at work. These things did not just happen; they were planned! The Lord of history was at work here, fulfilling his promises and working out his eternal purposes. He was the chief actor in the drama, using for his own ends first John's exposition of the law, then Andrew's expression of brotherly love. Let us look at God's strategy, then, for it embodies some principles that are of abiding relevance and application.

Finders, seekers

God's strategy is to use finders of the Messiah to be seekers of their brothers. Many Christians today are in danger of falling into the same basic error as the Jews of the Old Testament, who came under the severest disciplines and judgements of God for their sin. Their sin was this: they came to think of themselves as the end of God's dealings and God's mercies, rather than as the means to the fulfilment of an end beyond themselves. They came to think that God was blessing them so that they could keep the blessing. They failed to see that they were meant to be channels of blessing, canalizing the divine grace and the divine revelation beyond themselves to others. Ultimately they became too proud even to recognize their own need of salvation!

And many Christians today are in danger of falling into the same error. They love the Word of God, and if the preacher were not orthodox they would leave. They love to hear the hymns of Zion. They love the fellowship of God's people. But they think of themselves as the ends of God's gracious deeds, and not as means to an end. Therefore they take everything in to keep it. The gospel becomes imprisoned in their lives. Nothing spreads. Nothing goes

out. The seed does not bring forth fruit for the salvation of
others. Such Christians have not learned the lesson of history.
They have not become Andrews.

Failure to become Andrews and to seek our brothers
raises serious questions regarding our profession of faith.
First, such failure raises questions about *our intellectual
grasp of the facts* concerning the Messiah whom we claim
to have believed in and received. Can anyone claim an understanding of the person and the work of the Messiah on the
one hand, and of the plight and the peril of sinners on the
other, and then rationally and logically not become an
Andrew? Can we intellectually believe that God arranged
a plan of redemption in the Messiah because men and women
were lost without it, and then, having so believed, not seek
our brothers?

Second, failure to become involved in seeking the lost
raises questions about *our real personal fellowship with
Christ.* Can a person claim to be in vital life union and
communion with the Son of God, who left heaven's glory
for the cross of Calvary in order to seek and to save the
lost, and not show some of that same compassion, that
same active concern, even for his next of kin? In his great
high-priestly prayer, Jesus spoke to the Father in a way that
would answer my question in the negative: 'As you sent me
into the world, I have sent them into the world' (John
17:18).

God's strategy, then, is that finders of the Messiah should
become seekers of others. In common parlance we often
say, 'Finders, keepers!' That is all very well for a small
schoolboy to assume when he finds a coin. But when you
and I act this way with the treasure of the incarnate Lord,
the Messiah of God, when we keep him to ourselves, we
deny our very faith. Seeking is entailed by finding. That is
God's strategy.

Witnessing complements preaching
Another element in the divine strategy is this: God supplements the preaching of John the Baptizer with the witnessing
of Andrew; he reinforces the more general and, perhaps,
formal ministry of John with the more individual and

intimate ministry of Andrew; he complements John's pointing out the Lamb of God with Andrew's inviting Simon to come to him. That is the general strategy. Let me break it down a little.

1. Preaching and witnessing supplement each other in God's purpose. This means they are different. How? In preaching, the Word of God is declared and expounded to a congregated people of varying types, and it is applied in such a way as to elicit a verdict. That is what John did. He preached the Word of God and required a verdict, but a verdict in general terms, for he was preaching to the masses. In witnessing, the truth of the preached Word is affirmed individually by a believer to his brother or neighbour or friend. That is what Andrew did. Having discovered the truth preached by John to be true, he went to his brother Simon and joyously testified: 'It's true, man! He is the Christ. He is the Messiah. He makes a promise and he keeps it and I know it's true!'

The language of the Gospels corroborates this distinction between preaching and witnessing. The first three Gospels use two main words for the missionary enterprise of the church: *euaggelizō*, the word from which we derive our English word 'evangelism'; and *kērussō*, which means 'announcing as a herald does', 'to proclaim as a herald'. John's Gospel, on the other hand, does not use these words. In this Gospel the emphasis is upon that kind of missionary activity which is classified as witnessing. John's word is from the verb *martureō* which means 'to witness'. I find it very significant that the fourth Gospel in this way supplements the ministry of the preacher with the testimony of the believer. This is the divine pattern.

C. H. Spurgeon may have exaggerated when he allegedly said that one ounce of testimony is worth many tons of preaching, but his basic conviction was right. Much preaching is ineffective unless there are those who, like Andrew, act on it, discover the truth of it and then bolster the preached Word from the pulpit with a witness in the home, at work and everywhere. That is God's plan.

2. Thus we see that preaching and witnessing, the formal and the informal, the general and the intimate, are united

in common cause. John the Baptizer probably knew much
more than Andrew: his knowledge of Scripture and his
anointing and his unique ministry affirm that. But Andrew
was needed to get into Simon Peter's heart. It is still the same
today. A Welsh visitor wrote these words after he had come
to North America and visited Niagara Falls many years ago.
They illustrate the point being made here. 'The Niagara
excites our wonder, fills us with amazement, perhaps awe;
but one Niagara is enough for a continent. That same continent, however, requires tens of thousands of silver fountains
and lucid brooks; and let me tell you — those clear springs
and busy streams, whose names have never been registered
in any geography, prove an inestimably greater blessing to
the American continent than the mighty Falls whose fame
fills the world.'[1]

If John the Baptizer was a Niagara of a man, he still
needed the little stream, Andrew, to channel his divine
message into Simon's heart and soul. How much more does
every lesser preacher of divine truth need those who, having
entered into the reality of fellowship with the Messiah, go
out and tell the world: 'I've found him! I know him. He is
mine and he is true and he is alive!'

Do you know the Messiah like this? Have you found him?
Have you a real, personal conviction that Jesus *is* the Christ,
the only Saviour? Can you thus witness: 'We have found him
of whom Moses and the Scriptures spoke?' Is he the living
Lord to you? Have you something to tell? Have you a living,
ongoing and up-to-date testimony to bear to Jesus Christ?
How great are the possibilities of a church where there are
fifty people who on Monday morning are witnesses to the
truth proclaimed the morning before and who, like Andrew,
go for their brothers! Preaching and witnessing work together.

3. Neither John the Baptizer nor Andrew alone (nor even
both together) could create the faith that would lead to
Simon's salvation, but each had a part to play in bringing
Simon to him who is 'the author and perfecter of our faith'
(Hebrews 12:2). Through his words of correction and his
introduction of Jesus, John told Simon, in effect: 'There he
is! Go after him! Follow him!' Through personal sharing of
his convictions, and authentic compassion and concern,

Andrew added, 'Simon, come! I'll take you!' And Andrew brought him to Jesus. Less than that, we who know him dare not do; more than that we cannot. Jesus does the rest.

Reference
1. J. C. Jones, *Studies in the Gospel according to St John*, 2nd ed. (Ballantyne Press, Edinburgh and London), p. 123.

3.
Face to face with Jesus

*'Jesus . . . looked at him and said, "You are Simon
son of John [Jona]. You will be called Cephas"
(which, when translated, is Peter)' (John 1:42).*

The exposition of God's law by John the Baptizer and the
expression of God's love by Andrew have both made their
mark upon Simon. Together, these ministries have brought
him right out into the open, and now he stands face to face
with the Lord Jesus Christ.

Simon is in something of a turmoil. With his soul exposed
to its perils by the Baptizer's words, and his heart strangely
challenged by Andrew's testimony, he feels confused, convicted, even threatened. But if John and Andrew are right,
then this Jesus may be the very one who can heal such
brokenness of heart, the one of whom it was written in
the Scriptures: 'The Spirit of the Sovereign Lord is on me,
because the Lord has anointed me to preach good news
to the poor. He has sent me to bind up the broken-hearted,
to proclaim freedom for the captives and release for the
prisoners' (Isaiah 61:1).

This is the mighty moment in the life of Simon. Here
they confront each other, the seeking Saviour and the sinner
conscious of his need. Here they stand, face to face, eye to
eye, heart to heart, in what must be one of the most profoundly pregnant moments in human history. Everything
that has already happened in Simon's life has been preparatory to this; everything that is going to happen later will
issue out of this. And upon the outcome of this moment
hang the destinies of multitudes of men and women who
over the years will become debtors to the fact that Jesus
Christ saved Simon Peter.

At this point I feel very much that I can identify with Moses by the burning bush, being summoned by God to take off his shoes from his feet. The ground upon which we stand here is holy. It is with profound reverence and humility, then, that I invite you to examine with me the record of this momentous meeting. The text clearly refers to two main aspects of it: a look and a word.

The Saviour's look

The evangelist tells us that when Andrew brought Simon into the presence of Jesus, 'Jesus *looked at* him.' Now we naturally tend to gloss over that, but we should pause and notice that what John actually tells us here is that Jesus did more than look. Other translations bring this out. Moffatt writes, 'He gazed at him.' Rieu interprets it: 'Looking at him closely . . .' Knox's version is 'Looking at him fixedly . . .' Why do the translations vary? Because all three meanings are involved in the word. Jesus fixed his eyes upon Simon. Jesus gazed at the man. Jesus looked both *at* him and *into* him, as only God himself can look. Jesus, the one from whom nothing is hid, was reading Simon's heart. It was not a simple glance, or even a prolonged gaze — it was a penetrating, scrutinizing look.

Other uses of the same verb (*emblepō*) serve to underline this point. Let me give two examples, for if we miss this meaning we miss something that is vital to an understanding of the whole episode. Mark tells us that when Jesus was approached by a certain rich man who knelt before him asking the way of eternal life, 'Jesus *looked at* him and loved him . . .' (Mark 10:21). What did that mean? It certainly did not mean that Jesus was sizing up the fellow's physical appearance. Not at all. Rather, it meant that Jesus was reading his heart, considering his motives, weighing in the balances of his mind what Jesus alone could read there.

Again Mark tells us, to give an even clearer example, that as Peter some three years later stood in the high priest's courtyard while Jesus was being interrogated, 'One of the

servant girls of the high priest came by. When she *saw* Peter
warming himself, she *looked closely at* him. "You also were
with that Nazarene, Jesus," she said' (Mark 14:66,67). I am
not suggesting that the girl could read Simon's heart the
way Jesus could. I just want you to notice how Mark distinguishes between her 'seeing' Peter and her 'looking
closely at' him. She first saw him; but then she began to
puzzle and scrutinize and look very hard at him. And when
she had taken a really good look, she realized that he was
the person she had seen following Jesus right into the courtyard. This 'looking closely at' is the same kind of looking
as we have in our text: 'Jesus looked at him.' Here the looking represents the capacity of the Messiah, the Son of the
living God, to look into the mind, to examine the heart,
to scrutinize the soul and to search the deepest recesses
of a man's being and to read it like an open book. This is
the Saviour's look of unlimited penetration. There are
two things I want to note about it.

It expressed his knowledge of Simon
Our Lord's look showed that he knew Simon. That is obvious
from what we have said already, but it needs amplifying. If
you had been in Simon's shoes you would have experienced
the terrible realization that Jesus knew you. Any man who
has passed through the throes of conviction of sin will know
what that means. To all of us it is given, as we enter the
kingdom of God, to be singled out at some point; and in
that moment we know that God sees us and God knows us
and God reads us. I hope we all know something of that,
uncomfortable as it may be.

Imagine our Lord's deep look into Simon's soul. You
may have seen a pale reflection of this kind of look on the
face of a physician when, with tests and X-rays completed,
he comes back to the bedside, re-examines the patient and
suddenly knows exactly the meaning and significance of all
the symptoms which hitherto did not fit clearly together.
If you look at his face you see this sudden look of deep
comprehension, of expert knowledge.

Jesus knew Simon. And Simon recognized that fact from
his look. The Saviour knew not only his name and pedigree
('You are Simon son of John [AV, Jona]' — he could have

known this from Andrew), but he also knew his heart. Jesus knew all his peculiar tendencies and indeed all his uncertainties at this point. He saw how Simon was torn with conflict, as he weighed the teachings he had inherited as a Jew over against the principles taught by John the Baptizer about the King and the kingdom. And he knew how Simon was equally torn between the inherited caution of his fellow Jews and the uninhibited abandon with which his brother Andrew had owned Jesus as the promised Messiah. Should Simon make such a confession, too? Or should he remain carefully uncommitted like the Jews around him? Jesus knew all that was going on in Simon.

It explained Andrew's conviction

Jesus' look of unlimited penetration also served to explain to Simon, at least in part, why Andrew was so absolutely convinced that Jesus was the Messiah. Probably when Simon first heard Andrew's testimony, he felt it was premature, if not even a little bit crazy. Here was Andrew suddenly bounding in and claiming to have found the Messiah! How could it be? It seemed so implausible and dangerously revolutionary.

But now with the eyes of the Son of God upon him, standing fixed by that piercing, penetrating gaze that tore through every camouflage and mask, Simon must have experienced total, painful, relentless exposure. He must have felt like a worm unearthed from its dark hole, lying helplessly out in the light. Yet because of this experience he would find the testimony of Andrew taking on more credibility. Who else but the promised one could look like that into a man's soul? Who else could have such power? It might well be that this *was* none other than the Messiah, the Deliverer sent from God.

The Saviour's word

> '"You are Simon son of John. You will be called
> Cephas" (which, when translated, is Peter)'.

The silence prevailing as those holy eyes have searched and

scanned the hidden recesses of Simon's soul is at last
broken — broken by a word that is electrifying in its significance. The one who seems to know Simon through and
through now claims the right to give him a new name. More
than that, he assumes, in accordance with biblical tradition,
that he has the power to change Simon's very character. It
will be transformed from that which is signified by 'Simon
son of Jona' to that which is signified by 'Cephas, *Petros,*
rock'. The unstable son of a dove shall become the stable,
rock-like Peter. Jesus Christ is asserting that he has the
power, authority and grace to bring about a life-transforming
change in Simon.

By his claim of power and authority, Jesus is sub-
stantiating John's and Andrew's testimony. Did not John
prophesy, 'He will baptize you with the Holy Spirit and
with fire'? The Messiah's baptism is not the baptism of
water that can only touch the skin. His baptism penetrates
and transforms. And this is exactly what Jesus claims to be
able to do in Simon. Thus he identifies himself as the
Messiah. Jesus promises Simon: 'I'll change you. I'm exercising my authority over you and claiming you as my own.'
He assumes the right and the power to make what he pleases
out of the man in front of him, because he is Lord!

We need to get this clear. It is the Lord who stands before
us. We do not 'make' him Lord, as we so often tend to say.
He *is* Lord. He always was Lord (cf. Acts 2:36; Romans
14:9). He always will be Lord. We cannot 'make' him Lord;
we can only acknowledge his lordship. And we see here what
his lordship is like. He puts his hand upon Simon and tells
him, 'Simon, I'm going to change your name because you
are going to become my own man. The past is over and
done with; the future will be quite different. I'll not let
you be what you have been until now. I am Lord.' It is
his initiative and his power and his grace — that is the gospel.

We must notice two things in relation to our Lord's prediction about Simon Peter: in the background stands Jesus'
understanding of Simon; in the foreground stands the
revelation of the Christ himself.

The Saviour's realism about Simon

'You are Simon the son of Jona . . .' Underlying those

words is the claim to a personal, intimate and total knowledge of a man whom Jesus has just met for the first time. You and I cannot know each other like this; we shall never be able to. No human eyes can penetrate the soul of another in the way the eyes of the Lord Jesus penetrate the camouflage of Simon's life.

The point is that it is out of total knowledge, not out of misinformation, that Jesus makes the prophecy and promise which follow. When he says, 'You will be called Cephas,' he does not say it out of ignorance of what Simon really is like. He says it, knowing all the facts! This is not the false optimism of someone who has miscalculated a situation; rather, it is the solemn promise of one who knows everything there is to be known. Let me put it this way: our Lord does not promise the best because he does not know the worst; knowing the worst, he nevertheless promises the best. His prediction is based on the most realistic appraisal of the man. He *knows* Simon.

Simon will be tempted to doubt that time and time again before grace has completed the promised work. We shall discover in our next studies how Jesus reassures Simon and his friends that he does not make his promises lightly, without knowing men's character. There are incidents in each of the first four chapters of John's Gospel which prove precisely this point. Our Lord is not a physician who promises healing because his diagnosis is inaccurate or incomplete; his prognosis is absolutely sure even though he knows all of us through and through.

Let us take that to heart, for we shall need to be reassured of it many times in daily experience. Have we not often come to a point of discouragement when we have been tempted to say, 'O Lord, I'm such a failure! Haven't I disappointed you? Haven't I let you down? Did you really know what you were in for when you put your hand on me and called me? Are you sure you don't want to change your mind?' We may not say it exactly like that, but that is what we mean. We fear that the Saviour who began a good work in us will abandon us half-way through. We have disappointed him. He really did not know us in the beginning, we conclude. His appraisal of us, in other words, was inaccurate and incomplete, so we may imagine.

But we are wrong. While we may often surprise ourselves by our folly, we can be sure that we do not surprise our Saviour. He knows the human condition. And right at the moment of looking at Simon, our Lord sees his own entire future as well as Simon's. He knows that there will have to be a Calvary: Simon needs a saving Lord. He knows that there must be a resurrection: Simon needs a living Lord. There must be an ascension: Simon needs a reigning Lord. There must be a Pentecost: Simon needs an indwelling Lord. All these things must be, because nothing less can change Simon. Jesus knows all that. He knows that about each of us. And all that meaning lies hidden in his words: 'You are Simon . . .' That is realism — facing the brute facts squarely.

The Saviour's revelation about himself

'You will be called Cephas . . .' If Jesus really knows Simon's heart and everything in it, knows its hidden tendencies and evil propensities, knows its every latent mood and temper, how, then, can he proceed to make such an unqualified, positive prediction as he now makes? There is no 'if'. There is only the categorical 'You will be . . .' How can Jesus say this? Is such a prediction not precarious? He may lose his good name by making a prophecy like this about a man like that!

No, unequivocally not, and for this reason: the Saviour's prediction is not based upon who Simon is, but upon who he is himself. Fulfilment of the Saviour's promise depends not upon Simon's qualifications (or lack of them) to enter the kingdom, but upon the King's capacity to change and redeem Simon, irrespective of his past record, present tendencies or future lapses. Simon may be the roughest, most rugged, most lost of all men, but this doesn't matter. The Saviour knows himself. Therefore he can make this prophecy. And in making it he is also revealing himself as the one who can cope with the worst.

The Reformers, from John Calvin onwards, have been fond of referring to the messianic office as embodying in one person the combined ministries of Prophet, Priest and King. Only such a conviction about himself can explain Jesus' words now before us. Only because he knows himself to be Prophet, Priest and King can he realistically size up the life of Simon Peter and at the same time confidently promise that it will change. Without this knowledge about himself, our Lord would be a reckless promiser of good things which he cannot fulfil. But Jesus' consciousness (right at the beginning of his ministry, be it noted), is the consciousness of one who is Prophet, Priest and King.

1. Jesus knows himself to be the anointed Prophet who foresees the end from the beginning. He sees now the stability and the sanctity that will later stamp the life of the sinner before him. This is no mere guesswork. It is the assured, true knowledge of the Messiah as Prophet, for there is only one who can be at the same time both realistic and reassuring with regard to fallen sinners in a fallen world — that is God's Messiah. No one else can both face the facts (or even know them), and at the same time guarantee a work of grace. But *he* can. We can be sure that if he confronts us and says to us, 'You are . . . , you will be . . . ,' then one day he will bring us to the place where, with Peter, we shall confess, 'You are the Christ, the Son of the living God' (Matthew 16:16). That is the place where we shall know ourselves to be among the blessed.

2. Jesus knows himself to be the anointed Priest — High Priest after the order of Melchizedek (Hebrews 6:20). His one sacrifice for sin will bear away the sins of Simon so that they will no longer stand between him and God's purposes for him. Ultimately, pardoned and released from bondage, Simon will be free to serve God and his fellow men.

3. Jesus knows himself to be the very one of whom it was written: 'He will be great and will be called the Son of the Most High. The Lord God will give him the throne of his father David, and he will reign over the house of Jacob for ever; his kingdom will never end' (Luke 1:32,33). He knows himself to be the anointed King, of David's line, who has power over Satan, sin, circumstances and men. The King cannot fail to fulfil his promises, even in the face of the most stubborn traits of Simon's character. He does have to deal with these traits: we shall see in future studies how he has to discipline a rebellious Peter now and then — a man who has been changed but in whose heart there are

still pockets of rebellion. But the King does not fail. He cannot.

As we grasp the significance of so certain a future, let us make one or two points which relate to its application in our lives as believers.

1. First, let us notice that normally there will be more than one person involved in bringing a sinner to Jesus Christ. Neither John nor Andrew is capable of doing everything needful, though each has a necessary role to play. Are we, like them, part of a chain? It doesn't matter which link we are. It does matter that we should be links.

2. Notice next the balance here. John's emphasis upon the harsher aspects of the law, what Alexander Whyte used to call 'the dark lines in the Almighty's face', is counterbalanced by Andrew's manifestation of love and care. It is not law *or* love; it is law *and* love. The law of God must be declared in all its solemnity and all its eternal relevance, but so must the love of God be brought in all its healing strength to the sin-sick soul. Men need both law and love before they can properly appreciate the work and worth of Jesus Christ.

3. It is exceedingly important, also, that in our attempts to bring our fellow men to Christ we should be even more certain of the Lord's power to save them than we are certain of their need to be saved. In theological circles in recent years the emphasis has been laid almost totally on the necessity of 'knowing your man'. It is true that we should try to know people, and to understand their problems with as much psychological expertise as possible. I am not denying that. But there is one thing we need to know even better: we need to know the grace of Christ Jesus. We need to know that he 'is able to do immeasurably more than all we ask or imagine' (Ephesians 3:20), that he is able to resolve the problems of the person irrespective of the complexities of his need — problems which, even though we may be specialists, we can never fully unravel and understand. There is only one who knows all the depths and ramifications of sin; he does know, and he is able to save to the uttermost. This is what needs to be our deepest conviction as we look into the face of any man or woman, boy or girl, seeking spiritual guidance.

4. A final word: however much John and Andrew can do alone and together, even their combined labours cannot save Simon. Ultimately their most important work is to bring Simon to Jesus. Simon can be changed only if he comes face to face with Jesus. Let us, too, be content with nothing less; like John and Andrew we are intended to bring needy sinners to the Messiah. Let us tell, humbly and lovingly, of the Christ who is transforming our lives; this can yield a first glimmer of the light of the face of Jesus to those who do not know him. Let us pray for our friends, carrying them to him where he waits at the throne of grace. And let us bring them to the sanctuary where his people meet and he meets with them. There our friends can hear his Word declared, feel his Spirit present and, if God wills, yield themselves to him in life-transforming union. We never know the value to present society or to posterity of any one soul whom we bring to the place where he can stand face to face with Jesus. He may be only an ordinary fisherman now, but he may become a mighty fisher of men in the Lord's good grace and time.

4.
Jesus knows men

'He knew all men. He did not need man's testimony about man, for he knew what was in a man' (John 2:25).

Our Lord's promise to Simon that he would make him a new man and the claims about himself in that promise were all utterly breath-taking. But so also was his entire life utterly unique. There has been no other birth or ministry or death like his. There has been no other resurrection or ascension. And there never will be.

One remarkable characteristic of this unique life was its confirmatory nature: events in our Lord's life continually confirmed his testimony about himself. Read the Gospels from time to time with this in view. Notice our Lord making a claim, then pursue his footsteps. It is uncanny, and it would be altogether incredible if it were not so obviously true: the wheels of providence consistently move from a claim he makes to a corresponding confirmation of its truth. Each claim is substantiated.

Jesus Christ has spoken to Simon Peter: 'You are Simon the son of John. You will be called Cephas.' Implicit in these words are, as we have seen, two great claims of our Lord about himself — namely, that he possesses *total knowledge* of Simon, as he now is and as he will be, and that he has *all power* needed to change Simon into Peter. Out of his consciousness as Prophet, Priest and King, Jesus knows his own divine insight and power. But does Simon? Probably only in theory at the most. Probably he is in a state of total ambivalence. While Jesus' promise is breath-taking and the claims underlying it are such that only the Messiah could make them, are these things all really true? Can Simon stake his life on them? How can he know their truth? Simon would welcome some confirmations.

In the first four chapters of John's Gospel we find exactly such confirmations given. It is indeed uncanny: these chapters read like a commentary on our Lord's promise to Simon. Each event recorded in them serves to confirm and authenticate Jesus' claims to know men and to be able to change them. All of these events, by the way, *precede* the events with which the Gospels of Matthew, Mark and Luke begin their accounts of Jesus' public ministry. The incidents of John 1–4, therefore, occur fairly soon after Jesus' meeting with Simon. It is during the weeks immediately after this meeting that ever-increasing testimony to our Lord's wisdom and power becomes available to his followers, among whom most probably is Simon. In these weeks our Lord travels much with his growing group of followers — first north from the Jordan to Galilee, then south to Jerusalem, then out into Judea, then back north to Galilee through Samaria. That is the setting.

Let us then first examine the confirmations of his ability *to know* men. And what I want to emphasize is what our Lord by grace communicated to Simon through these incidents, or through others. My friend, whatever your name is, wherever you live, whatever your nature, whatever the sin is that so easily besets you, he knows you! And when he called you to himself, he knew everything that you could possibly do that was evil. And yet he called you, and he died for you and he made all the promises of grace over to you. He knows all things about all mankind. That is a word of encouragement and hope. Let us look at three incidents which show it to be true.

Nathanael

He who claimed to know Simon knew others also, and proved that he did. The first of these was Nathanael of Bethsaida in Galilee. Here we have a delightful record (John 1: 45–51). The same excitement which earlier sent Andrew bounding off to report, 'We have found the Messiah' to Simon, later sent a man called Philip with equal

enthusiasm to share his identical discovery with Nathanael.
'Philip found Nathanael and told him, "We have found the
one Moses wrote about in the Law, and about whom the
prophets also wrote — Jesus of Nazareth, the son of
Joseph."'

Quick as a trigger came the reply from frank, honest
Nathanael: 'Can anything good come from Nazareth?' It
seemed impossible to him at that point that the Messiah
should have any connection with Nazareth and, honest as
he was, he expressed his doubt. His scepticism was based
not on prejudice, but on two facts well known to him. On
the one hand, he knew of the glory and regal majesty of the
promised one of whom Moses and the prophets had written.
On the other hand, he knew of the commonness of Nazareth,
a caravan town, small and undistinguished. And so he simply
could not believe that the glorious Messiah would come
from inglorious Nazareth. Now, you cannot argue much
with honest doubt and Philip wisely did not even try but,
instead, invited Nathanael to 'come and see'. He did for
Nathanael what Andrew had done for Simon earlier on:
he took him to Jesus.

Just as Jesus had shown the Prophet's knowledge of
Simon when Andrew brought him, so he now showed
prophetic knowledge of Nathanael as he saw him coming,
saying, 'Here is a true Israelite, in whom there is nothing
false.' He spoke to him as one with whom he was personally
familiar. What was Nathanael's response?

There is hardly anything more revealing of character
and of the true condition of our hearts than our reaction to
praise. Far too often our ego is thereby so titillated and our
pride so aroused that we are prepared to dance to any tune
played by the person praising. But not so Nathanael! He
was as unmoved by Jesus' commendation as he had been
unimpressed by Philip's confession. His response was to ask
for the basis of Jesus' praise: 'How do you know me?'
He assumed that the best-sounding compliments are
meaningless unless based on facts. This was not equivo-
cating, nor wanting to wriggle out of the obvious truth of
a situation. It was honest doubt.

Now came the thrust. Now the Lord manifested his
omniscience: 'I saw you while you were still under the

fig-tree before Philip called you.' Whatever Nathanael had been doing under the apparent cover of a fig tree, it was known to Jesus. And that was enough for Nathanael: 'Rabbi, you are the Son of God; you are the King of Israel,' he cried. Why did he say those things? Because of the obvious ability of our Lord Jesus Christ to *know* him. Nathanael recognized this knowledge as supernatural and divine.

Thus we see that he who claimed to know Simon son of John (or Jona), without then and there proving his claim, confirmed his ability to know men through his wholly supernatural knowledge of Nathanael. How this would comfort Simon if he knew about it, as he very likely did!

Nicodemus

Moving from Galilee to Jerusalem, we find that the same one who professed to know Simon and proved he knew Nathanael also showed unerring knowledge of Nicodemus' heart (John 3:1–21). We cannot understand this episode in John 3, however, without understanding the closing words of John 2: 'Now while he was in Jerusalem at the Passover Feast, many people saw the miraculous signs he was doing and believed in his name. But Jesus would not entrust himself to them, for he knew all men. He did not need man's testimony about man, for he knew what was in a man' (John 2:23–25).

Because he knew men universally ('he knew all men'), and because he knew the nature of man ('he . . . knew what was in a man'), Jesus did not commit himself to those who committed themselves to him at Jerusalem. Another, and legitimate, way of expressing that would be to say that there were people in Jerusalem who believed in him, but he did not believe in them. He had no confidence in them, because he *knew* them.

However, if we rightly understand the meaning of the Greek particle *dē* ('but') with which chapter 3 opens, it would appear that John is telling us that there was one exception to the rule that Jesus made no response to those who apparently believed in him at Jerusalem. He did respond to Nicodemus. We could read the sequence as follows:

Jesus '. . . did not need man's testimony about man, for he
knew what was in a man. *But* there was a man . . . named
Nicodemus . . .' (John 2:25; 3:1). In his commentary on
John 3:1, B. F. Westcott writes, 'The word *man* is repeated
to emphasize the connexion with 2:25. Nicodemus offered
at once an example of the Lord's inward knowledge of
men, and an exception to this general rule which He observed
in not trusting Himself to them.'[1]

Jesus not only trusted Nicodemus, he opened his heart to
him. It is remarkable how he withheld his identity from a
responsive public and yet proceeded to reveal to this one
man a whole range of truth about himself — his descent
from heaven, the efficacy of his death, the way of eternal
life he would provide and the necessity for a person to
experience new birth in order to see his kingdom. Verses
3—21 are a sermon in themselves to Nicodemus.

Now, assuming that our Lord's assessment of the shallow
nature of people's response to his signs in Jerusalem was
correct and that, possibly, many of those same people
would later cry with the rabble, 'Away with him! Crucify
him!' what evidence is there that his view of Nicodemus'
response was also correct? And why do we say that Jesus
dealt differently with him because he *knew* him?

Well, take another look at the record. Do you notice
that, according to John, Jesus Christ answers a question
that Nicodemus has not audibly asked? Nicodemus
approaches our Lord with what is virtually a confession
of faith concerning him. It may be incomplete, but certainly
it is not flimsy; 'Rabbi, we know you are a teacher who has
come from God. For no one could perform the miraculous
signs that you are doing if God were not with him.' But
Nicodemus never finishes what he starts out to say. The
rhythm and flow of the language clearly indicate that
Nicodemus is in full verbal flight. Look at his words: they
are leading up to a conclusion. You expect a 'therefore . . .'
next. But it does not come. Instead, the only perfect gentle-
man of all time interrupts. Jesus breaks into the flow of
Nicodemus' talk.

Notice how John refers to this interruption: 'Jesus
answered him,' (RSV). But Nicodemus, as we said before,
has not verbally asked a question. And that is the point.

Nicodemus has been all talk about what is really a side-issue, as far as his heart of hearts is concerned. What he is really wrestling with deep inside, he has not mentioned — namely the puzzled longing to know how one can enter our Lord's kingdom. But Jesus knows Nicodemus' heart and he stops short the flowing compliments of his mouth in order to attend to this burning question of his soul.

Our Lord then leads Nicodemus step by step until he has disclosed to him that the life one must have to enter the kingdom is the life which will be mediated by his death on the cross, when he will be lifted up as Saviour. Men everywhere will have to be born again and there is only one way — through his death. When he is lifted up, those who will look and believe in him shall live. They shall have eternal life, the life of the kingdom.

We see, then, that Jesus knew the fundamental question of Nicodemus' heart and, in his great compassion and understanding, dealt with it. Can you imagine the impact of all this on Simon, when he heard about the meeting with Nicodemus? Here was yet another confirmation of our Lord's ability to see into a man's innermost being. There was yet another to come.

The Samaritan woman

The next chapter of John's Gospel relates how, on the way back north to Galilee from Jerusalem and Judea, Jesus and his disciples passed through Samaria and stopped to rest at the well near the village of Sychar. Weary, Jesus sat by the well while the disciples went to buy food. Though it was the hottest time of day, a time when you would not expect people to be outside, a lone woman appeared carrying a water jar, coming to draw water from the well. Seeing her approach the place where he was sitting, Jesus broke the silence that normally obtained between strangers in those parts, especially between Jew and Samaritan, man and woman. He made a request: 'Will you give me a drink? '

She was nonplussed: 'You are a Jew and I am a Samaritan woman. How can you ask me for a drink?' The text has an aside here, pointing out that Jews 'do not associate' with

Samaritans, a verb which may well literally mean that the
two groups 'never drink from the same cup'. Jesus' reply
was: 'If you knew the gift of God, and who it is that asks
you for a drink, you would have asked him and he would
have given you living water' (John 4:10). The plot thickens.
He had asked a drink of water from her because he had a
drink to give her. It was not primarily because he was thirsty,
but because he knew her thirst and could satisfy it, that
he wanted some of Sychar's water. He had better water to
give. Under the guise of quenching his own natural thirst,
he would quench the spiritual and moral thirst of the woman
before him. He *knew* her.

The conversation proceeded until the baffled woman
clearly sensed something of our Lord's unusual greatness
and grace. When he described the water he could give — water
that would become a spring welling up within her so that
she would not need to keep running hither and thither for
further satisfaction — she turned to him in anguished plea:
'Sir, give me this water so that I won't get thirsty and have
to keep coming here to draw water.'

Then came what was to her, at first at any rate, an alarm-
ing token of his knowledge of all her fast-locked secrets.
Apparently willing to grant her request, he made one prior
demand. He said, in effect, 'All right, but before I do, go
and call your husband and come back here with him.' Now
that touched a raw spot. Even though undoubtedly shaken
by this unexpected invasion of her private life, the woman
kept her composure and answered truthfully: 'I have no
husband.' Then came the devastating revelation of Jesus'
knowledge: 'You are right when you say you have no
husband. The fact is, you have had five husbands, and the
man you now have is not your husband. What you have
just said is quite true.'

Can you see it? He knew her, too! He knew her dark
past. He knew that she was burning herself out morally.
He knew all the grim story she hid beneath her talkative
camouflage. He knew her so completely that he could
unerringly guide the conversation step by step, as he did
with Nicodemus, until he had flooded her mind with the
glory of his person and satisfied the deepest yearnings of
her abused soul. He then and there changed the profligate

into a preacher. We read that she put down her water jar and went back to the village, summoning the people: 'Come, see a man who told me everything I ever did. Could this be the Christ?' And they came to see. Through the testimony of this woman the way was opened for the gospel to invade Sychar that day. Jesus' total and compassionate knowledge of this woman became the key to the hearts of many of her fellow villagers.

How graciously and gloriously, then, our Lord substantiated his claim to know men in his dealings with Nathanael, Nicodemus and the Samaritan woman! These three all experienced and responded to Jesus' infallible insight into their hidden selves. And Simon's faith must have soared as he saw or heard how, by penetrating the deepest recesses of these three souls, Jesus brought light and life and liberty to them.

He knows his sheep and he calls them by name. All of us, young and old, can take courage from that. Young Christians may feel that the temptations of the twentieth century are even greater than the temptations of previous times, and they may fall into doubt: 'What does he know about me?' And those of us who are on in years, drawing towards the end of life, as far as we can humanly see: 'What does he know of this? He lived only thirty-three years! What can he know about weary old age?' Everything. He knows everything. And he knows everybody. His understanding is accompanied by infinite love. And just as he promised to change Simon, so he promises to change us. As we yield to his love we shall be brought even 'to the whole measure of the fulness of Christ' (Ephesians 4:13).

Reference
1.   B. F. Westcott, *The Gospel According to St John* (Murray, London, 1898), p. 47.

5.
Jesus changes men

To make a promise is one thing; to deliver the goods is quite another. One wonders what really went on in Simon's heart when he heard Jesus address him by name and promise so confidently that he would become a new person requiring the new name 'Peter'.

In the last chapter we saw how various incidents from our Lord's early public ministry as recorded in John 1—4 served to confirm one of his claims — the claim *to know* men. In this chapter we shall look at the same narrative, John 1—4, for confirmations of Jesus' second implicit claim — the claim to be able *to change* men. And we shall see the truth brought out that he not only understands us through and through, but also has the power to make us into the kind of people he would have us be. Here is a physician come from God with both diagnostic powers that are unique, and recreative powers to bring a Simon to Peter, a sinner to sainthood, a child of Adam to a child of God. And this is salvation.

There is a third kind of power implicit in all this, which we need to draw out and elucidate: that is our Lord's astonishing ability to perceive the *need for change*. We have observed his diagnostic powers: he could see what was wrong. We are going to observe his recreative powers: he could right the wrong. But we need to note that underlying these powers was Jesus' insight into how things ought to be. Just as a physician knows how a diseased organ would look if it were healthy, so our Lord knows what we would be like if we became precisely what God meant us to be. And just as a physician's chief concern is to heal the diseased organ, so Jesus' chief concern is that we should be changed.

His passion for change

Have you noticed that, whereas no one else seemed to be concerned about the condition of things and people as described in these first four chapters of John's Gospel, Jesus was? Everyone else seemed to take things for granted; there was nothing very much wrong! But when he came, everything was wrong. He saw what was wrong because he knew what was right, and his concern was not simply to change things *from* what they were, but to change them *to* what they ought to be. He knew what was right. Therefore he could not tolerate what was wrong.

There are people who want to change things simply for the sake of changing them. The love of novelty characterizes their lives. If only they can change things, they are happy! But not so Jesus Christ. He did not desire change for its own sake: things needed to be changed because they were out of alignment with God's will. Change had a *raison d'être* beyond itself — namely, the accomplishment of the perfect will of God. Our Lord knew what God meant the world to be. He knew what God meant Simon to be. He knows what God meant you and me to be. That is the key to the changes he perceived to be needed in Simon, the Jerusalem temple, Nicodemus and the woman of Samaria. He wanted so to change each of them that they would become what God meant them to be. We shall look at them in turn.

Why change Simon?

Simon needed to be changed because he was not what God meant him to be. As Simon, he was alienated from God. Sin had made his life abnormal from the point of view of his Maker. Jesus saw all this. But he also had a clear conception of what the man Simon was meant to be in God's plan. Jesus' concern, let me repeat, was not for novelty but for normality — normality according to the divine standard. Nothing else was considered 'normal' by Jesus. Normality is not doing what other people are doing; it is being what God meant me to be.

As Jesus looked at that disorganized, disintegrated life of Simon's, he saw the lostness of it. And he could see the potential tragedy of Simon's powers of leadership — his

vast energies of soul and body being used just to shift around
on a fisherman's boat, bossing this man and bruising that
man, his sole daily concern being to count the haul of the
previous night. Our Lord could see the tragedy and the
waste of it, especially in the light of what God had intended
Simon to become — a fisher of men, a builder of churches
and one of the leading apostles of the reigning Lord!

Not that the fishing of fish is at all unworthy. It certainly
is not. But God had something bigger, something greater in
mind, in comparison with which Simon's present life was
lost. And Jesus was aware of that plan; hence his concern
to change Simon. It is so with us, too. It doesn't matter
how much we are like other people, or unlike them. The
question is 'Are we what God meant us to be?'

Why change the temple routine? (John 2:13–22)

There was a kind of justification for every commercial
activity that went on within the temple precincts. Doves
and animals were sold there because worshippers needed
them for making sacrifices. Money was exchanged there
because worshippers had to pay the temple shekel in the
coinage of the temple. So what's the point of changing anything? Why not leave things as they were? Remember the
beauty of the temple, and the ritual devotion it inspired!

But when Jesus came in, his soul blazed within him with
a holy zeal and a passion for change. He knew what the
temple was meant to be. The stench of the cattle and the
noise of the money-changers were ugly symptoms of a deep
human greed that traded on other people's religion. And
what was divinely ordained to be a house of prayer had
become a 'house of trade'. No amount of ecclesiastical
double-talk could alter that fact. Because Jesus wanted such
a change as would bring the whole of temple life into
harmony with the will of God, he forcibly expelled the
animals and the money-changers from the temple courts.
The presence of human greed was not part of God's plan
for the Jerusalem temple.

Why change Nicodemus? (John 3:1–21)

The same principle holds. Jesus knew what God meant
Nicodemus to be. Here he was, sophisticated, theologically

minded, *the* teacher in Israel, a ruler of the Jews, having a hand in organizing the life of the temple, a most influential man — why change him?

First, for his own salvation. Nicodemus had only been born once, born of the flesh, born of the will of man. And no man can enter the kingdom unless he is born again. Second, for the sake of the temple. If Nicodemus were changed he would then be qualified to work for the transformation of the temple as an inside member of the Sanhedrin. The mere purging of the outer courts was not radical enough. The temple leaders needed to be changed before the temple itself could assume its intended role.

Why change the woman of Samaria? (John 4:7–42)

She had a very different character from that of Nicodemus, morally and spiritually, but God had a purpose for her, and the Son of God always comes to the lives of the morally derelict knowing what a different life God has in mind for them. In what way should the woman of Samaria be changed? Well, it would be a good thing simply to change her way of life. That is true, and yet this was not God's only or ultimate goal. Something of his nobler purpose is revealed in these closing verses of the episode: 'Many of the Samaritans from that town believed in him because of the woman's testimony, "He told me everything I ever did." So when the Samaritans came to him, they urged him to stay with them, and he stayed two days. And because of his words many more became believers. They said to the woman, "We no longer believe just because of what you said; now we have heard for ourselves, and we know that this man really is the Saviour of the world"' (John 4:39–42).

Can you see what happened? In the purpose of God, this woman was to be the bearer of glad tidings. She was to open a gateway into that city of Samaria for the incoming of the Saviour of the world. Jesus knew that. Over and above his knowledge of her present degraded being was his knowledge of her potential glorious being as a messenger of the gospel. So it was also with Nicodemus, the Jerusalem temple and Simon: Jesus knew God's plan for them all, and his passion for change was the passion to see that divine will fulfilled in each one of them.

His power to change

Jesus not only knows all men, and knows God's plan for their lives; he also has power to change them so that their lives are in alignment with God's plan. Let us look at three incidents again from John 1—4, which show that Jesus has power over the entire human situation — over material things, over the human soul and over the human body.

His power over material things: water became wine (John 2:1—11)

When Jesus and his disciples were in Cana of Galilee (after Jesus' baptism by John, and before the Passover journey to Jerusalem), Jesus performed the first 'sign' of his deity and messiahship: he turned water into wine. What a delightful episode this is and what a remarkable indication of the range of his power! Through this miracle in the material realm, Jesus manifested himself as the Lord of nature.

Disappointment was probably the least consequence of the failure of wine at a wedding in the Near East of our Lord's day. According to J. D. M. Derrett (quoted by Leon Morris),[1] such a thing would mean much more than mere embarrassment for the hosts. It might well mean pecuniary liability for them, perhaps even a court case. This seems strange to us as Westerners. The point is, there was an element of reciprocity about everything that took place at a wedding: if one neighbour presented a son or daughter in a certain way, all other neighbours were expected to do the same; if one neighbour set the table in a certain way, all others were expected to do so, too. This amounted to a kind of stringent, if unwritten, social contract. Failure to provide what was expected and customary (enough wine, for instance), would be tantamount to breaking this social contract. It constituted robbing your neighbours of their due!

Thus the premature failure of the supply of wine at this wedding in Cana could have brought deep social stigma to the hosts. And so, at his mother's request, our Lord stepped in. What he does in every vineyard every year by means of a slow, natural process, he now did in one moment by his sovereign power: he caused the water to become wine. The Son of Mary manifested himself as more than Mary's son.

In addition to saving the situation for them, what would this miracle signify to the newly wedded couple? It would speak to them of a Friend who could help them meet every disappointment, who could, in fact, transform their whole life if they kept in touch with and were rightly related to him. What would the miracle signify to Simon? It would show him that Jesus was Lord of nature. As its Maker, he was also its Moulder, and could do with it whatever he deemed necessary in order to fulfil his Father's will. He who had promised to change Simon had changed water into wine, perplexity into peace, sadness into joy — and thereby shown that he had supernatural power over all creation.

His power over the human soul: the profligate became a preacher (John 4:7–42)
The sovereignty of Jesus Christ extends to a deeper sphere than the purely material. He has power over human souls, over the moral and spiritual realm of human life. We have already noted something of this power in relation to the woman of Samaria, as he changed her from moral decay into a woman with words of grace and healing.

Let us look more closely at this episode. As Jesus uncovers the camouflage and opens up the private life of this talkative, religious woman standing beside him at the well, we discover that beneath her friendly exterior she has been hiding a foul condition of heart. It is no wonder that she has had to come alone in the midday heat to get her water from the well: probably none of the decent women of the village will walk with her or even talk with her.

If we stop there, there is nothing but heartbreak. But see the end of the story! That mongrel community experienced a new tide of holy influence that flooded the town and purified it and brought salvation to it so that many of its citizens could say, 'We have heard for ourselves, and we know that this man really is the Saviour of the world.' How did they come to know? Through the salvation of this one woman. Changed by the Saviour's penetrating grace and power, she opened up the hearts of the whole village to change, to his incoming. And when he came to the people of the village, something of an

altogether supernatural change took place in them. Such was
his power over the moral and spiritual realm of human life,
over the human soul.

His power over the human body: the dying boy lives (John 4:46—54)

In this story a boy's life is fast ebbing away. He is the son of
one of Herod's officials who, since he was looking for a sign
(4:48), probably was a Jew. The location is again Cana of
Galilee, where Jesus turned the water into wine. He had
returned there with his disciples after his time in Jerusalem
and the countryside of Judea. Hearing that Jesus was back in
Galilee, the official hurried up into the hill country from
Capernaum on the Sea of Galilee, solely in order to beg Jesus
to come down to Capernaum and heal his dying son. Only a
father who has been in this situation can properly appreciate
the official's desperation. Death appeared certain and
imminent unless some power beyond the natural could
prevent it.

You will notice that the official lost no time introducing
himself, or apologizing for the interruption, or even pausing
to answer Jesus' reproach: 'Unless you . . . see miraculous
signs and wonders you will never believe.' The official's one
poignant plea was: 'Sir, come down before my child dies.'
And without moving from Cana, without lessening the
distance between himself and the boy by a solitary mile,
Jesus exercised his sovereign power. He told the father,
'You may go. Your son will live.' And the father believed him
and started off on the journey to find the miracle done.
Without even moving from where he was, Jesus had the
power to utter the word, and the healing followed.

What sovereign power this! And what comfort all these
confirmations of Jesus' power would bring to Simon as he
came to know them! They bring comfort to us, too. We
see that our Lord Jesus Christ can effect the change we
need in order to be what God intended us to be. In his
word there is power and authority. He is able to make
things different for us because he is able to make us different. His capacity to change us matches his ability to understand us. His passion for change keeps him pursuing his
efforts to fulfil God's will and likeness in us even if we

rebel, or are blind to his purposes for us. He is able to do *all* that he promises in his holy Word. His power suffices to bring Simon to Peter, and to bring each one of his people to glory.

Reference

1. Leon Morris, *The Gospel According to John* (Marshall, Morgan and Scott, London, 1972), p. 177.

6.
Called to be a fisher of men

'As Jesus walked beside the Sea of Galilee, he saw Simon and his brother Andrew casting a net into the lake, for they were fishermen. "Come, follow me," Jesus said, "and I will make you fishers of men." At once they left their nets and followed him' (Mark 1:16—18).

We come now to two episodes in our Lord's early ministry that describe his summons to Simon and his fellows to become 'fishers of men'. These episodes are recorded in the three synoptic Gospels, in Matthew 4:18—22, Mark 1:16—20 and Luke 5:1—11. The setting is the Sea of Galilee (the Lake of Gennesaret), located in the region of Galilee where, as we saw in the last chapter, Jesus has come with his disciples after a time of ministry in Judea.

Up to this point, Simon has been the passive recipient of several truths and promises. He has heard from John the Baptizer and from Andrew that Jesus of Nazareth is the Messiah. He has met Jesus and heard from him that he, Simon, is to become a new person with a new name. He has very likely witnessed the many manifestations (as recorded in John 1—4) of Jesus' power to know and to change men. Simon has learned much; now it is time for him to respond. We shall see how our Lord elicits response from Simon, first as he calls him to become a fisher of men, then subsequently as he promises Simon success in this undertaking.

There are two separate incidents to consider here: the incident described by Matthew and Mark is different from the one described by Luke. Whereas Matthew and Mark report Jesus as calling two pairs of brothers separately, Luke reports him as evoking response from one larger group of

50

fishermen. Whereas Matthew and Mark describe one of the pairs of brothers as 'casting a net into the lake', and the other pair as 'preparing their nets', Luke describes the fishermen as 'washing their nets' and, later, as all working together to land a miraculous haul of fish. In the first episode, Jesus appears to be walking alone beside the lake when he calls the two pairs of brothers to follow him; in the second episode, he is being so pressed by a great multitude of people that he has to move out onto the lake in a boat in order to preach to them. And, again, whereas the first incident culminates in an invitation by Jesus to follow him and become fishers of men, the second has as its climax more than an invitation — a categorical assertion by Jesus that Simon henceforth 'will catch men'.

These two separate incidents turn on one theme: becoming a fisher of men. In this chapter, using the combined narratives of Matthew, Mark and Luke, we shall try to see something of *the nature of the task* to which the fishermen were called, and *the necessity of training* for it. In the next chapter, concentrating on the incident recorded by Luke, we shall consider *the token of success* which our Lord gave these men, and the significance of it.

The task

Matthew and Mark record our Lord's summons to Simon and his fellows in terms of their becoming 'fishers of men'. Luke's phrase, also a fishing metaphor, is 'catching men', and this has a special meaning which we shall examine later on. But what does the general metaphor *fishing men* suggest?

It evokes a vivid picture. This fallen world is a vast, dark sea of sin, and men are dying in it. They are engulfed in an element that is choking and killing them. Imprisoned in this sea, they have no choice but to go round and round aimlessly and helplessly, trapped and confined. They suffer from darkness and distortion. They have no future except sure destruction. They live in hatred and in bondage: theirs is the kingdom of Satan.

In absolute contrast to this sea of death is the kingdom of God. This is the sphere of light and truth and righteousness,

of love and of salvation. Here, filled with the pure breath
of the Spirit, the redeemed find wholeness and eternal life.
Empowered by God, they have one clear life-direction and
the freedom to pursue it. They experience eternal joys
here, even in this life; yet they know these as but a foretaste of a whole eternity of joy opening out before them.
Theirs is the kingdom of heaven.

The New Testament uses many images to contrast these
two spheres of being. Paul testifies that Jesus sent him to
the Gentiles so that they might turn 'from darkness to
light, and from the power of Satan to God' (Acts 26:18).
He praises God that the Romans who were once 'slaves to
sin' have become 'slaves to righteousness' (Romans
6:16–18). And he testifies of himself that 'through Christ
Jesus the law of the Spirit of life' has set him free from
'the law of sin and death' (Romans 8:2). Peter, the changed
Simon, reminds readers of his first epistle that once they
were 'not a people' but now they are 'the people of God';
once they 'had not received mercy' but now they 'have
received mercy' (1 Peter 2:9,10).

To return to our picture, men in their natural state are
submerged in the sea of sin with no way out. They cannot
extricate themselves from this living death. They cannot
enter the sphere of the heavenly kingdom in their own
strength. And that is exactly why Jesus ordains that his
people should become fishers of men. That is why he
summons Simon and his fellows to move with him alongside
that sea of death, throwing out nets to gather in unsaved
men, and transferring them, by his Spirit, into the totally
different element of light and life and love which is the
kingdom of God. The redeemed are to gather in the un-
redeemed. The redeemed are to be fishers of men. That is
the picture.

Jesus' clear intention

Jesus' words are precise: 'Follow me and I will make you
fishers of men' (Mark 1:7). See how definite his intention
is! He knows exactly what he wants the disciples to do. But
we are always prone to clothe our Lord's clear, unambiguous
terms in qualifications of our own which change his meaning
or make it vague and imprecise. Nothing so militates against

the glory of God than our vagueness in spiritual things. The Bible is never vague. Even when it speaks in terms of general principles, it is never vague. And our Lord's terms here are clear. He has a positive goal in mind. He has a plan for Simon, and it is a fishing plan.

If we are not simply to play at religion, we must match our Lord's precise call with our own definite response. The call to Simon is equally a call to you and to me if we are followers of Jesus Christ. And the sea of death is larger today than it was in Simon's day, with more fish in it. The population explosion means that there are increasingly more people to reach out for, because increasingly more people are dying in sin without the Saviour. Therefore the call comes to the Christian church today as never before: 'Follow me and I will make you fishers of men.'

Unless we get this concept of our duty firmly fixed in our minds, we are not going to be about our Father's business. If we don't aim at catching men, we will rarely catch any. But if we take our Lord's call seriously, we will organize our lives so that the task of fishing men has its due priority. Insofar as the salvation of men is central to the divine plan, so should it also be central to the programme of God's people. If it is true to say that all the purposes of God crystallize down to one — the gathering in of the lost out of a fallen world — then your life and mine should be synchronized to that purpose. We cannot have fellowship with God unless we are one with him in purpose.

It is our Lord's definite intention, then, that we, like Simon, should become fishers of men. Let our intention be the same and as definite. Let our living be purposeful, with the end in view of gathering sinners out of the element of sin and death that engulfs them and, by the Spirit of God, transferring them into a new element — 'into his wonderful light' (1 Peter 2:9), the kingdom of God.

Jesus' masterful metaphor

Our Lord's approach to Simon and his friends was wonderful. He wanted to be clear, so he spoke to them very particularly, in a language they would understand. He spoke in terms of their own trade — fishing. No other metaphor could be so meaningful to them, and that in two distinct ways.

1. Jesus' fishing metaphor served to assure these fishermen that there would be an element of *continuity* between their old life and their new one, between the natural and the spiritual. They had been fishermen; they were to be fishermen still. Many of the old skills of fishing would be needed in the new calling of fishing men: the courage, the patience, the forethought, the perseverance of the fisherman and even the ability to face monotony.

We see here something very encouraging: the God of nature is also the God of grace. The God who made us yesterday is the God who calls us today. Yesterday he made us with natural abilities that today he wants to call into play. He does not want to make a fisherman into a farmer or a farmer into a fisherman. He says, 'Come with all the skills and experiences of your old life; come and use them for me.' It is only when we finally discover God's purpose for our lives that our natural gifts really come into their own. Only the redeemed truly know what fulfilment means.

2. However, Jesus' metaphor also suggested an element of *discontinuity* between the old life of Simon and his friends and the new. The metaphor communicated a kind of promotion to a new sort of fishing. Henceforth they were to catch men, not fish. And what an inestimable difference there is between men and fish! True, there are thinkers today who would have us regard men as merely highly developed fish, but in the Word of God we are taught differently. Man is the most glorious of God's creatures, the highest of all, made after God's image. Therefore, to gather in men is an infinitely graver and greater thing than to gather in fish.

In order to become a fisher of men, a fisherman must move into a wholly new world of values. So, while Simon would be comforted to know about the similarity of the skills involved in the two kinds of fishing, he would also be enormously challenged by the element of discontinuity entailed by his now having to deal with *men* — with the inestimably precious souls of his fellow men. To be a fisher of men is the ultimate privilege of this life. And this is our calling, as it was Simon's.

The training

The calling necessitates training. Listen to how Mark puts it: 'Come ye after me, and *I will make you to become* fishers of men' (1:17 AV). That is cumbersome English. Yet there is no more accurate way to convey what Jesus said. He meant precisely that: 'If you follow me, then I, for my part, will make you to become fishers of men. You will do the becoming, but I will do the making; you will change, but I shall do the changing.'

In other words, there is no way for us to become fishers of men other than by following the Saviour. He makes his followers into fishers of men. And if this is so, then, unless you and I have already become fishers of men, we cannot have been following our Lord very faithfully. Conversely, if we claim to be following Jesus Christ, then we should already be in some measure fishers of men. Insofar as we are not actively involved in this calling, there is something wrong with our following. This is the message of our text.

Training is necessary

Every believer should have compassion and concern for lost men and women, and every believer should feel responsible to seek the lost. It is one of the tragedies of the hour that we have very few concerned hearts in the church. When did we last shed a tear because men are unsaved? When did we last lose an hour's sleep over the plight of the lost? If the Spirit of Jesus Christ of Nazareth is in you and in me, then surely we shall show some of his concern. But far too often we are men of another spirit.

We should all feel responsible to seek the lost, then. But it is quite another thing to be *qualified* to do so. Anyone who presumes to engage in so intricate and delicate a task on the strength of his own natural resources is in for disappointment. Training is absolutely essential. Many people, however, have gone on record as positively denying the need for training, so let us examine two reasons for my assertion that it is necessary.

1. We all agree that those who attend to our physical needs must be trained and certified as competent in order to practise. By what process of reasoning, then, can we

conclude that physicians of the soul need no training? Is the
soul of man less complex or less valuable than the body? Or,
if those who educate the mind in secular things must themselves be taught and certified, by what process of reasoning
can we conclude that men who devote their lives to giving
spiritual guidance need no training? The soul is greater than
the mind, for it includes the mind.

2. That training in man-fishing is essential can also be
proved biblically. If there were no other text than the one
before us, we should need no further proof, especially in
view of the fact that our Lord spent over three years teaching and training Simon and his fellows. Many other texts
in the New Testament, however, spell out the need for this
training. Paul, for instance, urges Timothy to teach other
believers so that they 'will also be qualified to teach others'
(2 Timothy 2:2). And he writes to the Colossians, 'So then,
just as you received Christ Jesus as Lord, continue to live
in him, rooted and built up in him, strengthened in the
faith as you were taught' (Colossians 2:6,7).

The training is specialized

Training for man-fishing is not only essential; it is specialized
as well. We must be careful lest we falsely conclude from
the universality of the duty that it is easy or paltry,
requiring little care and thought.

1. The training is specialized because man-fishing, as
Luke points out, is itself specialized. Whereas Matthew
and Mark use a very ordinary word for fishing, Luke, as we
have already indicated, uses a different term which can be
translated as 'catching men' or 'taking men' or, literally,
'taking men alive'. The mark of the successful fisher of
men will be that he will catch men *alive*.

There were three methods of fishing in New Testament
times. First, there was line-fishing, where bait was put onto
a hook and cast by a line into the water. The fish was caught
by the hook. This kind of fishing is familiar to us today.
Then, second, there were two kinds of net-fishing. In one,
a cone-shaped net was put into the water and pulled towards
the fisherman. In the other, a dragnet was fastened between
two boats which moved in the same direction; as they moved,
the net dragged the sea for fish. Net-fishing brought the fish

in alive, without damaging them. Line-fishing, on the other hand, damaged or even killed the fish because the hooks necessarily had to cut into the throats or jaws or stomachs of the fish in order to pull them to land.

Luke's use of the term 'catching men alive' implies that our Lord wants us to be clear about this: we are not meant to engage in line-fishing with a hook. And that is one reason why we need special training in the art of fishing men. If the wrong method of fishing is used, men may be killed before they are landed. Personalities may be damaged; they may be overrun, bullied and mastered into a position from which, psychologically, they rarely recover. This is a mode of fishing that does damage to the souls God made, and our use of such a method is contrary both to the glory of God and to the good of the people we seek to save.

To change the metaphor, Jesus' concept of 'taking men alive' shows that he is interested in saving lives, not counting scalps. He is concerned to have lives netted for his glory — that is, whole lives, with hearts, minds and consciences intact. He wants a man to be able to serve his God with all that he is and all that he ever can be. Only net-fishing can bring him in undamaged.

2. Just as the training is exclusively for one kind of fishing, for taking men alive, so it is available exclusively in one school and from one teacher. The one infallible teacher of this noble and delicate art is our Lord Jesus Christ, and the one school is to be found in following his footsteps. Our only choice is either to follow Simon's Lord and be taught by him, or to fail. There is no other competent authority and there is no other school.

This specialized training entails more than just enlisting as a disciple of Jesus Christ. It requires the disciplined following to which he refers. The skill of fishing men is properly learned only through living with him daily. It is learned through working in conscious fellowship with him and in accordance with the principles that he practised in the flesh. Simon learned from the incarnate Son of God, the Lord of glory come among men. We learn from the same Lord who, by his Word and by his Spirit, perfects in us that which pleases him. That is the specialized training.

The training is conditional
The divine 'making' requires our 'following'; it is conditional
upon it. 'Following' demanded much more of Simon than
simply being present with Jesus Christ. That was the least
demanding of the stipulated conditions, though even that
meant a costly act of faith. But in addition to that, 'following' meant moving progressively forward with Jesus Christ,
learning each new lesson, obeying each new command
and generally maintaining fellowship with him. That was,
and is, the cost and condition of achievement in the Christian
calling.

Someone might object that this is really just the way of
Christian maturity — it is simply the call to be a good
Christian. Precisely! It *is* the way of Christian growth and
development; and for that very reason it is also the condition
of success in man-fishing. According to Scripture, Christian
character and Christian service are two sides of the same coin.
A man who is following Jesus Christ, and is thereby changed
and transformed in character, is a man who also becomes a
fisher of men. Sanctified character and successful service are
inseparable.

Simon and his friends, then, were called by Jesus Christ
to follow him and become fishers of men. 'At once they
left their nets and followed him' (Mark 1:18). 'Following'
would mean being sanctified; Simon would become Peter.
And though he would have to wait for some time, finally
on the Day of Pentecost he was to experience something
of the fulfilment of Jesus' promise that he would catch men
alive.

We, too, are called to follow Jesus and become fishers of
men. Does the concept discourage you? I should not be
surprised if it does, for Satan would have it so. If we focus
exclusively on the duty, then we have fallen already. But if
we focus on the one who calls us to the duty and who
promises, 'I will make you to become . . .', then we shall
know that his grace is sufficient. And that is our only hope.
Like Simon, we are to be God's fishermen. By his good
hand, we are to gather men out of the sea of sin and death,
lifting them through the gospel message into another sphere
of being altogether — the kingdom of God. Like Simon,
we can be trained only by following our Lord Jesus Christ,

by obeying his voice and learning to sense the movements of his Spirit. This will mean suffering, loneliness, deprivation and a sure cross, but this is the training. We cannot become fishers of men simply by taking courses in 'personal evangelism' or 'spiritual counselling'. We cannot become fishers of men without moving alongside the waters where the fish await us and actually following our Lord Jesus Christ as he leads us.

7.
The call confirmed

'Then Jesus said to Simon, "Don't be afraid;
from now on you will catch men." So they pulled
their boats up on shore, left everything and
followed him' (Luke 5:10,11).

In this chapter we shall examine the token of success in man-fishing which our Lord gave to Simon and his fellows in the form of a miraculous haul of fish. This is the episode reported exclusively by Luke (5:1—11). It took place at a stage in Jesus' public ministry when he was beginning to be popular, beginning to gather the crowds through his works of mercy and power. The timing of this sign to Simon is important, as is the testing of Simon that preceded it. But most significant of all is the token itself and the truth it taught.

The timing of the token

In addition to the fact that Jesus was now beginning to attract great crowds, we need to notice two other important things about the timing of this incident: from the point of view of Simon and his friends, it followed an apparent spiritual failure of the preceding days, and it came right after the evident material failure of the previous night.

Apparent spiritual failure
Let us go back a little. After arriving up north in Galilee, Jesus appears to have dismissed his little band of followers and sent them home to their families. That would be a natural thing to do: they had been down at the Passover

60

feast for a time, then they had been delayed with our Lord as he met the people and performed the miracles that we read about in John 1–4.

Then, after an unspecified length of time, came the incident we were considering in the last chapter. When Jesus was out by the Sea of Galilee one day, he found Simon and Andrew, James and John engaged in their fishing business, and he called them to become fishers of men. Instantly they left everything to follow him. Their response was decisive and whole-hearted (Matthew 4:20,22; Mark 1:18,20).

But, apparently, it was short-lived. Something happened that sent them back to their boats again, and here they were, in the Luke episode, washing their nets by the Sea of Galilee. What had happened? The Scriptures do not tell us, and when they are silent we can only conjecture.

And yet, do we not all know the kind of thing that happens when the Lord Jesus Christ calls us to a specific task? Do we not all know how everything possible intrudes into our lives just when Christ has summoned us to do something very definite for him? Friends and foes seem to unite in massive array to stand in the way. Enticements of the world — the love of ease, the love of pleasure, the desire for this, the lust for that — seem to spring to life when he calls, even though formerly we may not have experienced them. Everything seems to conspire together to distract us from what we have been called to do, and to hinder us from doing it.

Perhaps something of this order caused Simon and his friends to return to the familiar security of their secular life. But Jesus Christ, who had called them, did not leave them there. This is the thrilling note that we shall find running through Simon Peter's whole life: the one who called Simon always pursues him when he goes astray, and woos him back into the way of his will. Our Lord Jesus Christ always perseveres with Simon, fickle and floundering though he is, and redeems his spiritual failure.

Evident material failure
Whatever success Simon and his friends may have experienced at their fishing during the intervening days since they had turned their backs on the Lord Jesus and returned to

their boats, the night before this incident had been utterly
disastrous. They had caught no fish at all. Experienced fishermen though they were, and fishing in familiar waters (they
had been brought up here on the Sea of Galilee), they had
nevertheless *'worked hard all night and [hadn't] caught
anything'*. The fish kept strangely distant.

What a dismal state of affairs! The whole world seemed
to have turned against these men since they had come to
know Jesus Christ. They found it too difficult to obey
him and do what he asked of them, yet, having returned
to their secular vocation, they could make nothing of that
either. They were total failures. It looked as if Simon would
never become Peter at this rate! This was a time of deep
discouragement for him and his fellows. And this was exactly
the time when Jesus deliberately persevered with them,
especially with Simon, even to the extent of giving them a
token of ultimate success in the context of such abject
failure. Such is the divine timing!

The test that preceded the token

Looking at our text, Luke 5:1—11, we find the fishermen
back at their fishing again, cleaning their nets. Their two
boats stand empty near the water's edge. Through a remarkable providence, Jesus comes to the lakeside as he had on
the earlier occasion. This time, however, he is accompanied
by a whole crowd of people who are pressing in on him,
wanting to hear him speak. He is so pressed that he is driven
down to the edge of the lake and then into Simon's very
boat.

How graphic some life situations are when you see them
in perspective! While the very men who have been called to
be fishers of men are running away from their duty, the
'fish' whom they are meant to catch come crowding after
them. And while these men glumly clean the nets into
which no ordinary fish would swim last night, the very
catch for which they have not prepared nets stands eagerly
clamouring to be caught. What divine irony!

But Jesus is about his Father's business even if the fishermen are not. He steps into Simon's boat and asks him to put

out a little into the lake so that he can teach the people who are crowding around with such apparent spiritual hunger. The sight of the needy multitude and the sound of the Master's voice must stir Simon, and prepare him to some degree for what follows.

What follows is the double-thrust command from Jesus to Simon: *'Put out into deep water, and let down the nets for a catch.'* Jesus is commanding Simon to obey him – to do exactly what he says, even if it makes little sense. He is doing this because he wants to clarify Simon's precise relationship with himself. There is nothing more revealing of our real estimate of the person of Jesus Christ than our response to his commands. He will persevere with us, provided that in the depths of our hearts we have the right view of him.

That is exactly what Jesus wants to get clear: who does Simon really think he is? He is testing Simon, challenging him to show, through an act of obedience, what he thinks of Jesus. And on the basis of Simon's response to this challenge, Jesus will grant or withhold a token of ultimate success in Simon's calling. Let us look at the drama in action.

1. Already seated in Simon's boat, Jesus issues a command that is really a tacit claim to control Simon's boat and Simon's time. The boat is clearly Simon's, yet Jesus has taken it over. Simon has been washing his nets, yet Jesus has interrupted that important part of a fisherman's routine. How will Simon react?

Our Lord wants to expose his basic assumptions about himself. Does Simon see him as a mere man, as someone who has no right at all to be appropriating Simon's boat and his time? Or does Simon see Jesus as more than man, as the Messiah, perhaps, who has the rights and authority of a divinely appointed King over his people?

2. Look again. Jesus' command is also a tacit claim to have authority over Simon's natural wisdom and his personal will. When Jesus commands him to 'put out into deep water, and let down the nets for a catch', he is challenging Simon's wisdom as a fisherman: Simon is a good fisherman and knows better than to fish with nets during the daytime. Jesus is challenging his will as well: Simon had certainly not intended to fish right now.

Again, Simon's response will reveal his view of Jesus. If he sees him as a mere carpenter meddling in the affairs of a fisherman, Simon will mince no words telling him to mind his own business. Simon is under no obligation to do what is against his own better judgement at the peremptory command of a carpenter! What right has a carpenter to tell Simon what to do? Or is he the Messiah and has he the right? Jesus' challenge to Simon revolves around the one crucial question: 'Who is it that now commands me to do these things?'

What is Simon's response? The struggle is short-lived, even if it is sharp and deep. The grace of God suffices. He has begun a work in Simon's heart, as we can see by his response: *'Master, we've worked hard all night and haven't caught anything. But because you say so, I will let down the nets.'* Contrasting the 'we' with the 'you', Simon Peter yields greater wisdom and sovereign right to Jesus Christ. Simon acknowledges Jesus' authority over his possessions, his plans, his natural wisdom and his will. Simon is clearly convinced that the person who earlier taught the crowds from his boat and now bids him do what he personally considers futile, if not foolish — this person is more than a mere bungling human being. Jesus is of such an order of being that Simon can do no other than yield to his sovereignty and submit to his wisdom.

Grace has triumphed. This is what Jesus wanted: to force Simon to express in action, not in mere words, which can be glib, what he really thinks of him. And with that proof of grace in the fisherman's heart, vacillating and immature though the man still is, Jesus proceeds to carry out his plan to reassure the uncertain Simon of eventual success in his divinely appointed calling.

The token and the truth it taught

Luke describes what happens next in these words: *'When they had done so [let down the nets], they caught such a large number of fish that their nets began to break. So they signalled their partners in the other boat to come and help them, and they came and filled both boats so full that they began to sink.'*

The Master was indeed more than a carpenter. Whereas when Simon and his fellows had been fishing on that same lake the night before, all the fish had seemed to rush off in the opposite direction, now, as soon as the nets were cast, all the fish of creation seemed to rush into them. The fact that it was contrary to natural expectation made no difference. Drawn as by an unseen magnet, these fish made straight for the nets that were cast at the command of Jesus. The nets filled up to breaking-point. The men needed help to bring the huge catch to land. That was the token, overwhelming and overpowering in its abundance.

Simon's reaction was most revealing. Although he saw the bulk of the catch, he did not become absorbed with it. He would be glad to see it: it would change the whole fortune of the family for weeks. Had Simon been a materialist, he would have said something like this to Jesus: 'Lord, keep close to me so that I can keep on getting hauls of fish like this. Keep close to me so that I can go out again tomorrow and heap riches upon riches. In a few years' time I'll be able to retire on an early pension and then I'll be free to come and follow you!'

But Simon did not say anything like that. He asked Jesus to go away. Seeing beyond the bulk of the catch to the glory of the one responsible for it, he was overwhelmed by the holiness of that one and by his own unworthiness: *'When Simon Peter saw this, he fell at Jesus' knees and said, "Go away from me, Lord; I am a sinful man!"'* The one whom he had previously called 'Master' he now acknowledged as 'Lord'. He fell at his knees and offered to him what is due only to God. He begged him to go away, not because he did not know him or want him, but because he could not comprehend the unfathomable privilege of being pursued and disciplined by so divine an instructor. Simon acknowledged his own total unworthiness to receive such wonderful grace, such great love. That spirit is vital both for rightly honouring the Saviour and for effectively engaging in 'catching men'.

However dimly, Simon saw the truth taught by the token of the miraculous haul of fish. It was a twofold truth that we need to see, too.

1. Jesus is Lord over areas that, humanly speaking, were

not familiar to him. Though as a man he knew less than Simon about fishing, yet as God he held the key to Simon's success in fishing. It was he who now filled Simon's nets. It was also he, we are to understand, who kept the fish out of Simon's nets the previous night. The carpenter of Nazareth is Lord of the fishes and Lord of the sea.

This means that success is more a matter of following Jesus and being in fellowship with him than of having a natural capacity for what God calls us to do. When God calls us to do something, most of us protest, like Moses, that we lack the natural capacity required. But we need to learn Simon's lesson: first, our natural capacities can fail and, second, God's capacities cover every sphere of life and they cannot fail. Our part is to follow him.

2. Jesus is not only Lord over all creation but, as Lord, he is also absolutely trustworthy. As long as we submit to the Saviour's control and obey his commands, no promise of his need be unfulfilled in our lives. Like Simon, we may wonder why the Lord commands us to do this or that. We may sometimes quibble and argue and want to reject his commands outright. But let us notice that when Simon, even against his own better judgement, obeyed the Lord of glory, when he pocketed his pride and his sense of knowing it all and launched out into the deep, then he learned through the haul of fishes that he could trust Jesus.

If we, like Simon and his fellows, are running away from a calling which we consider far too difficult for us to fulfil, let us see that our doubts and fears are groundless. We can trust our Lord. He can enable us to catch men just as easily as he enabled those men to catch fish, as long as we are following him. It is in following that we discover the fulfilment of his promises.

Jesus said to Simon, 'Don't be afraid; from now on you will catch men.' And he did. In the book of Acts we see this very man Peter as a successful fisher of men, throwing out the nets and bringing them in again, full almost to the point of breaking. Three thousand souls are added to the church on the Day of Pentecost (Acts 2:41), all by the hand of the man who is himself in the hand of the Lord.

My dear fellow Christian, as surely as Jesus called Simon to be a fisher of men, so also does he call us. Take a good, long look at him outwitting the specialist in the specialist's field. Success and failure are in his hands; no task he gives us to do is impossible. He is Lord. All he requires of us is the confidence in him which is faith, and the obedience to his commands which is 'following'. Let him control our possessions and our wills, and we shall not know defeat.

Let us leave our nets and return to following him in fulfilment of his call to us. The need is overwhelmingly great. His promises and his power are at our disposal.

8.
In his steps

The directive which our Lord gave to those whom he called to be fishers of men was 'Follow me' (Matthew 4:19; Mark 1:17). It seems like a simple condition on the face of it, and without much significant content. But that is an illusion. In fact, its meaning is so profound and its implications are so wide-ranging that only a detailed knowledge of all the Gospel records of Jesus' subsequent ministry will fully reveal what is meant by it.

When we turn to the Gospel records in order to discover just what kind of pilgrimage is ahead for those who would follow the Saviour, we find that the road is steep and rugged, and there are many adversaries on it. Its landmarks are not geographical; they are the spiritual principles practised by our Lord Jesus Christ. Only by learning what these are, and by applying them to our own lives, shall we be enabled to press on, moving close at the heels of the Shepherd of our souls. This is the way. If Simon is to become Peter, he must follow in it. If we are to become fishers of men, we must follow in it. We learn everything we need to know by following Jesus. There is nothing we need to know that we cannot learn through following him.

Come, then, and let us see the Master about his holy business, looking particularly at the principles by which he acts or does not act, and then, by the grace of God, applying them to ourselves. Concentrating on the record in Mark 1:35—42, let us look at three outstanding principles which were clearly articulated and practised by Jesus throughout his whole ministry.

Communion with God comes first

Mark's initial observation about Jesus in this passage is that
he began the day after the sabbath in a place of communion
with God: 'Very early in the morning, while it was still dark.
Jesus got up, left the house and went off to a solitary place,
where he prayed.'

Simple, but essential! Here is a fundamental principle: the
pilgrimage from Simon to Peter necessitates daily communion with God. This is one daily practice that will be
required of any person who is to become a fisher of men.
There are no exceptions to this rule, not one. The pilgrimage
from the old to the new, from the men we were by nature
to the men God has promised to make us by grace, necessarily requires that we have a daily place of communion
with God. I am not speaking now of family prayer, nor of
the need to meet together regularly in public worship. I am
speaking of the daily need for each individual Christian to
come alone before God in prayer and worship, to meet him
and to wait upon him.

How significant it is that even our Lord, the incarnate
Son of God, found it necessary to leave aside both friend
and foe in order to commune alone with his heavenly Father!
Not that his link with God was ever ruptured; on the contrary, his daily life was one of unbroken and unclouded
fellowship with him. And yet he found it needful to begin
the day with this intensive, intimate, private communing
with his Father, apart and alone. If any person in the course
of human history could have done without this, Jesus should
have been that person. His heart was utterly dedicated to
doing the will of God. He was filled with the Holy Spirit,
whom he never grieved. He knew the will of God from
eternity. He had all power and all wisdom. Nevertheless he
began his day with prayer.

You and I are very different from Jesus Christ. Often we
don't know the will of God. Because we don't know it, we
have to seek to discover it. Even when we do discover it, we
are not always whole-hearted in doing it. And when we have
the Spirit within us, we often grieve him. How much more
than Jesus, then, do we need times of communion alone
with God, when in solitude and quiet we can bare our hearts

in his presence, and receive in return the grace he gives to all
who draw near!

A matter of priority

Notice that, with our Lord, this place of personal fellowship
with God had highest priority. This is revealed both in his
teaching and in his example. The passage before us provides
a particularly telling instance: the preceding verses (Mark
1:21–34) show how exacting the previous day had been for
Jesus.

It was a sabbath day, and Jesus had necessarily honoured
his Father's injunction to worship. He had gone to the
synagogue. He was invited to speak and he proceeded to
expound the Scriptures to men who had hitherto miscon-
strued them. Mark records that 'They were amazed at his
teaching . . .' That had been the first battle of the day:
opposing and correcting the scribal interpretation of Scripture by expounding it truly. 'Just then a man in their
synagogue who was possessed with an unclean spirit cried
out . . .' The second battle had followed hard on the first:
exorcising the evil spirit, which 'shook the man violently
and came out of him with a shriek'.

Then Jesus had gone with his little band of disciples to
Simon Peter's house. Upon entering, he was told that Simon's
mother-in-law was ill and he proceeded to perform another
miracle of healing. When Jesus healed, according to Luke,
the doctor, 'there went virtue [power] out of him' (Luke
6:19 AV). For the incarnate Son of God, healing was not a
simple matter of divine fiat: his energies were drained. He
gave of himself.

There then followed what appears to have been a quiet
afternoon in the privacy of Simon's home, and the sabbath
ended at sundown. But the conclusion of the sabbath had
involved Jesus in his most exacting labours yet, for at sundown, having been forbidden by the scribal understanding
of the sabbath to carry anything on their backs or in their
arms during the day, the Jews of Capernaum had 'brought to
Jesus all the sick and demon-possessed'. The area around
Simon's house was suddenly thronged with sick folk whom
their friends had been waiting all day to bring to Jesus:
'The whole town gathered at the door.' They were waiting

for one thing: the touch or the healing word of the Son of God. And he graciously and mercifully 'healed many who had various diseases. He also drove out many demons . . .' We are not told what time he went to bed that night.

Anybody who is aware of spiritual battles will know just how exacting that sabbath day had been for Jesus. It had been filled with a nearly continuous round of spiritual demands: preaching to people who had little sympathy for his message; spending his resources in many acts of physical healing; wrestling with the power of Satan to deliver many people from demons. And yet we read, 'Very early in the morning, while it was still dark, Jesus got up, left the house and went off to a solitary place, where he prayed.' We see that Jesus valued this meeting in prayer with the Father so highly that he put it ahead of every other consideration. The place of communion with God had priority of place with the Son of God.

A matter of consistency

Communion with God was also a matter of consistency for our Lord. Jesus Christ was the most consistent person who ever lived. And having publicly attended the synagogue for worship on the sabbath, he also privately attended to the same exercise early the next day. Why had he gone to the synagogue? It was not in order to be seen by men. He went there because it was his Father's house, the place where the faithful gathered, the place of worship. In other words, he had gone there to please God, to obey him and honour him.

And it was for these same reasons that our Lord engaged in private prayer with his Father very early the next morning. His motive was as compelling on the morning after the sabbath as it had been on the sabbath morning. For Jesus, communion with God was not a matter of day or season or social custom; it was a matter of heart and soul, of discerning the will of God. Therefore, it was consistently necessary.

To follow Jesus, then, is to be consistent in communing with God. To follow him is to have both a place of private communion where we worship God and hear his voice daily, and a place of public worship where we go loyally at the appointed hour. This is the way for Simon to become Peter. This is how a man is weaned away from material and

earthly things in order to become a fisher of men. This is the
way in which you and I must walk. There is no other way.
Communion with God comes first.

Communion with God yields a sense of direction

Mark's second observation about Jesus in this passage is that
he emerged from his place of communion with a God-given
sense of direction that governed his planning of the day:
'Simon and his companions went to look for him, and
when they found him, they exclaimed: "Everyone is looking
for you!" Jesus replied, "Let us go somewhere else — to
the nearby villages — so I can preach there also. That is why
I have come."'

It is important to be clear about the fact that Jesus Christ
came into the world *not simply* to do God's will: he came to
do it *in fellowship with God.* Jesus was not an errand-boy
sent by the Father to do certain things here on earth while
the Father remained aloof in heaven. Rather, he came to
live and act on earth as a man in communion with God.
They laboured together. They suffered together. They had
victories together. It was the Father *and* the Son, always.

That, of course, meant Jesus' constant conferring with the
Father in order to do the Father's will, in the Father's way
and at the Father's appointed time. Our Lord was not only
conscious of a call to be the Saviour of the world; he also
sensed a divine commission for each day's task. He moved
out of his daily place of communion with a daily sense of
God-given direction. He was aware of his daily duty.

Notice that Mark records both a negative and a positive
sense of direction in our Lord's approach to this particular
day. On the one hand, Jesus refuses to heed the demands
of the Capernaum multitudes that he go back to them for
the day. He resolutely turns down the plea of 'everyone'
at Capernaum. Without going into detail as to why or
wherefore, he simply makes it clear that the way for this
day is not backwards to the scene of yesterday's activity.

On the other hand, the way for this day is forward into
the other towns: 'Let us go somewhere else — to the nearby
villages — so I can preach there also. That is why I have

come.' Capernaum seeks Jesus for his miracles (if we rightly assess its present mood in the light of later teaching), but our Lord's primary task at this stage of his ministry is to preach. It was for this purpose, as the necessary preliminary to his dying, that he came into the world at his incarnation, and it is to perform this specific task today that he has come from communion with his Father in prayer. He intends to go on to the next towns to preach. The duty of each new day is always forward into the new, not backwards into the old.

Notice how the phrase 'That is why I have come' (AV, 'therefore came I forth') refers both to our Lord's larger calling and to his task for the day. Jesus *'came'* into the world at his incarnation to engage in the ministry of teaching and preaching that would ultimately lead to his sacrifice for the sin of the world: this was his larger calling, his life-goal. Jesus has also *'come* forth' from communion with his Father in prayer early this morning, armed with precise knowledge of where he must go *today*. In communion with his Father he has heard the bleating of the sheep in the other towns, and he knows that his specific commission for today is to preach to them. Thus our Lord has a double sense of direction — long-term and immediate.

The message for Simon

The Master's example of finding direction through communion with God was particularly relevant to Simon Peter just at that time. However clear and compelling his original call had been ('Follow me . . .'), and however well it had been confirmed, especially in recent days ('. . . you will catch men'), Simon was uncertain of his next step. He certainly did not know what he should be doing today. He felt the pull of two worlds. It was he, you notice, who came to Jesus with the request to return to Capernaum that day. Why? Because Simon's home was there! How much easier it would be for him to serve the Lord in Capernaum, where he could go back to his boats and his fishing if he so desired, than to move forward with Jesus into unfamiliar areas and difficult places beyond the home territory, in strict obedience to the Master's call! Would Simon take the easy or the difficult way? How would he decide? Simon as yet knew no clear sense of direction because he had not learned to follow in the Saviour's steps to a daily place of private communion with God. Simon lacked the daily reassurance of his appointed duty and the daily grace to do it, both of which come from prayer.

The message for all disciples

There are two things about which all of us, as prospective fishers of men, would do well to be certain. We need to be certain about our original call to follow Christ, on the one hand; and we need to be certain about the fact that, daily, we are doing the Master's will, on the other hand. If we are not certain of our call, we can hardly be sure of the Lord's daily will for us. If we are not certain of doing the Lord's will daily, we can hardly expect to make any impact as his followers. If we do, it will be despite our ignorant gropings. Jesus shows us the way whereby our original 'going forth' in fulfilment of God's call may be authenticated daily and related daily to the needs and the issues around us — that is, in the place of quiet retreat where we fellowship with God. The sense of divine direction that alone will carry us forward against the combined opposition of Satan, the world and the weakness of the flesh can only come out of a deep and abiding communion with him.

'That is why I have come.' Do you know anything of such a sense of direction, both long-term and immediate, that carries you along through the days, living a life which you know in your heart is a life of doing your Master's will? Do you know the reason for your existence? Do you know why God has preserved your life and redeemed you by the blood of Christ? Do you know what he wants you to be doing today? The one place to discover all this and know it and be reassured of it is in the daily place of quiet with the Lord. Blessed are those who have learned to follow in the steps of the Saviour in having this place of prayer. They not only sense daily the Reality who is God, but they also learn to be co-workers with him, moving fearlessly and confidently wherever he directs them, knowing that this is his will for the day. To the extent that we know intimacy with God, we know whether we are about our Father's business.

Communion with God yields a heart of compassion

Mark's third observation about Jesus in this passage is that he
came from his place of prayer with a heart full of godly
compassion: 'A man with leprosy came to him and begged
him on his knees, "If you are willing, you can make me
clean." Filled with compassion, Jesus reached out his hand
and touched the man. "I am willing," he said. "Be clean!"
Immediately the leprosy left him and he was cured' (Mark
1:40–42).

Jesus Christ did not simply do the will of God and heal
the leper; just as important, he did it in God's way, with the
compassion of God, with godly love. Our Lord emerged from
his communion with the Father resolved not only to move in
a certain direction, but also to act with a heart of compassion. His sense of duty, strong as it was, did not drive
him forward without regard for human feelings and sensitivities; his compassion was divinely inspired. What we have
before us is something far more precious than the mere
healing of the leper, wonderful though that was.

Before this incident took place, Jesus had gone the rounds
of the Galilean synagogues. These synagogues were not
comfortable places for the Messiah. He was not much wanted
there. Many of the Jews were becoming increasingly angered
against his ministry and the uncompromising nature of his
claims. But around to a whole range of synagogues he went!
If he had been just like us, how jaded and fatigued and short-
tempered he would have felt after such an exhausting round
of preaching to unreceptive people, and healing many demon-
possessed ones as well!

Then along came a man suffering from leprosy. If there is
any kind of person you would rather not meet at the end of
an itinerary like that, it is a person like this — a man with
such a loathsome disease (particularly in those days when
there was little or no remedy for leprosy) coming near you
and falling down at your feet and repeating over and over
again (it is a present tense, which is continuous): 'If you are
willing, you can heal me! If you are willing, you can heal
me! You can if you are willing! You can!' What a test of
patience!

But what did Jesus do? In spite of his fatigue, his

compassionate heart overflowed with love for the desperate man before him and he stretched out his hand and touched him. He did not simply heal him. Mighty though that act of healing was, it was the least thing Jesus did for the leper. Mark tells us that he '*touched* the man'. That touching of the man was no less precious than his healing. It was not necessary to the act of healing. Jesus could have declared, 'Be clean, go home, but don't come too near me!' And it would have been so. Jesus could have stood at a safe distance to heal the man, and there would have been nothing but rejoicing on all sides. But he did not do that. What the leper dared not expect anyone to do, Jesus did. He touched him.

Can you see that leprosy-ridden man, for a moment, as Jesus, in his compassion, saw him? He had not been allowed near any society for a very long time, ever since he had contracted this dread disease. He had been ostracized by everyone. No friendly hand had touched him for many a long day. And the Master wanted to assure him doubly of genuine sympathy. He wanted him to know that he had not come just to throw a miraculous gift at his feet, but to embrace him as well, and show the divine compassion of his Father. And so he touched him. The incident of healing was no mere act of power; it was suffused with the glow and grace of profoundest godly love as well.

I shall never in my life forget seeing this same spirit of love wonderfully expressed before my eyes when visiting a colony for those afflicted by leprosy in Africa. I did not know why these people were listening so receptively to the gospel, and responding so exceedingly beyond our prayers, until the following incident occurred. One morning as we arrived by car for a service, some of the women who had been eaten away by leprosy (though now it had been arrested) came running up to the lady who had driven the car. They put their arms around her and kissed her, and she kissed them. I looked at their unlovely faces and I felt a shudder. I could not have embraced them. But she could and did! It was no wonder they were responding so confidently to the gospel. The compassion of God had been declared and made real to them through the embrace of that God-fearing soul.

A place of communion; a sense of direction; a heart of

compassion. Do you see the principles and the connections between them? The clear sense of direction needs always to be matched by a heart full of love, and both are found in the place of daily fellowship with God in prayer. This was the pattern of our Lord's life and his dealing with men. It must be ours too. Simon, and every other follower of Christ, needs the spirit of love as well as the sense of duty that moved Jesus to heal the leper. As representatives of so great and gracious a God and Saviour, we owe it to the world to show rich compassion along with resolute will. Anything less, however apparently correct, is not worthy of our Lord.

We are doubtless challenged by so high a standard. 'Who is equal to such a task?' we cry with the apostle Paul (2 Corinthians 2:16). No one is equal to it in and of himself. Our sufficiency can only be from God, from the one whom we follow and who indwells us by his Spirit. His grace alone can produce a sense of duty and an attitude of compassion in any heart. Let me conclude with a story.

A gardener one day rescued a wild briar from the ditch where it had been left to rot and die and he planted it in a flower-bed where he was expecting a crop of flowers in the springtime. An onlooker imagined the briar's reaction in this way: 'How foolish,' the briar said, 'how foolish can a man be? Fancy placing a briar like me in a setting like this! I can produce nothing and I'll be out of place!'

But the gardener knew what he was about. He later returned and made a slit in the briar's stem, grafting into it the stem of a choicest rose. Later in the season, as flowers appeared elsewhere, so also were there lovely, perfumed roses on that old briar tree that had been left to rot in the gutter. Addressing the briar with the roses on it, the gardener said quietly, 'Now you understand! I did not plant you there for what you were going to give me, but for what I was going to make of you!' 'Christ in you, the hope of glory' (Colossians 1:27).

Let us learn to follow the Saviour. May the Lord grant to us to have a place of communion with him in which, daily, we shall know a sense of direction in doing the Father's business. And may he also grant to us hearts so full of compassion that we do not ride roughshod over other peoples' sensitivities, but instead, with care and love, do our Master's business in a God-honouring way so that the fragrance of the indwelling Rose of Sharon (Song of Solomon 2:1) may be shed abroad even from these once wild briars, from you and from me.

9.
When obedience leads into a storm

Three of the Gospels describe how, just a few hours after the miraculous feeding of the five thousand, a storm arose on the Sea of Galilee (Matthew 14:22–33; Mark 6:45–52; John 6:16–21). This storm must have left an indelible impression on the disciples, and especially on Simon Peter who, as so often, featured at the very centre of the action. The storm taught a great lesson. Every detail of its setting, both geographical and spiritual, seems to have been designed by God to convey a specific meaning. This storm was no accident, in other words. It was totally and purposefully controlled by God. And we can discover some important principles to take hold of in our own lives, by observing the disciples as they enter the storm, as they experience its fury, and as they react after it is over.

Entering the storm

> *'Immediately Jesus made the disciples get into the boat and go on ahead of him to the other side, while he dismissed the crowd' (Matthew 14:22).*

Immediately after the feeding of the five thousand, according to both Matthew and Mark, Jesus hurriedly summoned his disciples, telling them to get into their boat and go ahead of him to the other side of the Sea of Galilee. He did this with an evident sense of urgency: *'Immediately* Jesus *made* (AV, *constrained*) the disciples . . .'* And he did this contrary to his usual practice of leaving the disciples to dismiss the crowds. Having first dispatched the disciples to the boat, Jesus himself dismissed the multitude.

79

Why did our Lord feel this sense of urgency? Because he knew the hearts of the people. He knew that these five thousand men, besides women and children, 'intended' in John's words, 'to come and make him king by force' (John 6:15). They had just witnessed a miraculous act whereby Jesus had transformed five barley loaves and two fish, all of which together would not begin to fill one basket, into enough food to feed the whole multitude and to have twelve full baskets of fragments left over afterwards. What marvellous provision for the crowd's needs! 'Surely this is the Prophet who is to come into the world,' they concluded (John 6:14). Wouldn't it be wonderful to have him as their king?

Knowing that this intention was in their hearts, and that it was not God's purpose that he should become an earthly monarch, Jesus quickly saw to it that both he and his disciples evaded the self-interested scheming of the crowd. He sent the disciples into their boat, dismissed the crowd, then withdrew to the hills by himself to pray.

The disciples proceeded to the boat and began to cross the lake. To appreciate the significance of this whole episode, let us note carefully, first, that these men were, in fact, *disciples* of Jesus Christ. Despite all their faults and shortcomings, despite their great immaturity, they were disciples in the sense that they had taken the essential step of separating themselves from other men to be our Lord's known and acknowledged followers. Secondly, note that in getting into the boat and crossing the lake they were actually doing their Lord's bidding. They were *obedient disciples*. On this occasion, in contrast to some earlier occasions, they were acting in precise obedience to Jesus; they were not entering their boat out of self-will, or out of a desire to run away from their Master's claims. They were obeying him, *and yet* they ran into a violent and threatening storm.

This incident teaches us, therefore, that not all the storms of life are encountered because of disobedience or flagrant violation of divine law. It is true, of course, that 'the wicked are like the tossing sea . . .' and that 'there is no peace . . . for the wicked' (Isaiah 57:20,21). It is also true that some storms *are* encountered on the course of disobedience. Jonah learned that. Not wanting to declare God's message to

Nineveh, and setting sail in the very opposite direction, he ran into a ferocious storm. Simon Peter had the same experience, spiritually, when, in outright defiance of Jesus' command, as we shall see later, he followed him to the high priest's courtyard. Yes, there are storms on the way of disobedience. But there are also storms on the way of obedience, on the very route mapped out for his loyal followers by God's dear Son, our Saviour. And that is the kind of situation we have here in this incident. These were our Lord's own people, doing his will, and yet they met with a terrifying storm.

It is most important that we should always bear in mind that some storms are encountered in the course of obedience. Those who tell us (and they are usually found in evangelistic circles) that the Christian life is all sunshine do us a great disservice. They would have us believe that the Christian life is like an effortless drive in a marvellous limousine. We are cushioned with comforts on the inside, and we are quite unaffected by what happens outside. We do not need to worry about hills or storms or dangers on the road. There are no hills. There are no storm clouds. There are no difficulties. It is all a straight, easy course. In fact, it is downhill. We have nothing but comforts and provisions. There is no battle, no wrestling, no dimension that would involve us in a problem — *or a cross*!

That is a lie, fellow Christians. Even if it comes from the lips of an evangelist or a pastor, it is a downright lie and a contradiction of Scripture! Did not Jesus say, 'If anyone would come after me, he must deny himself and take up his cross daily and follow me'? (Luke 9:23.) A cross is not a decoration on your lapel; it is that on which you are going to die! It means blood and suffering. Our Lord and his apostles constantly warned men of the inevitability of suffering and sorrow and storms of one kind or another in the life of discipleship. We simply cannot follow the Crucified One very far without sharing his reproach or incurring the fury of his foes upon ourselves. If we are loyal to him in this fallen world, we shall be wounded sooner or later, be it in body or spirit. Perhaps it is significant that Peter himself later warned fellow Christians of this very thing: 'Dear friends, do not be surprised at the painful trial you are suffering, as though something strange were happening to you. But rejoice that you participate in the sufferings of Christ' (1 Peter 4:12,13).

Many Christians are confused about this issue. They have been taught that suffering necessarily presupposes sin: if you are sick, it is necessarily because you have sinned; if a storm comes upon you, it is necessarily because you have broken the law of God. But this is not necessarily the case! It is true that all evil (sickness, suffering, calamity) in our world exists, ultimately, because this is a fallen world, and when God finishes with the world there will be no tears, no heartaches, no sorrows. But to say that is quite a different thing from saying that the storms which overtake the saints on the way of obedience do so, really, because the saints are not obeying. That is both self-contradictory and untrue. The Gospels tell us that in our Lord's day his disciples ran into a storm because they obeyed him. In our day, too, his followers encounter storms through being obedient.

Let me give you an example. In a prayer letter from India a missionary tells about a young man who, after a period of deep consideration, became a Christian. That was just the beginning of the story. He then went home to his orthodox Hindu family, only to be beaten and kicked out. On another occasion his college friends tried to poison him. God be praised, he had been taught that it is costly to follow Jesus; in spite of all his suffering he continued to share his new joy and peace with others as he had been taught to do. Ultimately, too, his father accepted him. But he certainly met with storms and pain on the path of obedience. All of us need to be aware that we, too, may encounter storms because we are loyal to our Lord.

In the storm

> 'When evening came . . . the boat was already a considerable distance from land, buffeted by the waves, because the wind was against it' (Matthew 14:23,24).

As night approaches we see the disciples, obediently engaged in rowing towards the other side of the lake, suddenly overtaken by one of those boisterous, totally unexpected storms that are still commonly experienced on the Sea of Galilee because of its position below sea level. Matthew focuses attention on the severity of the storm; Mark, on the other hand, emphasizes the men's turmoil of body and mind: 'He saw the disciples straining at the oars' (6:48). They are really on the verge of giving up, in other words. Fishermen though some of them are, they are foundering terribly, they are badly frightened, and they are in evident danger.

Where is the Saviour? This is a question which naturally arises, especially in the minds of those who are not committed Christians, but also in the minds of thoughtful Christian people. Where is the Master who told these men to get into the boat and cross the lake? He has sent his disciples this way, knowing, probably, that the storm was brewing. Where, then, is he when they are in trouble? What is he doing when his saints are in the storm? The Gospel writers give us three answers to this question.

He is watching over the disciples

'After leaving [the crowd], he went into the hills to pray. When evening came, the boat was in the middle of the lake, and he was alone on land. He saw the disciples straining at the oars, because the wind was against them' (Mark 6:46–48).

This is a wonderful picture. There on the hillside overlooking the scene of his disciples' distress, their Lord and Saviour is watching and praying, praying and watching. Communing with his heavenly Father, he is also watching over his people in their little boat, and he is involving his Father in the same act of loving concern. The Father on the throne and the Son on the Palestinian hill together are watching over that storm-tossed boat. Together they are talking about it. Together they are listening to the sighs and the forebodings of the disciples. Together they see everything that is happening inside and outside the boat. Together they are keeping vigil through the first, second and third watches of the night, into the fourth watch. 'Indeed, he who watches over Israel will neither slumber nor sleep' (Psalm 121:4).

This is a lesson of cardinal importance: let us take it to heart. Though physically withdrawn from his followers, Jesus Christ is neither careless of their needs nor ignorant of their plight. He is awake beyond their vision, watching over them and praying for them. To step out into the Lord's service without knowing this is to be robbed of something exceedingly important and precious. Well does the hymn-writer express it:

> Oh, the deep, deep love of Jesus!
> Spread his praise from shore to shore;
> How he loveth, ever loveth,
> Changeth never, nevermore;
> How he watches o'er his loved ones,
> Died to call them all his own;
> How for them he intercedeth,
> Watcheth o'er them from the throne
>   S. T. Francis (1834–1925).

In this hillside vigil we have a faint picture of what is now taking place in the glory, in our Lord's present ministry of intercession for his people at the Father's right hand. While those who are obeying his commands are struggling, perhaps even with a furious storm that threatens their very destruction, 'he always lives to intercede for them' (Hebrews 7:25). You men and women who are going out into the storms of life because you are obedient to your Lord, please know that his eye never leaves you. Just as the seven churches in the book of Revelation are assured by our risen, ascended Lord, 'I know . . . I know . . . I know . . .' (Revelation 2:2, 9,13,19; 3:1,8,15) — he knows their circumstances, their enemies, their problems — so we should rest assured that he is watching over us with total knowledge of our situation, and with divine compassion for our suffering.

He is waiting to intervene
It may seem strange to us that our Lord actually *waits* to intervene. He could have stepped in as soon as the storm began! Are these not his own disciples, actually engaged in doing his bidding? Does he not want them to reach the other side of the lake in safety? Then why does he not come to their rescue?

The answer is that he waits until the storm has served its intended purpose. For the storm that our Lord allows to break upon his loyal servants is so allowed because it can bless and enrich them. When our Lord plans or permits a storm, he does so because he is able to make it a means of grace for his people: there is some valuable lesson, some enrichment of our spiritual life, some new knowledge of God, that we can receive through such a storm and that we cannot receive without it. The storm has a divine purpose. This is a certainty which we must learn to believe unwaveringly, difficult as that may be.

Well, then, what is the purpose of this particular storm? What are these disciples to learn from it? They are to learn, first, that their Lord has been mindful of them all the while, watching over them in their plight while communing with the Father. They are also to learn that the timing of his ultimate intervention is directly related to their own good. It is only when they finally accept the frightening truth of their own utter helplessness that they will rightly value his intervention to save them. They must first come to the end of themselves, to the place of acknowledged helplessness where, as Paul writes in his Second Epistle to the Corinthians, 'We were under great pressure, far beyond our ability to endure, so that we despaired even of life. Indeed, in our hearts we felt the sentence of death. But this happened that we might rely not on ourselves but on God' (2 Corinthians 1:8,9).

Many of the times of waiting for divine intervention are due to the fact that we have not yet come to the end of ourselves — we have not yet learned the limits of our own resources. And so, as in this incident, Jesus often delays his intervention until the fourth watch, so to speak (between 3 and 6 o'clock in the morning), first allowing the night as well as the storm to drive home to his people the sheer frailty of man. His delay gives his disciples time to learn that, familiar though they may be with the Sea of Galilee, with wind and rough water, perhaps with the very boat they are in, no matter how much natural ability and how much experience they have, they cannot negotiate these waters without his help.

Someone may protest that our Lord surely need not go

so far as to allow a storm to come into our lives just to teach us the trifling lesson that we cannot cope in our own strength. But this is not trifling: from the Christian point of view, it is one of life's major lessons. Our Lord Jesus Christ said, 'Apart from me you can do nothing' (John 15:5). But many of us, even as Christians, think we can! We do not really believe, in our heart of hearts, that we can do nothing apart from him. That is why we do not pray more. That is why we are not really seriously involved in the business of intercession. We read the Bible, we know how we ought to act, we have a 'spiritual' view of life and we make the mistake of thinking we can get on quite well with these resources — without him.

But we cannot. We need to learn to trust in his strength, to 'rely not on ourselves but on God'. It is only when we have experienced our own total helplessness that we can turn to him in faith and dependence. The ultimate lesson of any storm on the way of obedience is the lesson that God alone is the hope and the help and the Deliverer of his disciples. And it may take many storms to drive this truth home to us.

He is walking towards them

'*During the fourth watch of the night Jesus went out to them, walking on the lake. When the disciples saw him walking on the lake, they were terrified. "It's a ghost!" they said, and cried out in fear' (Matthew 14:25,26).*

Our Lord has been watching over his people and praying, and purposely delaying his intervention for their own good. Now he is at last coming to them, walking on the lake. This, of course, is totally unexpected; the disciples, their knowledge of Jesus still rudimentary, think they are seeing a ghost, and they cry out in their fear, for even though these men have been with Jesus for many months, their convictions about him are immature. There is a vast difference between an emerging idea or hunch that something may be so, and a firm conviction that it is in fact so. The disciples' impressions are just beginning to take the form of convictions. This means that they have not really learned to expect the unexpected from their Lord. Nor have they really learned that he is the Lord of nature. In a few short hours they have forgotten the miracle of the loaves and the fishes. In their obsession with the storm they have allowed that very sign of Jesus' lordship over nature to fade right out of their minds. They cannot have grasped its significance.

But he *is* the Lord of nature. Look at him! He comes, walking majestically on the water. He is in total command of the same waves that threaten to overpower the disciples. And he comes totally unsolicited; we read of no plea or prayer for help. If Jesus is answering any plea, it is the plea of fear rather than the plea of faith. According to the record, these frightened men have not prayed. They have not even known where Jesus was. But he knows the fear in their hearts and he sees their physical plight, and he comes to bring both their fears and the storm to an end.

What does this say to his disciples? Here are lessons being taught right in the very teeth of the storm. First, the fact that Jesus comes to these men in supernatural power shows that he can reach his disciples wherever they are. He comes walking on the waves. Here is the omnipotent Lord manifesting his sovereignty over nature. We are never beyond his reach and care.

One thing that worries many a Christian worker, I have found, is that he or she may get into such an out-of-the-way situation (geographically, morally or spiritually) that Jesus Christ will not be able to get there, too. This is a very prevalent fear — that if I walk in the path of obedience, I may ultimately land up in a place where the amazing grace of God cannot reach me, a place like this one where the disciples are, tossed up and down in the midst of the Sea of Galilee, unable to move either forward or back, dreading what will happen next, fearful for their lives: how can Jesus ever find them or help them here?

But look at the picture. Our Saviour comes walking over the waves. There is no place in life or in death where he cannot come alongside of me. There is no place where he cannot reach me to calm my fears and still my doubts and deal with the storm that is threatening me. Christian, you and I need to know that, just as Simon and his fellows did.

There is a second lesson here in the wake of the first one. The fact that Jesus can reach us wherever we are means, too, that he can save his people in different ways. He can

save them, as he shows Simon now, by imparting his power
to them, by enabling them to do what he does. Being, as
usual, the first disciple to speak, Simon challenges Jesus:
'Lord, if it's you, tell me to come to you on the water'
(Matthew 14:28). Jesus answers: 'Come.' Simon is out of
the boat in a flash, and for an instant he shares his Master's
power to walk on the water. His Lord's power enables the
disciple to do what the Lord himself does.

Then Simon, seeing the wind's strength, falls prey to
fear again and begins to sink. Our Lord now shows that he
can save his disciple in a different way. He lets him sink
deep enough to realize that he cannot save himself (just as
he had let the whole band experience the storm until the
fourth watch of the night); then he reaches out his hand
and saves Simon. There are limits beyond which the obedient
disciple will not be allowed to sink. Jesus will save him
with his own outstretched arm.

Yet another way in which our Lord can save his disciples
is through stilling the storm. We read that 'When they [Jesus
and Simon] climbed into the boat, the wind died down'
(Matthew 14:32). Or, 'He climbed into the boat with them,
and the wind died down. They were completely amazed . . .'
(Mark 6:51). Our Lord Jesus Christ can deal with the outward circumstances that threaten to overwhelm his people.

All of these lessons have been taught through the storm.
Were it not for the troubles of this terrifying night, the
disciples might not have learned what they did. But now
they know our Lord's great concern for them, and they
know his capacity to intervene on their behalf, no matter
where they are and how impossible the situation may seem.
No set of human circumstances need terrify them. The one
who came to Daniel in the lion's den (Daniel 6:22), and
to his three friends in the furnace of fire (Daniel 3:25),
can also walk over stormy seas to his own.

Let us take this message to heart. Is there anyone who
knows nothing of the storm encountered on the way of
obedience? Could it be that many of us Christians are spending our energies trying to *avoid* such storms? I know what
that is. It was my greatest difficulty before entering the
ministry: dare I do this? Dare I do that? Could I possibly
turn this person or that opportunity down? Well, the answer

is here in this account of the storm. Let us not try to evade
the storm on the way of obedience, for it is in the heart of
it that God has something to say to us that we will not
otherwise hear, something to teach us that will be worth
its weight in gold, not only on this side of death, but also
beyond.

Beyond the storm

Would these men ever be the same again? Having thus experienced their Lord's utter devotion to them and his un-
questioned dependability, would they ever again have doubts
and fears in the midst of a storm? Yes, they would. They
still had many miles to travel on the pathway of discipleship,
and they were to stumble many times. They did not learn to
live by faith overnight.

In fact, immediately after the storm the disciples were in
a strangely ambivalent state of mind. Matthew tells us that
when the storm suddenly ceased, 'Those who were in the
boat worshipped [Jesus], saying, "Truly you are the Son
of God"' (14:33). But Mark implies that this enthusiasm
was momentary and shallow, triggered by the miracle of the
storm's ceasing; it did not constitute any steady conviction
about Jesus' person. It came out of euphoria rather than
faith: 'They were completely amazed, for they had not
understood about the loaves; their hearts were hardened'
(6:51,52). Or, as the Authorized Version vividly expresses
it: 'And they were sore amazed in themselves beyond
measure, and wondered. For they considered not the miracle
of the loaves: for their heart was hardened.'

The reports of Matthew and Mark add up to the challenging
fact that the disciples were *unreasonably amazed* at our
Lord's mighty act of stilling the storm. They would not have
been so amazed if they had understood even something of
the significance of the miracle they had witnessed only a
few hours earlier — the feeding of the five thousand. If
they had not been so 'hard of heart', if they had but 'considered . . . the miracle of the loaves', they would have
realized something of the glory of our Lord's person. They
would at least have begun to realize that he was divine, the

Lord of nature; and then they would not have been so astonished at his wonderful deeds. But up to this point, our Saviour's deeds did not alert the disciples to the glory of his person so as to cause them to be amazed at him rather than at what he could do.

Here is something of vital significance and relevance to ourselves: there is a danger of becoming absorbed by our Lord's mighty deeds and their effect upon us, of failing to see beyond them to what they testify about his person. It is possible to experience the benefits of the miraculous acts without recognizing what they say about the Benefactor. But if Simon is to become Peter he will need to grasp what is implied by his Master's many signs and miracles. He will need to recognize and act upon the knowledge of his Lord's deity.

We must learn the same lesson. Through realizing what our Saviour's deeds say about him, we need also to learn to expect such things from him as his Word and promises warrant. We need to learn not to be unduly surprised even at his coming alongside our storm-tossed boat, all unsolicited and, having assured us that it is he, beckoning us to do the impossible with him. We need to learn that the outstretched hand of the Lord Jesus Christ is now, as it was in Simon's day, stronger than the pull of gravity.

10.
Forward with Christ without the crowds

*'From this time many of his disciples turned back
and no longer followed him. "You do not want to
leave too, do you?" Jesus asked the Twelve. Simon
Peter answered him, "Lord, to whom shall we go?
You have the words of eternal life. We believe and
know that you are the Holy One of God"' (John
6:66–69).*

The weeks preceding this incident have been exciting ones
for Simon and his fellow disciples. The significance of our
Lord's words of divine wisdom and his works of compassion
and power (the 'miraculous signs') has been dawning
gradually upon these men. They have begun to formulate
real convictions about their Master — not just ideas or
guesses, but real convictions about his uniqueness and his
deity. And they have begun to see that he requires of them
an ever new and ever-increasing dedication to himself.

The miraculous feeding of the five thousand seems to
have been a landmark. The disciples had failed to appreciate
its significance at the time it happened: we have read Mark's
frank admission that 'They had not understood about the
loaves; their hearts were hardened' (Mark 6:52). In retrospect, however, that miracle seems to have been a watershed
in the disciples' assessing of Jesus. Something, at last, seems
to have clicked. The storm and the disciples' rescue from
it by Jesus has doubtless also played a vital role, in retrospect, in convincing them of his unrivalled grace and glory.
And they have seen the crowds multiplying, following Jesus
wherever he goes, listening, expecting something new all
along the way. These have been weeks of discovery and
excitement and anticipation.

But now things change. The crowds are turning heel and going back, leaving only the Twelve to listen to Jesus' teaching and to accompany him wherever he plans to go. The disciples' growing confidence is challenged. Let us look at this crisis point in our Lord's ministry in terms of the people involved: the retreating multitudes, the resolute Lord, and the few disciples who remain.

The retreating multitudes

John describes the situation with solemn brevity: 'From this time many of his disciples turned back and no longer followed him.' They severed connections, totally reversing what had been their behaviour up to this point.

Remember how eagerly the crowds had followed Jesus until now. Many people in Jerusalem professed to believe in him at the first Passover he attended during his public ministry: 'Many people saw the miraculous signs he was doing and believed in his name' (John 2:23). His popularity grew to the point where it actually became an embarrassment to him in Judea, and he decided to go north to Galilee (John 4:1–3). The great numbers of people who were baptized as his disciples became a problem to him, because if the converts were going to grow in such numbers, the authorities would unleash a backlash. Jesus could not allow this to happen so early in his ministry when he had not yet taught all that he had come to teach. His hour had not yet come. So his popularity in the south sent him north to Galilee.

We have also had several glimpses of our Lord's increasing popularity in Galilee. Do you remember how the crowds on the shore of the Sea of Galilee so pressed him that he had to go out onto the lake in Simon's boat in order to find a vantage-point from which to preach? (Luke 5:1–11.) And do you remember how the multitudes thronged the street outside Simon's house in Capernaum as the sabbath day came to an end, waiting for Jesus to heal their sick? 'The whole town gathered at the door' (Mark 1:33). Then there were the five thousand men, besides women and children, who followed Jesus right across to the other side of the Sea of Galilee 'because they saw the miraculous signs he had performed on the sick' (John 6:2), and there they were miraculously fed on five loaves and two fish. Not satisfied with that great blessing, but eager to seek further benefits for themselves and dismayed to discover next day that Jesus had mysteriously vanished, they pursued him back across to the other side of the lake (John 6:22–24). They would not let him go. They were so intent, apparently, upon hearing his words and witnessing his deeds of power that they could not rest content unless they were with him. Our Lord had a great popular following in Galilee then, just as he had had in Judea.

The incident before us thus signifies a profound change. The crowds who only yesterday ate the miraculous food from our Lord's hand, who were so impressed by his miracles as to hail him as 'the Prophet who is to come into the world' (John 6:14), and who even planned to force him to be their king (John 6:15), now turn heel in total retreat, leaving only the Twelve to accompany him any further.

The 'hard teaching'

John tells us why. The crowds who had been pursuing Jesus were now suddenly put off by his teaching. They took offence at what he taught. They had been well pleased when he had been working miracles; that was exciting, thrilling, totally out of the ordinary. When their own kith and kin benefited, that was so much the better. And when they themselves were fed from his hand, that was better still! But when our Lord's teaching made explicit certain painful facts, both about themselves and about him, they were unwilling to listen. They complained, 'This is a hard teaching. Who can accept it?' (John 6:60). They could not take it, so they left it and left him, too.

What was this 'hard teaching' that drove the crowds away from Jesus? As the commentators will tell you, it was probably not just one statement that he made, but rather all of his teaching as we have it reported by John in a section of the sixth chapter of his Gospel (6:26–59). This section of John 6 is like a tapestry: it is an interwoven whole. We cannot isolate any one thread as being *the* one teaching which the Galileans found objectionable, but we can examine three of the main thrusts of his teaching as reported in this remarkable passage.

1. Jesus exposed the crude materialism and the false motives of the multitudes. Recognizing the real reason for their frenzied pursuit of him back across the Sea of Galilee, and pulling no punches about it, our Lord showed them their hearts: 'I tell you the truth, you are looking for me, not because you saw miraculous signs [notice, not just "miracles", but "signs" indicating that he was the Son of God], but because you ate the loaves and had your fill' (John 6:26).

This is a daring statement. Imagine looking into the faces of five thousand men, with women and children besides, and telling them straight: 'You are making all this fuss to find me because you want what I can give you, not because you want me. It is neither the truth I teach nor the person I am that attracts you; it is the power I have to multiply a few loaves and fishes to satisfy your material needs. You are after me for what you can get out of me. Your motives are false, your materialism is crass, and I know it!'

They do not want *him*. They want his power working on their behalf, and that exclusively in terms of providing 'the food that spoils'. Jesus adds, in effect, 'Don't waste your lives pursuing perishable, transient things, but rather use your strength and your intellectual energy and your moral power to labour for the imperishable, immortal things of my kingdom. You are using your strength in the wrong way. You are wasting your energy.'

Their motives were wrong and their goals were false. Jesus told them so, and they deeply resented the fact that he did. That is part of what they meant by calling his teaching 'hard'. It would be easier and more pleasant, would it not, for them and for us, too, to have a Saviour who would always tell us what we would like to hear? But he cannot be the Saviour of lost sinners without telling them the truth about themselves. Just as it is the function of a medical doctor to diagnose what is wrong and then tell a sometimes unwelcome truth to a patient, so our Lord Jesus Christ must always tell people the truth about themselves. And when he did so to these multitudes, they quit.

2. Jesus taught that no man has the power to come to him on his own; no man can simply choose, in his own strength, to come to Jesus and receive eternal life. On the

contrary, our Lord pointed in his teaching to the absolute sovereignty of God; without the call and the help of the Father, every man is morally impotent and naturally unable to come to the Son. For the crowds, in their arrogance and blindness, regarded Jesus as one of themselves. Was he not merely 'Jesus, the son of Joseph, whose father and mother we know'? Therefore, they thought they could opt for or against him at will. They could not recognize his divinity: 'How can he now say, "I came down from heaven"?' To which Jesus replied, 'Stop grumbling among yourselves. No one can come to me unless the Father who sent me draws him . . .'

Like these people we, too, like to feel that we can opt for Christ or against him, just as we please. We can vote him in or vote him out. We can bring about the success of the kingdom or we can frustrate it. But this is not so: a vote against Jesus is really a vote against oneself. The lesson of the New Testament is this: we can crucify Jesus, but God will not allow the crucifixion of his Son to spell disaster for his kingdom. He will raise him from the dead and see his victory through to the very end.

The success of our Lord's mission rests not in human hands, but in the sovereignty of God. And only insofar as God breaks the spell of spiritual death can men come to Christ and have life in him. Men can come only when he calls. This is a humbling fact — humiliating, even, for proud human nature. And this is part of the 'hard saying' that the multitudes could not accept from Jesus.

3. Jesus identified himself as 'the living bread' which men must 'eat' if they are to have eternal life. To the Jews of Jesus' time, steeped as they were in the Old Testament tradition, our Lord's reference to himself as 'the living bread that came down from heaven' would immediately communicate the disturbing truth that the manna which had sustained the ancient people was now superseded. That manna had been of an extraordinary nature: God himself directly provided what was needed for his people to survive in the wilderness. But now Jesus was claiming to be the bread of God come down from heaven to give life to the world. He implied, 'I am what the manna but faintly symbolized. And I have come down from heaven to bring life to

you. Without eating me, you have no life in you. You haven't even begun to live!'

'This is a hard teaching,' they said. That he should go so far as to make eternal life dependent upon the eating of his flesh and the drinking of his blood (even though he showed that by 'eating' and 'drinking' he meant *believing,* as John makes clear in verses 45 and 47), was extremely offensive to the multitudes. It was too exclusive and too demanding. For it made belief in him far more than just an addition to their present beliefs: it became the one thing essential to eternal life. Moreover, it required them to be rightly related to his person rather than to follow him for material advantage. And this was too much for them.

Notice that the crowds did not fail to understand what Jesus was saying. These three strands of his teaching did not constitute a 'saying' that was 'hard' in the sense of being intellectually too difficult to take in. That was not the real problem. What worried these people was not what they could not understand, but what they could and did understand! Their reaction of running away declared, as it were, 'You are talking so clearly to us in a language we understand that we see just as clearly how impossible it is for us to follow you. You are making yourself absolutely and exclusively the only Saviour. The moral implications of that claim are just too demanding for us to accept.'

The longer I live, the more firmly I am convinced that this is the cardinal reason why many people do not accept Christ and walk in his way. They are not so much deterred by some intellectual difficulty in understanding his teaching; what puts them off is the moral difficulty of walking in the way, of obeying his precepts. The cost of discipleship is too high to pay. This means, of course, that the 'hardness' is not in Jesus' teaching. Rather, as John Calvin wrote of these crowds, 'the hardness was really in their hearts'.[1] And so they turned back and followed him no more. And Jesus was left alone with the Twelve.

The resolute Lord

How did Jesus react when he saw that the crowds were

disappearing and the grim realities of the hour were dawning upon the Twelve? John writes, '"You do not want to leave too, do you?" Jesus asked the Twelve.' Calmly, quietly, with no attempt to persuade his disciples to stay, he simply asked, 'Are you going to go, too?'

Notice his uncompromising attitude. Although he knew that the retreating crowds spelled the end of his enormous popularity, he made no attempt to strike a compromise even with these twelve men who constituted his last apparent hope of a following. On the contrary, our Lord resolutely showed them that their only alternative to accepting his exclusive and demanding claims was the alternative the crowds had chosen — desertion: 'You do not want to leave too, do you?'

Underlying Jesus' attitude was his absolute certainty of his own authority and deity. This is clear from the claims he made in his 'hard teaching': he was the bread and drink of life; there could be neither life nor sustenance without him; his teaching about the way of salvation and his future work of atoning for the sin of the world had been 'given' him by the Father; everything he said and did came from the Father in accordance with his will: 'For I have come down from heaven not to do my will but to do the will of him who sent me . . .' What God had given him to do or say was, just exactly because it came from God, positively not negotiable. Our Lord could not compromise. He knew that those whom the Father gave him would come to him, and they would accept the cost of discipleship. If the Twelve, like the multitudes, boggled at what they called his 'hard teaching', then the Twelve, like the multitudes, would have to leave Jesus. Jesus gave them complete freedom to go away.

But it is important to a right understanding of the passage to notice that Jesus clearly did not expect his disciples to leave him. Knowing their minds and hearts, he framed his question ('You do not want to leave too, do you?') in a way that showed he anticipated a negative reply. In the Greek language you address a question like this in one of two grammatical forms, according to whether you expect a positive or a negative answer. The form of Jesus' question shows that he expected the answer: 'No, we are not going away!' He knew that these disciples were different from the others. He knew that, although his teaching did make hard spiritual and moral demands, this small group had come to have a measure of willingness to pay the price of following him. They had come to have some insight into the significance of his words and his works. They had the beginnings of a sure, if still imperfect, conviction about his person. They would not go away because they could not.

Why, then, did our Lord ask them whether they were going to leave him? The fact that he put the question at all served to show the Twelve how absolutely certain he was of his divine mission and, particularly, how uncompromisingly he would carry it out. Men must receive him on his Father's terms, or not at all. Jesus Christ could not negotiate the terms of the gospel.

It was important that future apostles should learn this: that our Lord was incapable of compromising his message to keep the crowds. Those of us who are in the ministry or in mission work always have to come back to this truth. It is tragically possible to modify the Word of God, or to mute some of his mighty declarations, in order to try to keep the peace or keep the people. And that is fatal. In asking the disciples whether they would go away, Jesus showed by his own example the hard fact that his teaching is beyond human modification. It is the very truth of God, unchanged, unchanging. And if the people will not come to the truth of God, which alone is saving, then the people cannot come to Jesus Christ at all.

The remnant few

As we have seen already, the humanly unbelievable had happened. He who only the day before had magnetically drawn men and women to himself from all directions, now had become actually repellent to them. Now only a few disciples were left — twelve men, and one of them a devil (John 6:70). There was to be yet a further narrowing down at a more poignant time in the future.

But remember that smallness of number or physical weakness is nothing new in biblical tradition. God seems to take a strange delight in doing his greatest exploits through only a few, or the weakest, people. He required, for instance, and this is only one of many biblical examples, that Gideon's army be pared down from 32,000 to 300 before he would allow it to fight the Midianites. God said to Gideon, 'You have too many men for me to deliver Midian into their hands. In order that Israel may not boast against me that her own strength has saved her . . .' (Judges 7:2). If they appeared to defeat the Midianites by the strength of their own numbers, the Israelites would become proud, and their whole disciplining and teaching would be undone in a moment. God therefore chose instead a remnant group that was weak enough to depend on his strength and so show forth his glory.

As the apostle Paul later expressed it, 'God chose the foolish things of the world to shame the wise; God chose the weak things of the world to shame the strong. He chose the lowly things of this world and the despised things – and the things that are not – to nullify the things that are, so that no one may boast before him' (1 Corinthians 1:27–29).

God was doing exactly the same thing here with our Lord's followers. He was letting the multitudes go – those who, in their blind arrogance, assumed that the kingdom depended on their strength. And he was taking the Twelve, and one of them a devil, in order to make out of them an army that the whole Roman Empire would not be able to withstand. He was taking the Twelve in order to gather through them a multitude of followers so great that no man could ever number it, coming 'from every tribe and language and people and nation'! (Revelation 5:9.) How this shows us the grace and the power and the wisdom and the might of God!

Notice, too, that Jesus had already warned his disciples that some men's initial response to the gospel would be short-lived. In the parable of the sower (Matthew 13), our Lord had shown that there will always be people who at first respond to the Word, whose apparent faith will then wither as soon as the heat of opposition is felt. They have had no root; the thing has not been real. And there will always be others who make an initial response and then wither because there is no room for roots to form: there is rock underneath that has never been broken. It comes to the same thing – an initial response that has not been real. This is exactly what happened to the multitudes who appeared to be following Jesus: their response was short-lived because it was shallow.

Forearmed by biblical precedent, then, and forewarned by Jesus' teaching, the twelve disciples were probably not altogether surprised by the fact that they alone were now left with Jesus out of literally thousands of former followers. This state of affairs was to be expected. But in any case, these men had very strong grounds now for remaining with Jesus. Speaking on behalf of them all (as he thought, although Jesus knew that Judas was no party to such a confession), Simon spelled out their reasons, saying, in essence, that the Twelve could not leave their Lord because of the view they had come to hold of his person, and the power they had come to discern in his message: 'Lord, to whom shall we go? You have the words of eternal life. We believe and know that you are the Holy One of God.' Simon was confessing that the Twelve had come to a point in their spiritual pilgrimage from which they could not in good conscience turn back. They could not betray what they had learned, even if they would have to go forward with Christ without the crowds. Their way could only be forward, crowds or no crowds. Let us examine Simon's words.

Their maturing view of the person of Jesus

Simon uses two titles to refer to Jesus, both of which express something deeper than mere respect for his person. First, he addresses Jesus as 'Lord', *kurios*. Though it was the resurrection which fully revealed the absolute deity implicit in this term, yet its use here implies that the disciples did already, however dimly, ascribe divinity to Jesus.

Second, Simon addresses Jesus as 'the Holy One of God'. This title occurs only twice elsewhere in the New Testament (Mark 1:24; Luke 4:34), but it is so reminiscent of the often-recurring Old Testament designation of God as 'the Holy One of Israel' that its use can only mean that the disciples believe Jesus to be God. To be the Holy One of God cannot mean less than to be the Holy One of Israel. In fact, it must mean more. However immature their concept of Jesus as God is at this stage, it is nevertheless on the right wavelength. The disciples see what others have not seen. They cannot leave Jesus because they know him to be divine.

Simon actually expresses the disciples' conviction more graphically than our translations indicate. When he says '. . . we believe and we know . . .' in Greek he is using the perfect tense, which expresses the *continuance* of their belief and their knowing. Dr Leon Morris translates those words in this way: 'We have come to a place of faith and continue there. We have entered into knowledge and retain it.'[2]

In other words, the disciples have now both believed and rested their faith in the fact that Jesus is the Holy One of God. This faith is constant despite the retreat of the crowds. The presence of the crowds had nothing to do with the disciples' faith in the first place. They had come to a place of faith because the Spirit of God had worked within their hearts. The crowds were and are irrelevant to the existence of their faith.

This is also true of their knowledge. It is not because of the crowds that the disciples have come to know something of who Jesus really is; it is because they themselves have believed, and have received and shared of his grace. A popular following or the lack of it is, then, as irrelevant to their knowledge as it is to their faith. The disciples' knowledge abides. It cannot be obliterated. Nor can it be denied: they know too much to go back, however difficult they may find it to go forward. To go back would be to betray what they know and what they are; it would strangle their intellects, tear their hearts and violate their personalities. Their knowledge of Jesus, like their faith in him, remains constant. It is now a conviction, even if only a budding and incomplete one as yet.

Their maturing view of the power of his message
Simon tells Jesus, 'You have the words of eternal life . . .' What does this mean?

To have the words of eternal life (or '*words* of eternal life' without the definite article, as in the better MSS) is to have the one message that recreates spiritually. It is the one message that brings life into being. And it sustains that life it has originated. This is not natural life stretched

out *ad infinitum*; it is a wholly new kind of life. Jesus'
Word gives new birth to men so that they enter a totally
new dimension of being.

There is no one else, then, whom the disciples could
follow even if they did leave Jesus. He has brought them
into a realm of spiritual experience that is entirely unique.
John the Baptist had a great word, but he could not bring
regeneration to men. He knew it, and he spoke of the
mightier one who would bring life by a greater baptism than
baptism by water (Luke 3:16). The disciples now know that
Jesus is this mightier one. He has begun something in their
lives which no one but he can continue and complete. They
confess, in effect, 'We know that you have the Word that
brings life to the dead — life of a new kind, eternal life, the
very life of God himself, given to men. Therefore we cannot
leave you. To whom else could we go? No one else is who
you are. No one else has what you have. It's not the bread
that you multiply in your hands that we mean; it's the bread
of life. We have no option but to go on with you.'

Simon and his fellows came to terms with the fact that
truth experienced and known may require us to be members
of an unpopular minority. They learned to accept the fact
that the claims of the Christ are to be assessed in terms of
their truth or falsehood, not in terms of their popularity or
their material consequences. The fundamental question is
this: 'Is Jesus Christ the Son of God and the Giver of eternal
life?' His being so is our only valid criterion — not the kicks
we may have from seeing his works, or the bread we may
receive from his hand. The crowds may vanish. The cross
may loom large on our path. But if we are given the faith
and the knowledge that he is the Son of God, then we are
given something that makes retreat impossible. Have we
learned this lesson? The learning of it is an essential landmark on the long pilgrimage from Simon to Peter. Blessed
are they who make Simon's confession their own: 'Lord,
who else is there? You have the message that gives life. We
have come to believe and do believe, we have come to know
and do know, that you are the one and only Holy One of
God!'

References
1. John Calvin, as quoted by Leon Morris, *The Gospel According to John* (Eerdmans, Grand Rapids, 1971), footnote 136, p. 382.
2. Leon Morris, *The Gospel According to John* (Eerdmans, Grand Rapids, 1971), p. 390.

11.
'You are the Christ . . .'

*'When Jesus came to the region of Caesarea
Philippi, he asked his disciples, "Who do people
say the Son of man is?" They replied, "Some say
John the Baptist; others say Elijah; and still others,
Jeremiah or one of the prophets." "But what
about you?" he asked. "Who do you say I am?"
Simon Peter answered, "You are the Christ, the
Son of the living God." Jesus replied, "Blessed are
you, Simon son of Jonah, for this was not revealed
to you by man, but by my Father in heaven. And
I tell you that you are Peter, and on this rock I will
build my church, and the gates of Hades will not
overcome it. I will give you the keys of the kingdom of heaven; whatever you bind on earth will
be bound in heaven, and whatever you loose on
earth will be loosed in heaven"' (Matthew 16:
13–19).*

There is no simple way to characterize what happened at
Caesarea Philippi. It was a time of intense confrontation,
first between our Lord and all of the Twelve, then between
our Lord and Simon Peter, each of them expressing profound
truth about the person and the work of the other, and doing
so in an atmosphere of great whole-heartedness and joy. It
was an event of reciprocal recognition and reciprocal
dedication. It was like a covenant-making. And it is a clearly
distinguishable turning-point both in the ministry of our
Lord and in the spiritual pilgrimage of Simon Peter. From
this time forward, Jesus began to teach his disciples many
things that he had been unable to teach them earlier. And
from this time forward, Simon lived his life as Peter, learning

to enjoy his new riches and to shoulder his new responsi-
bilities. This remarkable event also introduced a new age in
the history of the people of God: at this point our Lord
marked out the essential features of the church he was
dedicated to build.

A word of introduction: although there are some superficial similarities between this confession at Caesarea Philippi
and Simon's earlier one at Capernaum which we considered
in the last chapter (John 6:66–69) – and some liberal
writers have wanted to see the Gospel accounts of them as
variant presentations of one and the same event – these are
in fact two different confessions made on two different
occasions. An objective reading of Scripture will corroborate
this view. The present confession takes place at Caesarea
Philippi (Matthew 16:13; Mark 8:27) whereas the earlier
confession takes place at Capernaum (John 6:24) which is
about thirty miles to the south. All three synoptic Gospels
agree that this present confession answers a question concerning Jesus' identity, whereas John's Gospel shows that
the earlier confession answers a question concerning the
disciples' continued loyalty in following Jesus. Here in
Caesarea Philippi our Lord's question is not occasioned by
the pressure of outward circumstances; he is asking it in a
place of quiet retreat, far away from the scene of his
ministry. In Capernaum, on the other hand, according to
John, our Lord's question is occasioned by some very disturbing outward circumstances – by the sudden withdrawal
of the multitudes. In this Caesarea Philippi incident, people
generally are reported to have a high and respectful opinion
of our Lord, whereas in the Capernaum incident, the crowds
are disturbed and offended by his claims. Finally, although
there are evident similarities in the context of Simon's two
confessions, the actual words are quite distinct. The Caesarea
Philippi event, then, is a new situation altogether, and is not
to be identified with the earlier Capernaum one.

As we try to assess the significance of this great confession made by Simon at Caesarea Philippi, we need to
take into account the unique situation of the Twelve. They
were first-hand witnesses of the incarnation. They were also
first-hand recipients of our Lord's teaching in a unique and
unrepeatable manner. Jesus was physically present with

them to instruct them and he took a prolonged period of time — over three years — to do so. Over these many months, he taught them 'precept upon precept, line upon line' (Isaiah 28:10 RSV), eliciting some kind of response to each lesson taught and each deed performed. The fact that our Lord disclosed his message in this gradual, piecemeal fashion makes it difficult for us to know the precise significance of such reactions of the disciples as are recorded. For example, we cannot say with absolute certainty just exactly when these men became Christian in the full meaning of the term. Luke records Jesus as telling the returning company of seventy, whom he sent out to prepare the way for his coming into various towns and villages soon after this event at Caesarea Philippi, that their 'names are written in heaven' (Luke 10:20). That doubtless means that they were his redeemed people. Yet Peter's language in the book of Acts has been interpreted as implying that he traced the spiritual life of the church back to Pentecost as its 'beginning' (cf. Acts 11:15).

Another reason for our difficulty in assessing accurately the stages of the disciples' spiritual growth lies in the fact that we are living in a very different world from theirs. We can read in a few hours what it took them over three years to learn. We see things from a different perspective: we know at the beginning what they did not know until the end of their time with Jesus — that he died for our sins, rose again and sent the promised Paraclete to finish the work he initiated. Thus it seems illegitimate for us to apply many of the Gospel incidents to ourselves in the same way as they applied to the Twelve. And yet a knowledge of these records is essential to an understanding both of the gospel and of the faith of the apostles. And such knowledge must demand an appropriate application and response from us.

Now, with that introduction, let us turn to Matthew's account of what happened at Caesarea Philippi. The entire event hinged upon that probing question which Jesus addressed here to his remaining group of twelve followers: 'Who do you say I am?' No external circumstances forced him to ask this question at this time: the reason for asking it lay in his own heart and mind, and was related to the hearts and minds of the disciples. Our Lord saw that they had now come to the point in their pilgrimage where the question must be put to them. Everything in Jesus' ministry up to this time may be seen as preparatory to this question. Only when the disciples could answer it with accuracy and conviction could Jesus proceed to the next phase of his teaching ministry. Only when the disciples were fully convinced of his person could he teach about his work as Messiah and Redeemer.

And so he probed: 'Who do you say I am? You've had a long time to think about this. You know something of me and something of my work and something of my word. Now the time has come for me to ask you this question: "Who do you say I am?" Our Lord was aware that he was addressing to these men the most important question they had ever been asked. And it was for this reason, I believe, that he took so much trouble to provide the proper setting in which to ask it.

The setting for the question

'When Jesus came to the region of Caesarea Philippi, he asked his disciples, "Who do people say the Son of man is?"' Our Lord's ability to provide the most telling setting for an occasion is nowhere more strikingly apparent than here. Jesus was Lord of circumstances, even in the days of his flesh. And as Lord, he arranged appropriate settings for the questions he wanted to put, the lessons he wanted to teach, the things he wanted to do. But no other setting in the whole of the New Testament seems quite so magnificently prepared as this one. Over against it, both our Lord's questions and Simon's confession take on special significance.

Its geography
Caesarea Philippi was a town in the foothills of Mount Hermon, in the north-east extremity of Palestine. There, on the borders of Syria, it lay outside the domain of Herod Antipas, the Galilean Herod. It was far away from Jerusalem and its hubbub, where Jesus was certainly hated by this time. It was even reasonably distant from Capernaum,

where the retreating multitudes had disbelieved. It was in this largely non-Jewish community located in a remote and peaceful area where he was not the object of Jewish hatred and suspicion, that, after a season of prayer (Luke 9:18), our Lord posed his strategic question.

Its pagan associations

If Caesarea Philippi was remote from the main action of Jewish life, it had its own glut of religious associations. These were what made such an exceptionally telling background for our Lord's question about his identity. No other area in the entire country of Jesus' day was quite like this.

According to Thomson's illuminating record in *The Land of the Book*,[1] the whole district of Caesarea Philippi was dotted with shrines and temples of various kinds. Some fourteen, at least, were associated with the ancient Syrian worship of the Baal gods. A cavern in a hillside nearby was reputed to be the birthplace of the Greek god Pan, the supposed god of nature, and here a shrine had been erected in his memory and for his worship. This explains why the town had once been known as Panias, and later as Banias.

Another imposing edifice was a white marble temple in the town itself, dedicated to the cult and the worship of the Roman Emperor. This temple was built originally by Herod the Great, then given further adornments by his son, Philip the tetrarch, who changed the name of the town from Banias to Caesarea Philippi. 'Caesarea', of course, linked it with the Emperor. 'Philippi' linked it with Philip himself, and helped to distinguish it from another Caesarea, a town located on the west coast of Palestine (cf. Acts 8:40; 10:1).

And so this town, with its fourteen or more shrines to the Syrian god Baal, a shrine to the Greek god Pan, and a magnificent temple for the worship of the Roman Emperor, was full of religious tokens from the cultures of the three great nations of the ancient world. Jesus wanted to pose the question about his identity against this panoramic pagan background of the worship of dead deities. By placing himself and the Twelve in this religiously colourful setting, our Lord wanted to help them to get him in perspective — to compare and contrast him with these dead deities worshipped by men in their ignorance.

Its contrast with Jewish tradition

Jesus also wanted the Twelve to compare and contrast him with great men of their own Jewish tradition. Only when the disciples could view Jesus over against the Old Testament prophets as well as over against the pagan gods and the Roman Emperor, would they have him in accurate and complete perspective. And so, knowing that the disciples' answer would be in terms of the prophets of old, he asked them, 'Who do people say the Son of man is?' (By 'the Son of man' the disciples evidently understood Jesus to mean himself, even though, according to the best manuscripts and in contradiction to the Authorized Version, he did not specifically apply the term to himself.)

The response of the Twelve was illuminating. It made clear that, despite the retreat of the multitudes around Capernaum, men generally had a perceptive and high opinion of Jesus: *'Some say John the Baptist; others say Elijah; and still others, Jeremiah or one of the prophets.'*

People of those times regarded John the Baptizer as the one person who was an obvious mouthpiece of Jehovah. They knew that he wielded a power that was not of men or lifeless gods, but of the living God; and they apparently perceived this same kind of power in the word and the works of Jesus. Moreover, they undoubtedly remembered that early in his ministry Jesus had preached the same message as John: 'Repent, for the kingdom of heaven is at hand' (Matthew 4:17). Certain features of our Lord's life and work did resemble those of John the Baptizer.

So also were there similarities between Jesus' ministry and Elijah's. The same Syrian god Baal, to whom there were fourteen shrines here in Caesarea Philippi, had been worshipped in the prophet Elijah's time. We can recall how Elijah boldly gathered the prophets of Baal together at Mount Carmel and challenged them (1 Kings 18). Jesus also boldly challenged false deities: whenever he met demon-possessed people, he tyrannized and exorcized the demons, thus redeeming men from mental servitude. There was something of Elijah in him. And there was something of the weeping Jeremiah, too, in Jesus' deep concern for the spiritual well-being of a disobedient and hard-hearted people (cf. Matthew 23:37).

And so the people generally had an intelligent, respectful view of Jesus. They saw him as one who continued the line of Israel's great spiritual benefactors, or as one of those prophets raised from the dead and brought back to finish his work. They saw him as being on an entirely different level from their scribes or Pharisees or other contemporary leaders. So reported the Twelve. And in so doing, they verbally added another dimension to the panoramic background over against which Jesus wanted them to view him.

This, then, was the setting that our Lord arranged: a varied array of the objects of mankind's worship and veneration since the beginning of history — idols, mythical deities, human rulers, even men of real spiritual power sent by the one true God. This whole host clustered around Jesus and provided the perspective for the Twelve in assessing him. And Jesus looked them in the eye — these twelve men and one of them a devil — and said, in effect, 'All right, in this setting, over against this background, in the light of what men think of me, in the light of pagan religions, who do you say I am? We've lived together, we've eaten together, we've talked together, we've prayed together, we've faced opposition together all these months; now tell me, who am I?' Our Lord wanted his disciples to express their emerging convictions about his person in the form of a fuller confession than they had yet been able to make.

Simon's answer

'You are the Christ, the Son of the living God.'

As on many other occasions, Simon is the disciple who has the first word to say. It is just part of his nature to speak first. His high-spirited, volatile nature is such that it impels him always to say immediately and exactly what is on his mind.

But there is more to it than that: Simon does not need any time to formulate an answer to Jesus' question just now. The answer is already there in Simon's heart and mind. The Twelve have had due time to think about their Lord's identity; it has been their main preoccupation for about eighteen months. Jesus is not pressing for an assessment of his person without knowing the minds of his disciples: he knows that their earlier considerations have matured into convictions which need now to take the verbal form of a confession. And Simon is ready.

You will remember that, over the preceding weeks and months, Simon has already given voice to several unsolicited expressions of his view of Jesus. There was his reaction to the supernatural haul of fish, for example: 'Go away from me, *Lord*; I am a sinful man!' (Luke 5:8.) He perceived the awe-inspiring holiness of his Master's presence and he began to grope towards the truth. There was also Simon's response, along with that of the other disciples when, after Jesus miraculously stilled the storm on the Sea of Galilee, they spontaneously worshipped him, saying, 'Truly you are *the Son of God*' (Matthew 14:33). The truth was gradually dawning, little by little, even if sporadically, and even if expressed only in enthusiastic outbursts which did not yet betoken real conviction. Remember, too, Simon's expression of confidence in Jesus at Capernaum. As the disgruntled and disbelieving crowds moved away from our Lord, and he warned the disciples that he could not compromise his message to keep them from moving away, too, Simon answered, 'Lord, there is no one else we could go to! You only have the words of eternal life. And we have come to the conviction that you are the Holy One of God! You stand alone.' The truth was crystallizing towards becoming a settled conviction.

Simon had not been asked to express an opinion about Jesus on any of these occasions. This is important. It has, I believe, much to tell the church about methods of evangelism. We can press people to make a decision prematurely. A premature decision is a problem in itself, and it engenders further problems in due course. Let us take note that our Lord Jesus Christ waited eighteen months before pressing for a confession from the Twelve. I'm not sure that any one of us is better equipped than he was to press men!

But now, at Caesarea Philippi, the time has come when Jesus is actually asking for a decision. The time that Jesus alone can judge has come, when all the earlier impressions and hunches and budding convictions of the Twelve must be formulated into some credal confession. And this must be done, not under pressure of any external need, but solely

in response to the Lord's own question: 'Who do you say
I am?' Now let us look at Simon's reply. It is very wonderful:
'You are the Christ, the Son of the living God.'

'You are the Christ . . .'

With no equivocation or qualification, with no hesitation or
ambiguity, Simon speaks out and bares his soul: 'You are the
Christ . . .' With no 'if' and no 'but', he affirms Jesus to be
the Messiah. His words take us back to that astonishing
moment when Andrew, his brother, came bounding up to
Simon and said, 'We have found the Messiah!' (John 1:41.)
Much water has flowed under the bridge since then. Simon
has himself followed Jesus. He has heard for himself what the
Master has taught. He himself has witnessed the person and
the works of our Lord. Now, out of his own conviction,
and not because Andrew told him so eighteen months earlier,
Simon asserts categorically to Jesus: 'You are the Christ . . .'
Gone is his initial scepticism. Gone is his every intervening
doubt. Simon is now as convinced as Andrew had been then,
in fact more so, because Simon's conviction is based on more
substantial, cumulative evidence.

This term 'Messiah' or 'Christ' is one which combines the
ideas of Prophet, Priest and King. The Christ is the Anointed
of God as Prophet to teach, as Priest to make the needful
sacrifice for sin and as King to reign over his own and to
bring them home to glory. Simon thus sees Jesus as the
fulfilment of the Old Testament promises — as God's
anointed Deliverer, divinely qualified for every aspect of his
task. Not that Simon as yet fully understands all that is
implied by Jesus' messiahship; he does not, as we shall soon
have occasion to see (Matthew 16:21–23). He will still
need to be taught much more. He will need to be handled
carefully by this same sovereign Prophet, Priest and King
before he matures in knowledge. But at this point he does
have the certainty, the clear conviction, that Jesus is no less
and no other than the very Promised One of God. Jesus
Christ is no ghost of a past prophet; he is no mere continuation of that glorious line: he is the very one whom they
foresaw and foretold. 'You are the Christ . . .'

'You are . . . the Son of the living God'

Simon links Jesus directly with God. Which god — the Syrian Baal? The Greek Pan? The emperor? No, Jesus' identity cannot be explained in terms of pagan deities or human power. Then what god? The God of creation and the God of history. The God who called Abraham out of paganism and led him a thousand miles along the Euphrates Valley. The God who gave Abraham seed supernaturally, contrary to nature. The God who sent the law to Israel. The God who guided the nation through judges, prophets and kings. The God who was before the beginning of time and who will be after the end of time. The real God. Simon sees Jesus as related to him. Eighteen months of following Jesus have convinced Simon that he belongs on the side of the line of demarcation where God is, and God alone.

More than that, it is as if Simon, for one, has understood the significance of the Caesarea Philippi setting. It is as if he has recognized the sheer death that characterizes all of the gods made by man. The Syrian Baals are lifeless and dead. The Greek god Pan has no more life than the Baals, for he, too, is but a mythical being. The Roman emperor may live for a short while and be more powerful than anyone else in the world, but he is a mere man whose breath is short and failing. Jesus cannot belong with any of these man-made gods. To group him with them would be sacrilegious and idolatrous. No, he belongs with the self-sufficient, eternal God who speaks and acts and loves, the God who made all things and sustains all things. Jesus belongs with the living God.

How is Jesus related to this living God? He is no distant relative, if we may so express it. He is exactly who the living God himself proclaimed him to be at his baptism, namely, 'my beloved Son, with whom I am well pleased' (Matthew 3:17). Jesus is the Son of the living God. He shares his nature. He bears his likeness. He shows forth his glory. And Simon sees this. Blundering, arrogant, wayward as Simon so often is, he now confesses that he has arrived at the point where he sees the Lord Jesus to be exactly who and what God has said him to be. With this seeing and with this confessing, Simon becomes a new man.

And you who are reading, have you come to this point? Perhaps you have worshipped for many years. Or perhaps you have not been worshipping long, but you have been reading your Bible and watching Christians and reading Christian history. You know something about the great missionary enterprises of the Lord Jesus Christ, the working by his Spirit and his Word through feeble men. Perhaps you have gained the impression that there is no one else quite like him. Has the time now come for you to echo Simon's magnificent words: 'You are the Christ, the Son of the living God'? Say them, then, with prayer and adoration and trust. And may the Lord enable all of us to launch out into life afresh, and to look our difficulties in the face as the disciples now began to do, knowing this: if we have with us the Messiah — Prophet, Priest and King, Son of the living God — then neither in life nor in death need we fear, for he is all.

Reference
1. W. M. Thomson, *The Land of the Book* (Baker Book House, Grand Rapids, 1973), pp. 230 ff.

12.
'You are Peter . . .'

The fact that Simon sees and believes and confesses that Jesus is 'the Christ, the Son of the living God' has epoch-making consequences. Our Lord makes this clear in his response.

> '*Jesus replied, "Blessed are you, Simon son of Jonah, for this was not revealed to you by man, but by my Father in heaven. And I tell you that you are Peter, and on this rock I will build my church, and the gates of Hades will not overcome it. I will give you the keys of the kingdom of heaven; whatever you bind on earth will be bound in heaven, and whatever you loose on earth will be loosed in heaven"' (Matthew 16:17–19).*

Jesus answers Simon's whole-hearted, unqualified confession of his divinity with an equally whole-hearted, unqualified declaration of Simon's blessedness. He who earlier in his ministry had spelled out to his disciples the qualifications necessary for the enjoyment of blessedness (Matthew 5:2–12), now addresses Simon personally concerning his own particular blessedness. Jesus Christ looks into his face and says to him, 'Blessed are you, Simon son of Jonah.' He does not say, 'You may be blessed' or 'You will be blessed', but '*Blessed are you . . .*!' And our Lord then proceeds to explain what this means: Simon's blessedness lies in the revelation from God that occasioned it, the prediction of Jesus that is fulfilled by it, the mission which it inaugurates and the responsibility that is entailed in the working out of this mission.

The revelation

*'Blessed are you, Simon son of Jonah, for this was not
revealed to you by man, but by my Father in heaven'
(Matthew 16:17).*

It is God the Father who has revealed to Simon the truth
about the messianic mission and the deity of God's Son,
Jesus of Nazareth. Simon has not just happened to discover
this truth; he has not just stumbled upon a proper understanding of our Lord's person and work. Nor is his insight
fundamentally the product of his own reasoning, or of his
own attempts to solve the mystery of Jesus' identity
(although this is not to say that Simon did not use his mind).
Whatever probings and reasonings Simon may have used in
his attempts to discover who Jesus is, these have not brought
him the answer. The agency that has brought Simon to this
point of true understanding has been primarily divine. Jesus
is saying, 'Blessed are you, Simon! For however much you
sought the truth for yourself, or talked it over with other
people, no human effort of understanding has brought you
to this point, but my Father, who is in heaven.'

God's revelation to Simon Peter is a very precious thing.
Here was a simple, uncouth man, a rugged Galilean fisherman
who was as great a sinner as any of us. We are not doing him
an injustice: the record will show that, even though he had
all the privileges that the physical presence of Jesus could
provide, yet he was not above disobeying and cursing and
swearing and denying his Lord. Nevertheless, the omnipotent
Lord of all creation has come down to this one sinner, this
son of a nonentity, and opened his eyes and disclosed to
him what is hidden from the eyes of the wise and the
prudent, so that Simon sees Jesus for who and what he is.

This is the imponderable grace of God. He hides things
from men of high culture and great importance; it is not to
the Herods or the Roman emperors, to the scribes or the
Pharisees, that he unveils the most important truth of all
time. He conceals things from the supposedly wise and
understanding, while revealing his truths to babes (Matthew
11:25). And the revelation to Simon is all the more precious
when we remember that the one whose person and mission
have been revealed is the long-promised Saviour of the lost.

Standing before Simon, in flesh like his flesh, is none other
than the Messiah, the Son of the living God, the only Saviour
of men. And Simon knows it. There can be no blessedness
comparable to that knowledge, because it opens the way
to salvation and hope and glory and peace and joy and
fulfilment. Simon is blessed indeed.

The prediction

'*And I tell you that you are Peter . . .*' *(Matthew 16:18).*
The Father's revelation to Simon marks the fulfilment of
Jesus' promise made to him at the time of their first meeting. Jesus had said then, ' "You are Simon son of John
[Jona]. You will be called Cephas" (which, when translated,
is Peter): (John 1:42). What a remarkable thing to tell the
son of a dove — that, fluttering, feeble, frail, foolish, unstable
though his nature was, nevertheless he was going to become
a man of stability and strength and integrity, who would
legitimately bear the name '*Petros*' (rock)! Simon must
have wondered how this promised change would ever be
brought about. It sounded too good to be true.

But now, in this moment of truth at Caesarea Philippi,
'the Christ, the Son of the living God' is announcing the
fulfilment of his promise. 'You are Peter . . . ,' says Jesus.
He does not mean, of course, that the transformation from
Simon to Peter is total and complete. He does not mean
that there is no room for further change; on the contrary,
we know from the record that Peter still needed many a
word of reprimand and challenge. What Jesus is saying is
that the basic transformation has taken place; the new
man is born. Even though he is just a babe and will need
much training and care and teaching, he is born. *Petros*
has come into being.

And so this son of a nobody, this man who was as great
a sinner as anybody, hears the Saviour say to him, 'Simon,
you're a new creature. What I promised you a long time
back, which then seemed too good to be true, now has
actually happened. The new day has dawned. You are Peter!'
Simon is not only the recipient of the Father's revelation; he
is also a participant in the Son's redemption. He is a new

man because our Lord has redeemed him. This is blessedness indeed!

The mission

'You are Peter, and on this rock I will build my church, and the gates of Hades will not overcome it' (Matthew 16:18).

With these words, our Lord inaugurates an entirely new era in the history of God's people, a new era during which he is going to build his church. He implies that there is a clear distinction between the past and the period which he is inaugurating. He says, 'On this rock I *will* build my church.' Something is beginning, something new that has never before taken place exactly like this. Perhaps Matthew Henry's explanation will help us understand what Jesus means: 'God had a church in the world from the beginning, and it was built upon the rock of the promised Seed, Genesis 3:15.' (Every promise of God is a rock we can build on; that is what Matthew Henry is inferring.) 'But now that promised Seed being come, it was requisite that the church should have a new charter, as Christian, and standing in relation to a Christ already come. Now here we have that charter...'[1] The continuity yet discontinuity between the old and the new dispensations could hardly be better portrayed.

Standing, therefore, before the first person to confess his messiahship and his sonship, Jesus says, 'On this rock *I* will build my church.' Let us notice that 'I': Jesus alone is able to perform this great task. The New Testament everywhere affirms this. It is Jesus who calls every member of his church (Romans 1:6), gives life to each one (John 5:21), cleanses each one (Revelation 1:5), endows each one with peace (John 14:27), gives repentance to each one (Acts 5:31) and gives each one the right to become a son of God (John 1:12). He is the author and the perfecter of the faith (Hebrews 12:2). The Christ alone can build his church. And he points to two matters of extreme importance concerning the church that he pledges to build: its foundation and its future.

The church's foundation

What does our Lord mean when he says, 'On this rock I will build my church'? Jesus is speaking in Aramaic, and repeating a word that he used in the preceding clause when he said, 'You are Peter . . .' In Aramaic, the words 'Peter' and 'rock' are translated by the exact same word: *Kēpha* (not 'Cephas' as it is transliterated in most of our translations, as, for example, in John 1:42). What Jesus is saying, then, is, 'You are *Kēpha* and upon this *Kēpha* I will build my church.' This is no mere play on words, as our translations suggest; it is the repeated use of the same word. I am bewildered when I hear my best evangelical and fundamental friends evade this plain biblical fact. It does not do us good to try to evade what an objective reading of Scripture requires us to understand. We need the truth of Scripture, whatever it is. The moment we begin to quibble with Scripture, we are not on a rock; we have moved away from the rock. Jesus plainly said, 'You are *Kēpha* and upon this *Kēpha* I will build my church.' What does this repetition really mean?

First, our Lord clearly means to indicate that there is a very close relationship between Simon Peter, the confessor, and the foundation of the church which Jesus is pledged to build. It is not a remote or secondary relationship, but an intimate one. Jesus sees Peter as being, in some sense, the foundation of the church.

Secondly, Jesus is clearly distinguishing between Simon, the man he was by nature, and Peter, the man he is by grace. It is not about the old man, the natural man, Simon the man of flesh, but rather about the new man, the man of second birth, Peter the confessor, that Jesus says, upon him he will build his church. The reference is to Peter as the receptive believer and confessor of divine revelation about Jesus' person and work. 'To confess' means 'to say the same as' someone else. Peter's open confession is his saying out of his own conviction what God has first said to him. It is as the new man who now believes God and who now acknowledges Jesus to be the Christ, the Son of the living God, that Peter is to be the 'foundation' of the church.

But the question still remains: *in what sense* is Jesus referring to Peter as the 'foundation' of the church? The

New Testament speaks of the foundation of the church in more ways than one. It is in this differentiation of meanings that the real key to an understanding of Jesus' statement is to be found.

1. The major sense in which the New Testament uses the word 'foundation' is in an *essential, redemptive* sense. Essentially and redemptively, no one other than the Anointed One, the Messiah, Son of the living God, can possibly be the church's foundation. Paul's words are conclusive: 'For no one can lay any foundation other than the one already laid, which is Jesus Christ' (1 Corinthians 3:11). Notice the words 'than the one already laid'. Paul himself 'laid a foundation' (v. 10), but only in a secondary sense, in that he did the preaching and evangelizing which established the church at Corinth. The purpose of his teaching was to reveal the primary foundation, 'the one already laid'. Who laid it? The omnipotent God. What is it? It is Jesus Christ and him alone.

2. But the New Testament also uses 'foundation' in a *mediative sense*. The same apostle Paul, a man of mind and intellect second to none, finds no contradiction in stating at one time, as we have seen in 1 Corinthians 3, that there can be no other foundation than Jesus Christ, and then at another time, in Ephesians 2:20, that the church is 'built on the foundation of the apostles and prophets, with Christ Jesus himself as the chief cornerstone'. Paul is using 'foundation' in a different sense here: the foundation he now means is one composed of all the apostles and all the prophets together (not, you will note, just one or two or a few of them). What does he mean? In what sense are the apostles and prophets indispensable to the church?

In this sense: you and I can come to Jesus Christ only *through* the writings of the apostles and the prophets. We can only know the Christ as he was foretold by the prophets and as he features in the apostles' testimony to him. We can recognize him only when we read what the Old Testament says was going to happen and what the New Testament says did happen. We can come to the Christ whom God has laid as the church's foundation only when we accept the truth and the doctrines, the teaching and the witness, of the apostles and the prophets. Therefore, in a secondary and mediative sense, the apostles and prophets are the foundation of the church.

3. The New Testament also uses 'foundation' in an *experiential sense*. This is the meaning that Jesus intends to communicate in his response to Peter. The church has an experiential foundation which is perfectly represented in this new man, Peter. What is the church built on, in terms of human experience? What spiritual experience is entailed when a man enters the church? Unfortunately, in the ecclesiastical set-up of the twentieth century, people often join a church simply out of preference — because they like the building or the choir or even, perhaps, the minister — and they are accepted on this basis without any question at all! But in the church of the New Testament, becoming a member meant that something had happened to the people joining — something had happened in their minds, in their hearts, in their souls. They had been born again of the Spirit of God. Simons had become Peters, in other words.

For the church is built upon a saving knowledge of God in Christ. In terms of experience, this is its foundation. The church is built and it grows only where men and women come exactly to the point where Simon came, the point of knowing that Jesus Christ is Prophet, Priest and King, and Son of the living God — knowing it because God has revealed it and, having known it, believing it and, having believed it, confessing it to be so. This is the Christian experience upon which the church is based: a sinner who is blind by nature is divinely enabled to recognize Jesus of Nazareth as God's long-promised Saviour, sees him to be the only Saviour of mankind, flees to him for refuge, believes in him, trusts and confesses him. This is the only true basis for membership in the church of Christ.

We conclude that Jesus intends to communicate this third sense of 'foundation' when he says that he will build his church upon this '*Kēpha*'. Peter cannot be the foundation in the sense that Jesus Christ is the foundation; only the Anointed One of God can be that. But Peter is to be the first foundation member of the new church. He is to be the first brick in the building; all the other bricks will be built either upon him or around him and they will be linked to him and to one another the way all the bricks of a building

are cemented together. Or, in the words Peter was to write
later, he is the first 'living stone' of all the 'living stones'
which will be built up together into a 'spiritual house'
(1 Peter 2:5). 'On this [man] *Kēpha* I will build my church'
thus has this experiential meaning: the church will be built
upon the experience of men made anew in the way exemplified by the transformation of Simon into Peter, the
confessor.

The church's future

The other matter of extreme importance that Jesus points
to concerning the church that he pledges to build is the
matter of its future. What does our Lord mean when he
says, 'The gates of Hades will not overcome it'? This is
metaphorical language, the significance of which we cannot
rule on. It could refer to either of two things: the church's
mission or the church's ultimate destiny.

1. Our Lord could be referring to the church's mission as
the community charged with the duty of invading the territory of the damned and the dying to rescue them from
destruction. 'The gates of Hades' would then stand for the
stronghold of Satan. As the writer of the Epistle to the
Hebrews expresses it, speaking of the mission of Jesus Christ,
'He too shared in their humanity so that by his death he
might destroy him who holds the power of death – that is,
the devil – and free those who all their lives were held in
slavery by their fear of death' (Hebrews 2:14,15). Satan, who
has the power of death, holds men in subjection to himself
through fear of death. Death is his stronghold. From here
he can frighten and victimize almost anyone, apart from
the saints of God who know the Word and the power of
their God.

The picture suggested by 'the gates of Hades' might, then,
be this: through these gates the church, like an army, will
move into the territory of spiritual death and darkness to
rescue the perishing and to bring the prisoners of Satan out
of his domain into the kingdom of God's dear Son, the
kingdom of life and light. Our Lord would then be saying,
'I shall send my people into Satan's domain with the message
of grace and salvation, and the very gates of Satan's bastion
shall not prevail against them. Wherever my elect go,

ultimately they will return bringing their sheaves with them.'
Whether that is the truth meant by our Lord in this passage or not, it is a New Testament truth. And it underlies the words of this lovely hymn in which the writer prays:

> Free my soul from sin's foul bondage;
> Hasten now the glorious dawn;
> Break proud Babel's gates in sunder;
> Let the massive bolts be drawn.
> Forth, like ocean's heaving surges,
> Bring in myriads ransomed slaves,
> Host on host, with shouts of triumph,
> Endless, countless as the waves
> William Williams (1717–1791).

2. On the other hand, our Lord could be referring here (and I believe that he is) to the church's ultimate destiny at the end of time, the other side of death. Believers and unbelievers alike must pass through the dark gateway of death into the unseen world. Have you ever been puzzled by this? Here we are, believers in the Lord Jesus Christ. We have received the revelation. We have believed it; we have confessed it. But nevertheless we have to die. Saints and sinners alike suffer and die. Saints and sinners alike go under the cold sod of the earth. It might even appear that saints and sinners alike will remain in that same dark world.

But hear the word of our Lord concerning his church's destiny: 'The gates of Hades will not overcome it.' Though all men pass through death, the church of Christ shall not be imprisoned and ultimately contained by death. In the language of a fuller revelation, 'The trumpet will sound, the dead [in Christ] will be raised imperishable, and we will be changed' (1 Corinthians 15:52). In other words, there is a resurrection. And not all the powers of Satan can hold back the church and prevent it from arriving at this destiny appointed for it by its Head and Builder and Founder.

What blessedness was Simon's to know that all this applied to himself, and to all others who would be joined together with him in his faith, to constitute the church of Jesus Christ!

The responsibility

'I will give you the keys of the kingdom of heaven; whatever you bind on earth will be bound in heaven, and whatever you loose on earth will be loosed in heaven' *(Matthew 16:19).*

Let it be recognized clearly that the function here given exclusively to Peter is later given to the whole church then in existence (Matthew 18:18). To see this authority as a boon for Peter alone is, therefore, unbiblical and baseless, as is also the understanding of it as belonging only to a line of successors to Peter. There is no word here about any papal see, or about any successors to Peter. What, then, is meant by the gift of the keys and their use in binding and loosing?

The keys

The symbolism of the keys must have been familiar to Peter and the Twelve. It reflects such common Jewish usage as one finds, for instance, in Isaiah 22:20—22. The prophet describes how the key of David has been taken away from a man named Shebna and given to a man named Eliakim. The Lord says to Shebna: 'In that day I will summon my servant, Eliakim the son of Hilkiah. I will clothe him with your robe and fasten your sash around him and hand your authority over to him. He will be a father to those who live in Jerusalem and to the house of Judah. I will place on his shoulder the key to the house of David; what he opens no one can shut, and what he shuts no one can open' (Isaiah 22:20—22). The key, then, symbolizes authority. This same usage continues into the New Testament (cf. Revelation 1:18; 3:7). When Jesus entrusts Peter with the keys, he is entrusting certain authority to him, and later to others.

'Binding' and 'loosing'

Conceding that these are technical terms, a contemporary scholar explains, '*To loose* and *to bind* were very common Jewish phrases. They were used especially of the decisions of the great teachers and the great Rabbis. Their regular sense, which any Jew would recognize, was *to allow* and *to forbid*; *to bind* something was *to declare it forbidden*; *to loose something* was *to declare it allowed.* These were the regular phrases for taking decisions in regard to the law. That is in fact the only thing these phrases in such a context would mean.'[2]

We can conclude, therefore, that in giving Peter 'the keys', Jesus is bestowing upon him the authority necessary to declare to men what is right and what is wrong on the subject of the kingdom of heaven. This does not mean that Jesus, the Head of the church, is handing over his own distinctive, divine functions to a mere human being. On the contrary, he is giving Peter the authority to declare only what *by divine revelation* he has been given to know. It is in this sense, and no other, that Peter will exercise his authority, as will also his fellow apostles. In the book of Acts we see Peter doing precisely this, first in relation to the Jews at Pentecost (Acts 2:37,38) and later in relation to the Gentiles (Acts 10; 11; 15:14), admitting both groups into the same spiritual fellowship, into the church of Christ.

How very blessed Peter is to have the privilege of the keys! The fact that others are destined later to share in the exercise of this authority does not alter the stupendous fact that it is now, and first, vested in Andrew's brother, Simon son of Jonah, who has become the new man, Peter. All the blessedness of salvation is Peter's — revelation from God the Father, redemption through God the Son, foundation membership in the church and responsibility for guiding others, by the grace of God, to the place where they, too, may know such blessedness. Our Lord means all of this when he proclaims, 'Blessed are you, Simon son of Jonah . . .!' All that has happened here at Caesarea Philippi between our Lord and Peter means that the pilgrimage from Simon to Peter will now be seen in a new light. From now on we shall see Peter gradually appropriating his great blessedness and gradually coming into his own, but not without falterings.

References
1. Matthew Henry, *Commentary on the New Testament*, Vol. 1 (William Mackenzie, Edinburgh), p. 361.
2. William Barclay, *Gospel of Matthew*, Vol. 2 (St. Andrew Press, Edinburgh, 1957), pp. 160–161.

13.
On the wrong wavelength

'From that time on Jesus began to explain to his
disciples that he must go to Jerusalem and suffer
many things at the hands of the elders, chief
priests and teachers of the law, and that he must
be killed and on the third day be raised to life.
Peter took him aside and began to rebuke him.
"Never, Lord!" he said. "This shall never happen
to you." Jesus turned and said to Peter, "Out of
my sight, Satan! You are a stumbling block to me;
you do not have in mind the things of God, but
the things of men"' (Matthew 16:21–23).

This exchange between our Lord and Peter stands in stark
contrast to their dialogue at Caesarea Philippi. While only a
short space of time separates the two conversations chrono-
logically, an almost immeasurable chasm separates them
spiritually. What can be the cause of such a complete change
in such a short time? The basic answer: Peter's ignorance;
and its basic cause: his immaturity.

If the Caesarea Philippi event proved the reality of Peter's
coming into newness of life, this present event points with
equal clarity to the fact that he is only a babe. The new man
Peter *has* emerged in place of the old man Simon. But, as we
noted in the last study, this emergence signifies only Peter's
birth: it has not brought with it the mature man in Christ,
the finished product of the faith. Peter still has much of his
old life with him; this needs gradually to be cast away while
the new nature in him is nourished and trained towards
maturity.

Peter is still a babe, and as a babe he is still very ignorant.
While he has *some* knowledge, he does not have *complete*

knowledge. Alongside his area of certainty — that Jesus is the Messiah, Son of the living God — lies a whole tract of ignorance. The spiritual failure we see in this episode is brought about by Peter's blundering attempt to apply this very ignorance to a given situation. Let us never fall into the trap of thinking that because we are sure of one thing, we are therefore sure of everything. In the Christian life, as in life generally, it is quite possible to be absolutely certain of some things and, at the same time, to have a whole territory of experience concerning which we really know nothing. It is a wise man who clearly distinguishes between what he knows and what he does not know, and who does not let his uncertainties affect his certainties.

As we see him in this incident, Peter does not yet have this kind of wisdom. And he becomes so confused spiritually that he behaves in a way that might tempt us to doubt the reality of his recent glorious confession of Jesus' messiahship and sonship, or, at least, to doubt the accuracy of its chronological place in the Gospel narratives. But we need not doubt. Things are not as chaotic as they appear to be. Our Lord Jesus Christ will pursue his mighty work in Peter so that his many evidences of immaturity will ultimately disappear before the rising glory of the new man. That will be a long process, however, and the episode at which we are now going to look represents only one step in it.

Jesus' disclosure

'From that time on Jesus began to explain to his disciples that he must go to Jerusalem and suffer many things at the hands of the elders, chief priests and teachers of the law, and that he must be killed, and on the third day be raised to life' (Matthew 16:21).

The facts disclosed

Jesus Christ had the clearest possible insight into what his future involved. He foresaw the way along which he would travel; he knew the city where he would die; he recognized in advance the three main groups who would engineer his death and he knew that he would rise again from the dead.

Knowing all this, he nevertheless 'resolutely set out for
Jerusalem' (Luke 9:51). He did not turn in upon himself
in self-pity or lash out against his enemies in anger. He
firmly faced the realities of his future, and he began to
teach his disciples about them.

Matthew reports Jesus as showing his disciples 'that he
must go . . . suffer . . . be killed . . . be raised'. All four
predictions in his statement were grounded in this one
'must'. He *must* go to the holy city, so-called — to Jerusalem.
He *must* suffer there at the hands of the holy men, so-
called — the scribes ('teachers of the law') and elders and
chief priests who together constituted the Sanhedrin. He
must be killed. And he *must* be raised. Jesus thus unburdened
his heart and told his disciples of the divine 'must' which lay
at the heart of his mission of salvation. In doing so, he was
pointing away from all the subjective factors that might
distract the disciples' attention, away from all the sorrows
and sufferings that would be entailed, to the underlying
purpose and will of God.

The necessity for our Lord's death arose, of course, from
God's decision to save sinners. If God had not 'so loved
the world' (John 3:16), there would have been no need
for Calvary; Peter's wishes could have been granted and Jesus
could have gone another way. But God had set his heart
upon saving the lost. And if mankind were to be saved,
someone would have to pay the price. The only one who
could do that was the Anointed One of God, the Messiah,
Son of the living God. And he knew that. He knew what
messiahship meant. He knew that his every step — first
from God's immediate presence to Bethlehem, and now
from Galilee to Calvary — was necessitated by his involve-
ment in the love and compassion of the Godhead. Calvary
was no accident. It was at the heart of things, divinely
understood. God wanted to save the lost, and this was the
only way. This was a divine 'must' and our Lord willingly
submitted to it.

The timing of the disclosure

Matthew reports that '*from that time on* Jesus began to
explain to his disciples . . .' The Caesarea Philippi event
marked the beginning of a new phase in our Lord's ministry.

Whereas until now he had been concerned mainly to teach about his person and his mission, now he began to prepare his followers for his death. Earlier he had made a few veiled references to his pending death and resurrection (cf. John 2:19; 3:14; Matthew 12:40, etc.), but only now did he begin to fill in the picture with precise details — now, when the disciples had grasped the truth about his person, and Simon had confessed it at Caesarea Philippi. Now that these men knew Jesus as the Messiah, they must learn how he would perform his messianic mission. Now that they knew him as the Son of the living God, they must learn how his movements would be directed by the overmastering 'must' of God.

The purpose of our Lord's disclosure is not hard to discover: he wanted to spare his followers unnecessary shock at his death. He especially wanted to save them from being so overwhelmed by it as to fear that everything was lost. He wanted to assure them in advance that his sufferings and death were part of his divine mission. *He had come to die.* His death would not mean the failure or the end of his ministry; on the contrary, it would be a culminating point. And he would rise again. By teaching the disciples these things, Jesus wanted to prepare them for the events of his arrest, his crucifixion and his resurrection. His words would have spared them considerable anguish if they had simply believed them. As it turned out, of course, they did not.

Peter's disapproval

Here we come to one of the most audaciously arrogant deeds ever to be contemplated, let alone executed, by even the most arrogant of men. Peter reacts to his Lord's disclosure with an expression of unbridled disapproval: *'Peter took him aside and began to rebuke him. "Never, Lord!",* *he said. "This shall never happen to you!"'* 'Are you talking about dying? Are you talking about going to the holy city and there suffering and laying down your life? Never!'

Noble intentions
We may be sure that Peter's expression of disapproval is

not *intentionally* evil. There is no question but that Peter
means well; he assumes he is doing the right thing. This fact
does not excuse the deed, of course; the confessor of Jesus'
deity and messiahship is blundering terribly. But Jesus does
not question his motives and neither should we.

What exactly is Peter doing, then? Assuming that he is
wiser than his Lord, he is taking upon himself the role of
the mature counsellor of the Son of God. Peter is trying
to protect the very one whom he has recently acknowledged
to be divine from what seems to him the folly of his divinity.
Peter is trying to divert Jesus from the overmastering 'must'
which he has just disclosed as being indispensable to the
fulfilment of his mission. This fisherman, this man whom
we shall hear blaspheming fairly soon, thinks he knows
more than the Messiah. He begins to tell him, 'No, no, no,
not that way! You go the way I tell you!' In trying to shield
Jesus from the terrible events he has announced as necessary,
Peter is acting out of ignorant arrogance, and with the best
intentions in the world. He is, one might say, trying to save
the Saviour, to instruct him who is Truth.

Ignoble implications

Good intentions can cause as much grief as bad ones. The
good intentions behind Peter's disapproval are like that:
they suggest nothing but ignoble implications, because Peter
is acting out of the unqualified folly which assumes a right
to correct the Son of God.

1. Peter's disapproval of his Lord's plan implies *a contradiction of his great confession.* Logically, one cannot both
assert that Jesus is God's anointed Prophet, Priest and King,
and then deny that he understands God's will for his life.
But that is exactly what Peter is doing, and it is so self-
contradictory that if the Bible ended here we would be
likely to question the reality of his new birth. Yesterday
at Caesarea Philippi he seemed certainly to be a man of
God, but today where is he spiritually? He is denying today
what he professed to believe yesterday. For if Jesus is the
Messiah, then he is Prophet (Teacher) and Priest and King.
By protesting that Jesus' teaching about his death must be
wrong, Peter is implying that Jesus is not Prophet, not the
authoritative Teacher of God. This means also that he is

denying Jesus' kingship. Peter is trying to dictate to him, claiming that he has made a mistake and should revise his plans to accord with Peter's way of seeing things.

This is exactly the kind of thing that all of us do too often. Our lives are long-drawn-out contradictions of what our lips confess. We confess that Jesus is Lord, yet we often feel that we know much better than he does how things ought to be. We are scarcely less arrogant than Peter. In fact, we really outdo his folly, for we fail to learn our lesson even though we have the Gospel records of this incident to teach us.

2. Peter's rebuke *stems from ignorance*. We need to be aware both of our ignorance and of the sovereignty of God — of his infallible wisdom, his omnipotence, his omniscience. God makes no mistakes, and neither does the Son of God. He knows what is wisest and best at every turn of the road. But *we* make mistakes. *We* are not omniscient or infallibly wise. So when we are tempted to question the wisdom of God, let us rather question our own wisdom! This is exactly what Peter fails to do: he fails to take into account the possibility that he might be wrong. He fails to question his own wisdom. And therefore he remains ignorant of his own ignorance about what messiahship really implies.

In this, Peter is the child of his age and not the child of Scripture. Here is a warning for us. We need always to distinguish between these two things — tradition and Scripture. We are all brought up in a certain tradition and we inherit certain ideas about all sorts of subjects, even about the Bible and understanding the Bible. Sometimes it takes us many a long year to unlearn things that are purely traditional in order to learn what is really biblical and spiritual. Simon Peter stands at this point. His certainty that Jesus is the Messiah is accompanied by what, at this stage, is a coarse, materialistic concept of messiahship, the traditional concept accepted by the people of Peter's age. This concept is in fact unbiblical, because there is no place in it for divinely planned suffering or a divinely ordained death. Along with the people of his time, Peter seems to be ignorant of Old Testament prophecies concerning the Messiah's suffering (e.g. Isaiah 53). He seems also to have forgotten some of John the Baptist's main emphases, as well as references that Jesus himself has

already made to the necessity of his dying and being 'lifted
up' (John 3:14). Out of his ignorance, Peter thus turns to
his Lord and objects: 'You? Why, I confessed you yesterday
as Messiah, Son of the living God! You, suffering? You,
dying? Never!' And he puts his humanly protecting arm
around the Son of God and says, 'Never, Lord! This shall
never happen to you.'

3. Peter's attempt to oppose Jesus' plan is really an
attempt to exercise such authority over the Son of God as
the Son of God has called Peter to exercise over men. In
other words, Peter is *misusing his authority* — he is trying
to 'bind' the Son of God! But when Jesus gave him 'the keys
of the kingdom of heaven' and assured Peter of their 'binding' and 'loosing' powers, he was not thereby abdicating his
own sovereignty in favour of Peter's. He was not making
heaven subject to earth, or binding the Godhead to the
whims of a man!

Many people wrongly understand the gift of the keys in
that way — as if it meant that all heaven were to be subject
to Simon Peter! Heaven have mercy on us! If that had been
the case, there would have been no Calvary: Peter would
have diverted the Son of God from going to the cross. And
there would be no salvation: we should all still be in our
sins. But in giving 'the keys of the kingdom of heaven' to
Peter, Jesus did not, in fact, abdicate his own right to rule.
Peter will learn this in due time. But, meanwhile, he is
ignorantly trying to exercise his God-given authority over
God himself.

These three ignoble implications of Peter's rebuke to
his Lord all point to the important fact that knowledge
does not come all at once, even to an apostle. In our day,
we tend to expect instant results. We live in an age of coins
and slots; we put our coins into the slots and get out what
we want quickly, all at once. But real life is not like that.
Real knowledge does not come all at once. Peter's faulty,
inadequate understanding of the meaning of messiahship
will be corrected only gradually as he lives with his Lord
until his ascension, as he reads the Scriptures and as he
disciplines himself to apply the Word of God to himself
in life situations. This is true of any disciple of Jesus Christ:
real knowledge comes only gradually.

And there is great danger in assuming that all knowledge comes at once. In hindsight, we can see that Peter's blunder might have rendered him incapable of apostleship. His proud assumption that because he knew Jesus to be the Messiah, therefore he knew how the messianic ministry should be carried out, could have spelled spiritual disaster for him. This might well have been the case had it not been for the fact that our Lord's own infallible knowledge and understanding and compassion enabled him to rectify his disciple's gross folly.

Before we see how our Lord corrects his blundering follower, though, let us look again at Peter's situation. Yesterday's submission has given way to today's rebellion. Yesterday's spirituality has given way to today's carnality. Tuned into heaven yesterday, he is on the wrong wavelength today, and all because he is unable to distinguish between the certainty given him by God, and the remaining ignorance which is his. We all need to learn Peter's lesson: we all need to learn to embrace whole-heartedly the certainties that God gives us by his Word and by his Spirit and by his revelation and at the same time never to dogmatize on the basis of our own misconceptions and our own human ignorance.

Jesus' disciplining of Peter

No human being could have corrected Peter at this point. Armed with his divinely endowed authority, he would have argued his case against wise and foolish alike. He had received the revelation and the commendation of his Lord. He was spiritually bolstered. If any of the eleven had ventured to say a word to him, he would have made trouble in no time!

Only the Son of the living God could rectify Peter's grievous situation. Just as he had the power to call Peter from his secular involvements to follow as a disciple in the first place, so now he, and he only, had the power to correct him and build him up. The Saviour of men is also the perfecter of men. When he begins his 'good work' in a man, he goes on to complete it (Philippians 1:6). And this he does by direct, personal discipline. Let us observe how he dealt with Peter in this instance, noticing how he blended intolerance of evil with perceptiveness into the cause of Peter's behaviour.

'Jesus turned and said to Peter, "Out of my sight, Satan! You are a stumbling block to me; you do not have in mind the things of God, but the things of men"' (Matthew 16:23).

'Get behind me . . .' (RSV)

Jesus's first step in disciplining Peter was to command him to return to his rightful place, which was behind his Lord, not in front of him. Jesus was pointing out, in other words, that Peter's authority to lead men did not qualify him to lead the Son of God. Here Peter must learn to follow, never attempt to lead; he must get 'behind' his Lord and stay there. Indeed, only insofar as Peter learned strictly to follow his Lord would he be qualified to use his authority to lead men. In the very moment that he began to try to lead his Lord, he assumed the role of an adversary and a hindrance. He was then walking in the proud ways of Lucifer (Isaiah 14:12—20) and merited the designation 'Satan'.

Man at his best is always merely man at his best, and his place is always to follow his Lord, never to lead him. But isn't this a temptation to you and to me? All of us sometimes try to constrain our Lord to go our way; there is so much of Peter in us all. We need to remember that only insofar as we learn to follow our Lord have we any right whatsoever to lead men. I say that as much to myself as to anyone else: even though I am a minister called by a congregation, I have no right to expect any man to follow me unless I am following my Lord. The mere fact of office means nothing; it must be validated by the certainty that one goes ahead of us, and that we follow in his footsteps.

' . . . Satan!'

Secondly, Jesus pointed to the fact that Peter's attempt to lead his Lord revealed an alien influence. Behind the excited form of the confessor of Caesarea Philippi, Jesus sensed the presence of his chief adversary, Satan, and he rebuked him roundly. Remember, on a previous occasion, in the wilderness, Satan had tried to divert Jesus from the cross. He had tried to strike a bargain with him, promising him all the kingdoms of the world and the glory of them if Jesus would but fall down and worship him (Matthew 4:8,9). He had told Jesus, in effect, 'You don't need to die! You can avoid the cross! Abandon your plans and do what I say instead. Just worship me and accept my ways, and all will be well!' And Jesus had replied to Satan: 'Begone!' Now he perceived in Peter's rebuke that Satan was attempting a second, disguised version of his earlier plan. He sensed the same hideous presence coming to him not now directly, but indirectly, clothed in the form of the very foundation member of his church. For Satan can be very subtle. When he fails to influence us openly as an avowed enemy, he can come to us in the guise of a friend. How crafty! And how potentially destructive, both to our friend and to ourselves!

What did Jesus do? He rebuked Satan as he had in the wilderness, but this time with different words. Long ago in the history of the church, someone pointed to the similarity and the dissimilarity between our Lord's statements on these two occasions. His command in the wilderness was one of outright rejection: 'Away from me, Satan! For it is written, "Worship the Lord your God, and serve him only"'. His command to Satan (in Peter) here on this second occasion was just as resolute and clear, but it did not entail rejection of Peter. 'Get behind me, Satan!' Jesus was saying, in effect, 'I am not going to dismiss you because of this lapse, born of ignorance and pride. But I am commanding you to get to the place that I appointed for you, which is behind me, not in front of me.'

Because our Lord clearly named Satan and pointed to his influence on Peter, Peter must have caught a glimpse of the awful possibility of following in the footsteps of Lucifer, son of the morning, and of becoming so proud and arrogant as to displace God himself in his own imaginings. May God make us all sensitive to the presence of such influences as would make us presume to lead the one whom we are unworthy even to follow. Be they satanic or human, such influences make us hindrances. They disqualify us from being helpers or followers in any true meaning of the terms.

'You do not have in mind the things of God, but the things of men'

Jesus' third step in disciplining Peter was to draw a precise picture of his state of soul. He told Peter that, in opposing the divine plan for the Messiah, he was yielding his mind 'to the things of men' rather than to 'the things of God'. He was tuned in to earth, not to heaven.

One implication of these words to Peter is that all followers of Jesus Christ need to be attuned daily to the right spiritual wavelength. There is no guarantee that yesterday's recipient of divine revelation will not today be under carnal or satanic influence *unless and until* he learns to keep his mind and his spirit tuned exclusively to God's Word and God's Spirit. This is a discipline that needs regular practice; we are never safe unless we are freshly tuned to the Word and the Spirit of God.

Addressing students at Harvard University at the turn of the century, a renowned American spoke of the necessity for this spiritual tuning in terms of a metaphor.[1] He described a family out in a sailing boat which was becalmed on a glassy sea. The boat was not moving at all. Not a solitary breath of air was flowing to fill a sail. Finally, after much waiting and watching, someone noticed that a little pennant far up on the masthead was beginning to stir and lift. Though there was still no ripple on the water's surface and no trace of a breeze on deck, the little pennant kept flapping. Gradually the family came to the realization of what they should have remembered all along — that there are both upper breezes and lower breezes. Their sails were set to catch only the lower ones! When they adjusted the sails to catch the upper breezes, the boat began to move.

May we, too, be aware that there are upper breezes and there are lower breezes. Men who were yesterday borne along by the one kind may today be borne along by the other kind: it all depends how we set our sails. We must constantly examine ourselves to be sure that we are daily and primarily influenced by the upper currents of God's Word and Spirit. Blessed indeed is that person who can at any hour of the day or night echo the words of the late Dean Alford:

> My bark is wafted to the strand
> By breath divine;
> And on the helm there rests a hand
> Other than mine.

And blessed are we all that, despite the folly of men and the machinations of Satan, our Lord Jesus Christ 'resolutely set out for Jerusalem' to die for us. There would have been no Calvary, there would have been no gospel, there would have been no joy of pardon and peace for you and for me, if our Lord had not resolutely refused to heed the protest of an arrogant and ignorant disciple.

Reference
1. Dr W. B. Peabody, quoted in J. R. Miller's *The Upper Currents* (Hodder & Stoughton, London, 1902), pp. 11,12.

14.
On the sacred mountain

As we follow on the pilgrim way of this man Peter who, despite his many ups and downs, was ultimately to become an apostle and evangelist within the Christian church, we come now to another great landmark: the event of the transfiguration of our Lord. This was an event so overwhelming in its mystery and its glory that even in later years Peter could refer to it only with awe: 'on the sacred mountain' (2 Peter 1:18) something big happened. And it happened just at a time when all of the disciples, but especially Peter, badly needed the encouragement and the clarification that it provided.

Let us notice the context. Six days separated the events of Caesarea Philippi and the Mount of Transfiguration. In that time, Jesus had begun to teach his disciples what messiahship entailed and the necessity for his death in Jerusalem. And when Peter protested sharply at this, our Lord exposed the fact that Peter was now under the influence of Satan. Jesus went on to say that not only he, as Messiah, must suffer and be crucified and die; all of his followers must also take up their own cross and die their own death. These were his words: 'If anyone would come after me, he must deny himself and take up his cross and follow me. For whoever wants to save his life will lose it, but whoever loses his life for me will find it' (Matthew 16:24,25). He was saying, "It is necessary for me to die; but it is equally necessary for you to die your own death if you are to follow me and if you are to have fellowship with me in this life and the life to come.' Although the cross of Christ and the cross of the Christian are in most respects really incomparably different, they do share the common principle of self-sacrifice.

Thus Jesus had been presenting his disciples with one

hard fact after the other. But now the time had come for a different kind of teaching. Jesus summoned his three most highly favoured disciples to come with him up into a high mountain apart, and somewhere on the slopes of this un-named mountain the phenomenal event of his transfiguration took place.

Why did our Lord allow the disciples the privilege of witnessing his glory at this particular time? There may be many reasons. It seems apparent, for instance, that through certain truths revealed in the transfiguration event, our Lord wanted to clear up Peter's present spiritual confusion. Per-haps, too, recognizing that his insistence on the grim necessity of his death had cast a cloud of gloom over all of the disciples, he wanted to disperse it with something of an exceptional order, as the transfiguration event most certainly was. Perhaps he also meant it to serve as a re-assurance of his essential glory as he 'resolutely set out for Jerusalem' (Luke 9:51). Or perhaps he wanted to point to the glory that lay beyond the approaching ignominy and shame. Perhaps he had all of these things in mind, and much more besides. We cannot know for certain.

As we look, then, at the vast subject of our Lord's trans-figuration, let us focus on only two things: let us try to understand something of what really took place, and let us try to see both how this applied then to Simon Peter, and how it applies now to us.

The transfiguration event

> 'After six days Jesus took with him Peter, James and John the brother of James, and led them up a high mountain by themselves. There he was transfigured before them. His face shone like the sun, and his clothes became as white as the light. Just then there appeared before them Moses and Elijah, talking with Jesus . . . While [Peter] was still speaking, a bright cloud enveloped them, and a voice from the cloud said, "This is my Son, whom I love; with him I am well pleased. Listen to him!"' (Matthew 17:1—3,5.)

What really took place? We are treading on holy ground. There are mysteries here that are quite beyond our ken, and we can enter into them only insofar as the Word of God is our guide. Yet we dare not shrink from the challenge of trying to grasp at least something of what God, in his goodness, has revealed in this passage. Let us, therefore, try to discover what it is he wants us to see, and only those things that Scripture gives us unequivocal warrant in seeing.

The transfigured Lord

'There he was transfigured before them. His face shone like the sun, and his clothes became as white as the light.'

Words can be very simple on the surface, but beneath there can be an endless depth of meaning and significance. Such is the case here. The words themselves are simple: 'He was transfigured.' But what these words mean is anything but simple. 'Transfigured' comes from the verb *metamorphoō*, from which our English word 'metamorphosis' derives. By using it, Matthew, and Mark as well, apparently intend to point to a *substantial* change in Jesus; this is no superficial, external change, but a *substantial* transformation of his whole being. The Gospel writers' accompanying descriptions make this impressively clear. Matthew adds that Jesus' 'face shone like the sun, and his clothes became as white as the light'. Mark reports that 'His clothes became dazzling white, whiter than anyone in the world could bleach them' (9:3). Luke's version is this: 'As he was praying, the appearance of his face changed and his clothes became as bright as a flash of lightning' (9:29). The language points to a metamorphosis — an incomparably wonderful transformation of being that began right in the depths of our Lord's soul. It gradually manifested itself outwards through his face which was 'changed' and 'shone like the sun', and through his clothes, which became dazzlingly white, 'whiter than anyone in the world could bleach them', making our Lord a radiant light over against the night blackness of the mountainside. This marvellous change was more than just mysterious; looking back on it in later years, Peter wrote, 'We were eye-witnesses of his *majesty*' (2 Peter 1:16). The transfiguration revealed the majesty of Jesus to the three disciples. He now appeared before them as King — in fact, as God.

This, then, was no longer the familiar figure of the one whom the disciples had accompanied for so long. That figure was very ordinary, from the human point of view. He dressed in ordinary clothes. He spoke the ordinary language of the country. He was not taller than anybody else, or better-looking, according to anything we read in Scripture. He did not have any particular characteristic that set him apart from other people. He was just one of the disciples, humanly speaking — a common man from a common home. But that ordinary carpenter's son now had become the transfigured Lord, leaving the impression not only of a mysterious change, but also of a mystic manifestation of the very glory of God.

The appearance of the transfigured Lord stood in contrast not only to his own usual appearance, but also to any other exceptional appearance of a person in Scripture. Beginning, as it did, *from within*, as the verb *metamorphoō* apparently signifies, and then working outwards, Jesus' transfiguration was altogether unique to him. It was in a different category from Moses' appearance after Sinai (Exodus 34:29), and from Stephen's when he stood accused before the Sanhedrin and 'his face was like the face of an angel' (Acts 6:15).

We read that when Moses came down from Mount Sinai, 'He was not aware that his face was radiant because he had spoken with the Lord' (Exodus 34:29). He was bathed in the glory of God. Although he had caught only a glimpse of that glory — only the back of God and not his face (Exodus 33:23) — yet Moses' face reflected it. But, you notice, the glory was external to him. It did not dwell in his own soul and work its way out from there; it dwelt in Jehovah and shone upon Moses from him. As someone has put it, 'Whereas the glory of men like Moses or Stephen was like the glory of the moon reflecting a light that doesn't belong to it but belongs to another, the glory of the Lord Jesus is as the glory of the sun, exuding something that belongs to himself, albeit veiled in flesh and in the common things of life.'[1]

Jesus' glory came from within himself. It dwelt within him. This means it was always there, hidden behind his ordinary appearance and his humble life; it was veiled as he walked among men. His true glory was hidden by the ordinariness which clothed his extraordinary being.

Probably it was often or always evident as he communed with his Father, but no man had ever seen it until this day when our Lord chose Peter and James and John to see it, as he was transfigured *'before them'*.

The Lord's companions
'Just then there appeared before them Moses and Elijah, talking with Jesus' (Matthew 17:3).

As the three overwhelmed disciples looked at their transfigured Lord, they also saw two of the greatest of Old Testament leaders appear 'in glorious splendour' (Luke 9:31) and talk with him. The disciples saw these 'spirits of righteous men made perfect' (Hebrews 12:23) now coming out from the very presence of God and assuming a materiality that made them visible to human eyes. This is truly mysterious; I cannot explain it. But it is what the Bible says: Peter and James and John saw two men coming from another realm and speaking with Jesus.

Who were they? They were none other than Moses, the great lawgiver of ancient Israel, and Elijah, the first of the prophets who expounded and applied the law. Here we need to remember that, according to our Lord Jesus Christ's understanding of Scripture, Moses was one of the great heralds of the Messiah. The modern, liberal understanding of Scripture hardly sees Jesus in the Mosaic books at all, but Jesus himself, according to Luke, clearly referred to Moses as one of the heralds of his messianic sufferings. Speaking to the two disciples on the road to Emmaus, 'He said to them, "How foolish you are, and how slow of heart to believe all that the prophets have spoken! Did not the Christ have to suffer these things and then enter his glory?" And beginning with Moses and all the prophets, he explained to them what was said in all the Scriptures concerning himself' (Luke 24:25–27).

Here on the Mount of Transfiguration, then, was Moses, who had announced the coming of the Messiah, along with Elijah, the forerunner of the prophets who had brought the same message, immersed in discussion with the very Messiah himself. What were they talking with him about? Luke tells us unambiguously: 'They spoke about his departure', or, more accurately, 'of *his exodus (tēn exodon autou),* which he was about to bring to fulfilment at Jerusalem' (9:31). Moses, the leader of the Old Testament exodus, was rapt in conversation with Jesus, who was to accomplish another and more glorious exodus than that in which Moses featured as leader. Apparently Moses and Elijah had been given to know something of what was to happen at Jerusalem, and this was the thread that bound them together in conversation with our Lord. Discussing the same event that Jesus had earlier declared to be indispensable to his messianic mission, and to which Peter had so vehemently objected, these two illustrious figures from the old dispensation apparently saw it in a positive light and had no quarrel with Jesus about it. They evidently recognized its divine appointment.

Reacting to the idea of this 'exodus', Peter had cried, 'Never, Lord! This shall never happen to you' (Matthew 16:22). 'Oh, what a tragedy, Lord, if you go to Jerusalem and suffer there and die! And here I am. I've made my confession that you are the Christ, the Son of the living God. What's going to become of me? What a let-down for me! And what a let-down for you, too, because if you suffer and die at Jerusalem, that will be the end of the story. What about the church you were going to build on a rock? What are we all coming to?' But the two figures from the other world saw things very differently. They saw Jesus' approaching death in Jerusalem *not* as a tragedy for him and his people, but rather as an act of deliverance by him for his people. They saw that he would go to Jerusalem, not to be subject to human whims and fancies and to die because he had failed, but rather to accomplish the purposes of God. And this was the import of their conversation with Jesus, which Peter and James and John were given to hear.

The presence of God

'A bright cloud enveloped them, and a voice from the cloud said, "This is my Son, whom I love; with him I am well pleased. Listen to him!"' (Matthew 17:5.)

The gracious God who planned that the three disciples should see the Messiah's innate glory breaking forth and should witness his speaking with Moses and Elijah also ordained that they should see and hear something even more solemnly confirmatory of the messiahship of Jesus Christ and of his glory: 'A bright cloud enveloped them.' What does this mean?

Anyone unacquainted with Old Testament teaching would assume that the 'bright cloud' here is just an ordinary cloud, an advance warning of a shower on the way, its brightness caused by a star or some other natural source of light. But such a cloud would be meaningless in this context; this cloud has an entirely different significance, as the rest of the passage implies. This 'bright cloud' is none other than the Shekinah that marked the visible presence of God with his people in Old Testament days. It marked his presence on Mount Sinai: 'When Moses went up on the mountain, the cloud covered it, and the glory of the Lord settled on Mount Sinai. For six days the cloud covered the mountain . . .' (Exodus 24:15,16). It marked God's presence in the wilderness: 'The cloud of the Lord was over them by day when they set out from the camp' (Numbers 10:34); and in the Tent of Meeting: 'Then the cloud covered the Tent of Meeting, and the glory of the Lord filled the tabernacle' (Exodus 40:34); and in Solomon's temple at its completion: 'When the priests withdrew from the Holy Place, the cloud filled the temple of the Lord. And the priests could not perform their service because of the cloud, for the glory of the Lord filled his temple' (1 Kings 8:10,11).

This 'bright cloud', then, is something wholly supernatural. This is God, coming in the only way that a child of Israel would recognize him. In other words, not only are our Lord Jesus Christ and Moses and Elijah present on this holy mountain; God is also present — the God of Israel come down, the God of the burning bush, the God of the exodus, the God of the wilderness wanderings, the God of Canaan, God omnipotent. And he speaks out of the cloud. As on Sinai's slopes in the hearing of Moses and ancient Israel, so also he speaks here, on the slopes of this unnamed mountain, in the hearing of Peter and James and John, saying, 'This is my Son, whom I love; with him I am well pleased. Listen to him!' His words are no less clear now than they were when he spoke then with Moses. This time, however, he does not give the law; it has been given. This time he declares in unequivocal terms that Jesus is his Son and that he is well pleased with him. In other words, the Son's plans to go to Jerusalem are as pleasing to the Father as they are acceptable to Moses and Elijah. The Son has not veered out of the way in purposing to go to Jerusalem to die. The Father finds no fault with the Son; Peter does, but God does not.

The consequence is crystal clear: let his disciples and all men listen to what Jesus has to say. He is no blind leader of the blind. He does not say fanciful things that have emerged only in his human soul. He whom Peter has rebuked is commended by God as the disciples' unerring Guide. Let them listen to him and not think themselves wiser than he.

The transfiguration for Peter

The event of the transfiguration had particular relevance to Peter. It was he who had confessed Jesus to be Messiah, and then had undermined this confession by trying to put his Lord right. It was Peter whose thinking needed to be straightened out and whose faith needed confirming. What did it teach him that he needed to know in order to continue on his way as a disciple of Christ?

It corroborated his confession at Caesarea Philippi

Sooner or later God will always confirm the faith of his people. He will not stand aloof when one of his children witnesses so positively to his faith in the truth about Jesus as Peter did at Caesarea Philippi. Some of you may remember the first time you publicly acknowledged Jesus Christ to be your Saviour. Perhaps it was with great timidity that you stood before a congregation and confessed him to be your Lord. But as you did so, he sealed your soul with the certainty that can come only in the wake of obedience. God does that.

Through the transfiguration event he did that with Peter. At the time of his confession, Peter had been so courageous and so obviously in tune with heaven as to confess Jesus to be Messiah, Son of the living God. Now, in and through the transfiguration event, God came down to Peter and said, in effect, 'You were right there, Peter, and I'll prove it. I'll

come to your side, and I'll underwrite the whole thing with
my signature. I'll give you assurance and peace in your heart
and I'll enlarge your understanding.'

But more than that, God not only confirms the faith of
his people; he also more than compensates for the discipline
they accept from him. Imagine what must have gone on in
Peter's mind and heart and soul in the days after Jesus'
sharp reprimand. Peter must have smarted terribly under
Jesus' rebuke. How would you have felt if the Master himself
had looked you in the eye and said, 'Get behind me, Satan,
for you are not in touch with heaven now, but with the
things of earth'? You and I would not just shrug that off
with a smile and carry on. Neither would Peter.

The time between Jesus' rebuke of Peter and his transfiguration must have been one of the most painful periods
of Peter's whole life, a time when he was in a limbo of
tormenting uncertainty, oscillating between doubt and
faith, dread and hope. I can imagine his asking himself
such questions as these: 'Can I have been so right at Caesarea
Philippi and so wrong so soon afterwards? Can I have been
so right in confessing Jesus to be Messiah, Son of the living
God, and then so wrong in protesting against his plan to go
to Jerusalem to die? Was the first experience wholly wrong?
Wat it born out of my own ego in a moment of enthusiasm?
Should I have kept quiet at Caesarea Philippi? Exactly
where am I?' And imagine how severely Peter's pride was
wounded by the fact that Jesus called him 'Satan' so soon
after having called him 'blessed'.

Then came the summons to Peter, James and John to go
up on the mountain with Jesus. When they came to a place
and settled down, it was night (Luke 9:32). As their Lord
prayed, he was transfigured before them, his countenance
was altered and his garments were white with unearthly
light; his innate glory shone through every fibre of his being.
The three disciples witnessed a vision of the very light of the
world; they witnessed the embodiment of the glory of God.
And Peter would see that, whatever might have gone wrong
afterwards, his confession of the glory of Jesus had been
right. It would show him, in fact, that Jesus was even more
glorious than he had recognized at Caesarea Philippi; there
Peter had not yet witnessed the transfiguring glory that

welled up in Jesus' own soul. Now that he had witnessed it, Peter would be able to say with the hymn writer:

> 'Tis good, Lord, to be here,
> Thy glory fills the night;
> Thy face and garments like the sun
> Shine with unborrowed light.

It corroborated Jesus' teaching about his passion

Peter could be left in no doubt now about the necessity for Jesus' suffering and death. Neither the two illustrious visitors from the glory nor God the Father had any quarrel with Jesus Christ's plans to go to Jerusalem and be killed. As we have seen, they clearly saw his being killed as being 'the accomplishment of his exodus'. The Messiah was going to spoil the spoiler. He was going to tear proud Babel's gates asunder. He was going to liberate his people from a greater than Egyptian bondage. And the Father and the Son agreed about this plan.

Peter probably felt deep penitence upon hearing the divine corroboration of his Master's teaching. Certainly he later came to a whole-hearted acceptance of Jesus' own view of his own death. We know this from Peter's preaching as recorded in the book of Acts (cf. 2:22–33) and from his teaching as recorded in his epistles (cf. 1 Peter 1:18–21; 3:18), some of which shows familiarity with Old Testament prophecy that Peter had seemed to be unfamiliar with earlier: 'He himself bore our sins in his body on the tree, so that we might die to sins and live for righteousness; by his wounds you have been healed. For you were like sheep going astray, but now you have returned to the Shepherd and Overseer of your souls' (1 Peter 2:24,25; cf. Isaiah 53:5,6).

Peter changed his mind. He learned that God knows better. He learned that Moses and Elijah know better. He learned that heaven knows better than earth. Blessed is the man who can change his mind like that, in accordance with heavenly understanding.

It confirmed Jesus' authority in teaching his disciples

Peter's confused thinking was straightened out by specific truths taught by the transfiguration. But he had a further need: to learn to listen to Jesus, to trust his teachings and to obey his commands. This was the third lesson of the transfiguration event: the voice speaking out of the cloud about Jesus categorically commanded the disciples to 'listen to him'. That probably crushed the last vestige of rebellion in Peter's heart at that time — and well it might, for the whole vision was couched in terms that would assure his Jewish mind that he was here addressed by the very God of Israel himself. It was the God of the exodus who now demanded that his Son be accepted and obeyed without qualification.

And while it is not for us to climb the mountain with our Lord, or to see the magnificent vision recorded here, it is ours to be assured of its message to Peter and, through Peter, to ourselves. I have been grateful many times that the God who came down in the cloud spoke so clearly to the disciples, saying, 'Listen to him!' All of our problems emerge, really, because we do not listen to him, because we want to impose our own will and understanding upon him. But heaven says to us, as it did to Peter, 'Listen to him and not to yourselves. Listen to him in all circumstances. He is worthy to be heard and obeyed. He is the Prophet that should come.'

May God grant us grace to listen to him and obey him. And as we do, we shall find the glory of the mount in some sense repeated in our own lives, in the heavenly peace and grace and joy that will penetrate our souls. For the way of obedience is the way whereby we are 'being transformed into his likeness with ever-increasing glory' (2 Corinthians 3:18) so that the mind that was in him becomes the mind in us.

We cannot see the transfigured Lord as Peter saw him, and we cannot hear the words that Peter heard. But as we read the Gospels, as we see the emerging faith and confidence of Peter and the other disciples, and as we come to the fulfilment of the purposes of God later in the New Testament, we may know that behind it all is this sustaining vision of the glory of Jesus' person. As Peter himself later wrote: 'We did not follow cleverly invented stories when we told you about the power and coming of our Lord Jesus Christ, but we were eye-witnesses of his majesty. For he received honour and glory from God the Father when the voice came to him from the Majestic Glory, saying, "This is my Son, whom I love; with him I am well pleased." We ourselves heard this voice that came from heaven when we were with him on the sacred mountain. And we have the word of the prophets made more certain, and you will do well to pay attention to it, as to a light shining in a dark place, until the day dawns and the morning star rises in your hearts' (2 Peter 1:16—19).

Reference
1. Author unknown

15.
'For me and thee'

> 'After Jesus and his disciples arrived in Capernaum, the collectors of the two-drachma tax came to Peter and asked, "Doesn't your teacher pay the temple tax?" "Yes, he does," he replied. When Peter came into the house, Jesus was the first to speak. "What do you think, Simon?" he asked. "From whom do the kings of the earth collect duty and taxes — from their own sons or from others?" "From others," Peter answered. "Then the sons are exempt," Jesus said to him. "But so that we may not offend them, go to the lake and throw out your line. Take the first fish you catch; open its mouth and you will find a four-drachma coin. Take it and give it to them for my tax and yours"' (AV, 'for me and thee') (Matthew 17: 24–27).

This incident is neither as familiar nor, perhaps, as obviously important as many of the other incidents we have been considering so far. Viewed over against the momentous events of Caesarea Philippi and the Mount of Transfiguration, it may even seem trivial. Some would belittle its significance and see in it 'nothing more than a curious anecdote of a singular fish with a piece of money in its mouth turning up opportunely to pay a tax, related by Matthew alone of the evangelists, not because of its intrinsic importance, but simply because, being an ex-taxgatherer, he took kindly to the tale.'[1]

But this apparently simple incident played a major role in the formulation of Peter's faith and convictions. It served to mould him in a most remarkable way, leaving an indelible mark on his thinking and his acting as a servant of God.

150

The circumstances

The disciples' talk on the way to Capernaum
After our Lord's transfiguration and his subsequent healing of the demon-possessed boy at the foot of the mountain, while he and the Twelve were walking back towards Capernaum, the disciples, according to Mark, became deeply engrossed in conversation with one another. Jesus did not participate in the discussion, but he knew, of course, what was going on (cf. Mark 9:35). When they arrived at Capernaum, 'When he was in the house, he asked them, "What were you arguing about on the road?" But they kept quiet because on the way they had argued about who was the greatest' (Mark 9:33,34).

'Who was the greatest?' Why would the Twelve be concerned to discuss their relative merits? Let us go back a step further. All of them had been present at Caesarea Philippi and had heard Peter name Jesus as the Christ. Three of them had then witnessed his transcendent glory on the mountainside and had heard his authority attested to by Jehovah himself; they had seen 'the kingdom of God come with power' (Mark 9:1), albeit only its beginning. Whether or not the other nine disciples heard about the transfiguration experience of our Lord, they, too, witnessed something of his kingship and his power when, at the foot of the Mount of Transfiguration, they, along with Peter, James and John, saw him heal the epileptic boy whom they themselves had been unable to help (Matthew 17:14—21). Luke tells us that, because of this healing, 'They were all amazed at the greatness of God' (9:43). He adds pointedly, 'While everyone was marvelling at all that Jesus did, he said to his disciples, "Listen carefully to what I am about to tell you: The Son of man is going to be betrayed into the hands of men." But they did not understand what this meant' (Luke 9:43—45).

Instead of taking to heart Jesus' warnings that he was destined to go to Jerusalem and die, the disciples, it would seem, had seized on the many tokens they had witnessed of his kingship and had become absorbed by expectations of a bright future with him — a future when he would reign as king, and as the king's followers they would have a hand in

ruling the kingdom. That is why they were trying to decide
'who was the greatest' — who would occupy top place in
the kingdom. Who would be Prime Minister? for example.
Who would be Chancellor of the Exchequer (Minister of
Finance)? Who would be Foreign Minister? This kind of
discussion on the way to Capernaum forms one part of the
historical context for the incident we are considering.

The temple tax

The other issue relevant to this incident involves the question
whether or not Jesus paid the two-drachma tax to the
Jerusalem temple. One would like to know a little more
here. Why, for instance, did these 'collectors of the two-
drachma tax' not approach Jesus directly? He was very
approachable. But instead, they went up to Peter and asked
him, apparently meaning to insinuate that Jesus was a tax-
evader, 'Doesn't your teacher pay the temple tax?'

The two-drachma, or half-shekel, tax needs to be dis-
tinguished from two other kinds of tax: the civil tax, levied
by Rome on all citizens of the country, and another
capitation tax levied by Herod the Tetrarch on all Galileans.
Payment of these taxes was universally required by law. The
two-drachma tax was entirely different. It was an ecclesiastical, religious tax, Jewish in origin, based upon divine
injunction as recorded in Exodus 30:11—16: 'Then the Lord
said to Moses, "When you take a census of the Israelites to
count them, each one must pay the Lord a ransom for his
life at the time when he is counted. Then no plague will
come on them when you number them. Each one who
crosses over to those already counted is to give a half shekel,
according to the sanctuary shekel, which weighs twenty
gerahs. This half shekel is an offering to the Lord. All who
cross over, those twenty years old or more, are to give an
offering to the Lord. The rich are not to give more than a
half shekel and the poor are not to give less when you make
the offering to the Lord to atone for your lives. Receive
the atonement money from the Israelites and use it for
the service of the Tent of Meeting. It will be a memorial
for the Israelites before the Lord, making atonement for
your lives."'

This divinely instituted tax was modest in measure, not

legally enforceable, but required morally of every Jew twenty years of age and older, with the exception, apparently, of the Levites and the rabbis. And this was the tax referred to by the tax-collectors when they asked Peter, 'Does not your teacher pay the tax?' With his usual alacrity, Peter immediately replied, 'Yes,' and he clearly intended to say a word to his Master about the conversation as soon as he got home. Jesus, however, 'prevented' (AV) him. Obviously knowing what had happened, just as he had known what the disciples were discussing on the road to Capernaum, Jesus anticipated Peter's report with the question: 'What do you think, Simon? From whom do the kings of the earth collect duty and taxes?'

The Lord's humility

The gracious, selfless humility of our Lord stands out in stark contrast to the self-seeking ambition of the disciples, who saw themselves as rivals for the highest places of power in Jesus' coming kingdom, and in equally stark contrast to the officiousness of the tax-collectors who appear to have suggested that Jesus was a cheater. Though there is no valid reason for the tax-collectors to imply he is a cheat, he does not stand on his dignity and call the anathema of God upon them. Though there is valid reason why he should not pay the temple tax, he nevertheless takes steps to do so in loving condescension.

What did Jesus do that revealed his humility?

Negatively, our Lord declined to press his own rights. He had the right not to pay the required tax and to defend himself against the slanderous insinuation of the tax-collectors. But he did not act on either of these rights.

We live in an age when people are exceedingly, if not excessively, sensitive about their own rights. They will leap to defend them at the slightest provocation. They will do almost anything to get 'their' loaf of bread, even 'their' pound of flesh, if need be. Individuals and groups will go so far as to hold whole nations up to ransom so that they can have 'their' rights. They do not care who else suffers; they do not care about the welfare or the rights of others; they care only about getting their own rights. In contrast, we as Christians should be very much concerned to see that other people are treated fairly. To push aggressively for our own rights, and not to care how other people are affected by our doing so, can be very wrong. It is wholly opposite to the attitude of Jesus; it is totally unlike him.

Never did a man have such rights as the Son of God — the Ruler of the universe, the Judge of all men, the person to whom all things belonged. Yet he did not press his rights. Though he never treated lightly any attempt by one man to disregard the rights of another man, he never stood up for his own.

Positively, Jesus revealed his humility by setting about doing what he legitimately could have refused to do. He made provision to pay the temple tax though he could have claimed exemption on both scriptural and traditional grounds.

The Exodus passage shows that this temple tax had a special, *redemptive* function within its ecclesiastical framework. In the words of the Lord to Moses, a man paying the tax was giving 'a ransom for his life' to the Lord (30:12); he was making atonement for himself (30:15,16). This was essentially a sinner's tax; the entire ministrations, first of the tabernacle and then of the temple, were undertaken on behalf of sinners. All Jews were sinners, just as every Gentile is a sinner.

But Jesus was not a sinner. Jesus did not need to pay a ransom or make atonement for his sin. He whom Peter had identified as the Christ, the Son of the living God, and whom that very 'living God' had twice proclaimed as his Son, whom he loved, with whom he was 'well pleased' (Matthew 3:17; 17:5), he whom God found faultless, did not need to pay a sinner's tax or even a symbolic token of such a tax. He was exempt on scriptural grounds. But he did not claim his exemption.

Our Lord's own explanation of his freedom from this tax was couched in terms of human tradition: '*"What do you think, Simon? . . . From whom do the kings of the earth collect duty and taxes — from their own sons or from others?" "From others,"* Peter answered. *"Then the sons are exempt," Jesus said to him.'* Those words are capable of more than one interpretation, but the simplest and most natural one is probably the true one. It is based on the obvious fact that earthly kings and totalitarian rulers do not levy tax on their own families: they tax others, the nation at large, in order, fundamentally, to support their families and look after the realm. The temple tax in this incident was levied by God himself as King and Lord of his people (Exodus 30:11). Jesus was his Son, and not an ordinary citizen of the kingdom, therefore he was exempt from paying the tax. 'The sons are exempt,' he said. 'I am the Son of the King of all creation; kings do not tax their sons, therefore I am exempt from paying this tax.'

He was immune. He was free not to pay the tax. But Jesus Christ did not abuse his freedom. He concluded his explanation of his own legitimate exemption with the pivotal qualifying word: 'notwithstanding . . .' (AV). 'Notwithstanding,' said the humble, gracious Son of God, and he proceeded to pay the tax which, according both to Scripture and to traditional human precedent, he had no need to pay.

This 'notwithstanding' is a challenging word for us. Let us dwell on it a bit before we pass on. Are you a man or a woman who is known as always standing up for your own rights? There are times when this can be most offensive, when it is indicative of an arrogance and a selfishness that are out of all harmony with the spirit of the gospel and the person of the Christ. Let us remember that he to whom all things belonged nevertheless paid the tax, and not grudgingly.

When did Jesus show this gracious humility?

This second question puts the humility of our Lord into a different perspective, and helps us to see another aspect of the wonder and the grandeur of the 'curious anecdote' before us. Jesus' willingness to pay the temple half-shekel would have been amazing at any time and under any circumstances, as we have just seen. But it was doubly amazing in the context of this particular time. Why?

First, our Lord's experience of transfiguration before men had just recently taken place. What exactly that experience meant to him, we cannot fully know. But it must have heightened his awareness of who he was and why he had come. He must have been reminded particularly of the uniqueness of his mission — that he had come 'to give his life as a ransom for many' (Matthew 20:28). Therefore he, of all people, should not have to pay the ransom tax!

Yet he refused to stand upon his dignity. In spite of his knowledge that no mere tax could pay a ransom for sinners, and in spite of his awareness that it was his very mission in life to pay this ransom through his death, he paid the tax. This is the great grace of our Lord Jesus Christ, who, though he was rich, for our sakes became poor, so that by his poverty we might become rich (cf. 2 Corinthians 8:9).

Secondly, our Lord's healing of the demon-possessed epileptic boy had just recently taken place. This must have left him with a heightened sense of his divine power — a power which had caused 'all' to be 'amazed at the greatness of God' (Luke 9:43). Even now, as he talked with Peter in this incident, Jesus' consciousness of his power must have been intense: he knew that he could cause that fish to come to the very place where Peter would cast his line; he knew that he could make it respond to Peter's hook. He knew that the whole universe was at his command. But he did not press for his rights. Just at the time when his disciples were hoping to profit from his power, he himself declined to exploit it.

Thirdly, if ever there was a time when the ecclesiastical set-up supported by the two-drachma tax was unworthy, it was now. Meant to be 'a house of prayer', the Jerusalem temple had become 'a den of robbers' (Luke 19:46). Worse, it had become a place where murderers were gathering — not to murder mere men, but to crucify the very Son of God. The temple leaders were already plotting to get rid of Jesus; they were already setting in motion the machinery whereby they would ultimately crucify him. He was aware of all this and had been since Caesarea Philippi. Why, then, should he pay tax to a temple whose leaders were plotting his own death? Why should he support an ecclesiastical regime that was crooked? If ever there was a time when he legitimately could say, 'Not a penny!' it was now. But he proceeded to pay the tax. While his followers dreamed of thrones and crowns, he denied himself.

The Son of God asked for nothing. Yet we miserable

sinners tend to stand upon our supposed dignity, as if we had a right to everything! All that we actually have a right to is hell — the consuming fires of judgement. How arrogant, how unlike the Saviour we are!

The Lord's love

Why did our Lord refuse to press his rights? Why did he do what he legitimately could have refused to do? The answer is found in his overriding concern, first, for the glory of his Father and, following from this, for the spiritual well-being of both his friends and his enemies.

He acted out of concern for his friends

1. Here, as elsewhere, Jesus Christ chose to set an example for his followers rather than to find an easy way out for himself. He valued their spiritual welfare more highly than his own personal dignity. He loved his neighbours as himself.

For Jesus was training the Twelve. He had called them, and now they were in school, so to speak. He was going to send them out, not simply to bear witness, but to be witnesses as well. In Paul's later terminology, they were to be 'letters of recommendation . . . known and read by everybody' (2 Corinthians 3:1,2). They were to be salt; they were to be light (Matthew 5:13–16). Because the disciples' lives were to be witnesses to Jesus' life in them, he would not have them take one wrong step. No disciples should ever be able to point back to the Lord Jesus and say, 'Look, I did this wrong because I saw you do it first. Your example led me astray!' His example must always be helpful to his people.

This is very humbling for those of us who preach the gospel, or teach Bible classes, or lead others in some similar way. We can never wholly say that others should do as we do. But, by the grace of God, and insofar as it is humanly possible, we ought certainly *to aim* at a standard in our own lives which will be such that those around us can see exemplified in us the very message that we preach or teach.

Blessed is the one in whose heart God has kindled the kind of love for others that prompted our Lord to refuse to stand on his dignity. Blessed is each one who, as Paul admonishes, will gladly forego eating meat or drinking wine for the sake of a brother (Romans 14:21), or who, like Paul, will even refuse to draw support for himself from a divinely appointed source, lest it should cause some weaker brother to stumble (1 Corinthians 9). Paul refused to do something legitimate, something actually ordained by Scripture (Deuteronomy 25:4), lest it should be misunderstood. Like Jesus, his chief concern was to set an example for other men. The glory of God, the well-being of the saints and the gathering in of the lost came first. Any action that might appear to be out of alignment with these priorities, any action that might give offence to a person of less mature understanding, any action that might appear to reflect adversely on God or on one of his people must, therefore, be avoided, even at great personal cost. How much we need this grace, too!

2. We see here how Jesus' concern for his friends led him to open up what I call a 'joint account' for himself and his disciple. He told Peter what to do: *'But so that we may not offend them, go to the lake and throw out your line. Take the first fish you catch; open its mouth and you will find a four-drachma coin. Take it and give it to them for my tax and yours.'*

Jesus knew his servant's need as well as his own. He was as concerned about the fact that Peter had no money to pay the tax as he was that he himself had none. Peter owed the tax; Jesus was expected to pay it; there was no money in the kitty for either of them. The fish would provide four drachmas, a whole shekel — one half for Peter, one half for Jesus. Our Lord graciously linked their causes together, making himself responsible for his servant's need and his own: 'I am the Lord of all creation, and everything is in my hand. I want you to know that what belongs to me also belongs to you as my servant, as long as you are obedient to me and dependent upon me. This shekel is for us both: we have a joint account.' That was the message.

Peter never forgot that. We read in Acts 3, for example: 'One day Peter and John were going up to the temple at the time of prayer — at three in the afternoon. Now a man crippled from birth was being carried to the temple gate called Beautiful, where he was put every day to beg from those going into the temple courts. When he saw Peter and John about to enter, he asked them for money. Peter looked straight at him, as did John. Then Peter said, "Look at us!" So the man gave them his attention, expecting to get something from them. Then Peter said, "Silver and gold I do not have, but what I have I give you. In the name of Jesus Christ of Nazareth, walk."' Peter remembered, it would appear: 'I have no money, but my Lord's account is full. And it is full of better things than silver or gold! From it I can give you the kind of thing you've never even asked for! In the name of Jesus Christ of Nazareth, stand up and walk!' And the man did.

Thus we see our Lord's concern for the well-being of his friends: he would not do the least thing that might cause a disciple to blunder or stumble, but he would share his own resources with his disciples. He would have Peter know that, as long as he was obedient, he could depend on his Master's faithfulness. This is a message for us, too: all that is in Christ is at the disposal of those who serve him at his bidding. His account and ours are one and the same. If it was so in the days of his humiliation, how much more is it now that he is the exalted Lord?

He acted out of love for his foes

When Jesus said, 'But so that we may not offend *them* . . .', whom did he mean? I would suggest that the word 'them' included the tax-collectors. If Jesus did not pay the tax, they might go home and say, 'It's all very well for that preacher from Nazareth to go around preaching and working miracles. He may be some sort of magician, but if he doesn't pay the temple tax, he's not much of a man!' Jesus would not give them the least occasion to think this.

And I would suggest that the word 'them' also included the scribes and Pharisees and leaders of the temple, decadent and wayward though they were. Hatred was already seething in their souls; they were set upon a course to deny our Lord's every claim and to reject him; they were determined to get him out of the way because his views of messiahship were so different from theirs. But Jesus would not offend them by refusing to pay the temple tax; he would not make it

more difficult for them to recognize him and be saved.
Although they were bent on self-destruction, he would do
nothing to hinder even his worst enemies from seeing the
glory of God in him and the grace of God coming through
him.

Let us ask ourselves, how far do we emulate our Lord?
How far are you and I concerned not to cause any man or
woman to stumble? How far are we prepared not to press
our rights, but rather to abstain even from certain legitimate
modes of behaviour, simply because we care about the
spiritual well-being of our friends and our foes? The fundamental question we always need to ask ourselves is this:
whose glory means more to me — my own, or God's? This
is the question to put to people who always talk about their
own rights, who always argue the point, even though such
action is divisive: whose glory matters most?

May God give us grace and the Spirit of holiness in our
hearts to follow our Lord and to walk in this one narrow
path — to his glory, to the good of all disciples everywhere,
and even to the winning of our enemies. May God make
us strong to be and to bear what is pleasing to him, that
in all things we may show forth the excellency of him who
has called us 'out of darkness into his marvellous light'
(1 Peter 2:9).

Reference
1. A. B. Bruce, *The Training of the Twelve*, 6th ed. (T. T. Clark,
   Edinburgh, 1904), p. 215.

16.
The forgiven will forgive

'Then Peter came to Jesus and asked, "Lord, how many times shall I forgive my brother when he sins against me? Up to seven times?" Jesus answered, "I tell you, not seven times, but seventy times seven"' (Matthew 18:21,22, alternative reading).

As their first pastor, Jesus Christ had the well-being of his disciples constantly on his heart. He was concerned not only to initiate a fellowship of believers, but also to see that fellowship perfected — to see every individual believer brought to maturity, fulfilling his function and serving alongside his brother. Ultimately, he was concerned to enable his disciples to go into the world of need and sin, bearing and expressing in their lives the message of grace.

We saw in the last chapter how our Lord's example showed his concern for the well-being of his followers. In this chapter we shall see how his explicit teaching showed another aspect of his concern for them. His careful, unambiguous answer to Peter's question about forgiveness (Matthew 18:21–35) shows how deeply it mattered to Jesus to warn his people that the depth of their fellowship together would depend very largely on the quality of their relationships one to the other. Specifically, here, he taught that the failure to ask forgiveness of a brother and the failure to grant forgiveness to a brother when asked were two failures of personal relationship that constituted failures of Christian fellowship.

As we all know, it is not always easy for people to live and to grow together. It is one thing to have an experience of the grace of God for ourselves; it is quite another thing to live up to our Christian calling in a community, even

161

along with other Christians in the community of the church. Personal relationships are the key to Christian fellowship. The New Testament teaches that it is not enough that we should be doing the right things: we should be doing them in such a way as to cause no one to stumble, if that is humanly possible, and we should also be edifying one another, encouraging one another and helping one another on the pilgrim way. Growth in grace is not individual, isolated growth; it is growing *along with our fellows* in the body of Christ. And if we cannot grow in this way, there is something wrong with us.

In other words, both honesty and charity are required of those who would follow our Lord. By honesty, I mean the kind of honesty that is prepared to be judged by God at every turn in the road for every action, attitude and desire; the kind of honesty that makes us want to look into the mirror of God's law to see ourselves, and then to remember and to act upon what we have seen (James 1:23–25). By charity, I mean the kind of loving attitude that is willing to bear and forbear and, particularly, as we shall see in this chapter, the love that is always willing to forgive others.

We could summarize all this in terms of the Johannine twin concepts of *light* and *love* (cf. 1 John). We need to walk in the light of God's holiness and God's Word; but we also need to walk in the power and by the constraint of God's love. It is not an 'either . . . or . . .', it is a 'both . . . and . . .' Together, light and love, honesty and charity provide a wholeness to the climate in which Christian fellowship thrives, in which God is honoured and out of which we may witness for our Lord in a manner that is convincing to an unbelieving world.

Let us turn to Jesus' teaching about forgiveness, then, looking first at Peter's question about it, then at our Lord's answer.

Peter's question

'Lord, how many times shall I forgive my brother when he sins against me? Up to seven times?'

Whereas some Gospel passages are scarcely related to what goes before or to what comes after them, others have roots that go right back to the beginning of a chapter, or even to a previous chapter. This is that kind of passage: Peter's question grows out of everything that precedes it in the chapter (Matthew 18).

1. In verses 1—4, Matthew describes how Jesus addressed himself to the self-seeking, arrogant spirit of his disciples in their jungle-like battle for precedence: they were asking him, 'Who is the greatest in the kingdom of heaven?' This was the same spirit as had governed their private talk on the way to Capernaum (Mark 9:35—37). And apparently each of them had a claim to make. But Jesus did not rebuke them or dissociate himself from them because they were asking a question like this. Instead, he carefully explained that the greatest in his kingdom is the humblest, the highest is the lowest, the way up is down. Pride has no place here at all.

This is at one and the same time one of the most challenging and the most comforting passages in the Gospel of Matthew. Notice our Lord's patience with these foolish men. It is wonderful to see how he takes men and women like this, who want the uppermost places, who are arrogant and ambitious; he perseveres with them because he wants to mould them and bring them to a place where he can use them. He wants to transform them so that they fit into the fellowship of the church, standing not ahead of others, but alongside. This is our Lord's great grace — he perseveres with his disciples. He did then, and he does now.

2. In verses 5—14, Matthew reports that Jesus went on to speak against those who caused the least of his little ones to stumble. He saw a *necessary connection* between the attitude of pride (the attitude that tells me I deserve first place in the kingdom, for instance), and the sin of causing offence to a little one (the sin of belittling someone, for instance, who is, in my estimation, inferior to me). It is a developed thought: arrogance leads to offence; magnification of myself leads to disparagement of others. And Jesus seemed to imply that this is a particular peril for those who want authority over others within the fellowship — the peril of causing a little one to stumble. It is such a serious thing

that Jesus said, 'If anyone causes one of these little ones who
believe in me to sin [to stumble], it would be better for him
to have a large millstone hung round his neck and to be
drowned in the depths of the sea.' However deserving a man
may be in his own estimation, if his haughtiness hinders
one of Christ's little ones, that man might better be dead.
In fact, it would be better for a man to amputate an offending hand or foot, or get rid of an offending eye, rather than
to allow any one of these to hinder a humble Christian.
It is as serious as that.

To elevate oneself implies derogating one's brother, and
God prizes even his least child too highly to let anyone get
away with that. His least child counts with God. His least
child has an angel in heaven, constantly seeing 'the face of
my Father', and ready to move if the Father sees that the
child has any need. But that is not all: God's least child is
sought after by the Father himself on earth. The Great
Shepherd leaves the ninety and nine sheep on the mountains
and goes off in search of the wandering one. 'Your Father
in heaven is not willing that any of these little ones should
be lost.'

God puts a price on the head of the least of his children.
Therefore, you who think you are better than another, be
very careful. If you cause the least of his little ones to
stumble, you will arouse the holy anger of your Father in
heaven. You cannot undervalue a brother and get away with
it: God values all of his children.

3. Following on in verses 15—20, Matthew shows how
Jesus then turned the subject of his teaching from those
who give offence to their brethren, to those *who are
offended* by them. Our Lord taught them the duty of trying
first to show the offending person his sin privately. This
private approach is motivated by the desire to heal (rather
than to aggravate) an incipient rupture in the fellowship.
The fewer people who know about the issue, the better:
'Love covers over a multitude of sins' (1 Peter 4:8). If your
offending brother listens to you and sees that he has done
wrong and is sorry, then you should just forgive him and
forget the matter, and thus heal the fellowship.

If, however, this private approach fails, and if you are
quite sure of having a legitimate grievance that needs to be

put right, not just for the sake of the two of you, but also for the sake of the fellowship at large, then you should repeat the procedure in the presence of one or two witnesses. If this, too, fails, then you should repeat the procedure before the whole fellowship, gathered in the presence of the one Lord and Head of the church, who is always there with the two or three who meet in his name. If the offending brother is still recalcitrant, and expresses no penitence or guilt, then he is in no position to be forgiven. Using the power of the keys in the presence of the Christ, the church must exercise discipline, either in that it expels the offending brother from its membership, or in that it excludes him temporarily from fellowship.

That, then, is the context of Peter's question. Let us notice carefully that this whole unhappy sequence (vv. 1–20) arises out of the disciples' talk about *who was the greatest* in the kingdom of heaven. When you meet a Christian who wants to be first, you are in the presence of danger: make no mistake about that! This attitude may come from the minister in the pulpit, or it may come from the member in the pew. But wherever it comes from, the devil is there. We have just seen how Jesus spelled out all the dire consequences that inevitably follow from the attitude that asks, 'Who is the greatest?' We have seen our Lord describe the brood hatched before it was born. Let us learn from his foresight.

With that background in mind, let us see how Peter's question disclosed his soul. Perhaps the abrasiveness of his personality had evoked harsh words from his friends from time to time, and he was hurt by them. Perhaps, too, the special privileges he had been granted by Jesus — for instance, the promise that he would found his church upon Peter — had made the other disciples a bit jealous. Perhaps they had been complaining in his hearing: 'Why should *he* lead us? Why should *he* have authority over us? We're as important as *he* is!' And Peter was feeling discouraged. Apparently he had already forgiven his friends many times, but the whole situation was getting to be too much. So Peter turned to Jesus and asked him, in effect, 'How long is this going to go on, Lord? How many times do I have to forgive any one of these fellows? Up to seven times?'

Notice the magnanimity of Peter's soul. To forgive once is a very beautiful thing. I deliberately use the word 'beautiful' because it speaks of the beauty of godliness: a person is never more Godlike than when he or she forgives and forgets. But Peter would exceed that 'once': he was willing to forgive even up to seven times. When we remember that the rabbinic teaching of Peter's day forbade a man to ask for forgiveness more than three times (hence a man needed to grant it only three times), we can appreciate how generous Peter's attitude was. Grace alone could be responsible for this magnanimity. Peter was willing to double the rabbinic three, and even to add an extra one for good measure, coming up with the perfect number seven.

But Peter's soul is also shown to be immature, judged from a Christian point of view. Despite his advance on rabbinic thought and practice, and despite the fact that his generosity showed the undoubted influence of the Lord Jesus and his grace in Peter's heart, Peter was still thinking of forgiveness in terms of an arithmetic figure. He was circumscribing forgiveness. He was seeing it as an action repeatable up to a certain number of times, rather than recognizing it as the expression of an illimitable attitude of soul.

Forgiveness is never circumscribed in Scripture. God never says, 'If you sin seventy times, I'll forgive you; but at the seventy-first time, I won't, or even at the seven hundred and first time!' Divine forgiveness is not numerical in nature, and it has no ceiling. This is what Peter had still to learn. And he still needed to learn that forgiveness among the people of God is a matter not of arithmetic, but of a constant attitude that belongs to me as someone forgiven of God, so that whenever a brother pleads for my mercy, I should be ready and willing to forgive, even as my Lord is.

Our Lord's reply to Peter

Our Lord considered Peter's question to be so vitally important, and a clear answer to it to be so essential to the well-being of his church, that he replied both in parable and in the plainest of plain language.

The parable (18:23–34)

Describing the kingdom of heaven in terms of a king settling his accounts with his servants, Jesus tells of one servant who owed his Lord the fabulously large sum of ten thousand talents. Whether these talents were made of gold or silver, and whether they were Jewish, Attic or Syrian, they amounted, scholars tell us, to nearly three million pounds, calculated in our currency. Our Lord is talking of a gigantic debt.

Threatened with the enslavement of himself and his whole family for the rest of their lives in order that something of the debt should be paid, the debtor began to plead with the king for time. In response, the king did more than give him time: he actually forgave the man his entire, enormous debt. How would you feel? A three-million pound debt cleared in a moment! The joy and freedom of it would be overwhelming!

But look how this man reacted. On his way out from settling his account with the king, he met a fellow servant who owed him a trifling debt equivalent to less than ten pounds. Without any compunction at all, the forgiven servant seized his fellow servant by the throat and demanded immediate payment of this small debt. When the fellow servant sought mercy he received none, but was summarily put into prison until he would pay the whole amount.

News filtered back to the king, who was seriously and justly angered by what he heard. Calling his forgiven servant back, he denounced his unforgiving spirit: 'Shouldn't you have had mercy on your fellow servant just as I had on you?' And the king cast him into prison ('delivered him to the tormentors' AV) until he would pay his debt to the very last farthing. That is Jesus' way of teaching about forgiveness by parable.

In trying to understand a parable, we need always to remember two things. The first is not to press every solitary detail in order to try to find some correspondence to it in reality. To attempt to do that is inevitably to get into doctrinal trouble. If, for instance, we try to apply to God everything that is attributed to the king in this parable, we shall strip God of his deity. This king was deceived: he was blissfully ignorant of what was going on in his servant's heart when he pretended to be repentant; but God is never deceived, never ignorant. Our God 'cannot be mocked' (Galatians 6:7). Our God knows each of our hearts like an open book, and he cannot be fooled. Moreover, this king had to change his mind and cancel the pardon he had given his servant, but God never has to do that: 'For the gifts . . . of God are without repentance' (Romans 11:29 AV). Our God never has to call back what he has given because he knows everything before he ever gives.

The second thing we need always to remember in trying to understand a parable is that a parable usually conveys only one main message. The message of this parable, I suggest, is this: if you are a person who cannot or will not forgive your fellow human being (when he is penitent and seeks forgiveness), then you are in a very precarious position, because such failure or refusal to forgive is morally incompatible with your having been forgiven of God. To put it another way, failure or refusal to forgive your fellow man his debt against you, which of necessity is a trifling debt compared with your debt against God, signifies that something is radically wrong — you are not in fellowship with God; you are not in his kingdom; you are not under his rule. Your lack of forgiveness makes you so inconsistent with the person of the God you claim as your Father that you cannot genuinely be what you profess to be.

The plainest of plain language

How can we be sure that this is the parable's message? Because our Lord prefaces and ends his parable with two plain statements which, taken together, unequivocally assert this same message.

1. The first statement precedes the parable. When Peter asks how many times we should forgive an offending brother, Jesus immediately replies, *'I tell you, not seven times, but seventy times seven'* (see NIV footnote). We miss the point, of course, if we think that Jesus means the arithmetical total of 490 here. Our English translations seem to imply this. By failing to bring out the idiomatic usage of his language, they make it appear that Jesus is saying, 'Peter, you're not going far enough. There is a ceiling, but it is much higher than your suggested ceiling of seven. It is 490! You must

forgive your brother 490 times, Peter, and then you may stop.' But Jesus is not saying anything of the kind!

The idiom that Jesus uses is a synonym for *unlimited* forgiveness. Forgiving a man 'seventy times seven' times does not mean forgiving him 490 times, full stop. It means, rather, forgiving him *whenever* he repents of the wrong he has done, as long as the need for forgiveness obtains, and as long as he asks for pardon. Our Lord is saying that a divinely forgiven man cannot put limits to his forgiveness of others; he cannot set a ceiling to the number of times he will forgive. The man forgiven of God must forgive others, and his forgiveness must spring from a constantly willing attitude rather than from a sense of duty to go so far and no further. What makes such an attitude possible? Let us look at Jesus' second plain statement.

2. At the close of his parable, having just said that the king handed over his unforgiving servant 'to the jailers [tormentors], until he should pay back all he owed', Jesus adds, *'This is how my heavenly Father will treat each of you unless you forgive your brother from your heart.'* The crucial words here are 'from your heart'. Forgiveness is a matter of attitude, not a matter of arithmetic, nor is it simply a matter of doing what God requires of us; it is something that every member of God's kingdom should be able to do and should want to do *from his heart.* For the heart of a child of God is different from the heart of a child of Satan. The heart of a child of God is regenerate — it is renewed after the image of the Father's heart and it has the Holy Spirit in it. Therefore, because his heart is different, the child of God is expected to forgive repeatedly and willingly *from his heart.*

Every man who has settled his accounts with God knows the enormity of his own transgressions against God. He knows both the immensity of his own debt to God and the corresponding triviality of every debt of other men to him. A Christian man is a man who has settled his accounts with God. For my sin to be forgiven I must repent, and one thing at the heart of repentance is that I recognize the gravity of my transgression. I recognize that not only have I broken the law of God at every point, but my attitude, too, is wrong. I recognize that 'Nothing good lives in me, that is, in my flesh' (Romans 7:18, see footnote). I am sinful through and through (cf. Psalm 51:4,5). I know how much I have sinned against God.

Moreover, I see that I have nothing whatsoever with which to make amends for my past sins, or to wipe out my enormous debt to God. I understand my utter spiritual poverty. And I see that I am totally lost — not just endangered, but lost — mortgaged for eternity, unless God himself saves me. I have come to the end of myself. I see my need for grace. And then, when I plead for mercy, God comes to me in the extremity of my lostness and he wipes out my whole incalculable debt.

'Blessed are the poor [bankrupt] in spirit,' says Jesus (Mathew 5:3). Only they are blessed. Acknowledgement of one's own utter poverty is the place where all blessedness begins. When I learn that I have nothing with which to pay back what I owe — *nothing* — only then do I find the beginnings of grace. If you have not come to that place of acknowledged poverty, then the question is whether you have ever really been forgiven; if you have never learned the desperateness of your situation, then you have never learned your need for God's grace and pardon. Every Christian has gone through some such process of seeing himself bankrupt spiritually; this discovery has made him plead for forgiveness, and God has forgiven him his whole debt.

But every Christian remembers all too well what a stupendous debt it was. Therefore he cannot, without violating every moral instinct in his new heart, refuse to forgive other people their comparatively small debts against himself. No matter how many people wrong him and no matter how many times they do so, the forgiven child of God cannot prosecute them. Having been freed of a nearly three million pound debt himself, he cannot be morally free to press his neighbour for the ten pounds he owes him. Anyone who *can* do that shows that he does not understand anything about divine forgiveness. Unlimited forgiveness 'from the heart' is, then, a necessary consequence of having been forgiven.

Or, looking at it another way, every truly forgiven person will readily forgive 'from the heart' because the Spirit of his Father dwells in him. God forgives us because his very Spirit is forgiving, and when he forgives, he gives us more than forgiveness. Divine forgiveness is always part of a larger grace that includes penitence, regeneration and the gift of the Holy Spirit. This means that every forgiven person is 'a new creation' in Christ (2 Corinthians 5:17), and is indwelt by the Holy Spirit. This is true without exception. Therefore, as he dwells within each child of God, the Spirit of the forgiving Father will urge and constrain and even pressurize the child of God to forgive others. That is a second sense in which every Christian will forgive 'from his heart'.

What of the person who dearly nurses the memory of someone else's wrong against him and, when asked for pardon, refuses to forgive and forget? In effect he is taking more offence at another's sin than God himself does at the sins of men; and he is taking another's sin against himself more seriously than he takes his own sin against God. Any man who does that shows that he has never come to know himself in a way that would lead him to repentance. Furthermore, he shows that he is a stranger to the Spirit of God who never turns down a penitent's plea for pardon. Therefore, this unforgiving person can, himself, never have been forgiven. That is what Jesus is saying.

To say that the forgiven of God must be, and will be, forgiving of others is not to deny that sometimes there will be a very serious struggle involved. Satan exists, and he is very subtle in making a person feel justified in withholding forgiveness: 'For the sinful nature [the flesh; footnote] desires what is contrary to the Spirit, and the Spirit what is contrary to the sinful nature. They are in conflict with each other, so that you do not do what you want' (Galatians 5:17). Whereas the new man will want to do what God requires, Satan will come and tell him a thousand reasons why he should not forgive his offending brother: 'Haven't you forgiven him before? Didn't he insult you very badly? Didn't he embarrass you in front of other people? Why should you forgive him now?' Our Lord says, 'Because you have a new heart and another Spirit'.

The forgiven of God must be, and will be, forgiving of others. And this is how the Christian church has borne its witness throughout the ages. From Stephen, the first Christian martyr, to the five missionaries murdered by the Aucas, that spirit of forgiveness has been so complete that, for instance, the widows of those missionaries returned to the Indians with the message of forgiveness. This is true Christianity: the flower of Christian grace in the soil of a human heart. They shared their very costliest treasures with those who had robbed them of their partners' lives.

And how goes it with you? Do you belong to that sad company who do not and cannot forgive? Do you carry a dossier in your memory in order always to have a reason why you should not forgive a personal offence? My word to you is this: seek the face of God, that you may know yourself and the immensity of your sin against God. Pray for a new heart. Pray God to renew a right spirit within you. Your point is, of course, that the offending person does not deserve forgiveness. But remember this — by that principle, none of us would be forgiven. In the New Testament church, as in the New Testament gospel, the principle is not that of merit, but mercy.

What a reply to Peter's question! Jesus has not only stretched the seven to a limitless number; he has also shown that forgiveness is a necessary fruit of the forgiven life. Thus the words of the New Testament make a consistent pattern: 'And when you stand praying, if you hold anything against anyone, forgive him, so that your Father in heaven may forgive you your sins' (Mark 11:25). 'So watch yourselves. If your brother sins, rebuke him, and if he repents, forgive him. If he sins against you seven times in a day, and seven times comes back to you and says, "I repent," forgive him' (Luke 17:3,4). 'Get rid of all bitterness, rage and anger, brawling and slander, along with every form of malice. Be kind and compassionate to one another, forgiving each other, just as in Christ God forgave you' (Ephesians 4:31,32).

The forgiven of God must forgive. May God give us grace always to be ready to pardon anyone who asks pardon of us, to his everlasting praise and glory. Such an act, however often repeated, will still not merit salvation for anyone, of course, but it will mark out those in whom the Spirit of Christ is evidently re-embossing his Father's image.

17.
'We have left everything—What shall we have?'

> 'Peter answered him, "We have left everything to follow you! What then will there be for us?" Jesus said to them, "I tell you the truth, at the renewal of all things, when the Son of man sits on his glorious throne, you who have followed me will also sit on twelve thrones, judging the twelve tribes of Israel. And everyone who has left houses or brothers or sisters or father or mother or children or fields for my sake will receive a hundred times as much and will inherit eternal life"' (Matthew 19:27—29).

In this incident recorded at the end of Matthew 19, we will see how Jesus revealed a further aspect of his concern for his followers' well-being through explicit promises — promises which were meant to encourage his people both then and now, even in the face of loss and persecution. This is yet another incident in which Peter features; it must have left a deep impression on him, and indeed on the whole group of disciples, for all three synoptic Gospels refer to it (cf. Mark 10:28—31; Luke 18:28—30).

Peter's question about compensation

'We have left everything to follow you! What then will there be for us?'

The claim made by Peter
Notice first of all the claim that Peter makes in these words: 'We have left everything to follow you!' Peter is not boasting

here; nor is he stating something that is palpably untrue. His words are absolutely true to fact, and they apply not only to himself but to every other member of the Twelve besides. Each one of them did, indeed, leave everything he had in order to follow after the Son of God. Luke tells of the very occasion when this decisive break was made (5:4–11). Having worked all night without catching any fish, the disciples rather sceptically and half-heartedly obeyed Jesus' command to try again, only to be overwhelmed by such an incredibly great haul of fish that their nets began to break under the strain of it. The impact of this miraculous event on the disciples was so great that 'they pulled their boats up on shore, left everything and followed him'. Or, as the Authorized Version expresses it, 'They forsook all, and followed him.'

What was the value of what they left behind? We could try to assess it. With some research, we could probably calculate the value of Peter's boats and nets, and with a little more research, we could perhaps establish how much Matthew earned at tax-collecting. But such information would not really be to the point, for the important fact is that each disciple forsook his *all*. Whether a man leaves behind ten thousand pounds or ten pounds, a man's all is his all: he is leaving everything he has, and he has nothing left. Each disciple left his all; each made an identical sacrifice. This is Peter's claim: each disciple has made a complete break. Each has left everything behind – his means of livelihood, together with such home comforts as he enjoyed. All of these men have done so because they have realized that Jesus Christ offers something better than material security.

The contrast assumed by Peter
'We have left everything'

Peter's claim that the Twelve have left everything is, indeed, a true claim. But what prompts him to make it? It looks like a boast, taken by itself. Taken in its context, however, it appears in a different light. For Peter has a specific contrast in mind when he says 'we': he is thinking of the Twelve in contrast to a certain young man who has just consulted Jesus about what he must do to have eternal life (Matthew 19:16–22).

What a wonderful question to be asked! This was just

the kind of question that Jesus must have been waiting for! The young man who asked it was ostensibly willing to do anything or go anywhere, if only he could possess eternal life. He was obviously a God-fearing man who lived a righteous, upright kind of life. He might well have seemed to be an excellent candidate for discipleship. But our Lord Jesus Christ, in his omniscience, knew differently. Perceiving that the young man worshipped a false god, and hoping to rid him of its hold on his life, Jesus said, 'If you want to be perfect, go, sell your possessions and give to the poor, and you will have treasure in heaven. Then come, follow me' (Matthew 19:21). The young man could not do these things. He was so shackled to his gold that he could not contemplate breaking free of it even for the sake of the knowledge of God which is eternal life (John 17:3). He could not leave his gold behind even though he had the promise of 'treasure in heaven'. And so, we read, 'He went away sad, because he had great wealth.'

But the Twelve have fulfilled both conditions demanded of the young man by Jesus, even though their 'all' has not been the great fortune which he would have had to give up. They have left everything and followed Jesus; the young man was promised 'treasure in heaven' if he would do that; therefore, what shall the Twelve have — 'treasure in heaven', too? That is the gist of Peter's thought sequence.

The concern behind Peter's question
'What then will there be for us?'

We must not suspect that Peter had become mercenary at this point, for, had that been the case, Jesus would have chided him. Jesus never hesitated to rebuke Peter when rebuking was necessary, as, for instance, on that earlier occasion when he had told him, 'Out of my sight, Satan! You are a stumbling block to me; you do not have in mind the things of God, but the things of men' (Matthew 16:23). On this occasion there was not a word of reprimand. Why?

It appears likely that Peter had not thought in terms of reward or compensations until this very moment. He and the rest of the disciples had followed Jesus for other reasons — because they believed him to be the sole author of 'the words of eternal life' (John 6:68), and because

they had come to recognize him as 'the Christ, the Son of
the living God' (Matthew 16:16). They had not followed
him for what they could get out of him materially, but
rather, because of who he was and what he taught. Now,
though, the issue has been raised. Jesus has just told the
wealthy young man, 'You get rid of your possessions, sir,
and give the proceeds to the poor, and you shall have treasure
in heaven!' And Peter's ears prick up, and he looks surprised,
and he says, 'What? What's all that about? You are talking
about treasure? Well, *we* have left everything and followed
you. What, then, is this treasure you are talking about? What
shall we have?' How honest and unselfconscious Peter is!
If only he knew it, he is raising a very basic question here,
namely, what difference does it make whether or not we
leave everything to follow the Saviour?

In hindsight, we can see that if he had taken the time
to think about it, Peter might never have dared to ask this
question. But he did ask it in all innocence, and Jesus
answered it without the least trace of a rebuke, assuring
Peter and his friends, and all successive ages of our Lord's
followers, that he will never be in debt to anyone.

Jesus' promises of compensation

*'Jesus said to them [the twelve disciples], "I tell you the
truth, at the renewal of all things, when the Son of man
sits on his glorious throne, you who have followed me will
also sit on twelve thrones, judging the twelve tribes of Israel.
And everyone who has left houses or brothers or sisters or
father or mother or children or fields for my sake will receive
a hundred times as much and will inherit eternal life!"'*
(Matthew 19:28,29.)

What a remarkable passage! And how challenging to the
kind of person whom you sometimes meet even within the
Christian church who believes, really, that Christians have
made a pretty poor bargain in agreeing to follow Jesus
Christ. For the principle enunciated here by Jesus is this:
'Peter, Peter, if you only knew what you have gained in
following me, you would not even ask the question! If
you only knew what in my heart I have planned for you,

and what in his heart the Father has prepared for you, you would rejoice with joy unspeakable, whatever you've left behind! For that which you've forsaken is nothing in comparison with that which awaits you!' Our Lord's words refer first to the Twelve (v. 28), and second to all of his cross-bearing followers in every age (v. 29).

The promises to the apostles

'I tell you the truth, at the renewal of all things, when the Son of man sits on his glorious throne, you who have followed me will also sit on twelve thrones, judging the twelve tribes of Israel.'

This promise explains both *when* the apostles of Christ[1] will be honoured, and *what form* their honour will take.

1. *When* will they be honoured? Jesus describes that time in two parallel concepts: 'at the renewal of all things' and 'when the Son of man sits on his glorious throne'.

In the first of these concepts, when saying that the apostles will be honoured 'at the renewal of all things', or 'in the regeneration' (AV), Jesus uses a word (*paliggenesia* = *palin* + *genesia*) which literally means 'the new genesis'. The first book of the Bible is, of course, called 'Genesis' ('emergence', 'coming into being', 'origin') and it refers to the beginnings of the world as we know it. But there is going to be *another* new beginning, a different condition of things — something which does not yet obtain when our Lord is speaking, whether a state of being or a period of time. This will be 'the new genesis', 'the renewal of all things', 'the regeneration', and then the disciples who have left all to follow Jesus will sit on twelve thrones, reigning over the twelve tribes of Israel.

Now what era, exactly, is Jesus referring to with this phrase 'the new genesis'? Commentators make many suggestions, but, in summary, they suggest that Jesus could be referring *either* to a more immediate state of things, *or* to an ultimate state of things, *or* to both. My personal inclination is to see in his words a reference to *both*.

Since the word Jesus used here (*paliggenesia*) is found only once elsewhere in the New Testament, and there for *spiritual* regeneration (Titus 3:5 where Paul speaks of 'rebirth and renewal by the Holy Spirit' upon individual people), it can legitimately be seen as referring to a 'spiritual genesis'—specifically, to the time of spiritual renewal that was to follow the Pentecostal effusion of the Holy Spirit. Pentecost was to inaugurate a whole new beginning in the history of the Christian church, a new era in which renewal and regeneration would be experienced by an ever-increasing number of people from Jerusalem to Judea to Samaria to the uttermost parts of the earth. Interestingly enough, Pentecost was later referred to by Peter himself quite specifically as 'the beginning' (Acts 11:15).

Moreover, Scripture clearly refers elsewhere to a material regeneration of the cosmic order to take place in the end time, and Jesus may well have this in mind when he speaks of 'the renewal of all things'. This is the kind of thing that Paul refers to, for example, when he writes, 'The creation itself will be liberated from its bondage to decay and brought into the glorious freedom of the children of God' (Romans 8:21). This is the time when 'the wolf will live with the lamb, the leopard will lie down with the goat, the calf and the lion and the yearling together; and a little child will lead them . . . for the earth will be full of the knowledge of the Lord as the waters cover the sea' (Isaiah 11:6,9). This is the time when 'the heavens will disappear with a roar; the elements will be destroyed by fire, and the earth and everything in it will be laid bare [or burned up]' and 'a new heaven and a new earth, the home of righteousness will have arrived' (2 Peter 3:10,13).

'At the renewal of all things', then, 'in the regeneration', the apostles of Christ will be honoured — whether we think of this renewal in terms of its spiritual inauguration at Pentecost, or in terms of its cosmic consummation in the end time, or in terms of both.

The second concept that Jesus uses in his description of the era when the apostles will be honoured is 'when the Son of man sits on his glorious throne'. Again it has both a more immediate reference to the period following our Lord's resurrection and ascension, and an ultimate reference to his coming again in glory and in power to judge the world and to complete his work in his people.

The New Testament speaks of the resurrection and ascension of our Lord as entering into his kingship. The writer of the Epistle to the Hebrews, for instance, announces, 'After he had provided purification for sins, he sat down at the right hand of the Majesty in heaven. So he became as much superior to the angels as the name he has inherited is superior to theirs' (Hebrews 1:3,4). Paul writes of God's 'mighty strength which he exerted in Christ when he raised him from the dead and seated him at his right hand in the heavenly realms, far above all rule and authority, power and dominion . . . And God placed all things under his feet . . .' (Ephesians 1:19—22). Peter proclaims to the Jews at Pentecost: 'God has raised this Jesus to life, and we are all witnesses of the fact. Exalted to the right hand of God, he has received from the Father the promised Holy Spirit and has poured out what you now see and hear . . . Therefore let all Israel be assured of this: God has made this Jesus, whom you crucified, both Lord and Christ' (Acts 2:32—36).

There are sections of the Christian church that seem to minimize the significance of the fact that Jesus Christ is crowned today. He is victorious; he is not waiting for victory. He is on the throne; he is not merely on the way to the throne. Already at Pentecost he was King of kings and Lord of lords! His sending forth of the Holy Spirit signified that: only deity can command deity! Let us see the significance of this: *Jesus reigns now.*

But even though our Lord's reign was to begin at his ascension, and ever since then he has been high over all, yet Jesus himself and some of his apostles also sometimes used the language of 'sitting on the throne' to refer to the time of his ultimate return: 'When the Son of man comes in his glory, and all the angels with him, he will sit on his throne in heavenly glory. All the nations will be gathered before him, and he will separate the people one from another as a shepherd separates the sheep from the goats. He will put the sheep on his right and the goats on his left' (Matthew 25:31—33).

In interpreting 'when the Son of man sits on his glorious throne', then, we may again legitimately understand Jesus as referring to two ages or two states of being — to the period begun by his exaltation and ascension, and to the end period when he will return to oust his foes and consummate his purposes. The apostles are to be honoured throughout this whole time, and the passage proceeds to tell us how.

2. *What form* will the honour take? *How* will the apostles be honoured? Jesus answers, 'You who have followed me will also sit on twelve thrones, judging the twelve tribes of Israel.' Just as the timing can be more immediate and/or ultimate, so, too, can the honour take an immediate and/or an ultimate form.

First, our Lord means that in the immediate era introduced by his exaltation, with the resulting Pentecostal outpouring of the Spirit, the apostles are to enter upon their unique, spiritual reign in the church. Now I can almost hear someone objecting: 'Surely that's not right! No one ever saw the apostles reigning! They had no crowns or sceptres or other paraphernalia of kingly office!' No, that's quite true. But let us not confuse the paraphernalia of office with the reality. As there are so-called 'kings' today who have all the trappings of office but no real authority, so, conversely, the apostles reigned with real authority, but without its trappings.

And never did men reign like the apostles! In every church in New Testament times they ruled by their teaching and by their epistles. What they declared to be wrong was acknowledged as wrong, and what they declared to be right was obeyed; otherwise men were excommunicated or disciplined. The apostles had the power of the keys. Their authority was such that the whole church of apostolic and post-apostolic times bowed to their rule. If it did not, it was heretical.

The apostles ruled 'on twelve thrones', therefore, and they are reigning still. Through their writings and teachings they still exercise the power of the keys of the kingdom so as to open its doors to penitent, believing Jews and Gentiles alike. They still exercise spiritual rule over the entire Israel of God. For under whose government do we, as a church, stand today? Under the government of the Head of the church, who rules it by his apostles (cf. Ephesians 2:20). Our doctrine of eldership is such that it must always be subservient to the Word of God and his apostles. Today we have no apostles: there are no apostolic successors in the full sense of the word. The apostles of Jesus stand alone, for they beheld the Lord risen from the dead. They all witnessed his resurrection, and by virtue of this unique position they are reigning still over the whole household of God.

Someone may want to point out here that other people besides the Twelve are called 'apostles' (*apostolos*) in the New Testament (cf. 2 Corinthians 8:23; Philippians 2:25). Yes, but not in this technical sense. The others are apostles of the churches, that is, messengers sent by the churches. These, on the other hand, are the apostles of the Lamb. There is a world of difference between being sent as a messenger by a church, and being commissioned as an apostle by the Head of the church.

'You . . . will also sit on twelve thrones, judging the twelve tribes of Israel.' Jesus is saying that the apostles are to reign in the era that is to begin at Pentecost. And wherever there is a church of Christ today, the apostles are still reigning. Wherever they do not rule in this spiritual sense, doctrinally and morally through their teaching, there the church of Jesus Christ is falling into disrepute and decay and will soon, if that state of affairs continues, lose its light and its witness.

Yet that is not the only thing that our Lord has in mind here. The present rule of the apostles is but the precursor of their future reign. There is a time coming when their honour will be so great that they will sit alongside the great Judge himself. This is the ultimate reference of Jesus' promise that they will 'sit on twelve thrones'. Remember Paul's question to the Corinthians: 'If any of you has a dispute with another, dare he take it before the ungodly for judgement instead of before the saints? Do you not know that the saints will judge the world?' (1 Corinthians 6:1,2.) If that is a privilege awaiting the saints in general, then it is certainly a privilege awaiting the apostles in particular, according to the glorious promise of our Lord.

So Jesus reassures Peter that he is no man's debtor. To Peter's question as to what the disciples will receive, who have left everything to follow him, our Lord points to the positions he has appointed for his apostles both in the more immediate and in the ultimate future. He is saying, in effect, 'Ah, Peter! You have left your boat and your nets, but let me tell you that there are honours awaiting those who have left the things of this life to follow me, the nature of which I cannot now paint in full for you because your minds would boggle at the picture!' And here is the essence of Christian faith: to believe your Lord even though you do not always understand everything he says, and to go on expecting in due course the fulfilment of his every promise.

The promise to all of Christ's disciples

Our present text does not end with the promises made by Jesus to his future apostles. He also makes promises of sure compensation for the sacrifices of *all* his followers, both then and now. Far from chiding Peter for his question, 'What then will there be for us?', Jesus Christ goes on to reply to what may well be a question in the heart of any child of God: 'Am I a loser if I follow Jesus Christ?' No! No one is a loser who follows him. You may have to take up your cross daily; you may even have to die, but even your death means no loss, but gain.

This is how Jesus puts it, according to Matthew: *'And everyone who has left houses or brothers or sisters or father or mother or children or fields for my sake will receive a hundred times as much and will inherit eternal life.'* Mark adds two significant clarifications: every follower of Christ who makes sacrifices 'for me and the gospel' will receive a hundred times as much *'in this present age . . . and with them, persecutions . . .'* (10:30). Let us look at two main points here.

1. First, the promised compensation is over and above the gift of eternal life: 'Everyone . . . will receive a hundred times as much *and will inherit eternal life.'* These five words are deceptively simple, but I wonder whether we are really aware of what they mean? They refer to the most infinitely precious gift that any man anywhere can ever possess — eternal life! Nothing that God can give us is more precious than this.

Eternal life is the life of God himself. It is life without any flaw, without any disappointing factor, without any cause of grief or sorrow, in itself. It belongs exclusively to God and to those to whom he imparts it in Jesus Christ.

Nothing can surpass it in beauty or glory or joy. It is *all* grace and fulfilment and righteousness, and peace in the Holy Spirit. It is the embodiment of every perfection, without the possibility of diminution, either at death or beyond death. And even as it includes all good, so it excludes all evil. Eternal life may fill and flood our souls now and hereafter in such a measure as we simply cannot now comprehend. That any of Adam's fallen race should have eternal life is a matter of divine grace. It was necessary for the Son of man to die in order to procure eternal life for sinners. It was necessary for God's Holy Spirit to come into the world to perform the delicate task of renewing and recreating men, in order that sinners should personally possess eternal life. Through these means, in his infinite grace, God made provision to share his very life with us.

Therefore, this great gift of eternal life is the pearl of great price (Matthew 13:46). It alone is more than ample compensation for any denials we have to make, for any deaths we have to die and for any desolations we have to experience. And yet we see in this passage that eternal life is *the minimum* that any follower of Jesus Christ is given. The wonder is that the 'hundred times as much' mentioned in our Lord's answer to Peter is *over and above* the gift to each saint of eternal life. Well may our worship and praise be inspired by such abundant generosity!

2. Secondly, the promised compensation goes infinitely beyond offsetting our temporal losses and sufferings: '. . . a *hundred* times as much in this present age . . . and with them, persecutions . . .'

The first thing that may strike us about Jesus' words is his honesty. He could have left out the reminder of persecutions, especially in this context of rewards and compensations, but he does not. He does not gloss over the inevitable consequences of following him in a fallen world, knowing that persecutions are as unavoidable for his faithful followers as the cross is to himself. He also knows that both the glory of eternal life and the liberality with which he will compensate each follower for his sufferings ultimately will outweigh the sufferings themselves.

But there is perhaps an even more sublime reason for Jesus' mention of persecutions here: part of the wonder of our gospel is found in the fact that Jesus Christ takes persecutions and uses them for our good. Persecution is not just something that the Christian suffers and manages to endure; it also works out the purposes of God in an individual's life. Our Lord takes the briar of persecution, with all its flesh-cutting properties, and he makes it bring forth roses. He takes the flinty rock of some of our sufferings, and he makes it gush forth with water in a desert. He declares, 'Blessed are you when people insult you, persecute you and falsely say all kinds of evil against you because of me. Rejoice and be glad, because great is your reward in heaven, for in the same way they persecuted the prophets who were before you' (Matthew 5:11). We should rejoice in the moment of persecution? Surely that would be foolish? Yes, unless we believe this: Jesus Christ makes persecution work out for our good.

His servants agree that he does: 'Consider it pure joy, my brothers, whenever you face trials of many kinds, because you know that the testing of your faith develops perseverance' (James 1:2,3). Persecution is productive: it produces steadfastness, character, glory. Peter says the same thing: 'If you are insulted because of the name of Christ, you are blessed, for the Spirit of glory and of God rests on you' (1 Peter 4:14).

Even in the context of the rewards of the Christian life, then, Jesus is able to refer to persecution, and he is able to be honest about its inevitability for his followers, because he has mastered it. He can make it work for his own glory and for our good. This in itself is a form of recompense.

But let us look too at our Lord's liberal compensation: 'Everyone . . . will receive *a hundred times as much.*' How are we to understand this?

It is no *quid pro quo:* we should not be enslaved to a purely literal interpretation of 'a hundred times as much'. Jesus does not mean that he will give Peter one hundred boats in place of the one he has left behind in order to follow him, for example. Nor does he mean that he will pay Matthew exactly a hundred times as much in wages as he earned while collecting taxes. Such a literal interpretation is neither required by the text nor substantiated by the facts! For what the New Testament clearly teaches is that Jesus

Christ does not pay his 'hundred times as much' in any one currency. It is true that when people like Paul had to turn their backs upon their families in order to follow and to serve Christ, he provided for them many homes, many fathers and mothers, many brothers and sisters and many children. Rufus' mother became Paul's mother, he tells us (Romans 16:13); Onesimus was like a son to him (Philemon 10) and more homes opened to him in his journeys than he needed.

This precious truth is tellingly illustrated from the experience of Egerton Young, who preached to the Indians of Saskatchewan many years ago, when they knew very little about the gospel. An Indian chief asked him, 'Did I hear you call God your Father?' 'Yes,' replied the preacher. 'And,' retorted the chief, 'is he my Father?' 'Yes,' came the reply again. 'Then,' said the chief, putting out his hand, 'we two are brothers!' What a great discovery! They had found each other. Christians have brothers and sisters everywhere. Jesus does repay in kind.

But let us go beyond that: Jesus does not pay his 'hundred times as much' in just *one* kind of currency, valuable as that one may be. He pays it in many others as well. He pays some of it in the currency of 'the peace of God, which transcends all understanding' (Philippians 4:7). He pays some of it in the currency of a contented spirit (cf. Philippians 4:11,12), and some in the currency of 'godliness with contentment' which is 'great gain' (1 Timothy 6:6). He pays some of it in the currency of freedom from care and anxiety (Matthew 6:33), even in the face of danger (Hebrews 10:34), some in the currency of his joy (John 15:11), and some in the currency of his own felt presence with us (Matthew 28:20).

And he pays some of his 'hundred times as much' in the currency of personal fulfilment. Let us not overlook this. Men and women in the Christian church who are serving the Lord have found themselves. Until they came and left all and followed him, they were like square pegs in round holes. They did not know either what they should do or what they wanted to do. They could not make heads or tails of themselves or their lives. Then suddenly the grace of God came to them and put them in their right places, suddenly all that they had and all that they were blossomed forth, and they found they had gifts galore! It is a priceless thing to know that you are in the place where God meant you to be. And this is one of the currencies in which he pays his 'hundred times as much'.

And so, far from chiding Peter for his question, our Lord inundates him with promises and assurances that to follow him cannot mean loss. To lose for Christ's sake is to gain; to die is to live; to go down is to go up, for Jesus Christ repays a hundredfold in this life, quite apart from the fruits of persecution that he nurtures and the gift of eternal life that he freely grants those who trust and follow him. Well does the Scottish paraphrase express it:

> A hope so great and so divine
> May trials well endure,
> And purge the soul from sense and sin
> As Christ himself is pure.

'No, no, Peter: you have not left anything comparable with that which in the fulness of time you will reap.'

Therefore, rather than allow crippling doubts to dampen our zeal, let us, with Peter, believe the Saviour's promises, trust his faithfulness and never flinch from any sacrifice he may ask of us as we follow him. He cannot fail. And he will never be our debtor.

Reference
1. Judas Iscariot, of course, forfeited this privilege. The identification of the 'twelfth' apostle — whether it be Matthias or Paul or both — is beyond the scope of these studies.

18.
Two lessons in one

Thoughtful readers of the Gospel narratives repeatedly find themselves awestruck as they meditate upon various experiences of the Twelve in their nearness to the Lord. Take, for example, the washing of the disciples' feet by Jesus (John 13:1−17). At first sight this seems to be an incident of sheer beauty and uncomplicated simplicity. But further consideration reveals it to be much more meaningful than that; it is a sermon in action, an incident as profound as it is beautiful. Here Jesus is speaking and acting on two levels at once — physical and spiritual; on each level he is making clear what it is that all of us, saved or unsaved, must do to be in fellowship with him.

The physical action

What Jesus knew
John, the Gospel writer, takes considerable pains to fill in the context here. He uses three whole verses to give preliminary information before coming to the main point. Whenever we find such a full context given in Scripture, we should sit up and take notice, because it is usually a signal that something important is about to happen. Here John is signalling to us that Jesus is about to do something very remarkable, and he is giving us some necessary background information first.

> 'It was just before the Passover Feast. Jesus knew that the time had come for him to leave this world and go to the Father. Having loved his own who were in the world, he now showed them the full

187

> *extent of his love. The evening meal was being*
> *served, and the devil had already prompted Judas*
> *Iscariot, son of Simon, to betray Jesus. Jesus*
> *knew that the Father had put all things under*
> *his power, and that he had come from God and*
> *was returning to God . . .'*

Here John tells us a great deal about the mind of our Lord on this occasion. Jesus was aware of four main things.

1. *'It was just before the Passover Feast. Jesus knew that the time had come for him to leave this world and go to the Father.'*

Our Lord was aware of the *time*. With his outer eye on the calendar (the feast of the Passover was imminent), he had his inner eye on God's schedule. He knew that his time, his hour, had come. Other people did not know this, but he did. Until now he had been waiting for this time; many things could not take place until it arrived (cf. John 7:30; 8:20). But now it had come. And so he was aware that at this Passover something singular was going to take place. The one mighty hour, the unrepeatable hour upon which the destiny of all mankind rested — that hour had arrived.

2. *'Having loved his own which were in the world, he loved them unto the end' (AV).*

Our Lord was aware of *his love* for his friends. These men had been difficult to teach and lead: what they learned one day, they forgot the next; their failures and their follies were innumerable. If any one of us had been their leader, we might have felt nothing but disappointment in them at this stage; we might even have felt positive relief at the thought of leaving them. But not so our Lord! His thoughts of his disciples were full of compassion and affection. Out of the depths of his soul he cared for them. And it was not without pain that he contemplated the necessity of leaving them, even to go to the Father.

3. *'The evening meal was being served, and the devil had already prompted Judas Iscariot, son of Simon, to betray Jesus.'*

Our Lord was aware that his final battle with Satan was about to begin. He knew what was going on in Judas' heart. As he looked into it, he could see something sinister already set in motion there: Satan had planted a seed that had taken root and was about to bring forth fruit. Judas was already calculating in his heart: 'For how much will I sell my Lord?'

4. *'Jesus knew that the Father had put all things under his power, and that he had come from God and was returning to God.'*

Jesus was aware of his own personal glory, of his origin and destiny. He was conscious of who he was in the purposes of God. He knew that everything in the whole world belonged to him. He was conscious of his lordship, in other words, and this consciousness remained undimmed throughout the ensuing incident.

What Jesus did and the contrast it revealed

> *'So he got up from the meal, took off his outer clothing, and wrapped a towel round his waist. After that, he poured water into a basin and began to wash his disciples' feet, drying them with the towel that was wrapped around him.'*

Through this brief description, John shows what a great contrast there was between our Lord's attitude and that of the Twelve. For they had begun to eat their meal without anyone making a move to do what was the customary chore before meals in Palestine then — the washing of everyone's feet. This was a custom necessitated both by the heat of the climate and by the dustiness of the roads on which people walked in open sandals. But it was not only a matter of hygiene; it was a token of welcome as well, and it was a means of physical refreshment after the heat of the day. It was performed by a slave, if there was one in the household.

Supper had begun, then, and Jesus had allowed it to begin without one single disciple offering to wash the feet of his Master or his fellows. Why not? Because each of them was intoxicated with a false sense of his own importance and greatness! Why should any of them stoop to do menial service? They had been quite preoccupied lately with the question of who among them was the greatest (Mark 9:34;

Matthew 18:1), and each of them had a claim to stake, apparently. Being in that frame of mind, they were certainly not prepared to wash their brothers' feet!

But he who was heir of all things, who had come from God and was going to God — the lowly Son of God, in full consciousness of his own eternal glory and deity — *was* prepared to do so. And so *during* supper (not, as the Authorized Version wrongly translates, 'supper being ended'), the Lord Jesus Christ rose from the meal, dressed himself in the appropriate servant's garb, and set about washing the feet of his disciples. What a contrast between his attitude and theirs!

Jesus' conflict with Peter

Everything now seems to centre on Peter. When he saw the Lord Jesus Christ dressed as a slave with a towel around his loins and a basin of water in his hands, something triggered in Peter's soul which set off the most violent kind of opposition. His impetuous nature swung from one extreme to another in confused, intense reaction to his Lord's humble deed.

1. First, Peter frustrated his Lord's action: *'He [Jesus] came to Simon Peter, who said to him, "Lord, are you going to wash my feet?"'*

Authorities tell us that it is almost impossible to give an accurate translation for Peter's words here. They carry a tone of horrified disbelief which might be expressed as: 'What, *you*? *My* feet?' The emphasis is on 'you' in the one breath and on 'my' in the next breath. In other words, Peter clearly saw the situation as totally incongruous. He recognized that there was something altogether wrong about Jesus' washing his followers' feet.

Why did Peter act and speak like this? True, the incongruity was there, but even more, when Peter saw his Lord coming to do for him what he himself had disdained to do for anyone else, his conscience began to bother him. When he saw his Master about to put his hand on Peter's own dirty feet, he rebelled because he saw exactly what he himself should be doing. His pride was condemned and his conscience was stung. And in his resulting confusion of mind, his one desire was to prevent his Lord from performing this humble act.

2. Then Peter rejected Jesus' promise of a later explanation: *'Jesus replied, "You do not realize now what I am doing, but later you will understand." "No," said Peter, "you shall never wash my feet."'*

See how understanding our Lord was. He did not come down like a ton of bricks on Peter; instead he calmly said, 'All right, Peter, I can understand that it may be a bit of a shock to you to see me doing this. It seems incongruous to you. But let me tell you, Peter, that though now you don't understand what I am doing, later on you will. There is a reason for this, and you shall have the reason from me when the right time comes.' Fully aware of Peter's struggle with his pride and his conscience, Jesus offered him some comfort. He tried to assure Peter that his action in washing the disciples' feet was not primarily meant to show up their own failure. Rather, it had a deeper meaning which would later become clear.

But what was Peter's response? One is almost ashamed to report it, because it is so often the response of all our hearts. For humanly we cannot conceive of the possibility that we might not understand the reason for something our Lord does. We acknowledge him to be the Christ, the Son of the living God, but when he does something that is beyond our ken, we deny that there can be a valid explanation. This is what Peter did: he rejected Jesus' assurance that there was a reason, and he flatly stated, 'You shall never wash my feet.'

For Peter was rattled. A man with a guilty conscience always tends to be rattled so that he cannot think clearly. Any pastor knows that. And because Peter, in his guilt, could think of no other possible reason for Jesus' washing their feet than to show the disciples' fault in not doing it, therefore he rejected Jesus' own assurance that there was another, deeper meaning to his action. Peter was in the unhappy, ambivalent condition of being both humble enough to recognize the incongruity of his Lord's washing his feet and proud enough to reject his Lord's word and promise!

3. But he did ultimately yield to the Saviour's requirement. For Jesus is not only very understanding, he is also resolute, and he will deal with arrogance and defiance in

any disciple. He is King. When once he has begun to work in a man, he will pursue him with one means or another. He *will* be Lord! This is a fact that we seem to have forgotten today. Men now tend to represent Jesus as a beggar at the mercy of the whims of every man and every power. But he is not so — he is Lord!

And with Peter he now used another approach — a threat. Jesus Christ is very slow to make threats. There are times when he has to do so, as we see throughout the New Testament, but his normal method is to disclose his promises and to say, 'Look, here is my promise! Believe me, receive me, trust me and obey me!' It is only when his promises fail to register that his chastisements begin.

What Jesus' promise to Peter did not accomplish, his threat did: *'Jesus answered, "Unless I wash you, you have no part with me." "Then, Lord," Simon Peter replied, "not just my feet but my hands and my head as well!"'* Jesus was saying, in effect, 'Peter, look! You and I cannot go on in fellowship together unless I wash your feet!' And this threat worked; it snapped the spell of Peter's rebellion.

Peter loved his Lord too dearly to be able to bear the thought of life out of fellowship with him. True, he would yet say and do some very outrageous things before Jesus' death on the cross, but they would be due largely to his impetuosity and thoughtlessness. Peter's real heart was such that he loved his Lord far too much to be able to think of living or dying without him.

And so, bless him, Peter went from one extreme to the other. He did a complete about-face! Typically, he blurted out words of surrender that were more rash than rational: 'Take me and wash me all over, Lord! Don't just wash my feet — bath me!' He was just as irrational and thoughtless as before. But this time there was a point to his exuberance: it showed total capitulation. Peter was saying, 'Lord, all right, then. I didn't accept your promise of an explanation by and by, but, my, I take your threat! Do anything you like with me!' He was presenting his body, as it were; he was offering his head, his hands, his all to Jesus. This episode must have electrified the disciples. Yet there was still much more to it that would move them profoundly later on when they understood it.

The spiritual application

The fact that Jesus is speaking and acting on two different levels at once — the physical and the spiritual — becomes very evident as soon as he tells Peter, 'You do not realize now what I am doing, but later you will understand.' Here is Jesus coming with water and a towel to wash Peter's feet. Peter is only too well aware of what Jesus is doing, physically. Yet Jesus says, '*You do not realize now* what I am doing.' He is telling Peter that there is a significance to the feet-washing other than the physical one. This becomes clearer still when we hear Jesus saying, 'Unless I wash you, you have no part with me.' Jesus cannot mean that his physical washing of Peter's feet is *in itself* a necessary precondition for fellowship with him. He must be referring to something that is greater than, and beyond, the mere physical experience of having one's feet washed by him.

This kind of double reference is not strange to any student of John's Gospel. In fact, it is typical of Jesus' way of teaching as John portrays it. Using words like 'birth', 'life', 'thirst', 'bread', etc., all of which have plain physical meanings, Jesus speaks of spiritual things. He speaks of spiritual birth (John 3:6) and spiritual life (3:16); he speaks of spiritual thirst and spiritual water (4:14); he speaks of spiritual hunger (6:35) and spiritual bread (6:33). Therefore our Lord is not introducing any new principle into his teaching method when, here in John 13, he speaks of spiritual uncleanness and the need for spiritual cleansing. What Peter does not realize is that in his action of washing the disciples' feet, Jesus is doing something that is symbolic or parabolic. His external, physical action portrays profound spiritual truth.

A symbol of salvation

1. Salvation, viewed from one angle, is nothing other than the washing away of the filth of sin; and Jesus' washing of the disciples' feet here in this episode represents this washing of salvation which he has come to make possible in 'his hour' that is now ticking away. Five times between verses 5 and 10, we meet the verb 'to wash [a part of the

body]' (*niptō*); once we meet the verb 'to bath' or 'to bathe
[the whole body]' (*louō*); and once we meet the adjective
'clean' (*katharos*). The whole passage hinges on the concept
of *cleansing*. Behind the physical action, then, we are seeing
the humble willingness of the Son of God to become the
servant of man. We are seeing his willingness to lay aside
the glory that he had with the Father in order to come down
to the dirty feet and the dirty hearts of his miserable
creatures. We are seeing the cleansing blood that he comes
to pour forth for us to make us clean from the defilement
of sin, and to wash our stains away.

This concept of salvation as *cleansing* is amazingly prevalent even in books of the Old Testament. For instance,
thinking of the messianic age to come, the prophet Zechariah
says, 'On that day a fountain will be opened to the house
of David and the inhabitants of Jerusalem, to cleanse them
from sin and impurity' (Zechariah 13:1; cf. Psalm 51:2;
Jeremiah 33:8; Ezekiel 36:25,33).

This same imagery is used by New Testament writers.
Peter, for example, points out that God made no distinction
between Jew and Gentile in his gift of grace: 'God, who
knows the heart, showed that he accepted them by giving
the Holy Spirit to them, just as he did to us. He made no
distinction between us and them, for he purified their hearts
by faith' (Acts 15:8,9).

Salvation involves being cleansed. The apostle Paul says
the same thing: 'Husbands, love your wives, just as Christ
loved the church and gave himself up for her to make her
holy, cleansing her by the washing with water through
the word, and to present her to himself as a radiant church,
without stain or wrinkle or any other blemish, but holy and
blameless' (Ephesians 5:25—27). And he writes to Titus of
God's love: 'But when the kindness and love of God our
Saviour appeared, he saved us, not because of righteous
things we had done, but because of his mercy. He saved us
through the washing of rebirth and renewal by the Holy
Spirit, whom he poured out on us generously through Jesus
Christ our Saviour' (Titus 3:4—6).

The writer of the Epistle to the Hebrews (9:14; 10:22,
etc.) and the apostle John (1 John 1:7,9; Revelation 1:5)
use this same concept of salvation as cleansing through the
blood of Christ.

Jesus Christ came in humility to wash away our sins in his own blood, and to make us clean for the presence and the service of God. This is biblical Christianity. This is salvation. And this is what the hymn-writer had in mind when he wrote,

> There is a fountain filled with blood
> Drawn from Emmanuel's veins,
> And sinners plunged beneath that flood
> Lose all their guilty stains.

The most damaging dirt is not the dirt that clings to the hands or the face or the feet. It is the moral pollution that seeps into the crevices of the mind and the heart and the soul. There is no other cleansing under heaven for that uncleanness than that provided by the Christ of the cross. Only his blood can cleanse the heart and mind and soul of mankind born in sin. Without his cleansing we cannot be clean. 'Unless I wash you, you have no part with me.' When Jesus says that, he is not referring to the physical feet-washing, but to the spiritual reality it symbolizes. This is the truth he is expressing: you and I must be purged through the precious, atoning blood of Christ or we have no fellowship with him and no salvation.

2. *'Jesus answered, "A person who has had a bath needs only to wash his feet, his whole body is clean."'*

Jesus is making a distinction here. When Peter's complete about-face expresses itself in his offering of his whole body to be washed, Jesus pulls him up short and says, in effect, 'No, no, Peter! You don't know what you're saying! Look, the person who has had a bath' (*literally*, not 'washed', but 'bathed' which is a different word) 'needs only to wash his feet and then he is completely clean again. There are two aspects to this cleansing work that I have come to do in this mighty hour at the Passover. The one is total and unrepeatable — it's like having a bath! It takes the form of a total cleansing of the entire being of a person, and it needs no repetition.'

The experience of becoming a Christian is like having a moral bath. One's whole being is submerged, as it were, in the cleansing blood of Christ, and is washed and made clean. This is that act of divine forgiveness and purging away of sin which takes place when we repent of our sins and place our faith in Jesus Christ as Saviour. It makes a person totally clean in the sight of God. And such a total cleansing is not again necessary. Theologically speaking, this refers to the sinner's justification, in which God no longer imputes his transgressions to his charge, but forgives all his sin.

But there is a second aspect to the cleansing work of Christ that is more limited in scope and that does need to be repeated: 'A person who has had a bath *needs only to wash his feet.*' In his physical action of washing the disciples' feet, Jesus is telling them by analogy: 'You may have had a bath before coming out to this supper tonight, but in walking through the dusty streets you have made your feet dirty. You need to have *them* washed, and then you will be totally clean again.'

And for us who belong to Christ, though we have been washed in his blood and are clean, nevertheless we become sullied; our thoughts become impure, our consciences become dulled. They need to be cleansed again and again by our Lord's cleansing blood. Each new day Jesus comes to each of us with his provision for cleansing every sinful stain. There is not a child of God who does not need it! Let us not push him away like Peter, or say like the Pharisee, 'I've no need of you! I'm clean.' 'If we confess our sins, he is faithful and just and will forgive us our sins and purify us from all unrighteousness' (1 John 1:9). Jesus continually comes to wash and cleanse and purge us so that we may enjoy continual fellowship with him and serve him.

A symbol of sovereignty

Jesus' washing of his disciples' feet is a sermon in action not only about salvation, but also about the complementary notions of sovereignty and submission — Christ's sovereignty to save and our submission to be saved.

1. Jesus Christ as Sovereign expects the submission of his people to his ministry of feet-washing. Our Lord approached Peter in the expectation that he would yield. Indeed, he refused to be put off by Peter's objections. In fact in his coming to Peter with the basin of water, Jesus was making the judgement that Peter's feet needed washing.

And so he comes to his children still. When he comes to you and to me with the cleansing blood of his cross, he is passing judgement upon us. He infers that we need cleansing. And when he comes with the provision for this cleansing, Jesus, as Sovereign, expects us to submit. He expects us to accept his judgement of us as he comes to show us our stained feet, our soiled minds and imaginations and consciences. And each time he comes, it is to offer his cleansing. Let us therefore yield to him every stained area of our beings, for maintaining fellowship with him necessitates constant cleansing by him.

2. Jesus Christ as Sovereign expects the submission of his people to his will, even when they do not fully understand what he is doing. If he has given his promise that he will provide an explanation in due course, that should be enough for us. The man of the world cannot believe him, but the man in whose heart is the Spirit of God can and should. Let us trust our Lord, then, and believe that he always has a reason for what he is doing.

3. Finally, Jesus Christ as Sovereign expects the submission of his people in following his example of lowly service.

> '*When he had finished washing their feet, he put on his clothes and returned to his place. "Do you understand what I have done for you?" he asked them. "You call me 'Teacher' and 'Lord', and rightly so, for that is what I am. Now that I, your Lord and Teacher, have washed your feet, you also should wash one another's feet. I have set you an example that you should do as I have done for you. I tell you the truth, no servant is greater than his master, nor is a messenger greater than the one who sent him. Now that you know these things, you will be blessed if you do them."*'

a. The verbal confession of Christ's disciples demands a corresponding practical expression. Those who call him 'Teacher' must heed his precepts; those who call him 'Lord' must honour and respect him as such. If we call him 'Teacher', then, rather than being shocked by any action of his, or by any demand that he makes of us, we should try to learn what he is teaching through that action or demand. If we call him 'Lord', we should never disobey him or dishonour him. These titles are no mere courtesy titles (as someone has said). They demand whole-hearted respect from those who use them.

b. Men who believe that Jesus Christ is Teacher and Lord must logically learn to see themselves as his disciples and servants. The disciple is not greater than his teacher, nor is the servant superior to his lord. Therefore, no disciple of Christ ought to be above doing such menial, humble service for another as his Lord and Master did here for his disciples. We should follow his example.

Some people have gone to the extreme of believing that this passage means we must physically wash one another's feet, at services of worship, for example. What I would say is this: if our brother *needs* his feet washed physically, then we should do it. But whether or not that physical need is there, we are certainly to get down and serve one another in lowly situations of many kinds. The point is, if our divine Master humbled himself to do such menial acts, it cannot be beneath our dignity to do the same. If we think otherwise, then either we esteem Jesus Christ less than we confess with our lips, or we fail to relate our view of him to our view of ourselves.

That this message left its mark on Peter is evident from a passage in his First Epistle. Knowing the tendency of the young to pride and self-will, he writes, 'Young men, in the same way be submissive to those who are older. Clothe yourselves with humility towards one another, because "God opposes the proud but gives grace to the humble"' (1 Peter 5:5).

Let us ask ourselves now, where are we today? Can we receive the deeper lessons of this apparently simple episode of the feet-washing? Jesus comes to us with a washing for the soul and the spirit — with an initial washing that is for those who repent and turn away from sin, and come to him, and with a repeated washing of the parts that continually become soiled — a washing that is for all of his children. Let us willingly receive what the Master would do for us. He comes as the sovereign Lord and Teacher, and he tells us, 'I've left you an example. Follow me!' May God grant us grace to do so, to his honour and his praise.

19.
Sifting times

A man's elevation to high office in the church of Jesus Christ does not exempt him in the least from having to pass through trials and tribulations. On the contrary, it is only by going 'through many hardships' that any of us enter into our Lord's kingdom at all (cf. Acts 14:22); and if that is true of all the people of God, it is especially true of those who are called to be leaders. In fact, it would even appear that the more exalted the office to which a man is called, the more exacting the testings are through which he must first pass in order to become the kind of vessel that our Lord wants him to be.

Listen to Jesus speaking to Peter in Luke's Gospel: *'"Simon, Simon, Satan has asked to sift you as wheat. But I have prayed for you, Simon, that your faith may not fail. And when you have turned back, strengthen your brothers." But he replied, "Lord, I am ready to go with you to prison and to death." Jesus answered, "I tell you, Peter, before the cock crows today, you will deny three times that you know me"' (Luke 22:31–34).*

The disciples, and especially Peter, have already been promised positions of authority and honour in the church of Christ. Peter will be the first foundation member of the church (Matthew 16:18). The Twelve will 'sit on twelve thrones, judging the twelve tribes of Israel' (Matthew 19:28). And now, having just celebrated the Passover feast with Jesus (this being the occasion on which he instituted the Lord's Supper), the disciples have heard another similar promise from their Lord: 'You are those who have stood by me in my trials. And I confer on you a kingdom, just as my Father conferred one on me, so that you may eat and drink at my table in my kingdom and sit on thrones, judging the twelve tribes of Israel' (Luke 22:28–30).

But Jesus immediately turns to Peter and warns him that such a high calling has a high price. The disciples must undergo testings before they can qualify for such privileged authority. They must be tempted and tried and sifted; they must pass through the refiner's fire of much tribulation. And Peter especially, as leader among the Twelve, will have to be squeezed through the finest mesh in the sieve of divinely approved circumstances in order to come into his own, and to be fitted to fulfil his appointed ministry. In the dramatic situation of our text there are three chief figures: firstly, Simon Peter, the young disciple, called to be one of the greatest leaders of the Christian church, secondly, Satan, the seducer and tempter and accuser of the brethren and, thirdly, our blessed Lord Jesus, the faithful and infallible Saviour of his people.

Simon Peter, the disciple

The painful truth is that, despite all the blessings and privileges and opportunities that have been showered upon them, Peter and his fellow disciples are still very immature. Immediately after they participated in the first Lord's Supper, they broke into a dispute about which of them was the greatest (Luke 22:24). How insensitive they are to spiritual realities, and how preoccupied with themselves! This is true of them all, but notice one or two characteristics that are particularly evident in Peter.

He is impetuous
Human nature does not become transformed overnight. Despite the fact that Peter has been with Jesus for many months now, and has heard his Lord's teaching and seen his gracious example, Peter is still naturally impetuous. We see this above all in the fact that he still feels compelled to comment upon everything that happens. He doesn't think much — his lips move before he has taken time to consider what he is going to say — but he talks! He simply has to say something; he cannot remain quiet.

So, on this occasion, when Jesus warns Peter that a satanic assault will be made upon the entire group of twelve disciples, Peter impulsively and arrogantly retorts, 'Lord, I am ready to go with you to prison and to death.' He is saying, in effect, 'I don't know about these other fellows, Lord, but I know you can count on *me*! Satan can't scare *me*! I am so devoted to you that I'll go even to prison and to death with you! That's how great my loyalty is!' Peter will have to pay dearly for the rashness of that statement. One day in the not too distant future, Jesus will ask him, 'Simon, son of John, do you truly love me more than these [other disciples do]?' (John 21:15). The question will be a reminder to Peter of this very boast, and it will be a *bitter* reminder in the light of what has happened in the intervening time. In that time Peter is going to have to face the reality of his impetuosity. The battle will be long and challenging, and it will wound his spirit deeply, but it will have to take place. Peter has spoken rashly, out of a proud and competitive spirit. His notion that at this stage he loves his Lord better than the other disciples do simply is not true.

We have seen Peter's impetuosity on many other occasions, of course — after Caesarea Philippi, for example, when he tried to dissuade Jesus from going to the cross (Matthew 16:22), on the Mount of Transfiguration when he spoke and 'did not know what he was saying' (Luke 9:33) and in the episode of the feet-washing, when he at first flatly refused to let Jesus wash his feet, then went to the opposite extreme and begged Jesus to wash not only his feet, but his head and his hands as well (John 13). In each case, Peter spoke unadvisedly. He gave voice to the first thing that came into his head, without stopping even to consider the possibility that his words might not really suit the occasion. What always mattered to him most was that he should be the first to comment on everything that happened, even though he had not really grasped the issues at stake. And he has not changed by the time of our text.

He does not know himself

Peter is still impetuous, then, but his intentions are consistently good. In his heart he always aims at the highest, even when acting most incoherently and unwisely. In his heart he always wants the best for his Lord. When he speaks of his willingness to face prison and death with Jesus, he clearly means it. The trouble is, Peter does not yet know himself. He has not yet learned from his past, sometimes even stingingly painful experiences (cf. Matthew 16:23). Humility is not yet part of his spiritual vocabulary.

He is still imperfect
In summary, Peter at this stage is still a babe in Christ, still immature. It is necessary to emphasize this fact in order to counter the mistaken idea some people have that the first disciples were sanctified and perfected almost in the twinkling of an eye! They were not. The human clay took a long time to be shaped, and moments of extreme pressure were required in which all of the disciples, and Peter in particular, were disciplined to yield to the perfect will of their Lord. For Peter has come almost to the end of Jesus' earthly ministry without having gained any insight at all into the reality of the spiritual warfare that faces him. In consequence, he thoughtlessly responds to his Master's warning of imminent peril with blasé, carnal self-confidence. This is Peter's anomalous position: he is destined to ascend to great heights of service for his Lord, yet he is still a babe.

Satan the tempter

We shall not go very far on our mission in life before we meet the arch-enemy of Christ and his church astride our path. When Jesus graciously forewarns Peter of the inevitability of this encounter, he reveals the existence of a struggle that is constantly going on between powers in realms of experience beyond our knowledge. Here he discloses the invisible struggle going on between God and Satan in relation to the spiritual well-being of the twelve disciples, a struggle between the good and perfect will of God, on the one hand, and the forces of evil, on the other hand, championed by Satan. There are three things we may note here about Satan, the tempter.

Satan's general intentions
Jesus, who himself was cunningly tempted by Satan as he was about to begin his public ministry, announces that his

followers can expect nothing less than what he had to undergo. As he met the enemy, so must they. Satan has a plan for the whole group of disciples (as he has, of course, for the church). Jesus says, *'Simon, Simon, Satan has asked to sift you [plural] as wheat . . .'*

Although he is speaking to Simon Peter alone, our Lord reports Satan's purpose for *the whole group* of disciples; for the word 'you' here is in the plural. Another translation makes the meaning clear: 'Simon, Simon, Satan has claimed the right to put the loyalty of all of you through the mill . . .'[1]

Addressing Peter by his old, natural name 'Simon', and repeating it to emphasize the seriousness of what he is going to say, Jesus warns Peter, perhaps in the hearing of the others, that the followers of the Messiah have a foe to encounter. The Hebrew name 'Satan' (which means 'adversary') marks him out as the implacable opponent of God and his purposes. It was Satan who incited David to be so unwise as to number the people of Israel (1 Chronicles 21:1). It was Satan who stood at the right hand of Joshua the high priest to accuse him (Zechariah 3:1). And Satan has not lost his passion for all that is unholy and opposed to God's will. Here he is, waiting, full of evil intentions, and armed with a special plan for attacking the entire group of twelve disciples.

This persistent dedication of Satan to evil — a dedication that marks his activity throughout the whole Bible — is something that we, as Christians, need to take very seriously. The writers of Scripture tell us about Satan, not because they have some strange interest in him, but because he is the enemy, and the moment we come onto the side of God and his Christ, we are going to encounter this enemy. Here he is, demanding to test the whole company of the disciples, and on the same basis as he tested Job. The episode here is remarkably reminiscent of the opening chapters of the book of Job (1:6–12; 2:1–6). Job was a righteous man. And so Satan said to God, 'Aha! Does Job honour and respect his God for nothing? Not on your life! It's for what he gets out of it! Look how good you have been to him: you have put hedges around him and his house and all that he has, on every side! You have given him large

possessions and a big family! But take away all that and
you'll soon see how much Job really honours and respects
you!' What Satan is really saying, in fact, is that Job is
more chaff than wheat. And God, who knows the heart
of a man better than Satan does, permits him (within certain
limits) to test Job to find out whether he is, in fact, more
chaff than wheat.

The devil never really changes. He has no new card in his
pack. In principle he does the same things over and over
again, and if you know Scripture, you know all of his
strategies. They may appear to be different sometimes, but
that is only because our circumstances are different. Satan's
basic approaches hardly vary. And so here he comes again
to God with the same allegation against the disciples that
he made long ago against Job: 'Aha! Here are these twelve
disciples whom you are going to elevate to such high
positions in your church! Well, let me tell you that they are
really more chaff than wheat! Let me test them in my
sieve, and you'll see! There will be nothing to show but
chaff!'

Now from one point of view there is much common
sense in what Satan is saying here. What *is* the use of counting on these men for leadership when they have not yet
proved themselves loyal? And isn't it a good thing for
disciples of Jesus to be tried and tested? God himself tests
us, doesn't he? Satan is showing a lot of wisdom here! But
it is exactly there, at the point where the devil appears to
be most wise and sensible, that he is most deceptive and
dangerous. His apparent good sense is a clever smoke-screen
behind which he hides a pernicious plan.

Satan's motive in showing up the weaknesses of the
disciples is not to promote their growth, or even to prove
his own point. He wants to sift them, not to get rid of
the chaff in them, but rather, to get rid of the wheat and
leave only chaff for Christ. He wants to expose the
disciples' weaknesses in order to cut short the work of
grace in all of them, and to make it more difficult, if
not impossible, for them to serve Christ and his church.
When God tests us, he does so for our good — to get rid
of the chaff in us; but when Satan tempts us, he hopes to
harm us and destroy the work of God in us. Satan's sieve
is perverse.

You may remember these words of a hymn:

> Oh, not for thee my weak desires,
> My poorer, baser part!
> Oh, not for thee my fading fires,
> The ashes of my heart!

The hymn-writer speaks in a previous verse of the sad possibility of someone having spent all of his energies on the swift errands of the world and having nothing left for God but slow, feeble minds and bodies. That is exactly what Satan wants. He wants us to spend all our energies on other things. He wants us to waste our time and our talents and everything we have on other things so that there is nothing left but ashes to be employed for God. That is his intention concerning Christ's followers generally — he wants to strain out our wheat.

Satan's concentration on Peter

But notice, the devil has not declared his case completely. He never does! He always conceals a part of what he has in mind. He has appealed to the Almighty for permission to test *all* of the disciples but, according to what we have before us in the text, he has not mentioned the fact that he has particular designs on Peter. Jesus, however, who knows all the secrets of Satan, knows that he has his eye especially on Peter. And that is why he addresses his words directly to Peter, with such urgency, adding, '. . . but I have prayed for you, Simon, that your faith may not fail. And when you have turned back, strengthen your brothers.' This time the 'you' is singular, denoting Peter alone.

Now why should the devil have a special purpose in attacking Peter, or any other individual, for that matter? Why should he want to concentrate more on some people than on others? There are many possible reasons.

1. Sometimes it is because of a man's *past glory*. In this case, Satan is interested in attacking Peter because he has been given special privileges and graces. To cite one example, Peter was the first to receive God's revelation of his Son as the Deliverer and Saviour of mankind (Matthew 16:17). Peter received the revelation and believed it and confessed

it and thereby became the foundation member of the church. Though we are conscious of his faults and follies, we cannot help but be aware of his many positive characteristics and his great potential.

Now wouldn't it be a strike in favour of the kingdom of darkness if Satan could discredit that unusually honoured disciple, Peter? Wouldn't it be a score against the kingdom of God if the devil could make Peter look unreliable and untrustworthy, unfit to be a leader? Think how many people Satan could keep away from Christ by casting a cloud over Peter's past glories! And Satan is still the same. He still has special designs on those who have risen to high places of spiritual usefulness and service. They may be ministers or Bible School teachers — leaders of men through whom God has spoken and brought blessing. It would greatly enhance Satan's cause if he could humiliate these people. The greater their past glory, the greater his present victory would be!

2. Satan's concentration on one person rather than on another may be due to that person's *present position*. The devil does not usually waste time on those who do not threaten his kingdom. And why should he? There is no point in his attacking people who are not attacking him, who are not trying to liberate any of his prisoners or to do anything else that would greatly harm his cause. He can let these people go by; they may not even be aware of Satan's existence!

Satan aims his energies at those who actively speak against his interests, or zealously support and serve the cause of his arch-enemy, Jesus Christ. Satan wants to silence them and curtail their service. He will do anything he can to counter their effectiveness for God. He has a special eye for those in key positions of influence.

3. Satan may concentrate on a particular man because of his *potential value* as a future leader in the church of Christ. The prospect of men and women dedicating themselves to the service of Jesus Christ makes Satan furious! He covets their abilities for other purposes — for *any* purpose other than the service of the crucified and risen Lord! Satan wants our best powers and possessions used for his ends, and if we will not change sides and come back under his control, he will make things difficult for us. He

will concentrate on lessening our potential as servants of Christ, be it by one foul means or another.

It is unclear how far Satan can see into the future. He is not omniscient, certainly, yet he possibly could see quite clearly what this man Peter could become. For Peter is a natural leader, with all the energies of a gigantic soul, and when he is in his right mind, he is going to put everything he has on the altar for his Lord. His intentions are always good. If Satan lets a man like this succeed, that man will become a menace to Satan's own cause: therefore Satan must concentrate on stopping him. Let me ask you who are reading this, do you have gifts by nature and by the Spirit of God? Are you aware of your capacity to lead people, to give spiritual food and direction? Then do not be surprised if the devil is concentrating on you!

Satan's limitations

Though Satan is interested in all the saints, and particularly in Peter, he is not free to do whatever he pleases with his enemies; he is limited in his power. Notice what Jesus discloses here: 'Satan *has asked* to sift you all as wheat.' Satan must ask. He must obtain God's permission before he can attack his saints. His power and authority over men are limited by God.

Someone may ask, 'But if God grants Satan's request, what comfort is there in knowing that he has to ask? What difference does it make?' Much every way. From the fact that Satan must ask permission to test us it follows, first, that no man is in Satan's sieve by accident, without divine permisson; and, second, that God is *aware* of what one is suffering in the sieve. That is one thing that every tempest-tossed Christian needs to know.

But something else also follows: if God allows a person to be placed in Satan's sieve, then the testing that follows must have the capacity to do the good that God plans, rather than the evil that Satan purposes. When God permits a saint to be put into Satan's sieve, he does so *not* in order to give Satan what he wants, but in order to prove his accusations to be wrong. He makes the wrath of men and the anger of Satan praise him and serve his purpose.

This is surely one thing Paul had in mind when he wrote,

'No temptation has seized you except what is common to man. And God is faithful; he will not let you be tempted beyond what you can bear. But when you are tempted, he will also provide a way out so that you can stand up under it' (1 Corinthians 10:13). In other words, when God lets us go into Satan's sieve, it is to outmatch the strategy of Satan. God is not only aware of what is going on; he actively guides and guards and watches. It is God, not Satan, who is in charge.

Jesus Christ, the Saviour

If the struggle here were confined to Simon Peter and the other disciples, on the one hand, and Satan the accuser and tempter of men, on the other hand, then the outlook would be grim. If human strength were the only combatant in the battle against evil, we would all be lost before we ever started. In our trials and temptations as Christian people we must see a third party in the struggle if we are to have any hope at all. That third party is the Saviour, our Lord Jesus Christ, guiding his disciples by his presence, knowledge and power.

The Saviour knows the battle

Jesus Christ is aware of a dimension of reality that is unknown to us. He perceives higher echelons of power and deeper conflicts between powers than we can ever conceive. If this were not so, he would not be in a position to tell Peter what is going on — that Satan 'has asked to sift you [all] as wheat'. We human beings know what goes on in the spiritual world only insofar as it is revealed to us indirectly; Jesus Christ knows everything personally and directly.

The instinctive human reaction to such a claim is 'Piffle! There can be no realm of experience unknown to us!' But that is a mistake, born of ignorance and pride, and made by many people. They simply cannot conceive of the possibility of there being anything in the whole realm of existence, here or there, past or present or future, of which the human mind does not know something. And they are wrong.

There are whole realms of reality and struggle that scientists do not know anything about as scientists, philosophers do not know anything about as philosophers, and psychiatrists and psychologists do not know anything about from their professional standpoint. No man knows about these realms but the Son of God, and acceptance of this truth is involved in our acceptance of him as the Christ. Furthermore, if our Lord knew this unseen dimension of reality in the days of his humiliation when he lived as a man in the flesh, how much more does he know now what goes on behind the scenes, raised as he is 'far above all rule and authority, power and dominion' (Ephesians 1:21), King of kings and Lord of lords!

The Saviour announces Satan's plan

The fact that Jesus Christ is aware of what goes on in the unseen world is in itself comforting because, as our Saviour, he is pledged to save us. He is our Shepherd; we are his sheep. There are many things the sheep cannot know or see or understand, but if the Shepherd knows and sees and understands them, we are safe. We can have peace.

But there is something more here: in his grace, our Lord tells his people some of the things that he knows about Satan's plans. He does not tell us everything, and we should not want him to. We must take our place as his creatures. It was his refusal to accept his creaturely limitations that led to Satan's downfall. He wanted to be omniscient and was cast down into hell (Isaiah 14:12—15). But Jesus discloses to us anything that in his wisdom he sees is necessary for our good and our safety and our ultimate glory.

Remember the story of the stripling David, coming to maturity and approaching the throne that had been promised him by God but which, as yet, was still occupied by Saul. In his jealousy, Saul would time and time again get terribly angry at David because he was stealing the hearts of the people away from Saul (cf. 1 Samuel 18:9; 20:42) and he would plot to kill David by one means or another. But David had a friend at Saul's court who told him things that Saul was planning. This was Jonathan, Saul's son and David's bosom friend, who listened to the plans of his evil father, then informed David of them, thereby saving him from harm.

It is wonderful to have a Friend, not in Satan's palace, but one who nevertheless sees all that goes on and knows everything that is being plotted in realms of reality and struggle that we humans cannot discern. And we have a Friend who is able by his Word and by his Spirit to communicate to his people what is afoot behind the scenes. This is exactly what our Lord does and what the Bible does and what the Holy Spirit does, if we walk in the light of the Word: he helps us to understand the kinds of things that Satan may be up to, so that those who are attuned to his voice may be prepared for such battles as are imminent.

The Saviour assures Peter of safety

Looking into Peter's face, Jesus says, *'But I have prayed for you, Simon, that your faith may not fail. And when you have turned back, strengthen your brothers.'*

Our Lord wants Peter to know that Satan's asking permission to test him and his friends is matched by Jesus' own high-priestly intercession. Opposite the plea of Satan, Jesus places his own prayer. Satan has to plead: the verb 'to ask', or 'to ask excessively' (*exaiteō*) implies this. But our Intercessor needs only *to ask* that Peter's faith should not fail; and on the basis of his asking, in full knowledge of Peter's coming testing and its consequences, Jesus adds, 'When you have turned back, [When thou art converted, AV] strengthen your brothers.' This is extremely significant. Jesus is not saying, 'I've prayed for you, Peter, and you're going to have a bad time of it; but *if* you get through, I'll have a job for you to do!' Instead he is saying, *'When* you are converted, there will be a task awaiting you.' Not *'if'* but *'when'*. Jesus not only foresees Peter's temptation and failure, but he also foresees his conversion, his 'turning back'. Let us look closely at this metaphor.

Jesus' message to Peter is this: 'Satan is going to make a special bid for you, Peter, and you are going to leave the main highway of obedience and go a long way with him up a side-road. But I am coming with you, and when you have *been turned around again with*' ('conversion' in its Latin root means 'turning around with'), 'I'll have a job for you to do. What is it? To weep over your sins and failures? Yes, there will be a place for penitence, most certainly. But beyond the tears and the shame will be the task of strengthening your brothers. And I am going to make you strong enough to do that in and through the very sifting that Satan meant for your undoing!' For the trial that God allows is not going to weaken Peter. It is going to strengthen him so that he in turn can strengthen others. Jesus will turn apparent defeat into certain victory. He will use Satan's sieve to serve a noble end. By his own presence, he will turn the humbled, tested believer around again so that he can use him in his service.

Let us be sure that our Lord Jesus Christ is no less powerful or less committed to his followers today. We all need to take Satan seriously, and to learn what our Lord has said concerning his strategy and motives. But at the same time we need to learn to fix our gaze upon the one whose gracious promises and almighty power are more surely for us than Satan is against us. It is wonderful to know that there is one with this grace and knowledge and power, who, by the Spirit, is able to accompany us into any sieve where Satan may place us, so that all things may yet 'work together for good to them that love God, to them who are the called according to his purpose' (Romans 8:28 AV).

What is your situation, as you read this? Are you sufficiently menacing to the enemy's position that he should have an interest in you? Are you perhaps being shaken in the sieve so that you do not know where you are, and life is desperately confusing for you as a Christian? Listen to the promise of the Lord, and the Lord of the promise, who has pledged, and cannot fail: '*When* you have turned back . . .' There is a limit beyond which he will not allow his disciple to go. He will turn him back again, and when that disciple has come out of the trial, he will be able to be something that he never could have been apart from it. He will be more wheat than he was, and less chaff.

Reference

1. William Barclay, *The New Testament, A New Translation*, Vol. 1 (Collins, London, 1968), p. 183.

20.
Forewarned but not forearmed

Writers of Scripture never blush to expose the faults and failures even of the most important people. They spare no one, without exception. There is only one person whom they present as flawless; and had there been a solitary fault in him, these honest writers would surely have recorded it. So, in the Gospel accounts of his denial of Jesus (Matthew 26:36—75 and related texts), as in many earlier episodes, Simon Peter appears in a humbling light. In his rebellious denial of his Master and Saviour, Peter experienced the most desolating of all the many spiritual lapses of his life.

The essence of our Lord's ministry cannot be limited to his high-priestly work, vital as that was and is. As High Priest, he made atonement for our sins, and now intercedes for us at the right hand of God. But he is Prophet and King as well as Priest. As King, he rules over all things; it is only because he is King that we can say, 'All things work together for good to them that love God . . .' (Romans 8:28 AV). As Prophet, our Lord is the Revealer of the Father and the Teacher of his people; he is the 'Wonderful Counsellor' (Isaiah 9:6). The prophetic, counselling aspect of our Lord's ministry is particularly relevant at this point in Peter's life. Ever since Caesarea Philippi (Matthew 16:21), Jesus had been teaching the disciples about the necessity of his death. Now, as the hour drew nearer, he had been warning all of them, but especially Peter, to be on guard against certain specific perils. Through forewarning these men our Lord wanted to forearm them. He knew what tremendous commotion of heart and mind his death was going to cause, and he wanted them to be prepared.

Peter, then, received special counsel from Jesus. But the tragic thing was that he arrogantly ignored it. Acting as if he were blind and deaf to everything our Lord told him, Peter fell into the very trap from which obedience would have saved him. In fact, he nearly forfeited his life, and when the crucial hour came he was utterly unarmed.

The warnings that Peter disregarded

Are you disregarding a divine warning in your Christian life right now? This is perhaps the most important question we can ask ourselves and one another, in the name of the Lord. What do we do with divine warnings? Gloss over them? Put our hand over the page of the Bible that says, 'You shall not . . .'? This is a very serious matter. If the Bible is the Word of God, then the warnings of God need to be taken to heart. What are we doing with them? What did Peter do with them?

The two warnings that Jesus gave to Peter

1. First, as we saw in the previous chapter, our Lord had warned Peter of Satan's insidious plan to attack all of the disciples, but especially Peter himself. Without unnerving him by saying too much, Jesus was also warning that there existed for him the special danger that his faith would fail, but our Lord had prayed for him in order to counter that danger. One would expect Peter to be grateful beyond words for such guidance, and to arm himself for whatever battle was brewing.

But what, in fact, was Peter's reaction? He disposed of Jesus' counsel with a cocksure boast: 'Lord, I am ready to go with you to prison and to death'! (Luke 22:33.) It was as if he meant to say, 'Why are you talking about dangers, Lord? I am ready for anything! You can always count on me!' Peter dismissed the divine warning with a thoughtless affirmation of his own self-sufficiency. There was no hypocrisy in this: his good intentions and his sincerity were genuine. The fault lay in Peter's wilful rejection of divine counsel, and his woeful ignorance of himself. In fact, he was arrogantly suggesting that he knew himself better than his Lord did.

We need to take this to heart. Through his Word and

by his Spirit, Jesus Christ continually gives us the same warning that he gave Peter — the warning that Satan has a sinister
plan for each and all of us. Let no one think that he or she
can evade the snares and subtleties of the tempter! Anyone
who does think that lives in a fool's paradise. To consider
ourselves exempt from danger, and to reject our Lord's
warnings, is to tell God that we know ourselves better than
he does. It is to say, in effect, 'I'm all right, Lord! Don't
worry about me! I can cope!' But we *cannot* cope, and if
we think we can, we are self-deluded, miserable wretches.
God is omniscient. He knows us better than we know ourselves. And on this basis he gives us his prohibitions and
warnings.

2. Jesus' second warning to Peter was not to follow him
into the events that followed the Upper Room discourse
(John 13:16), his high-priestly prayer (John 17) and the
Gethsemane vigil. Jesus knew Peter's heart. He knew that
Peter was well-intentioned, loyal (to a degree), fond of
his Lord, but impetuous still, so that he would want to
follow Jesus wherever he was going, no matter where that
was. And so, when he was still with the disciples in the
Upper Room, Jesus tried to make clear to Peter that he
ought not to attempt to follow him then: *'Simon Peter
asked him, "Lord, where are you going?" Jesus replied,
"Where I am going, you cannot follow now, but you will
follow later"' (John 13:36).*

When we think of Peter's following 'at a distance'
(Matthew 26:58), we need to remember that Peter should
not have followed Jesus at all at this point; his fault lay in
his following Jesus at all, not in any failure to keep physically closer to him. Preachers like good texts, and 'Peter
followed afar off' makes a good sermon title, but we may
misinterpret it: Jesus told Peter *not* to follow. He would
tread the winepress alone, as it had been written of him
(Isaiah 63:3).

But Peter's response again shows his refusal to take his
Master's words seriously: *'Lord, why can't I follow you
now? I will lay down my life for you' (John 13:37).* And
when Jesus replied with a forceful prophecy of Peter's
threefold denial of him before the cock would crow (John
13:38), Peter asserted yet more strongly his determination

to be loyal to his Master (Matthew 26:35; Mark 14:31). Under no condition would he ever betray Jesus! He was saying, in effect, 'Master, I am ready for anything!'

Peter had evidently not learned the lesson of submission that he had appeared to grasp from the episode of the feet-washing. Acting upon his own high estimate of himself, he again defiantly determined to go in the very direction his Lord had forbidden him. Many Christians make this same mistake of failing to take our Lord's prohibitions seriously, and especially those biblical injunctions that tell us that in certain respects we should be separate from the world. We too often reply, 'Don't worry about me, Lord! I can cope! I can do these things and not fall!' And the results we know, or, if we do not, we shall learn about from Peter's experience.

Peter's fatal mistake

One of the saddest things about Peter was his total inability to see what his past history had to say about him. He had passed through experiences that could have taught him much about his character, but he did not learn from them. Whatever the reason, he repeated the same mistakes again and again. Even at this late hour, Peter continued to blunder along on the strength of a groundless faith in himself. He was like a sick man incapable of reading his own symptoms.

For a man's history reveals a man. Our past history makes a pattern. That is why it is good to keep a record (in memory or in a diary) of how the Lord has led us and how we have reacted. If we look back honestly over the days and weeks and months, in the light of God's Word, we will see a picture of ourselves emerging. And if we have the least grain of wisdom, we will learn from that picture.

But Peter had made no such assessment of himself. In all the things that had happened to him, even though they added up to the picture of an impetuous man who was in constant danger because of his self-will, Peter just did not see any pattern. He was well-intentioned; he knew that his motives were good. And he saw no need to assess himself further.

Peter seems to have learned little, for example, from Jesus' sharp rebuke after Caesarea Philippi, when he tried

to dissuade him from going to the cross (Matthew 16:21–23).
Our Lord went so far as to call him 'Satan', but Peter seems
eventually to have shrugged off the hurt of that experience
without seeing what his fault had been. Neither did he profit
from his blunder in wanting to stay on top of the Mount
of Transfiguration (Matthew 17:4) — forgetting his commission, forgetting the fact that Jesus had put the keys of
the kingdom into his hands, forgetting that there was work
to be done, there were souls to be saved and a church to
be built. Peter wanted to build a camp on the mountain!
That was sheer impetuosity, but Peter did not learn from
his blunder. Nor did he long bear in mind Jesus' warning
at the scene of the feet-washing — the warning of being
out of fellowship with his Lord unless he submitted to
his sovereignty (John 13:8).

Such experiences, one would think, should have
punctured Peter's pride and blunted his self-will, at least
to the extent of enabling him to learn that there was a
rational basis for our Lord's warnings when he gave them.
But no. Peter completely disregarded every warning,
believing that he knew himself at least as well as Jesus knew
him. But, in fact, he did not know himself at all.

We need to ask ourselves, 'Do I know myself? First of
all, have I taken seriously what the Bible says about me?
Have I seen it corroborated by my history? And have
I accepted it?' There is a streak of sheer dishonesty about
any of us who say we believe the Bible when, in fact, we
do not believe what it says about us. And that is what is
turning off our twentieth-century young people who, whatever their faults, want to be honest. I know many people
who swear that they believe the Bible, yet simply do not
do so and who have enough blind spots to turn the whole
world against our Lord. This is a serious issue. This is no
time to trifle with God, as many of us do by not taking his
warnings seriously. If the Lord has seen fit to incorporate
warnings into Holy Writ, he has done so exactly because
he knows us better than we know ourselves. Let us listen
to him!

Peter's ensuing failure

Peter lived to regret bitterly the pride that made him think
he knew himself better than his Lord knew him. The path
of disillusionment was, as always, stony, cruel and harrowing,
but Peter had to walk it because of his own self-will. Sadly,
so many of us have to go this same way. We would save many
a heartache and many disciplinings from God if only we
would take the Bible seriously the first time we read it. But
often we do not; like Peter we think we know better, and
we rebel.

And so it was necessary for Peter to come to know himself
and, in doing so, to be broken. For God can do nothing with
a man until he is really broken. The trouble with us human
beings is not that we lack self-will, but rather that we have
too much of it. If you are a child of God, then because he
loves you, God will break you sooner or later so that you
come to yourself. Just as standing wheat is no use as food,
but must be broken and threshed before it can fulfil the
purpose it is meant to serve, so it is with us as children of
God. The trouble with men and women in the church, even
in the evangelical church, is that we are like standing wheat —
erect and cocksure. We are arrogant with the Lord and with
one another. We have not yet been broken; but broken we
must be if we are to be useful to God. So it is that God had
to let Peter fall and fail in order to deliver him from blind
self-will, so that ultimately he could be made into 'an instrument for noble purposes, made holy, useful to the Master
and prepared to do any good work' (2 Timothy 2:21).

Peter's failure to watch and pray

The failure to watch and pray is almost inevitably the first
vital failure that precedes spiritual or moral disaster. With
Peter it happened in the Garden of Gethsemane after Jesus
took him and James and John aside and spoke to them of
his overwhelming sorrow: *'Then he said to them, "My soul
is overwhelmed with sorrow to the point of death. Stay here
and keep watch with me"' (Matthew 26:36).*

Going by himself into the interior of the garden somewhere, our Lord spent some time in ardent prayer to the
Father. When he returned to the three disciples, what did

he find? Where was the cocksure Simon? Where was the proud, self-sufficient Peter? Where was the man who was ready to go to prison and to death with his Lord? He was fast asleep.

Jesus spoke directly to Peter: *'Could you men not keep watch with me one hour? . . . Watch [keep awake] and pray so that you will not fall into temptation. The spirit is willing, but the body is weak' (Matthew 26:40,41).*

But the same pattern was repeated again, twice. Jesus went off into the garden by himself to pray, only to find the disciples asleep when he returned. They could not watch with him 'because their eyes were heavy'. Those three favoured disciples could watch neither with their Master nor for themselves, and Peter was one of them. His boasting came to nothing.

Let us take this warning to heart. We who have professed loyalty to our Lord need to realize that our drowsiness or our absence in the hour of prayer betrays a terrible state of soul. Failure to pray is generally the precursor of many other failures. If we sleep in the hour of prayer, a landslide begins that will soon desolate the individual, the church or the community. For failure to watch and pray means that we really do not believe Satan is abroad. And yet we say we believe the Bible! We must be consistent. If we do believe the Bible, we must act on that belief; the doctrine of sin and the devil is not simply for our minds, but for our lives!

Peter's failure to walk by faith

The landslide had begun. Peter's failure to watch and pray led to his failure to walk by faith (Matthew 26:47—56). Wakened out of his sleep to the harsh realities of the hour which his Master had foretold, he was entirely unnerved by the sight of temple guards coming into the Garden of Gethsemane, armed with swords and clubs. How nightmarish it must have been! What were these guards doing here? The answer would dawn upon Peter when he saw Judas walking among them, then approaching Jesus and greeting and kissing him! When the temple guards laid their hands on Jesus to seize him, Peter could remain passive no longer. He reached for his sword and cut off an ear of one of the guards (John 18:10).

In the hour when a man has lost the sense of power that prayer brings, when he is unnerved like this and spiritually unprepared, he always falls back on what in his heart he really considers to be the strongest thing in his life — his last line of defence, his chief security. For a strong, masculine fisherman like Peter, this security lay in his physical strength; therefore his first impulse was to resort to violence and fight the matter out with brute force. If it were not so serious, the futility of his action would be laughable. And how greatly it contrasted with the attitude of his Master! He who had spent the hours in prayer and intercession would have nothing to do with the sword, or with intrigue, or with lines of defence formed even by the legions of angels whom he could summon at will (26:52,53).

'For the weapons of our warfare are not carnal . . .' (2 Corinthians 10:4 AV). Whenever we resort to carnal methods of any kind, we show that we have lost sight of the spiritual realities that Jesus knew. When we engage in intrigue of any kind to get our way, we have lost all sense of the power of prayer — we are substituting some kind of human prop for faith in God; we are relying on our own self-sufficiency. This failure to walk by faith is the inevitable result of the failure to watch and pray. For one failure leads to another.

Peter's failure to witness as a disciple of Jesus

This third failure was the direct result of the first two. Relying solely on his own resources, Peter next explicitly disobeyed his Lord's warning not to follow him where he was going. Albeit 'at a distance', Peter pursued the temple guards as they led their prisoner from the Garden of Gethsemane into the city (Matthew 26:58). Peter went as far as the high priest's courtyard, from which he could see, if not hear, his Lord's interrogation. In a state of spiritual failure, physical fatigue and emotional turmoil, shuddering from the early morning cold and probably also from a terrible fear of soul, Peter drew near a charcoal fire to warm himself (John 18:18).

Then came the testing:

'A servant girl came to him. "You also were with Jesus of Galilee," she said. But he denied it before them all. "I don't know what you're talking about," he said. Then he went out to the gateway, where another girl saw him and said to the people there, "This fellow was with Jesus of Nazareth." He denied it again, with an oath: "I don't know the man!" After a little while, those standing there went up to Peter and said, "Surely you are one of them, for your accent gives you away." Then he began to call down curses on himself and he swore to them, "I don't know the man!"' (Matthew 26:69—74.)

The proud man who only a few hours earlier had pledged his loyalty to Jesus, even to the extent of going to prison and to death with him if that were necessary, now denied his Lord three times over, adding an oath, and invoking a curse upon himself if his denial were not true.

Thus the prophecy was fulfilled: *'Immediately a cock crowed. Then Peter remembered the word Jesus had spoken: "Before the cock crows, you will disown me three times." And he went outside and wept bitterly'* (Matthew 26:74,75).

Peter must have remembered Jesus' warning, too: 'Where I am going, you cannot follow now . . .' (John 13:36). And, seeing at last what a self-willed sinner he was, he poured out his soul's anguish in tears. No one can know the depths of his despair. It must have been abysmal and desolating, for his threefold denial was painful enough in itself, but the memory of his earlier professions of loyalty, his position as leader among the Twelve and his many special privileges must have been like salt to an already smarting wound.

There is a progression in evil which is found in most of our lives. If we fail to watch and pray, then we fail to walk by faith; closed to spiritual realities, we rely on our own devices. The next step is the failure to witness as followers of Christ: wanting to save our own skins, we become ashamed of him. More concerned about ourselves than about truth itself, we abandon our loyalty to Christ. Our professions of faith, so sincerely and confidently and fervently made, now dissipate into denials with oaths and cursing. And we become sick with guilt. This is the ultimate wretchedness to which anyone slides who fails to watch and pray.

Peter's witness to us

The record does not end there, of course. Jesus died as it was foretold he would and as he purposed to do. But he rose again and he is alive for evermore. And no sooner was he risen from the dead than he commissioned someone to tell Peter, especially, of that glorious fact (Mark 16:7). Then he appeared to Peter privately, personally, face to face (1 Corinthians 15:5). And many times after this, before his ascension, he appeared to Peter along with other people. Jesus Christ forgave the humbled blasphemer, the foolish self-willed man. He healed him and restored him to his service, so that in due course Peter became the altogether different man — the great herald of the gospel that we see in the book of Acts and hear in his epistles.

But Peter would never forget his threefold denial of his Lord, and the soul-rending awareness of sin that followed it. And if Peter could speak to us directly today, as a man who failed miserably but was ultimately retrieved, forgiven and restored by his Lord, I think he would bear witness to the truth of the following three principles.

Our Lord's prohibitions and warnings are for our good
Peter might say to us, 'If your Lord sees fit to say, "You shall not . . ." he has good reason. Time was when I thought it unnecessary to listen to divine prohibitions, but I learned bitterly to regret that. Time was when I thought I knew better than Jesus what was for my good, but I learned differently through bitter experience.' We live in a world that frowns on authoritative commands of all kinds, especially on prohibitions, and so we need to learn from Peter. As sure as Jesus Christ is the wise Counsellor of Isaiah's prophecy (9:6), he knows us and our circumstances better than we do, and we need to take his prohibitions as seriously as his positive commands.

Sincerity is no substitute for obedience

Peter was sincerely devoted to Jesus. Yet again and again he refused to act on his Master's commands and warnings. Like Peter, before he came to know himself better, we, too, tend to assume that if we are well-intentioned, nothing else is very important. We like to justify ourselves on the basis of our sincerity. But Peter would tell us that in and of itself, sincerity is no adequate test of loyalty to our Lord. It needs to be lived out in our willingness to obey what he commands us to do or not to do; it loses its virtue if it violates a known command.

Our Lord is patient and persevering

Peter might also like to look us all in the face and say, 'I know that you may do as I did, and you may fall as I fell, but listen! There is something which is much bigger and much greater than my sin, and that is the grace of my Lord. He did not give me up. He would not let me go. He did not abandon me to my sin and rebellion, but came after me! True, he let the vessel be broken to shards, but when I came to myself and my senses, he made a new man of me — a man who could take in all of the fulness of the Pentecostal blessing, and who could start to act as the rocklike man he promised I would become at the very beginning. My Lord is patient and persevering: "The one who calls you is faithful . . ."' (1 Thessalonians 5:24).

Forewarned but not forearmed: that was the sad truth about Peter up to this stage, and his self-will and arrogance and dependence upon human methods had to be corrected. May God grant us to learn from the folly of this great man. May we learn what our past histories tell us. And may we learn more about our Lord: that he is wise in his counsels, and full of grace in his pursuit of those who go astray. For he intends to fulfil in every man and woman whom he has called to himself the original purpose of his calling.

21.
'Go, tell Peter'

'But go, tell his disciples and Peter, "He is going ahead of you into Galilee. There you will see him, just as he told you"' (Mark 16:7).

The spiritual journey of all the disciples, but especially of Simon Peter, was very much a matter of ups and downs. It was a chequered pilgrimage on which there were as many setbacks as there were advances, and sometimes the setbacks were so severe as to seem to make the divine promise of ultimate victory unfulfillable. It was simply not the case, as some interpreters seem to think, that these disciples entered upon their Christian life and then lived it out in one clear, straight line upwards towards glory. These were not men of straw — they were real men, in real situations, facing a real foe. And there were times when they failed miserably.

Peter's denial of his Lord was, as we have seen, a case in point. It looked like a final triumph for Satan, a total renunciation of Peter's earlier confession and an absolute nullification of his entire profession of faith. But it was not. Why? Because our Lord is a risen Lord, and he pursues his straying disciples even when they wander into the wilderness of rebellion. He comes right after his own, even right into Satan's sieve. For the wonder of our gospel is *not* that it totally transforms a person today so that he will never be tempted again; rather, it begins a work in men and women today which continues unremittingly until, at last, through many struggles, our Saviour brings us to our appointed destiny of glory.

The story is told of a person in the eighteenth century who was suspicious of the theology of a certain Puritan. In

his suspicion, he approached this man one day and asked,
'Do you believe in the perseverance of the saints?' Realizing
that he was under interrogation, the Puritan decided to
answer appropriately. 'No,' he said, 'I do not!' 'Aha,' said
the questioner, 'I knew there was something amiss! You
do not believe in the perseverance of the saints! Then you
are not true to the Word!' Said the Puritan in reply:
'I believe in something far better than the perseverance of
the saints — I believe in a persevering God!'

And that is really the message of this chapter, as well as
of the next two. We will see the Good Shepherd rising from
the dead and immediately pursuing the neediest among
the Eleven — Peter, the disciple who has failed most miserably. Easter Day changed everything for Peter. The risen
Lord found him and began to reverse his whole process of
sin and rebellion into a process of enlightenment and hope.
Something new started in Simon Peter's life: a sun was now
to rise which nevermore would set.

Midnight darkness

Darkness — thick, black, oppressive darkness — is the only
appropriate way to describe the bleak desolation that
enveloped Peter after he denied all association with Jesus.
This was not the darkness of ignorance, but the darkness
of guilt: it was the darkness of a man who knew his Lord,
yet failed him. Having denied his association with Jesus
with an oath and a curse (Matthew 26:70–74), Peter
suddenly heard the cock crow and saw his Master turn to
look at him from the other end of the courtyard (Luke
22:61). At this, the fountains of deep remorse broke forth
in his soul, and 'he went outside and wept bitterly' (Luke
22:62).

We cannot more than superficially describe this darkness that overwhelmed the disobedient, disloyal Peter.
We cannot really know what he was thinking, or how pain-
fully his conscience was working, or how incisively the
Spirit of God was dealing with him. What we do know is
that his anguish sent him apart to pour out his soul in tears:
the big fisherman was a broken man. But the tears and the

circumstances that bring a man to the place of brokenness are blessed, for no man can be made after God's image until he is broken. And Peter's brokenness was the harbinger of a new wholeness in his life.

Besides guilt and shame, Peter must have felt a terrible sense of separation from his Lord. Just as Jesus had warned him it would (John 13:8), Peter's lack of submission violated their fellowship. It created a chasm between him and the one he had been near to, the one who had befriended him and had brought him hope and joy and gladness over the past many months. Now they were out of touch with each other. How bleak and lonely this place of darkness must have been, and how far removed from the place of privileged communion with God and his Son that had been Peter's at Caesarea Philippi and on the Mount of Transfiguration and elsewhere! All that now lay in the infinitely distant past, and must have seemed unreal, for Peter had denied it all. There was nothing and no one to comfort him.

Peter needed no one to come and tell him the nature of his sin. He knew what he had done. He knew the gravity of it, and he could hardly have underrated its consequences; in fact, he probably bordered on total despair at the thought of them. If Judas knew that he had betrayed innocent blood (Matthew 27:4), Simon Peter certainly knew that he had sinned against the very Messiah, Son of the living God. He knew that his cowardice, his untruthfulness, his unaccustomed profanity and his irrepressible persistence in it all were absolutely at odds with his privileges and his high calling. How he must have hated himself, and loathed the self-will that had made him walk right into Satan's trap! Moreover, he had proved himself disloyal, cowardly and totally ineffectual just at the time when his Lord was being taken away to be crucified — he, Peter, the man who had boasted of being ready for anything, and who would even go to prison and to death with his Lord! (Luke 22:33.) His pride must have suffered a shattering blow at the realization of all this.

It could well be that some readers are in such a plight of midnight darkness, just yearning for a ray of light, as Peter must have been. Nothing is clear. You cannot see ahead or behind. A curtain of black seems to separate you

from your former experience of God. You, too, had your
Caesarea Philippi, when you made your confession and
could not do otherwise. You, too, saw the glory of the Lord
on the mountaintop. But then you denied him, and not only
once. And the heavens are black to you now, and there is
little for you in the means of grace. You read your Bible,
but it seems like an ordinary novel; you shoot your prayers
into the distance and the throne of grace seems unoccupied.
This is your midnight darkness, like Peter's.

This is an experience that the people of God *may* pass
through. The Bible does not say that we *must* pass through
such an experience: God did not call us into darkness but
into light; he did not call us into misery but into joy and
peace and fellowship with himself. But such an experience
is possible for us. And if you are experiencing something
like it now, it does not necessarily mean that you are not
a child of God. But it may mean that you have rebelled
and sinned, as Peter did. The ensuing experience of guilt
and shame, of self-knowledge and brokenness may be
terribly painful. Even so, God can make that the foundation
for a whole new life.

Twilight dimness

The second stage of Peter's experience on Easter Day is of
twilight. The dictionary describes twilight as being 'the
light from the sky when the sun is below the horizon either
in the morning or in the evening'. At this time and in this
light, nothing is clear. Objects can be discerned only vaguely
and imperfectly. Although twilight is a great advance on
the pitch-blackness of a starless night, it is still far short of
full daylight. Its effect is partly physical, partly psychological, especially when it is a sign of a rising, not a setting,
sun: it is the herald of better things. Peter's 'twilight' experience on that first Easter Day was an occasion of graduallly
dawning knowledge and hope. It was a prelude to sunrise in
all its glory. It consisted of three hopeful signs.

The tomb was empty
Mark (16:1—8) describes the first trace of light that was to

bring hope to Peter's heart. At twilight, 'very early' in the morning on the first day of the week, a group of women-folk, including Mary Magdalene, came to the garden tomb where their Lord had been buried. They wanted to anoint his body, and so complete the last rites that they had hurriedly begun to perform before his burial on the evening before the sabbath (Luke 23:54–56). But a great stone had been placed by the Romans over the mouth of the tomb and secured with a Roman seal. The problem in the women's minds as they approached the tomb was: 'Who will roll away the stone for us from the door of the tomb?' But, to their great amazement, they found that the stone had already been removed and they could enter the tomb effortlessly. There, inside, two things startled them: first, the absence of their Lord's body; secondly, the presence of someone else — a 'young man' dressed in white, who said to them, *'Don't be alarmed . . . You are looking for Jesus the Nazarene, who was crucified. He has risen! He is not here. See the place where they laid him. But go, tell his disciples and Peter, "He is going ahead of you into Galilee. There you will see him, just as he told you."'*

John tells us how the news of this first trace of light was carried into the darkness of Peter's misery. He describes Mary Magdalene running to find Peter and John: *'So she came running to Simon Peter and the other disciple, the one Jesus loved, and said, "They have taken the Lord out of the tomb, and we don't know where they have put him"'* (John 20:2).

Mary ran all right, as only a forgiven soul that loves the Lord can run. But she ran more out of frightened amazement than out of any certainty that her Lord had indeed risen from the dead. Her word to Peter and John was not very hopeful: it was a pessimistic misconstruction that revealed Mary's terrible fear that 'they', some unnamed persons, had done something amiss with her Lord's body. Her report was objective only insofar as it revealed that Jesus' body was no longer in the tomb. Mary did not remember the young man's words — either to the effect that Jesus was risen, or that 'the disciples and Peter' should be told he was going to Galilee and would meet them there as he had promised. She did not deliver that message.

Even in its minimal objectivity, however, Mary's report did convey the first trace of hope to Peter. The news that the tomb no longer held a body was the first sign that a new day was about to dawn. And it sent Peter and John running to the tomb to see for themselves what had happened.

The graveclothes were intact

It was still twilight. Nothing was clear as yet. But the first light brightened somewhat as Peter and John ran to the garden and to their Lord's tomb. Arriving first, John stooped down to look into the tomb: all he could see were some linen cloths lying there, and he did not go inside in order to see better. But when Peter came up to the tomb he typically went straight inside. There he was able to see that the linen cloths were lying in a strange, orderly way, exactly where Jesus' head and body had lain — having been undisturbed, apparently, when the body left them.

> 'Then Simon Peter, who was behind him, arrived and went into the tomb. He saw the strips of linen lying there, as well as the burial cloth that had been around Jesus' head. The cloth was folded up by itself, separate from the linen. Finally the other disciple [John], who had reached the tomb first, also went inside. He saw and believed. (They still did not understand from Scripture that Jesus had to rise from the dead)' (John 20:6–9).

What did all this mean? It was not the resurrection glory: no one except the 'young man' had yet seen the risen Lord. It was twilight still. But Jesus was, indeed, no longer in the tomb and his graveclothes were lying in that significant way. John first 'saw and believed' and he undoubtedly shared his insight with Peter. What did John see and believe? Probably this: the fact that the cloth that had been wrapped around Jesus' head still lay where his head had rested, and was still 'rolled up' in its original folds, meant, first of all, that the grave had not been plundered. No thief would have taken the time or trouble thus to refold and replace any of the graveclothes. Secondly, it looked as though

Jesus' body had somehow mysteriously slipped away —
evaporated, so to speak — leaving the cloths and the napkin
just where they had been when the body was inside them.
It looked as though something supernatural had taken
place, with the cloths left behind as a testimony. No human
being could have done this; this was something of a different
order. That is what John seems to have perceived.

It was still twilight. But Peter now knew that the grave
was indeed empty and that, possibly, something transcendent
had taken place. As yet he did not know what, but 'he
went away, wondering to himself what had happened'
(Luke 24:12). His hope was very slowly growing.

There was a message for Peter

In that early morning atmosphere of sorrow and doubt
and mystery, a third sign served to brighten the sunrise
twilight in Peter's heart. This was the message given to
Mary Magdalene for the disciples generally, but for Peter
particularly, that Jesus was risen and had gone ahead to
Galilee where he would keep his appointment to meet
with them. Whenever Peter received this message — and
we do not know when that was — it must have lightened
his burdened soul considerably. It must have been a vivid
reminder of the promise that Jesus had given to the disciples
when they went out to the Mount of Olives together
(Matthew 26:32; Mark 14:28). Peter must have wondered:
'Can it really be true? Can he really have risen and gone
ahead to Galilee? Will we really see him again? Did he
really mean the message to be for me particularly? Is there
any hope that he will have something to say to me now,
after all this terrible separation and desolation?'

We all make appointments with people in the daily
routine of our lives, but we don't make engagements for
the day after the resurrection, do we? We do not arrange
for people to come to our offices the day after we rise
from the dead! Anyone who schedules a meeting for that
day is either a fool, or the Lord of glory. Jesus Christ had
scheduled such a meeting, and now here was a message
especially for Peter that he was on his way to it. Even
though it was still twilight, and no one had as yet seen
Jesus except the 'young man' in the tomb, the sky had

brightened considerably. Peter knew that the tomb was empty, he suspected that something supernatural had taken place and he could believe by faith that his Lord would indeed meet him in Galilee.

Daylight brightness

Peter and his fellow disciples as yet knew nothing definite. While the signs of resurrection kindled hope in their hearts, they probably also added to the bafflement and doubt that haunted them. For the testimony of the empty tomb, the graveclothes and the message from Jesus was as yet unconfirmed.

Dawn

Real dawn came to these confused men only when they were actually face to face with the risen Lord. Their new day did not arrive until they unmistakably recognized Jesus as alive after his suffering (Acts 1:3) — until they were together again with their familiar Friend, their crucified Lord, their buried Master and their risen God incarnate. Our Lord met time and time again with the Eleven, and with smaller groups, during the forty days between his resurrection and his ascension and, most importantly, Jesus had a private meeting with Peter.

We do not know exactly what happened when he first appeared to Simon Peter. The Bible always tells us what we *need* to know, but it does not always tell us everything we *want* to know. Perhaps what happened at this meeting was too sacred or too precious or too moving to be put into writing. But we can probably rightly assume that when Jesus and Peter met, the big fisherman was so broken with shame and penitence that he opened up his heart and confessed his sins to the risen Lord, and the blessed, crucified Saviour turned to him and showed him his wounds and assured him of mercy and forgiveness and the possibility of a new beginning.

The narrative tells us two things only, the first of which is that this meeting did take place. That Jesus appeared to Peter before the others is made clear by the apostle

Paul: 'For what I received I passed on to you as of first importance: that Christ died for our sins according to the Scriptures, that he was buried, that he was raised on the third day according to the Scriptures, and that he *appeared to Peter,* and then to the Twelve' (1 Corinthians 15:3–5).

That his appearance to Peter meant the dawning of a new day for the other ten as well is made clear by the enthusiasm with which they greeted the two men who returned from Emmaus: 'It is true! The Lord has risen, and *has appeared to Simon!*' (Luke 24:34.)

The narrative shows us, secondly, that after this private meeting with Jesus, Peter was never the same again. The fact that he was now a man of totally changed attitudes and behaviour is written into the rest of the Gospel accounts, and on into the book of the Acts of the Apostles and into Peter's own epistles. From this point on, the upward trend in Peter's life becomes evident. It would still need to be encouraged and promoted through further dealings with our Lord, but it was already plainly there. Satan had not sifted out Peter's wheat, as he had hoped to do; only the chaff had stayed in his sieve!

Never again would Peter boast of his self-sufficiency, or claim to be more trustworthy than his fellows. Never again would he stand on the ground of his self-assurance and self-will. From now on, whenever he spoke dogmatically, it would be because he knew the power of the Spirit of God, or the presence of the Son of God, or the sufficiency of the grace of God. Never again would it be because 'I can do it, Lord! You can count on me!' It is a great turning-point in any man's life when, having learned the truth about himself, he finally comes to the end of himself and ceases to rely on his own strength. Peter had now reached that point.

His fellow disciples noticed the change right away. These were puzzled, frightened men at the time, and they neither understood nor believed everything they were told. Luke tells us, for example, that the ten did not believe the women's report that Jesus was alive, for it 'seemed to them like nonsense' (Luke 24:11). The two men on the road to Emmaus had no faith in it either (Luke 24:22–24). But the same ten who could not accept the women's story did

believe Peter! (Luke 24:34.) Why? Was this sex dis-
crimination?

No, the more likely explanation lies in the effect that
the meeting with Jesus had had on Peter. Something had
happened to him. Not only were his faith and hope revived,
but his sense of guilt was relieved, his anxiety about the
future was gone, his tears were wiped away. His self-will
had been broken, and he showed it. His sins had been forgiven, and he showed it. What made Peter's report credible
to his fellows was the fact that *he had been changed*, and
the transformation could only be explained by the fact
that he had met the Christ of God risen from the dead.

Noonday glory

Let us look ahead now. The resurrection of Jesus Christ
inaugurated a whole new era. It was the dawn of a new
day that has never set, but has cast its light down through
the centuries on all the people of God everywhere.

'For we know that since Christ was raised from the
dead, he cannot die again; death no longer has mastery
over him' (Romans 6:9).

'Do not be afraid. I am the First and the Last. I am the
Living One; I was dead, and behold I am alive for ever and
ever! And I hold the keys of death and Hades' (Revelation
1:17,18).

During the forty days between his resurrection and his
ascension, our Lord would not only assure his disciples
that he really was alive by many infallible proofs; he would
also assure them that he was the Lord of all destiny, the
Lord of life and death. He would transform this entire
group of disciples from a company of downhearted, worried
men into a team of devoted crusaders who were evermore
ready to live and to die for him: 'All authority in heaven
and on earth has been given to me. Therefore go and make
disciples of all nations, baptizing them in the name of the
Father and of the Son and of the Holy Spirit, and teaching
them to obey everything I have commanded you. And
surely I will be with you always, to the very end of the
age' (Matthew 28:18—20).

And so persuaded were these men that Jesus Christ was
indeed alive, and that he was indeed Lord, with a message

to proclaim to the nations, that they explicitly followed this further command of his: 'But stay in the city, until you have been clothed with power from on high' (Luke 24:49). They patiently waited in Jerusalem until he sent forth the Spirit. They might have said to themselves, 'We've got the message, what more do we need?' But instead, they waited, because they knew that he who kept his promise to meet them in Galilee after he was raised from the dead would also keep his promise to come to them again in spiritual form, with that mighty power they needed in order to be dynamited into all the world with his message and to be effective in their ministry.

The Lord was risen indeed! The black darkness of despair had turned to dim twilight, and finally to the light of a new day, whose sun would never set again. But one day there will come a further blaze of glory, the like of which we have never seen or imagined. For in the glory of his crowning day he will come again, Jesus our Lord! May God help us to rise with him to newness of life, so that, fearless of life and death, we may show a devotion to him and his message that will continue unabated until that day when we are finally 'with Christ, which is better by far' (Philippians 1:23).

22.
Vital reassurance

Over and over again we see how amazingly patient our Lord is with his disciples. Nothing is too much for him, neither the stubbornly ingrained traits of human nature that Satan would so dearly love to preserve in them, nor the enormous sins of denial and desertion that Peter and the others had recently committed against Jesus as he was taken to be crucified. But where his people's sin abounds, his grace abounds far, far more. A particularly moving illustration of this saving love of Jesus Christ for his own is found in an episode recorded by John; it took place by the Sea of Galilee some time during the resurrected Lord's forty days on earth (John 21:1—14).

This was a critical time for the Eleven in their training as a group, and it was especially critical in Simon Peter's individual training. For at long last Peter had come to a knowledge of himself, and yet neither Jesus' private meeting with him, nor his subsequent appearances to him along with others (Acts 1:3) completely rehabilitated Peter spiritually. He was certainly not yet ready to assume the tasks of an apostle of Jesus Christ. He was anything but sure of his direction; he was plagued by new doubts and fears, in fact; and he was still unnerved by the reality of his sinfulness and failure. And we can identify with him, for if we had come to know ourselves as men or women capable of denying our own Lord with an oath and curses, we would surely feel shaky and uncertain. The other disciples were in much the same state of insecurity. And so, as the forty days of our Lord's post-resurrection appearances to his people drew near to their close, these eleven men were a somewhat desolated, directionless group. Which way would they now turn? That was the crucial question at this point in their lives. And in this episode we see our Lord seeking to bring them the vital assurance they still need.

The disciples in semi-retreat

> '*Afterwards Jesus appeared again to his disciples by the Sea of Tiberias. It happened this way: Simon Peter, Thomas (called Didymus), Nathanael from Cana in Galilee, the sons of Zebedee, and two other disciples were together. "I'm going out to fish," Simon Peter told them, and they said, "We'll go with you." So they went out and got into the boat . . .*' (John 21:1–3).

The disciples were going fishing. Why? They were not now turning their backs on Jesus primarily because he had been crucified. The mere fact of the crucifixion was no longer seen by them as a tragedy, for God had omnipotently reversed the situation: the very worst that man could do to him had become the greatest deed of God. Jesus was alive, and the disciples knew that. Though crucified by men, God made him a Prince and Saviour.

Why, then, were they evading any form of spiritual ministry? Surely the knowledge that Jesus was risen should have saved them from any such withdrawal? Yes and no, for the truth is that the resurrection of our Lord created some new, strange problems for his disciples, especially during this forty-day period. They were in considerable uncertainty both about Jesus' person and about his programme.

Their uncertainties about Jesus' person
Though they had heard repeated warnings about the necessity of their Master's crucifixion, the disciples were left numbed and baffled by the event when it actually occurred. Now he was indeed risen from the dead, but could they put their trust in someone to whom that had happened? There were times when he had seemed so full of power and authority before he was crucified, yet he was taken away like a lamb to the slaughter without a protest

(cf. Isaiah 53:7). Could that not happen again? Moreover, were they themselves safe from his enemies? If the Shepherd could so easily be smitten, what about his sheep? If the Master could be nailed to a cross, what about the Master's men? Should they risk their lives by continuing to follow him? Would they not be safer to return to the security of their old life?

There were other tormenting questions. Yes, the disciples knew that their Lord was risen, but they also knew how different he was now. There was something strange about him that they could not fathom. They were puzzled by his mysterious appearances and disappearances. For example, he would come into a room that was bolted and barred against all intruders (John 20:19,26), then he would suddenly take his leave again. No one knew where he spent his time or what he was doing when he was not with the disciples. They were puzzled also by the fact that the nail-prints in his hands and the spear-wound in his side felt real (John 20:27,28), yet his body moved in that spirit-like way in and out of nowhere. He was at once substantial and insubstantial. How could he be? Was he real? Was he really Jesus? The disciples could not conceive of a Saviour who was no longer dwelling in a normal physical body, who was no longer limited by the ordinary laws of nature. They were mystified by his glorified body.

But all of this had meaning: there is never anything that is meaningless in the unfolding drama of divine redemption. If only the Eleven knew it, the strange phenomena of those forty days were a necessary introduction to the new age that had dawned with our Lord's crucifixion and resurrection, and would come to its noontide at Pentecost. This would be an age when the Christ who had hitherto been present among them in the narrow, tangible confines of a physical body would come to be equally present and powerful among them apart from such a physical frame, by the Holy Spirit. Now during these forty days, God was preparing the disciples for the age of the Spirit, through the mysterious fact that Jesus was present when he was apparently absent as he physically came and went, yet he was always among them in power when they needed him. These forty days introduced another era. But failing to realize this, the Eleven became again baffled and uncertain about the person of the risen Lord.

Their uncertainties about Jesus' programme

Another troubling question for the disciples at this time was whether or not they still had a place in whatever plans Jesus had for the future. He sometimes spoke as if they did: 'Again Jesus said, "Peace be with you! As the Father has sent me, I am sending you . . . If you forgive anyone his sins, they are forgiven; if you do not forgive them, they are not forgiven"' (John 20:21,23).

But even if they still featured in his programme, what kind of church could they build around someone who was so elusive and so unpredictable? What kind of kingdom could they build around a King like this? How could they launch out on a programme of evangelism when they were still plagued by so many questions?

The disciples were in a quandary. They had experienced too much to unbind themselves abruptly from the yoke of Christ. The three years' teaching and the repeated evidences of Jesus' grace and power had left an indelible mark on their lives. But on the other hand, they also had too many doubts and uncertainties to be able to go right on. What should they do, then?

Their answer was to go fishing. Nervous people cannot long remain inactive; the disciples had to do *something*. And it was Peter who led the way: 'I'm going out to fish,' he announced. His idea found a response in the hearts of his friends: 'We'll go with you,' they answered. Even in his spiritual uncertainty Peter was the leader still. The potential and the power of leadership were still with him; the human charisma was there, if not the divine. This is a danger we need to watch out for in our own day: there are men and women who can be leaders, even in their most backslidden state.

And so the disciples followed Peter and went fishing. Wanting a change of scene, an escape from their spiritual problems, these men got into the boat. The former fishermen among them probably welcomed the prospect of doing something at which they were sure to be successful. Perhaps the thought even crossed their minds that fishing was something they could always return to as a permanent occupation if they decided not to go on following Jesus. Perhaps.

I have often counselled people who, if they were honest enough to admit it, were in this identical situation. They knew too much to make a clean break away from Christ, but they were equally unable to go aggressively forward in his name. He had said something, or done something, or allowed something to happen, or required something of them that puzzled or frightened them. And because of this mystery of his providence they had made for some area of life which they saw as a spiritual 'no man's land' — a place of safety and escape from conflict. They went back temporarily to their familiar former trade. They were now up some cul-de-sac, hoping that things would somehow work out for the best. Such withdrawal might have been brought about by sheer rebellion, by lack of knowledge, by faithlessness, by adulation of a humanly charismatic teacher, or by something else. In any case, they knew too much to go back, and not enough to go on; there was no passion of truth in their souls, no fire of the Spirit in their hearts. They were stymied. Does this state describe any of us?

The Saviour in full pursuit

Knowing the mind of each disciple who had gone fishing, the risen Lord came after the group in full pursuit. He came right into their cul-de-sac in order to teach three very necessary lessons which he would still teach to those today who are in a similar spiritual dead end.

'That night they caught nothing'

> 'So they went out and got into the boat, but that night they caught nothing. Early in the morning, Jesus stood on the shore, but the disciples did not realize that it was Jesus. He called out to them, "Friends, haven't you any fish?" "No," they answered' (John 21:3,4).

The disciples caught no fish. Why? Were there none in the lake? Or had the fishermen among them lost their former skill? No, not at all, as we shall see later on. The answer is that the Lord of oceans and tides, the Lord of men and beasts, the Lord of angels and demons, the Lord of the fish of the sea and the birds of the air — *he* was in command of that lake and those fish, and he ordained that the fish in the Sea of Galilee should stay out of the disciples' net that night. For he was and he is Lord; he is in command. There is no gospel apart from this truth. You cannot understand the Bible or the Christian faith unless you rest on the basis that our Lord is sovereign. The fact that the disciples caught no fish that night was no accident: it was planned in order to give these men an object lesson.

Our Lord wanted to teach them that life outside his will is utterly futile. He graciously, firmly showed his security-seeking followers that *the very best skill, exercised in the most familiar of circumstances, is no guarantee of success, outside his will.* The fishing failure was love's way of showing that there are as many perils in withdrawing from the Lord as there may be in going on with him. He is the Lord of success and failure. Therefore it is safer to go on with him with his blessing than to return even to the most familiar pursuits when such a return is against his will and his purposes.

This is one warning which Satan does not want any of us to hear; yet it is one that we desperately need, and perhaps especially those of us in middle life. Men and women at this stage of life tend to want to 'go fishing' spiritually, that is, they are afraid to go on in an entire abandonment to the will of God in case they might lose something. They avoid giving too much time or energy, too much money and too much of themselves, above all, to the work of the Lord. Better to be careful and not get too involved! But is this not 'the plague that destroys at midday'? (Psalm 91:6.)

Our Lord wants us to know that we can no more succeed in the material realm than we can in the spiritual without his permission. He is creation's Lord: if he does not see fit to let the fish enter our net, we will catch nothing. This is not to deny the fact that God allows some people to

prosper even when they are in rebellion against his law:
'I have seen a wicked and ruthless man flourishing like a
green tree in its native soil' (Psalm 37:35). Yes, but when
the accounts are finally settled, the very success of the
wicked will make their condemnation all the more terribly
just. Ultimately there are no exceptions and no qualifications to this truth: life outside our Saviour's will is futile.
The dangers of going back out of his will in dependence
upon our natural abilities are greater than the dangers of
going on with him and risking everything, in dependence
upon his grace.

'The net full of fish'

> 'He said, "Throw your net on the right side of the
> boat and you will find some." When they did,
> they were unable to haul the net in because of the
> large number of fish. Then the disciple whom Jesus
> loved said to Peter, "It is the Lord!" As soon as
> Simon Peter heard him say, "It is the Lord," he
> wrapped his outer garment around him (for he had
> taken it off) and jumped into the water. The other
> disciples followed in the boat, towing the net full
> of fish, for they were not far from shore, about a
> hundred yards' (John 21:7–9).

The second truth that Jesus wanted to demonstrate to his
nervous, insecure disciples was that *victory is absolutely
certain if it is his will to give it*. Arriving near the shore
towards break of day, having caught nothing during the
night, these men must have been doubly miserable. Added
to their spiritual problems, which were still there, un-
resolved, was now this material failure in a realm of
experience that was familiar to at least several of them.
Having lost any hope they might have had of finding security
in fishing, they must have been tired and disheartened and
not in any mood for conversation with a stranger. But a
stranger was there on the shore who insisted on conversing
with them. He called out, 'Friends, haven't you any fish?'
They had to say 'No'.

I wonder what the disciples thought when the stranger then proceeded to counsel them, saying that if they threw their net on the right side of the boat, they would catch fish. Probably they were indignant: 'Who does this man think he is? What can he see from the shore? We're not blind! We can see from the boat here that there are no fish around. Is this some kind of bad joke? Is he seriously implying that we don't know how to fish?' But in spite of their natural indignation, some impulse made them take his advice to heart and, through moving their attention from one side of the boat to the other, they moved from sheer failure to unqualified success. Scores of fish crashed into the net until it was at the point of breaking.

John was the first disciple to realize that this was a miracle, the work of only one person: 'It is the Lord!' he said. He undoubtedly recalled the almost identical miracle that Jesus had performed early in his public ministry (Luke 5:1–11), a miracle which so astounded the disciples that 'they . . . left everything and followed him' (Luke 5:11). What a vivid reminder of their earlier total abandonment to his will! Now, because the two miracles of the great hauls of fish are very similar, some of us might be tempted to treat the two scriptural accounts as merely variations of one and the same event. But that would be a great mistake. In fact, I want to go so far as to say that Jesus was now deliberately duplicating the earlier miracle in order to show the disciples that death had shorn him of nothing. Now he was alive again he could do the same things as he did before he died; his power was unchanged. He was telling these men, in other words: 'Even though my physical body is a mystery to you, don't let it blind you to the fact that I am Lord still. I'm Lord of death. I'm Lord of life. I'm Lord of all creation. And I can give success when it is my will to do so.'

In spite of their fears and uncertainties, then, the disciples came to see that the outlook was far brighter forwards with Christ than back in the most familiar scenes of past success without him. Let every disciple who is tempted to withdraw out of fear take serious note: we may be persecuted and despised, wounded and even killed for our faith, but there is something bigger even than death: 'Blessed are you when people insult you, persecute you and falsely say

all kinds of evil against you because of me. Rejoice and be
glad, because great is your reward in heaven, for in the
same way they persecuted the prophets who were before
you' (Matthew 5:11,12). His is the Word that gives victory.

'Come and have breakfast'

> 'When they landed, they saw a fire of burning
> coals there with fish on it, and some bread. Jesus
> said to them, "Bring some of the fish you have
> just caught." Simon Peter climbed aboard and
> dragged the net ashore. It was full of large fish,
> 153, but even with so many, the net was not
> torn. Jesus said to them, "Come and have break-
> fast." None of the disciples dared ask him, "Who
> are you?" They knew it was the Lord. Jesus
> came, took the bread and gave it to them, and
> did the same with the fish' (John 21:9—13).

Jesus Christ not only warned his disciples of the futility of
life outside his will, and showed them the certainty of
victory when he is pleased to grant it; he also demonstrated
to them that his care and love and plans for them continued, despite their faithlessness and waywardness. He
had not washed his hands of them. He had not changed
at all.

Not only did the disciples have grave doubts about Jesus,
they probably also feared that he had grave doubts about
them: one of their number had sold him for thirty pieces
of silver; their leader had denied him three times with oaths
and cursing; all of them had forsaken him and fled (Matthew
26:56). Wouldn't he want to wash his hands of them and
put the business of the kingdom into the hands of new
men? But no, our Lord Jesus Christ loves his people even
in their sin and rebellion. He will not let them go! He still
plans the future with them in mind! If they are in semi-
retreat, he is in full pursuit.

Even the simple fact of Jesus' presence there on the lake-
shore at this very early hour of the morning shows his concern for these men. They are evidently on his mind. He isn't
out for a morning's walk; he is there because they are there

and he has an interest in them. And, of course, he especially proves that he cares through teaching the two lessons about failure and success. But all that is almost dwarfed by the stupendous action that follows. Jesus Christ, the Son of God, risen from the dead, now makes himself the servant of these none-too-worthy followers: he prepares a hot breakfast — not just a roll and butter and marmalade, but a hot cooked breakfast — for his backsliding disciples. For he has thought of their empty stomachs as well as their dimmed spirits. There is no need for him to do this, only the need of love; it is self-kindled love, the cause being in him, not in them. He loves these men whatever their present state. He wants to lavish the best on them and make abundantly clear to them that he will not let them go!

There is something terribly humbling here: the Lord of life and of death has been on a shopping expedition. He has brought bread and fish to the shore for this meal, just as a slave-servant would do. He has brought some charcoal from somewhere, built a fire and set it aglow. Can you see it — the Son of God blowing a charcoal fire into existence, kneeling there with his mouth to the sand? And it is all out of love for his wavering disciples. He who washed their feet as the climax of his pre-Calvary ministry, now again shows himself to be the servant of his people. He has not changed. Now in resurrection power he demonstrates that even though he is Lord of all, and can grant or withhold success at will, yet he is also servant of all his disciples. He has everything they need at his command, and he will not grudge even to cook their meals when that is their need. If his previous appearances in the Upper Room have proved the reality of his resurrection, his cooking of breakfast here proves the continuing sufficiency of his grace — grace to have compassion on his wayward people, and grace to strengthen them in their every need, be it physical weakness or spiritual uncertainty. He is able, indeed, 'to make all grace abound' (2 Corinthians 9:8) to those whom he has called.

Jesus Christ still pursues his wayward, fearful, half-believing disciples today. He still prepares a meal for them and demonstrates his love. He still shows that nothing can frustrate him:when it is his will to give the victory, he can and does give it. Meantime, despite his disciples' failures,

he only asks for brokenness, penitence and a turning afresh
to him in faith. Then they will know the flood of grace and
love that his sustenance provides; then they will know as
well the joy of being recommissioned, as we shall see in
the next chapter. For the plan that he had in mind for his
own from the very beginning he will never abandon. The
risen Lord says, 'Come, I've prepared a meal for you. On
the strength of it you can go forward anywhere, with me.'
This is the safest and best way, even if it means death, 'for
death no longer has mastery' (Romans 6:9).

23.
The basis for recommissioning a failure

'When they had finished eating, Jesus said to Simon Peter, "Simon son of John, do you truly love me more than these?" "Yes, Lord," he said, you know that I love you." Jesus said, "Feed my lambs." Again Jesus said, "Simon son of John, do you truly love me?" He answered, "Yes, Lord, you know that I love you." Jesus said, "Take care of my sheep." The third time he said to him, "Simon son of John, do you love me?" Peter was hurt because Jesus asked him the third time, "Do you love me?" He said, "Lord you know all things; you know that I love you." Jesus said, "Feed my sheep"' (John 21:15–17).

We have been noticing for some time now that at this stage of his life, Simon Peter was a moral and spiritual failure. His self-will made him tend to go absolutely contrary to his Master's will: what Jesus told him to do, he did not do; and what Jesus told him not to do, he did. Soon the great confessor had become the great repudiator, three times denying all association with Jesus Christ his Lord. But if Simon Peter was a failure, his Lord and Saviour was not. The crucified Lord rose from the dead. He then followed Peter into the wilderness of his anguish, both to comfort him with his blood-bought pardon and to banish his fears with the peace of his presence. In several meetings with the disciples, the risen Jesus reassured them that the grave had shorn him neither of grace nor of power; he still cared for his fearful, faithless people and he was able to transform their failure into success.

And then, on that same beach early on the same morning,

Jesus turned to Peter alone. He had set the stage for this
point at which he would finally elicit from Peter's heart
the kind of confession which could alone be a valid basis
for recommissioning him. For Jesus Christ always has a
message for the individual as well as the group. He always
calls a man or a woman by name, and pursues his work in
that person in order to bring him or her to a new beginning.
Let us watch him do that here with Peter and let us take to
heart what he says, both for our own benefit and for the
benefit of others. There are many spiritual failures in the
world today who desperately need this healing, renewing,
rehabilitating ministry of Jesus Christ. There is a whole
multitude of professing Christians who are yearning for
a new beginning, yet may not be aware that it is available
to them. They do not know where to turn. They do not
even know how to look others in the face. They set out
well in the beginning, but they have fallen by the wayside.
Jesus Christ does indeed have a message for them: he would
come to each of them individually with the same questions
that he put to Peter.

The threefold interrogation and confession

There is no stage-manager like the Son of God. He never
lets the action begin until the stage is so perfectly set that
each of its features is eloquent in meaning. On this occasion,
one of our Lord's purposes is to remind Peter of the gravity
of his iniquity and waywardness. But instead of flaying
Peter verbally with the details of his denial, Jesus finds
other ways to remind him of its grim nature. He skilfully
sets a stage that will speak for itself.

The most obvious feature of the stage-setting is the
charcoal fire that glows there in the pre-dawn light. It will
vividly remind Peter of that other early morning and that
other charcoal fire where he warmed himself just before
denying his Lord in the high priest's courtyard (John 18:18).
And just as Peter then denied Jesus three times over, so Jesus
will now question Peter three times over: 'Simon son of
John, do you love me?' It will grieve Peter to be questioned
three times, but the terrible persistence of his denial must

be brought home to him. Finally, a threefold confession and a threefold commission will follow from the threefold question. That numerical correspondence is no matter of mere chance; it, too, is sovereignly arranged by the Master of meaningfulness.

Our Lord causes the entire interview with Peter to revolve around the repetition of one basic question: 'Do you love me?' Before we delve into the text, there is a grammatical point that we should note: the language changes in the third question. In the first two questions, the word for 'love' is a form of the verb *'agapaō'* which corresponds to the familiar Greek noun *'agapē'*. This denotes the highest and noblest form of love. It is defined by the apostle Paul in 1 Corinthians 13. Jesus' first two questions to Peter mean, then, 'Do you love me with *agapē*-type love?' Then, very significantly, in the third occurrence of his question, 'Do you love me?' Jesus changes to Peter's word for 'love'. He asks Peter whether he really has this great affection for him: 'Do you really have the kind of love for me that you say you have, Peter, even if it is *philia* rather than *agapē*?' And, repeating the word *'philia'* for the third time, Peter strongly affirms that he has.

Scholars are divided as to what Jesus' use of these two different words for 'love' really means. Some say that it is purely a stylistic matter: the two words are used interchangeably, with no difference in meaning. It is a good stylistic device to use a synonym that will vary the vocabulary, rather than repeating the same word three times in an immediate context. Other scholars, however, insist that the use of the two different terms for 'love' means that two different meanings of 'love' are clearly intended. When Jesus speaks of *agapē*-type love, and Peter replies that he loves his Lord but not in that way, Peter is really frankly admitting that he does not come up to the standard that Jesus is asking for. And when Jesus ultimately changes his word for 'love' to *'philia'*, and comes down to Peter's level, something very significant is happening. It is on this second view — or something akin to it — that our analysis will be based.

The first question

'Simon son of John, do you truly love me more than these?'

With his first question, Jesus would challenge the hitherto boastful Peter at two points. Does he have the highest kind of love for his Lord, the kind of love designated by the word *'agapē'*, and does he love Jesus more than his fellow disciples do, as he once claimed? There are other possible interpretations of Jesus' question: the phrase 'more than these' could have a number of different references. It could refer to Peter's boat and his love of fishing, for example — does he love Jesus more than he loves *them*? Or it could refer to Peter's relationship with his fellows — does he love Jesus more than he loves these friends with whom he has just spent the night fishing? My personal impression is, however, that Jesus' question refers back to Peter's claim to be a far more reliable and devoted disciple than any of his fellows were: 'Then Jesus told them, "This very night you will all fall away on account of me, for it is written: 'I will strike the shepherd, and the sheep of the flock will be scattered.' But after I have risen, I will go ahead of you into Galilee." Peter replied, "Even if all fall away on account of you, I never will"' (Matthew 26:31—33).

Before he learned otherwise, Peter had been so sure of himself that he even imagined himself to be the only disciple, ultimately, on whom Jesus could rely. He believed this fiction in spite of Jesus' own prophecy that the disciples would *'all* fall away'. Peter thought he knew better: 'It's not so, Lord! The others may all desert you and scatter, but I won't! You just don't know the stuff I'm made of!' But now the risen Lord faces Peter with his past. He says, in effect, 'Look, Peter, you know what has happened over the past few days. You know what you've said and what you've done. Now tell me, do you in fact really love me more than the other disciples do?'

Now Peter expresses in honest terms exactly what he finds in his heart. Now his reply reveals a genuine attempt to come to terms with reality. He says, 'Yes, Lord; you know that I love you.' This reply is really a bundle of contradictions. Peter is saying 'Yes' and 'No' at once! He is saying, 'Yes, Lord, I really do have love [*philia*] for you; but no, Lord, I do not have the kind of love [*agapē*] that you are asking for.' For Peter's bubble of arrogance has been pricked. He knows that he cannot claim to love Jesus with the highest kind of love; that he must deny. But he also knows that he has genuine affection for Jesus, and that he must confess. He has nothing at all to say, now, about the other disciples' love for their Lord. He does not compare himself with them at all. Gone is the arrogance of former days, and in its place is emerging the first bloom of a different spirit — a spirit of sober-minded realism and humility.

There is nothing in the whole world that is more important than honesty with God. I know young Christians who have come to real disaster in life simply because they have exaggerated their early experience in the faith. Then Satan has come to them and pointed out their misrepresentation: 'Do you remember what you said to so-and-so at such-and-such a place? Do you remember what you professed? Well, the thing is not real, and you know it!' And they did know it, and they then became discouraged and bewildered, fearing all was lost. That is why it can be very dangerous to ask a young Christian to bear witness to the grace of God in his life before he really has found his feet.

Peter had learned through bitter experience that dishonesty with God leads to disaster. His boast that he was Jesus' only loyal disciple was an empty boast; it exaggerated the true state of Peter's heart and it caused him to fail miserably. Now we hear a humbler, wiser man speaking to his Lord. In this interview with Jesus, Peter says only what is honest and true and accurate: 'Lord, I haven't got the highest form of love for you, and I am certainly in no position to compare myself with these fellows, but there is something here in my heart, and I'm appealing to your knowledge of that fact. You know that I have great affection [*philia*] for you.'

The second question
'Simon son of John, do you truly love me?'

Without changing the word for 'love' [*agapē*], which he used in his first question to Peter, Jesus now drops any further reference to a comparison of Peter's love with that of the other disciples. He simply drives home his main challenge: 'Do *you* truly love me?' It is as if the Saviour is urging Peter to take another look into his heart, and then either to repeat or to retract what he has just said about loving Jesus. The time is past when a slick, easy answer to such a fundamental question will do. And if Peter can no longer claim to surpass his fellows in loving Christ, can he still claim to have any kind of genuine love for Jesus at all?

Yes, he can. Peter sticks to his guns. He replies very simply, 'Yes, Lord, you know that I love you.' Saying this with an open heart, Peter is not simply asserting the truth as he honestly sees it. He is also tacitly appealing for Jesus' correction on the matter: 'Lord, I'm saying it, and if I'm wrong, then please correct me. But as far as I know myself, I do have genuine affection [*philia*] for you, even if I do not have the *agapē*-type love that you are looking for.'

The third question
'Simon, son of John, do you love me?'

This is the question, where Jesus changes his word for 'love' from the verb '*agapaō*' to the verb '*phileō*', the same word that Peter has insisted on using in each of his two replies so far. Jesus drops all reference to love of the *agapē*-kind. He is wanting to ask Peter, 'All right, Peter, you disclaim any superiority over your fellow disciples, and you say that you have genuine affection [*philia*] for me. Now listen, man, are you absolutely sure of that? Are you certain that what you are confessing, even though it is not what I've asked for, is real and honest and true to fact?'

As John reports, Peter is 'hurt' that he should be questioned yet a third time about his love for his Lord. He is smarting, and he shows it. In reply, as if to protest quite vehemently that he is now indeed being extremely careful to claim nothing more for himself than Jesus knows to be true, he makes a still more ardent appeal to his Master's omniscience: 'Lord, you know all things; you know that I love you.' In other words, 'Lord, you know better than I do myself! Please correct me if I'm wrong, for I certainly want to be honest. But I do indeed have genuine affection for you!'

Harsh and gruelling as this kind of interrogation must have been for Peter, it was as necessary as it was painful. The truth for any fallen disciple whose lips and life may have denied the Christ whom you once loved and served is this: only when you have discovered in your soul a grain of real love for Jesus Christ are you in any position to be recommissioned to do your Lord's work. It is absolutely essential that his disciples love him: if there is no love in our hearts for Jesus Christ, then we cannot be entrusted with his business. We must be very sure of our own hearts. Rigorous self-examination is basic to discipleship, and is especially necessary to the recommissioning of any disciple who, like Peter, has failed.

Not only is it essential that we should know the presence in our hearts of real love for Jesus; it is equally essential that we should be clear about the *quality* of this love. There is nothing more dangerous in the whole of the Christian life than our assuming that we have something which, in fact, we do not have. If, for example, we imagine ourselves to have fully fledged love for Christ when, in fact, we have only immature love, then we do not seek the grace of further love. We think that all is well — we have 'arrived'! We do not sense the reality of our need, nor do we pray with any urgency. If, on the other hand, we examine our hearts carefully and find that our love for Christ is imperfect, then we are driven by our sense of need to ask for the grace to love him better. And what Christian does not need more grace? We are all needy, and must learn to recognize our need.

Self-examination is an essential. And here in this episode, however painful the process may have been for Peter, Jesus has skilfully brought him through to the place where he makes an honest, realistic appraisal of his relationship with his Lord. There is no substitute for this sheer honesty of soul that asserts what is true, and no more. And when such honesty can claim the presence of even a grain of genuine love for the Saviour, this love, albeit immature and imperfect, is, in the Saviour's estimation, a sufficient basis for recommissioning a failure. When genuine love for him is present in the heart of his disciple, Jesus Christ will hand over his whole flock to his care.

Let us examine ourselves. As the Spirit of God searches our hearts, do we find real love for our Lord there? 'If I speak in the tongues of men and of angels, but have not love, I am only a resounding gong or a clanging cymbal'

(1 Corinthians 13:1). Love is the first of the fruits of the Spirit (Galatians 5:22). Love is the best and the greatest fruit of the Spirit (1 Corinthians 13:13). Without love, all else is vain. With love, every other grace and gift comes into its own.

The threefold commission

On the basis of Peter's honest love for himself, immature though it still is, Jesus reinstates his fallen disciple. Our Lord values genuine love for himself so highly that it is sufficient basis for recommissioning even a disciple who has three times denied his Lord. It will not be until Pentecost that Peter really comes to understand the Scriptures. The one indispensable prerequisite for recommissioning is not full or perfect knowledge, therefore; it is real love for Jesus Christ. This love will seek and will find knowledge in due course. Now, as Jesus recommissions Peter, he clearly enunciates three principles of Christian service.

Love for Christ must be expressed towards his people

In response to Peter's threefold confession of love, Jesus gives his disciple a threefold commission to 'feed my lambs . . . take care of my sheep . . . feed my sheep'. Our Lord does want his followers' love to be expressed directly to him; he does desire us to tell him face to face how we feel about him. But most of us find this quite natural: we love to praise God, to express our adoration and our thanksgiving, and to say that we love him. He is the 'lily of the valleys' and the 'rose of Sharon' (Song of Solomon 2:1). There is no fault in him.

The difficulty comes with the next step. Jesus says to Peter, 'If you love me, then feed my lambs, take care of my sheep and feed my sheep.' In other words, the love that we confess for Jesus Christ personally and directly must then be expressed in action and attitude towards his people. This is where the shoe really pinches for many of us Christians! It is easy to love Jesus, for there is no fault in him; but it is not always so easy to love his sheep, for there are many faults in them. Some sheep are very difficult: they butt you at every corner, they have horns and they can even bite!

Yet our Lord says that we must love them; our love for him must be expressed towards his people. Three times over he repeats this to Peter. He meets each confession of love with this same demand that the disciple's love be expressed to other people. Philip Doddridge puts it well:

Jesus, my Lord, how rich thy grace,
Thy bounties how complete!
How shall I count the matchless sum,
How pay the mighty debt?

But thou hast needy brethren here,
Partakers of thy grace,
Whose names thou wilt thyself confess
Before thy Father's face.

In them thou may'st be clothed and fed,
And visited, and cheered,
And in their accents of distress
Thy pleading voice is heard.

Thy face with reverence and with love
I in thy poor would see;
Oh, let me rather beg my bread,
Than hold it back from thee!

This is the first principle of Christian service that Jesus enunciates in his recommissioning of Peter: love which is first expressed directly to him and for him must then be manifestly exemplified towards his people.

Love for Christ must be expressed towards all of his people
The Saviour points Peter to his duty both to his lambs and to his sheep. That covers the whole flock. It covers every single member of his fold, near or far, old or young, black or white, rich or poor. No one is left out. In other words, if I love my Lord, then I have no right to withhold my service from any section of the church of Christ. And this means that all of our walls of prejudice and favouritism must come down; we are to serve *all* of Christ's people, not just those whom we like and would choose to serve. In fact,

it is not even for us to do the choosing; it is for him whom
we love to choose whom we shall serve. As he presents us
with the need and opportunity, we must be the servants
of all of God's people. Bang goes our love of a clique! Bang
goes our preference for an exclusive group! Says Jesus
Christ, 'The lambs are waiting, the old sheep are waiting
and everybody in between is waiting; the whole flock consti-
tutes the scope of your service.'

For this reason there is potential danger in sectionalizing
within a church. It is necessary, of course. Young people
have specific needs and aged people have different specific
needs, for instance. But when we sectionalize, we run the
risk of erecting walls, with the result that members of each
group think only of their own group and its needs. God
have mercy on us! The *whole* church is to be served because
we love the Head of the church!

How are we to serve others? In what way are we to
'strengthen our brothers', as Jesus told Peter to do when
he would finally emerge from Satan's sieve? (Luke 22:32.)
If we are to judge from our Lord's own example, the love
that we ought to express in our service of his lambs and his
sheep is the kind of love that pursues any erring members
of the flock until they are brought back to the fold. This is
how Jesus loved Peter, and this is the kind of love that the
early Christians felt constrained to emulate.

It was this kind of love that earned such a reputation for
the apostle John. Clement of Alexandria reports that John
was always on the alert for a wayward, needy sheep, whom
he rarely failed to serve for Christ's sake. For instance, he
took an interest in quite a rebellious young man in a church
near Ephesus. John loved this young man into life. He
introduced him to the Saviour and tried to ground him in
the truth. But then John had to leave this church, so he
looked around for somebody else into whose hands he
could commit the boisterous youth. Finally he found a
middle-aged man who, as John thought, was mature in the
faith and would nourish and care for his new-found brother.
When John came back, among the first of his questions was
one asking after the young man. To his dismay, John discovered that the lad had rebelled against the disciplines
of the gospel, had left the fellowship and had last been

heard of roaming the mountains with a gang of thieves and robbers. 'What, up in the mountains?' John gasped. 'Then I must climb!' And he did. The aged saint, probably in his nineties by now, climbed up into the mountains to look for the rebellious sheep. He looked until he found him; then he brought him back down from the wilds and loved him back into the fold. And so for us, too, our love for Christ must be expressed in loving service to all of his flock — from the youngest lamb to the oldest sheep.

Love for Christ must be expressed towards all of his people in their every need

The scope of Christian service not only embraces both 'sheep' and 'lambs'; it also entails both 'feeding' and 'taking care of'. These two terms cover all the needs of every sheep and lamb. Nothing is omitted: everything is included that a shepherd does for his flock from birth until death, from morning until night, from night until morning. We are to lead the lambs and the sheep; we are to feed them, nurse them, care for them when they are sick. We are to minister to their every possible need, be it spiritual or material. Our love for Christ must express itself in any and every possible service to his own. And this love has its own logic. Let me illustrate with a story.

Emerging from the rubble of a demolished house following one of the German air raids on London, there appeared a short, cockney lad, carrying a fellow nearly twice his size. A policeman on the scene turned to the lad and said, 'Mate, leave your burden there! He's far too heavy for you! I'll give you a hand in a moment!' But the cockney lad looked up in his cockney way and replied, 'Cop, 'ee ain't 'evy; 'ee's me bruvver, and I'm tak'n 'im 'ome!'

Do we know anything of that logic: 'He isn't heavy; he's my brother and I'm taking him home'? That is the logic of Christian love. And because we have brothers in Christ, and because the Lord has commanded it, the way should be clear and easy, albeit difficult. That may sound like a contradiction, but it is true to fact. The actual task before us may be obviously difficult to tackle, but the inner propulsion of a heart that is ablaze with love for Christ more than matches the challenge. Love never fails. Has the love of Christ that inspires us to sing his praises also begun to constrain us to serve the lambs and the sheep of his fold in all their needs? Never were burdens heavier or needs greater than they are today. The scope is unlimited.

If you are a floundering believer today, as Peter was, Jesus Christ has the same word for you as he had for him. He comes to make you face yourself: have you any real love for him? Don't profess what is not true, but tell him if you find in your heart any genuine love for him. That is all he asks for as yet, before showing you his needy brothers all around, and the need for you to love them and serve them because of your love for him. May God grant us all to walk in the way of his love.

24.
The Holy Spirit and Peter's speech

'When the day of Pentecost came, they were all together in one place. Suddenly a sound like the blowing of a violent wind came from heaven and filled the whole house where they were sitting. They saw what seemed to be tongues of fire that separated and came to rest on each of them. All of them were filled with the Holy Spirit and began to speak in other tongues as the Spirit enabled them' (Acts 2:1—4).

The Peter whom we see for the last time in the Gospels (John 21) is a greatly humbled man. He is able to look at himself objectively; he has learned not to make claims for himself that are less than true. He has come to a new self-knowledge and a new honesty about himself. It is on the basis of these that Jesus recommissions him, bidding him prove his love for the Saviour through service to his Saviour's people — a service that will ultimately result in Peter's martyrdom (John 21:18,19).

When we turn from the Gospels to the book of the Acts of the Apostles, the transformation in Peter is still more apparent. In fact, it is almost unbelievable in its sudden completeness, because the pouring forth of God's Holy Spirit at Pentecost brings about a remarkable and decisive change in Peter's life. Graces and natural gifts already present in Peter not only come to full bloom, but they become controlled, held together by a mighty hand, and used now not for Peter's glory, but for the glory of his Lord and the extension of his church. What is more, graces and gifts that Peter never had before are now lavished upon him by the Holy Spirit so that we see him fully endowed for the fulfilment of his ministry. Here at last, in the book of Acts, we find Peter armed and ready, greatly transformed into 'an instrument for noble purposes, made holy, useful to the Master and prepared to do any good work' (2 Timothy 2:21).

If I had to choose one word to describe the difference between Peter in the Gospels and Peter in the early chapters of the book of Acts, I would naturally think in terms of his mellowing. With the pouring forth of the Holy Spirit upon him at Pentecost, Peter suddenly *mellows* into spiritual maturity. As the mantle of leadership descends upon him, everything in his thinking and his action somehow falls into place. As he comes under the Spirit's control, Peter finds his true direction and his true self. The man who was earlier cowardly, ignorant and impetuous when driven by the whims of his self-will, now is unbelievably courageous, wise and balanced as he is controlled by the Spirit. And nowhere is this transformation more evident than in the way Peter speaks: the Spirit's wholly supernatural influence upon Peter's speech is nothing less than miraculous in its effect.

This startling change in Peter's speech manifests itself in two different ways. In the first place, Peter (like his fellow disciples) receives at Pentecost an altogether new ability to speak in a language he has never learned. Neither Peter nor his friends need a teacher or an interpreter to communicate with the multitudes that throng Jerusalem. Remember the reaction of the 'God-fearing Jews from every nation under heaven' (Acts 2:5), the Jews and proselytes gathered in Jerusalem out of many different countries in the Mediterranean region for the Feast of Weeks? 'A crowd came together in bewilderment, because each one heard [the disciples] speaking in his own language. Utterly amazed, they asked: "Are not all these men who are speaking Galileans? Then how is it that each of us hears them in his own native language? . . . we hear them declaring the wonders of God in our own tongues . . . What does this mean?"' (Acts 2:6–8, 11,12.) The people get the message, indicating a wholly supernatural work of the Spirit.

But secondly, and equally supernaturally, Peter also receives the capacity to explain the significance of Pentecost in a language (probably Aramaic) common to himself and the gathered crowds of Jews, in such a clear, convincing manner that three thousand souls are gathered into the gospel net that day (Acts 2:41). This man who has always been a mere talker is now a preacher of the gospel of grace. This man who has hitherto been a wayward, vacillating disciple is now an apostle of Jesus Christ, with a Spirit of grace upon him and the Word of God like a fire within him. Above all, this former fisher of fish is now a fisher of men! The Lord's promises may tarry awhile, but his every promise is true. Months ago he promised Simon and Andrew: 'I will make you fishers of men' (Mark 1:17); now Peter casts out the gospel net and draws the thousands to land.

We find two keys to an understanding of what the Spirit has done for Peter in the following words: *'All of them were filled with the Holy Spirit and began to speak in other tongues as the Spirit enabled them' (Acts 2:4).* The Holy Spirit is the controller of those whom he fills and the communicator of truth through those whom he controls.

The Holy Spirit as controller

The Spirit's fulness involves his control
When the Bible speaks of a person being *'filled with* the Spirit', it means that he is *under the control of* or *mastered by* the Spirit. This control affects the entire person — all of his capabilities, his will, his whole life. Being controlled by what one is filled with is a common human phenomenon: if you are filled with grief, for example, you are controlled by it; if you are filled with joy, you are overcome by it; if you are filled with wine, as some people charged the disciples with being on this occasion (Acts 2:13), you are under its alien control. Similarly, if you are filled with the Spirit, you are necessarily under the Spirit's control.

The fact that Peter and his fellows are suddenly able to speak in languages they have never learned is, in and of itself, secondary to this control by the Spirit. The power of the Spirit is no less evident as Peter proceeds to explain the significance of the Pentecostal happening in a language which he and his listeners understand. The primary factor is this: Peter's speech is so much under the control of the

Spirit of God that Peter speaks whatever the Spirit wants him to speak, now in an unknown tongue, now in Aramaic — first, telling of 'the wonders of God' (Acts 2:11), then explaining why it is that the disciples are speaking in unknown tongues (Acts 2:17–36).

If being filled with the Spirit means being controlled by the Spirit, it will be significant to recognize that people may be born of the Spirit and influenced by the Spirit without being filled with him. The difference is evident. Our churches are full of people who have been merely influenced by the Spirit, not filled with him. And that is why our churches are so impotent!

The Spirit's control involves mastery of the tongue

How do we know when a person is filled with the Holy Spirit? When he or she does the work of the Spirit and of no one else, be it in speech or in any other way. And how do we know what is the will and the work of the Spirit of God? The simple answer is that the will of the Spirit is whatever is in accordance with the Word of God. And that is why the church of today is rarely in a position to judge who is filled with the Spirit and who is not: our knowledge of the Word of God is too inadequate to enable us reliably to judge.

Some people would claim that the only proof of a person's being filled with the Spirit lies in his speaking in 'tongues' that he has never naturally learned. Now I do not want to grieve the Spirit of God by disparaging his gift whereby a person is enabled to speak in a language foreign to him. But I do want to emphasize that the mere fact that a man speaks in tongues *does not necessarily mean* that he is filled with the Spirit of God. 'Speaking in tongues' or *'glossolalia'*, is not an exclusively Christian phenomenon: the old pythoness of Delphi, for example, in the fifth century before Christ, used to attract thousands of people to hear her speak as the oracle of the gods in an unknown tongue, and Plato mentions the same phenomenon in many of his dialogues. In our present-day society, moreover, there are many instances of speaking in tongues in an utterly pagan setting. We must conclude that the mere fact of speaking in an unknown tongue does not prove that the Spirit of

God is present in a person at all, let alone present in his fulness.

The only infallible evidence that a person is filled with the Spirit is that he or she is fulfilling the Spirit's will as it is revealed in Scripture. And what makes us certain that Simon Peter here in the book of Acts was filled with the Spirit of God is this: everything that he did was born out of Scripture and confirmed as right in the light of Scripture. That is the major and objective test of any subjective experience, including speaking in tongues.

All of us will agree that a supreme miracle of grace is required to bring any human tongue under the control of the Holy Spirit. James tells us that the tongue is humanly uncontrollable: 'Consider what a great forest is set on fire by a small spark. The tongue also is a fire, a world of evil among the parts of the body. It corrupts the whole person, sets the whole course of his life on fire, and is itself set on fire by hell. All kinds of animals, birds, reptiles and creatures of the sea are being tamed and have been tamed by man, but no man can tame the tongue. It is a restless evil, full of deadly poison' (James 5:5–8).

It is a wonderful thing to see a person whose whole speech is so guided by the Spirit that he says only what the Spirit wants him to say, now in one language, now in another. Are you filled with the Spirit of God? Is your tongue under his control? For if not, then you do not know the gift of the fulness of the Holy Spirit. 'Fulness' means *full control* by the Holy One, and nothing less.

The Spirit's control involves mastery even of a tongue like Peter's

Whereas every person's tongue is naturally evil and humanly uncontrollable, some tongues appear to be particularly difficult to control, let alone to use for a holy end. And Peter's tongue is a case in point, for it had always wagged endlessly; it had always said things that Peter's mind had not considered first. Peter could speak arrogantly, thoughtlessly and defiantly; Peter's natural tongue was a runaway, wild and uncontrolled tongue. But now Peter's tongue is so mastered by the Spirit that it becomes his instrument to speak whatever language and whatever words he needs to fulfil his gracious purposes. What a miracle of grace that even a tongue like Peter's can be made thus 'useful to the Master'! (2 Timothy 2:21.)

And we need to ask ourselves, 'Is my mouth under control? Am I filled with the Spirit?' Or could it be that this is a major point of controversy between me and the Spirit of God — I want freedom of the tongue? If so, I must recognize that I will live forever on less than God's best.

The Holy Spirit as communicator

God communicates with men

As we hear Peter explaining to the people in Jerusalem what the events of Pentecost really mean (Acts 2:14—36), we witness the wonderful phenomenon of God communicating with men. For our God is a communicating God: Elijah proved that at Mount Carmel (1 Kings 18). Baal could not communicate with his people. The prophets of Baal would have done anything just to get one word from their god. They tried everything: they cried out to him, prepared a sacrifice for him, cut themselves until the blood flowed and 'continued their frantic prophesying until the time for the evening sacrifice. But there was no response, no one answered, no one paid attention' (1 Kings 18:29). But our God answered his prophet. Elijah had proclaimed, 'The God who answers by fire — he is God' (1 Kings 18:24). And our God answered by fire. The genius of our faith is that, if we are in touch with the God of the Bible, we are in touch with the God who communicates. Jesus Christ is 'the Word' who 'became flesh' (John 1:14). He is the Word of God, the mind of God, the expressed reasoning of God. What is happening in Jesus Christ is that God is talking to us, bidding us be silent and listen to what he is saying.

We hear much about the problem of communication. People are separated from God and from one another. Great chasms exist between people of different generations, different cultures, different races, different social classes, even different stages of growth within a family. It has become increasingly difficult to communicate across these gaps in such a way that people really understand one another. But here in the book of Acts there is no problem of communication: the Spirit who has filled Peter and who has taken control of the whole man now communicates his mind and his message through Peter's lips. This Galilean fisherman, who does not know the languages of the foreign Jews gathered in Jerusalem at this Pentecost, is nevertheless able effectively to communicate with them. For God never meant us to communicate the gospel by means of our natural powers. The divine plan is different. The Spirit of God is the only adequate communicator of the gospel, and his method is first to secure control of our lives, and then to communicate the gospel through our lips. Is God silent today because some of his people rebel against his lordship over their lips?

The Spirit's message through Peter

What is being communicated through Peter is not something that Peter has composed. It is the message of the Scriptures, the Word of God, coming from Peter's mouth only because he is under the Spirit's control. The message has two themes.

1. As the amazed Jews report, it concerns 'the wonders of God' (Acts 2:11), or, in the words of the Authorized Version, 'the wonderful works of God'. The Spirit is speaking about God as living and active in the events of this Pentecostal hour. In the context here, the phrase 'the wonders of God' probably refers to the fact that God is fulfilling his promise made hundreds of years earlier through the prophet Joel: 'And afterwards, I will pour out my Spirit on all people . . .' (Joel 2:28–32).

Well might Isaac Watts sing:

> Begin, my tongue, some heavenly theme
> And speak some boundless thing,
> The mighty works or mightier name
> Of our eternal King.
>
> Tell of his wondrous faithfulness,
> And sound his power abroad;
> Sing the sweet promise of his grace
> And the fulfilling God.

Engraved as in eternal brass
The mighty promise shines;
Nor can the powers of darkness raze
Those everlasting lines.

His very word of grace is strong
As that which built the skies;
The voice that rolls the stars along
Speaks all the promises.

This is our mighty God! He makes a promise and he fulfils it in the fulness of time — as in the birth of the Saviour, so also in the coming of the Spirit. He is, indeed, a God of 'wonders'.

2. But more particularly, the Spirit of God stresses through Peter that the wonderful works of God *centre in Jesus Christ*. The outpouring of the Spirit at Pentecost is essentially bound up with *the person* and *the work* of God the Son. To see what this means, we may pose two questions.

a. *Why has the Holy Spirit been sent forth at this particular point in time?* The Spirit of God himself replies to this question through Peter's words, by showing that God could not fulfil his promise to send the Spirit until he had first accomplished other things through his Son. Christ first had to die, that sinners might be saved, and that the Scriptures (e.g. Isaiah 53) might be fulfilled. 'Jesus of Nazareth was a man accredited by God to you by miracles, wonders and signs, which God did among you through him, as you yourselves know. This man was handed over to you by God's set purpose and foreknowledge; and you, with the help of wicked men, put him to death by nailing him to the cross' (Acts 2:22,23).

b. *What does Pentecost mean?* Its significance hinges on *the person of Jesus Christ.* He has done his saving work, and God has 'raised him from the dead, freeing him from the agony of death, because it was impossible for death to keep its hold on him . . . God has raised this Jesus to life, and we are all witnesses of the fact. Exalted to the right hand of God, he has received from the Father the promised Holy Spirit and has poured out what you now see and hear . . . Therefore let all Israel be assured of this: God has made this Jesus, whom you crucified, both Lord and Christ' (Acts 2:24,32,33,36). God has raised Jesus from the dead to his own right hand: he has made him both Lord and Christ. In this capacity Jesus has both received the promise of the Holy Spirit from the Father, and he has sent the Holy Spirit down upon his people as he promised he would do (John 16:7). The sending forth of the Spirit means, then, that Jesus is both Lord and Messiah: Pentecost is a supreme witness to his person.

It is a historical fact that this message of the Spirit came through to those who were listening on that day with the power and the shock of a thunderclap. Through it they saw the Scriptures come alive and the recorded promises of God suddenly become both relevant and meaningful. They saw their own sin in rejecting and crucifying Jesus of Nazareth: 'they were cut to the heart' (2:37). And they saw that there was only one way to be saved: by repenting of their sin and turning to embrace Jesus Christ as Lord and Messiah (2:38). For on that day in Jerusalem the Spirit of God communicated the truth of the gospel through Peter to multitudes of Jews gathered there for the Feast of Weeks. He made God immediately real. He made the Scriptures vocal. He made sin so painful and so challenging that he convicted thousands of souls. And he did all this through the feeble lips of that uneducated Galilean fisherman, Simon Peter. This feat was, in itself, a wonderful work of God!

We may ask, why is it that God seems so silent today? There is no easy answer to that question. There are times when God is silent because he is sitting in judgement over the nations; he is withholding his Word from a people who have despised it, who prize actors and sportsmen and clowns far above the preacher of the gospel or the gospel of the preacher. But wait a moment: there are also times when God is not heard speaking because people's lips are not under his control, because lives have not been humbled and subdued and harnessed by him. They have come the easy way into the church and they walk the easy way along what they think to be the Christian path, but they have never really been mastered by God. Are *we* under God's control? Could it be that God's voice is muffled today because some of us do not want to be controlled by the Spirit in his fulness? For we dare make no claim to the Spirit's fulness if it is not evident to readers of Scripture that we are mastered by him. Progress along the pathway from Simon to Peter, from spiritual babyhood to spiritual maturity, is impossible apart from the Spirit's control. This is a serious and challenging fact, for it involves the glory of God and the salvation of man. God still has a message for this generation. Can he utter it through you? Through me?

25.
The Holy Spirit and Peter's personality

Think back to the words of our Lord to Simon Peter when they met for the first time — the words that initiated the whole pilgrimage from Simon to Peter: ' "You are Simon the son of John? You will be called Cephas" (which, when translated, is Peter) [i.e. "rock"]' (John 1:42). Jesus' promise meant that, in due time, the vacillating, impetuous Simon would be transformed into the new man Peter, the man of rock — stable and strong in spirit to serve his Lord. The personalities of Simon and Peter would be as different as chalk and cheese.

It is in the book of Acts, beginning with the remarkable second chapter, that we find the new Peter emerging very clearly and dramatically. We have already seen the miraculous change that the Pentecostal fulness of the Spirit brought about in Peter's speech. In this chapter, still looking at Peter on the Day of Pentecost, we shall see the Spirit's equally miraculous transformation of his whole personality so that he was enabled both to take his place within the community of believers and to fulfil his destined ministry there as leader.

'Then Peter stood up with the Eleven' (Acts 2:14).

There is much more to this phrase than a merely factual comment. True, Peter and the Eleven[1] were standing together physically, shoulder to shoulder, in battle for the gospel. But they were also standing together spiritually, heart to heart and soul to soul, standing as one man in a fellowship created by the Spirit of God. They were joined together in a concerted effort to move forward as one in the way of the Lord.

This sense of unity and direction was new. Even during our Lord's last few days on earth before he ascended to the Father, it seems the disciples had very mixed feelings. Though they knew that Jesus was risen from the dead, and he had not died in vain, they had many questions. They were perplexed, for example, by his earlier announcement that he was going to leave them, and that this would be to their profit (John 16:7). Had he simply told them that he was going away, they would have been grieved enough; but their grief was aggravated by this mysterious insistence of our Lord that his departure would be to their benefit. How could it be?

The disciples must have been further perplexed by the terms of Jesus' commission to them before his ascension. He told them exactly what they were to do: they were to be witnesses to 'all nations, beginning at Jerusalem' (Luke 24:47); they were to 'make disciples of all nations' (Matthew 28:19). But they were not to begin this ministry until they were 'clothed with power from on high' (Luke 24:49). They were to wait in Jerusalem 'for the gift my Father promised, which you have heard me speak about. For John baptized with water, but in a few days you will be baptized with the Holy Spirit . . . You will receive power when the Holy Spirit comes on you; and you will be my witnesses in Jerusalem, and in all Judea and Samaria, and to the ends of the earth' (Acts 1:4,5,8).

It must have been difficult for the disciples to wait like this. Grieved as they were by Jesus' departure, and unsure of when they should act, they must have been further disconcerted, and probably even frightened, by the prospect of this mysterious event that was to prove their Lord's absence to be to their profit.

But then, in due course, the Day of Pentecost arrived, and the Spirit of God came down upon that ancient community in a manner that was wholly unique. And when he came down, he fulfilled the promise of power — power that was as mighty as the disciples' need was great. With sovereign strength, as we saw in the last chapter, the Spirit took control of the disciples' lips, using them to communicate his truth in many languages to the gathered multitude. And with mighty power the Spirit extended his control over the many idiosyncrasies of these men's personalities and temperaments. It is almost unbelievable how creatively and unifyingly the Spirit of God dealt with these individuals so that each was enabled to take his rightful place within the community of believers. The community became a communion: the Holy Spirit fused these men into an organic oneness in which heart beat with heart, mind thought with mind, and each individual will was subject to the holy, perfect will of God.

The Spirit's power to control the disciples' personalities was vital. The ability of these men to communicate the good news could have been rendered null and void if they had begun to quarrel among themselves, for example. The whole message of Pentecost could have come to nothing if the members of that early Christian community had started to bicker and argue among themselves — something which is too often seen in the church. That this did not happen is due to the Holy Spirit's dealing in power with each of their personalities, blending them together into one cohesive whole through which God could work; and the record shows how heavily he sometimes needed to rest his hand on those personalities in order to '. . . keep the unity of the Spirit through the bond of peace' (Ephesians 4:3).

This was especially true, of course, in relation to Simon Peter. For Peter's personality was anything but an easy one. He was an extreme individualist. He never saw other people's feet or considered other people's corns — he just stepped on them! A man of this temperament and personality could easily have torn the emerging church to shreds if the mighty Spirit of God had not come down to deal with him at the basic level of his personality weaknesses. But he came down with such a supreme miracle of grace that Peter was set free from many of his faults and enabled to fit into the community of believers to fulfil his mission there — not only in a negative sense, without hindering the others, but also in a positive sense, bringing them along with himself, so that all grew in grace and the knowledge of God together.

Our interest in the power of the Holy Spirit to deal with men's personalities is not purely historical; it is also practical. For you and I belong to a church, and unless the Spirit of

God is abroad to restrain and transform the individual church members into a true fellowship of faith, 'strong' personalities are potentially just as divisive today as they were in Pentecostal times. In any church, in any age, only the Spirit of God can enable a Peter to fit into a fellowship so that he finds the exact niche for his developing gifts and temperament, matures spiritually and helps those around him to do so at the same time.

Integrated into the community

Peter did not simply come to have his name on the membership list of believers in that early Christian community, but rather *he belonged.* He belonged to the others and they belonged to him. This is exactly what Christian fellowship is all about. We say that the Lord is ours and we are his, and that is wonderful, but Christian fellowship also entails that you are mine and I am yours, in Christ. We do not know anything at all about fellowship until we can honestly say to one another: 'Man or woman in Christ, I'm yours and you're mine!' Being in fellowship means that we are inextricably bound together by God's grace and energizing power. We are integrated into a whole, parts of the one body of Christ.

Integration into a community is, of course, a two-sided affair. It makes demands both upon the incoming individual and upon those who receive him in, and there must be considerable give and take on both sides. This is especially true when a community is as yet in its infancy, as the church in Jerusalem was at this stage, and this church had the further drawback of having recently experienced the traumas surrounding our Lord's crucifixion. At Pentecost the disciples were still emotionally somewhat tense.

But that early Christian community learned to receive Peter as one of their members. Despite his history of blustering and failure, and despite his gross individualism, they managed to accept him. No one knew Peter's faults better than the other eleven disciples did. They had lived with him for over three years, and theirs were the corns he had constantly stepped on. Their task of accepting Peter was like that of fitting a rough, unhewn, mammoth stone into a wall of smaller, trimmed, more regular stones. Peter was not made to measure — he was rough; he was an individualist. To fit him into the community was a task that called for enormous wisdom and grace and self-control on the part of his fellow believers.

Looked at from Peter's side, the task was no less challenging. He knew how his tongue could get out of control. Also he knew his tendency to act out of turn. Probably he had often been at his very worst when out in the fishing boat with his companions. There must have been many lacerated spirits from time to time among those who fished with him. And some of his Galilean fishing companions were right here with him in Jerusalem now, standing in front of a crowd of thousands, with everybody looking on. But the miracle has taken place: all sense of isolation is gone and Peter speaks out of a deeply felt unity with his fellow believers. They are one in Christ, made one by the Spirit.

Actually, all of these followers of our Lord, in their different ways, had been very much solitary believers up until Pentecost. Of course, they had been identifiable as a group because of their common loyalty to Jesus: they were following the same Master, listening to the same teaching, coming under the same influence. Sometimes two or three of them would act together, and at other times they would be sent out two by two. But in spite of all that, the marks of individuality were always strongly there. Each disciple was very much a man for himself. One proof of this fact lies in their constant competition with one another, in their incessant concern as to who was greatest in the kingdom, for example (Matthew 18:1; Mark 9:34; Luke 22:24 etc.).

But now at Pentecost, through the power of the Holy Spirit, the disciples changed. Being united through the Spirit into one body, their concern ceased to be each man for himself, and became each man for the others. They were no longer like beads on the same string; they were now more like branches on the same vine. They shared the same life. They belonged together. Indeed they even brought their material goods together and pooled them!

(2:45.) To express it in terms of Ezekiel's vision in the valley of dry bones, not only were the individual bones now brought close together, 'bone to bone' (Ezekiel 37:7), but the whole body was now animated by one controlling Holy Spirit: 'Breath entered them; they came to life and stood up on their feet . . .' (Ezekiel 37:10).

And we, do we know anything of this? We are members of a church, most of us. We have been officially received into membership somewhere and have our names on a register. But far more fundamental than whether or not we thus belong to a church is whether we actually belong to the saints. Just as your hand belongs to your arm and your arm belongs to your body, do you belong to the saints? Have your excessively individualistic traits been trimmed so that you fit into the community of God's people? This is the indispensable baptism of which Paul writes in Romans 6:3,4 and 1 Corinthians 12:13. And if you do not know this baptism, hear Peter's words at Pentecost to those outside the Christian community: 'Repent and be baptized, every one of you, in the name of Jesus Christ so that your sins may be forgiven. And you will receive the gift of the Holy Spirit. The promise is for you and your children and for all who are far off — for all whom the Lord our God will call' (Acts 2:38,39).

Acknowledged as leader

Through the power of the Holy Spirit, Peter was enabled not only to become integrated into the Christian community, but also to assume his destined role of leadership within that community, and to do so without causing any rupture in the fellowship. For Peter was divinely chosen by God to be a leader. He was both naturally and spiritually endowed to serve his Lord in this way. But a crucial question arises: how can a man like Peter ever win the confidence of his fellows so that they concede to him the place of leadership? Does he have to rule with a rod of iron and impose himself upon the people, or is there some way whereby they can be brought willingly to acknowledge him as leader, and gratefully to accept him in the position to which God has called him?

The answer to that question is clear: only the Holy Spirit who initially fuses individuals into a fellowship can maintain the communion within that body. Only the power of the Spirit of God, acting both upon a potential leader and upon the rest of the community, can make possible the right kind of acknowledgement and acceptance of that leader. In the text before us we have clear evidence that the Spirit's power was so mighty upon both Peter and the Eleven (and others) that they conceded to Peter the place that was his due. Nor did he ride roughshod over them but dealt with them as with the Lord's own sheep.

For that initial nucleus of believers recognized Peter's gifts and calling just as surely as they saw his faults. When we know someone's faults, the memory of them tends to colour, if not becloud, our whole view of that person. And that might well have happened here; the other disciples might have staked their claims to leadership in opposition to Peter. After all, none of them had sunk to the depths of sin that Peter had in denying Jesus, and the Eleven could have argued very cogently that such failure automatically disqualified Peter from leadership. How could they rely on a man like him?

But these Spirit-filled men also remembered how their Lord had reinstated Peter (John 21:15–17). Most of them had been present that morning around the charcoal fire beside the Sea of Galilee. They had heard Peter's threefold confession of his real affection for Jesus and had heard Jesus' threefold commission to Peter to feed his lambs, take care of his sheep and feed them. Remembering these things, the Eleven staked no counter-claims. They did not try to stand in the way of God's will. Instead they marched forward with him so that he was found standing 'with the Eleven' in unbroken fellowship.

Recognition of other believers' gifts is a very necessary grace in the life of the church. We are often tempted to allow other people's faults to blind us to their divine calling; sometimes we even go so far as to stand in the way of its fulfilment. And when that happens, God is truly grieved and the fellowship is badly marred — especially so when we court for ourselves what God has purposed for another. Blessed are they who can see the gifts and callings of others,

as well as the nature and the limits of their own. Martin
Luther had this grace: he would not try to do what he knew
belonged to someone else to do. He knew, for example,
that he was less gifted in certain respects than the great
scholar and charming personality, Philip Melanchthon;
knowing this, he neither attempted to do what was his
brother's part, nor neglected to do what was his own. Somewhere he said, 'I was born to be a rough controversialist.
I clear the ground, pull up the weeds, fill up ditches and
smooth the roads. But to build, to plan, to sow, to water,
to adorn the country belongs by the grace of God to
Melanchthon.' Undoubtedly there were times when Luther
might have envied Melanchthon his great mind and his
popularity. But seeing the grace of God in him, and the
calling of God for him, and knowing clearly what he himself
was ordained to do, Luther was satisfied with his own part
while gladly acknowledging God's work in his brother.
That is the attitude we see here in the other disciples'
obedient acceptance of Peter's gifts and calling.

But Peter's attitude is important too. It is most significant,
here in Acts 2:14, that although Peter was spokesman for
the community, he was standing with the other members.
He was not apart from them as a leader on a pedestal.
Instead, he was carrying them with him and winning their
confidence so that what was done and said by him was
done and said in the name of the whole body. The impetuous
self in Peter was so controlled by the Spirit of God that
Peter could now lead those who were meant to support
him, without offending any of them. The fellowship was
enriched as each member of it yielded to the Spirit's control
and the church grew larger as the fellowship grew richer.

Released from innate fears

The Holy Spirit of God not only enabled Peter to fit into
the community of believers and to assume his destined role
as leader there; he also enabled Peter to break away from a
native fearfulness that, had it remained, might badly have
impeded his ministry. There are some aspects of Peter's
personality which we rarely fail to notice, such as his

impetuosity and his talkativeness. But there are other equally obvious traits which we tend not to notice, and one of these is his fearfulness. For despite his 'big fisherman' stance, Peter was afraid. Most of his blustering and boasting and apparently quick, courageous action was, in fact, sheer reaction, coming instinctively out of fear. At the basis of his whole being were underlying fears. This is not the first time that a torrent of words and a flurry of busyness had hidden great fearfulness of heart! And three of Peter's fears in particular are relevant to the fulfilment of his ministry and his destiny.

Fear of drowning

The story in Matthew 14:22—33 tells us that the disciples were caught in a storm on the Sea of Galilee. Jesus was not with them. He was watching and praying on the slopes nearby, in the moonlight. But he could see his disciples toiling and rowing and, at last, when they thought they were finally doomed, he walked on the waves towards them. When Simon Peter, impetuous as usual and always the first to speak, bade Jesus prove his identity by enabling him to walk on the waves just as he was doing himself, Jesus agreed and told him, 'Come.' At first Peter could walk on the waves just as his Master did, but 'when he saw the wind, he was afraid' (14:30). He began to sink out of sheer fright. Peter was a fisherman, a man of the sea. But he had yet to master all his fear of the Sea of Galilee! 'Lord, save me!' he cried out (14:30). He was afraid of drowning.

Fear of derision

Peter had a fear of being mocked. That is why, in the high priest's courtyard (John 18:25—27, for example), he so vehemently and persistently denied that he knew Jesus. Other factors, such as the fear of death, may also have been involved here, but basically what seems to have been in the foreground of Peter's soul was fear of derision. He flinched when he was laughed at as the foolish follower of the one who was now totally at the mercy of his enemies. Peter simply could not take people making fun of him; he was afraid of ridicule.

Fear of speaking the truth

Peter had a fear of declaring an unpalatable truth when it needed to be declared. We see this in John 20:19. Along with others, Peter spent considerable time on that glorious resurrection day, and beyond it, shut up in a house, 'with the doors locked for fear of the Jews'. The disciples knew that their Lord was risen, but they were afraid to broadcast the fact. Imagine Simon Peter, this physically burly man, being afraid to tell the enemies of Jesus that they had failed to get rid of his Lord! What would happen if he and the others went out into the streets of Jerusalem to tell the Jews that the one they nailed to the cross was now the Lord of glory, risen from the dead? Peter was afraid to proclaim this unwelcome truth.

Peter's basic fearfulness was short-lived, however, once the Spirit of God fell upon him and his friends. Jerusalem was still the headquarters of those who had killed Jesus, and Jewish worshippers from all parts of the then known world were in the city for the Feast of Weeks. In fact Pentecost was a no more opportune time to declare the resurrection than that first day of the week after Passover when Jesus rose from the dead. But when the Spirit came down upon Peter he was changed. The power of the Spirit within him was more than a match for the presence of any fears that lingered in his heart. Peter marched out into the street which was teeming with people and, standing 'with the Eleven', exercised the power of the keys that Jesus had given him, directing thousands of Jews into the kingdom of God and his Christ. Fear of men and fear of death were gone, allowing Peter to move forward to his destined ministry. Whether in life or in death, he was now totally free to be at his Lord's disposal.

What has God called you to do? Has he called you to something specific, yet you are afraid to move forward? Don't feel ashamed of that — Peter, too, was afraid during the days of his training. But when the Spirit of God filled him, he went out, not like Abraham who 'did not know where he was going' (Hebrews 11:8), but knowing that one day he would be bound and martyred (John 21:18). And even so he was enabled by the power of the Spirit to live courageously under the shadow of death as he marched forward to fulfil his ministry.

The Holy Spirit of God has not changed. Our God is still the great 'I am'. No matter what our needs may be, he can still enable us to fulfil our callings. He can smooth off the rough edges so that we fit into a community of believers. He can make leaders assume leadership without destroying the fellowship. He can strengthen us to move forward, despite all the fears and tyrannies that may have broken our hearts and silenced our tongues in days gone by. Let us open all the windows of our souls towards the heavenly Jerusalem then, so that we may receive every grace and gift that God wants to give us, to his honour and his glory.

Reference
1. The Eleven refers to the initial group of our Lord's disciples after the lapse and death of Judas, and before his successor was chosen.

26.
The Holy Spirit and Peter's understanding of Scripture

When the Spirit of God came down at Pentecost, he illumined Peter's mind, giving him both a new understanding of Scripture and, through that, a new understanding of the Saviour. As the disciples were enabled to speak in different languages to the thousands of Jews gathered in the Jerusalem streets, they caused a great stir.

> *'Amazed and perplexed [the crowd] asked one another, "What does this mean?" Some, however, made fun of them and said, "They have had too much wine." Then Peter stood up with the Eleven, raised his voice and addressed the crowd: "Fellow-Jews and all of you who are in Jerusalem, let me explain this to you; listen carefully to what I say. These men are not drunk, as you suppose. It's only nine in the morning! No, this is what was spoken by the prophet Joel . . ."'* (Acts 2:12–16).

'This is what was spoken by the prophet Joel,' for Peter knows what the Pentecostal event means. He is able to explain a phenomenon that utterly mystifies even the most devout of Jews. How is this so? Because the Holy Spirit, who has come down upon Peter and flooded his whole being, has thereby illumined his mind, giving him the key to a new understanding of Scripture (cf. Luke 24:45). Now this unlettered man from the lower or lower-middle stratum of society, this man without a university degree, this man who is not authorized by the Sanhedrin to teach — *this* man understands the mighty phenomenon of Pentecost. Here we see the power of the Holy Spirit to enlighten the mind of the humble.

We are now moving into a different sphere of the Spirit's great work in Peter at Pentecost. Whereas his influence upon Peter's tongue and personality was largely a matter of curbing and controlling things that were natural to Peter, his influence upon Peter's mind was largely a matter of imparting new gifts that certainly were not natural to him. What we have here is not the refining of a natural capacity, but the divine conferring of something new upon the recipient. The Holy Spirit granted to Peter a supernatural understanding that flooded his mind with light, and as this happened, Peter was enabled both to see new dimensions of truth and to communicate them to those around him whose understanding was limited.

Peter had had a taste of such illumination of the mind earlier on. At Caesarea Philippi, Jesus asked his disciples, 'Who do people say the Son of man is?' (Matthew 16:13.) The replies were given. He then challenged his followers: 'But what about you? Who do you say I am?'' (16:15). And Peter replied for the whole group: 'You are the Christ, the Son of the living God' (16:16). This was our Lord's response to that confession: 'Blessed are you, Simon son of Jonah, for this was not revealed to you by man, but by my Father in heaven' (16:17). In other words, 'You haven't deduced this by your own reasoning processes or learned it from any human teacher. God has revealed it to you!' And that experience was but a foreshadowing of the marvellous illumination of mind which at Pentecost was to become a more or less settled, permanent work of the Spirit in Peter.

The importance of the mind in the life of any Christian

What is the place of the mind in Christian experience? Scripture makes clear that the whole person is to be involved in response to the gospel. Jesus said, 'Love the Lord your God with all your heart and with all your soul and with all your mind and with all your strength' (Mark 12:30). Those terms cover the whole person; nothing is left out, no matter how you care to categorize the various aspects of human life. Our Lord is saying that God requires *the whole of us,* both in our initial response to the gospel, and in our continued, daily response to God. The whole of us includes, of course, our minds. In fact, a whole personal response is *dependent upon* the mind. It is not enough to have a mere emotional experience; it is not enough to go to meetings that give us 'kicks'; it is not enough to feel happy or to feel better. Feelings by themselves can be very misleading. Our Christian gospel makes its primary appeal to the mind, and then, via the mind, to the conscience and the will and the heart. If this were not so, why would God have given us a Bible? He surely meant us to use our minds to read and absorb and understand it, so that we should then know how to live! The whole of biblical religion is addressed primarily to the mind.

This does not mean, of course, that Christian experience amounts to some kind of arid intellectualism: Christian experience involves the whole man, but the mind is central to all else. Man is a thinking being and what he does not properly understand, he cannot properly respond to. We must *think,* therefore. We must read and study and come, by the grace of God, to an understanding of the truth before we can respond to the truth. Then, when we respond, we must respond with our whole selves. Years ago a Princeton professor pointed to the dangers inherent in either a purely intellectual or a purely emotional response: 'Commitment without reflection is fanaticism in action. But reflection without commitment is the paralysis of all action.'[1] We might ask whether much so-called 'keen' Christian activity is not, in fact, largely unreflecting fanaticism. It is not thoughtful. It is often inspired by a mere emotional hunch. It does not know the Scriptures of truth or the will of God and if it involves the mind at all, it only does so in a very secondary way.

Over the last number of years, three main movements in the church have tended to ignore or to downgrade the intellectual side of Christian experience.[2] *Ritualism* is one such movement. We have always had ritualism in the church, especially in medieval times, and it can be found in all kinds of places, even in the Protestant church in the twentieth century. Here is the love of the ornate and the symbolic, the love of what the eye can see, of beauty and proportion and good taste. Now, our God is no patron saint of ugliness. How could he be, having created a world like ours? Beauty has its undoubted place in his scheme of things. But ritualism gives too high a place to beauty: it elevates it above the rational to the neglect of reason. Where ritual is afforded such a degree of importance, the doctrines of the Word and the preaching of the gospel generally recede in importance. History will show this to be true.

Another movement in the church today that often downgrades the intellectual side of Christianity is *social activism.* That there is a necessary application of gospel principles to social and political life is clear enough for the blindest to see — an application which is always relevant and currently urgent. There are some, however, who tend to equate what has been called 'Christian social action' with the gospel itself and thereby cause no little confusion to the unwary. Apart from the unjustifiable equation involved in this process, it often further results in the equally unjustifiable downgrading of the value of truth and of the knowledge and application of sound doctrine. Correct doctrinal thinking about God, man, salvation and much else appears to be less important than a frontal attempt to change the structures of society. The real significance of revealed truth for the true worship and acceptable service of God, as well as for ethical and moral behaviour, is obscured and man becomes the focus of all things. This is a serious misconstruction of the Christian message.

A third movement in today's church that minimizes the importance of the mind in Christianity is the movement that emphasizes the value of *experience.* This is a form of pragmatism which says, 'It really doesn't matter what you believe, as long as you have an experience of God.' That might be all right if the Holy Spirit were the only spirit abroad in the world! But he is not. Just as there were evil spirits in the days of Moses and of our Lord, so there are evil spirits abroad today, and just as the magicians of Egypt could produce counterfeits and ape God's work (Exodus 7:11,22; 8:7), so can evil powers today produce counterfeits to the genuine experience of God. Experience, therefore, cannot be the touchstone of truth.

Ritualism, social activism and pragmatism in religious

affairs must all be brought to the bar of truth, namely, the teaching of Scripture. The test of Christianity is not whether it appeals to my sense of beauty or gives me an ecstatic 'spiritual' experience; the test of Christianity is not whether it brings a better social order: the test of Christianity is whether or not it is *true according to Scripture.* If it is thus true, even though we may suffer politically, socially and economically, we must proclaim it, and even die for it if necessary.

We are living in an age when so many secondary things are being emphasized, to the detriment of truth. The minimizing of the importance of the mind in Christian living has resulted in a frightening downgrading of the biblical and apostolic ordinance of preaching, for example. In some evangelical circles it has become heretical to ask people to think. Great doctrines and issues that occupied the best minds of the ages have now been abandoned as inappropriate for serious consideration, on the grounds that Christians are unable to cope with them. The mind is placed in abeyance.

This state of affairs creates great problems for parents of young children, for instance. Because so many churches have succumbed to the idea that biblical teaching is 'too heavy' to understand, or largely irrelevant, and have wellnigh abandoned doctrinal teaching, only the most superficial spiritual food is often made available to growing children. Thus many parents are faced with a dilemma: are they going to teach the full-orbed faith of the Scriptures to their own children, involving their children at home in the discipline which this entails, or are they going to entrust their children's spiritual education to Sunday Schools where they may be fed on the most superficial spiritual diet?

Here in Acts 2 we have the divine corrective to the anti-intellectual trends in the church. The answer to people's would-be inability to grapple with, and to profit from, divine truth lies in the control of their mind by the indwelling Holy Spirit, and their subsequent obedience to him. Just as he illumined and taught Peter, so also may he be our illumination and our Teacher. There is no other key to the proper understanding of Scripture. We must, therefore, acknowledge this power of the Holy Spirit, and pray for it in our lives and in the lives of the churches.

Indeed, it was fundamentally *because of* the Holy Spirit's illumination of his mind that Peter became a leader. Of course, he also wrought miracles and spoke in other tongues through the power of the Spirit, but Peter became the man he did fundamentally because the Holy Spirit illumined his mind, so that he became a man of understanding and could therefore open the doors of the kingdom to thousands of other people. If only we had more men and women of understanding in the Christian church today, we would be able to do things which are wholly impracticable in our present condition of sloth.

The Holy Spirit and Peter's new understanding of Scripture

In Acts 2, we see that Peter's new understanding of Scripture stands out in stark contrast to that of even very devout Jews, and certainly to that of some less devout ones.

The perplexity of the devout

There was in Jerusalem at this time a very remarkable gathering of Jews from all parts of the then known world. There were 'Parthians, Medes and Elamites; residents of Mesopotamia, Judea and Cappadocia, Pontus and Asia, Phrygia and Pamphylia, Egypt and the parts of Libya near Cyrene; visitors from Rome (both Jews and converts to Judaism); Cretans and Arabs . . .' (2:9—11). These people are referred to as 'God-fearing Jews' (2:5). They were Jews of the best kind, very serious about their faith. But they were absolutely at a loss to understand the phenomenon of Pentecost. They simply did not know what it was all about: *'Amazed and perplexed, they asked one another, "What does this mean?"'* *(2:12).*

We must fully acknowledge the religious zeal and enthusiasm of these good people. They had come all the way from such distant places as Mesopotamia and Rome in order to observe the Feast of Weeks in Jerusalem, and that was quite a feat because travel was slow and dangerous in those days. These people were sincere. They were worshipping God in the only way they knew how. As far as their knowledge went, they were obedient. They were prepared to pay the price of their devotion by coming all the way to Jerusalem in accordance with the requirements of Scripture at this time of year.

But their zeal was 'not based on knowledge', to use a Pauline phrase (Romans 10:2). Even though they had read the prophets who had foretold God's sending forth of his Spirit upon men, these God-fearing Jews were incapable of recognizing the fulfilment of that prophecy taking place before their very eyes. Even as others of their kind had been bewildered by the coming of the Son of God some thirty-three years earlier, so these dedicated men were amazed and perplexed by the coming of the Spirit of God at Pentecost. They did not understand the Scriptures; therefore they did not know what to make of the disciples' speaking in tongues to them, and they responded with sheer perplexity.

The mockery of the less devout

'Some, however, made fun of them and said, "They have had too much wine"' (Acts 2:13).

These others were abusive and sceptical. Too arrogant to contemplate the possibility that there might be anything good in the despised followers of the crucified Nazarene, they were also too blinded by prejudice to recognize even the greatest of divine gifts when it was given. Their hostility to the disciples was as great as that of those other Jews who had charged the disciples' Master with casting out demons by 'the prince of demons' (Matthew 12:24). These Jews now charged the Spirit-filled disciples with being drunk, thus dismissing the entire Pentecostal event as something unworthy of serious thought. There could be nothing for respectable worshippers of God to learn from the frenzied actions of drunkards! For these people were out of their depth. They not only did not understand, but in the superficiality of their alleged devotion to God they even reverted to mockery.

The certainty of Peter

In contrast to the reactions of these Jewish listeners, Peter's certainty is magnificent: *'Then Peter stood up with the Eleven, raised his voice and addressed the crowd . . .' (Acts*

2:14). The very fact that Peter stood up and addressed others in public was itself something big and new.

'Fellow-Jews and all of you who are in Jerusalem, let me explain this to you, listen carefully to what I say . . .' (2:14). He was telling the Jews that he had something very definite to teach them. Notice the tone of authority in his request that they should listen to him!

'These men are not drunk, as you suppose. It's only nine in the morning! No, this is what was spoken by the prophet Joel: "In the last days, God says, I will pour out my Spirit on all people. Your sons and daughters will prophesy . . ."' (2:15–17). Peter was able to explain to the gathered crowds exactly what the event of Pentecost was all about. And the source of his understanding was twofold: his prior instruction in the Scriptures and the present illumination of the Holy Spirit.

1. *Before the Spirit could illumine Peter's mind, Peter had become instructed in the Scriptures.* Just as a knowledge of facts precedes an understanding or interpretation of those facts in any field of learning, so instruction in Scripture always precedes and provides the basis for the illumination of Scripture. For the Holy Spirit does not give to men that knowledge of Scripture which they can acquire naturally by means of discipline and study. Thus, before the Spirit came upon him in power, Peter had learned what Joel had said; and when the Spirit eventually came, Peter then learned the significance of what Joel had said. Although we are not specifically told this, we may legitimately assume that Peter had studied the book of Joel. How else would he know Joel's words of prophecy? And it was only because Peter had this prior knowledge that the Spirit had the materials at his disposal for showing Peter the true meaning of the Pentecostal event. Up until Pentecost Joel's words would have made no sense except as a vague pointer to something too mysterious to comprehend. But the fact that Peter already knew what Joel had written now made possible the Spirit's work of illumination. This underlines the vital importance of instruction in the Scriptures, and the indispensable need for every believer to know the Word of God in all its completeness. For instruction precedes illumination.

2. Peter's certainty about the meaning of Pentecost sprang

from this *subsequent illumination of his knowledge of Scripture by the Holy Spirit*. What happened to Peter at Pentecost was not unlike what happened to the two unnamed disciples on the road to Emmaus (Luke 24:13–32). On that first day of the week, that resurrection day, these two companions were walking away from Jerusalem, discouraged and disillusioned by the events surrounding Jesus' death. A stranger joined them on their way and asked them what it was they were talking about. At last, having listened to their tale of woe, the Lord said to them, "How foolish you are, and how slow of heart to believe all that the prophets have spoken! Did not the Christ have to suffer these things and then enter his glory?" And beginning with Moses and all the Prophets, he explained to them what was said in all the Scriptures concerning himself' (Luke 24: 25–27). And later on in the breaking of bread the two disciples recognized Jesus because the eyes of their understanding had been opened by him.

Here in Acts 2 it is the Holy Spirit who explained to the humble believer, Peter, how the Scriptures that had spoken of the coming and the suffering of Christ had also foretold his own coming and his ministry. And this revelation made Peter wise to matters which were otherwise beyond his grasp too.

I remember hearing of a farmer on the British side of the Atlantic who lived in a very dilapidated old farmhouse and decided that the time had come to replace it with a new house. This was in a very remote district of the country where there was as yet no electricity, but there was talk about 'power' coming that way before very long. So, in spite of much mockery, and even against the advice of his builder, this man decided to have all of the rooms in his new house wired, complete even with switches, in preparation for the coming of electricity. Finally, about eighteen months later, power did come that way. The poles were erected and the wires were put in their place. Now the wise man needed only to link up his house with the source of power to have heat and light throughout his home! He did so with the result that, one happy day, he was able to go around to every room and switch on the lights. The house was now ablaze with light, because it had been previously wired for it.

We might say that Peter had the house of his mind wired with knowledge of God's Word prior to the Spirit's descent in power upon him at Pentecost. The home, the synagogue and probably the ministry of John the Baptizer had begun a process of wiring that was continued by our Lord himself. And when the Spirit eventually came, all that Peter had learned came aglow with meaning and certainty. Indeed, the same thing was true of the apostle Paul. How could a man like Paul become almost overnight the man he appears in the New Testament — teacher, preacher, witness that Jesus Christ was Messiah? This is how: Paul was nurtured in the Scriptures. He had studied the Law and the Prophets. Therefore he had the necessary wiring for the Spirit's illumination!

We need to take this lesson to heart: the illumination of the Spirit only comes in its robust fulness and freshness along the 'wiring' of the mind by the Word of God. If it is treasured there from youth, and if it is learned and memorized, kept there and added to as the years go by, then, when the Spirit comes, there is something for him to illumine. Our children need to be equipped with basic biblical truth so that when the Spirit comes he will light up every room of their minds. Let us not be deceived, therefore, by anti-intellectual trends in the church. The man or woman, boy or girl, who does not know the Scriptures may all too easily become a person who is caught in the quagmire of false teaching and false experience. But men and women who would know the real power of the Spirit in their minds do well to acquire a basic knowledge of Scripture today. Only then can the Spirit of God illumine their whole beings and make them lights in their generation — cities set on a hill that cannot be hidden (Matthew 5:14).

References
1. J. R. W. Stott, *Your Mind Matters* (Inter-Varsity Press, Downer's Grove, Ill. 1972), p. 7.
2. *Ibid.,* pp. 7—11.

27.
The Holy Spirit and Peter's understanding of the Saviour

There can be no such thing as a mindless Christianity. It is very significant that, in his First Epistle, Peter the ex-fisherman writes to his fellow Christians that they should 'prepare [their] *minds* for action' (1 Peter 1:13). For Peter learned that to be an effective Christian you have to use your mind. And when the Holy Spirit comes upon someone in power and in grace, the mind is never in abeyance; in fact, it is activated and inspired by the Spirit to fulfil its true function. So when Peter's mind came under the inspiration of the Holy Spirit at Pentecost, the first and major thing that happened was that he gained a new and an almost unparalleled understanding of Scripture. And, following from this, the Holy Spirit gave him a new appreciation of the chief subject of Scripture, our Lord and Saviour, Jesus Christ. The body of Peter's sermon to the crowds of Jews in the Jerusalem streets (Acts 2:22–36) reveals this new understanding. The sermon ends with an explosive truth that sums it all up.

> *'Therefore let all Israel be assured of this: God has made this Jesus, whom you crucified, both Lord and Christ' (2:36).*

It is no exaggeration to say that all of Peter's subsequent ministry and teaching emerged out of this Spirit-given conviction concerning his Lord. For once the Spirit of God has given us to understand the Scriptures, we are in a position to recognize the glories of the Saviour. And then we have the answer not only to our own questionings, but also to those of other men in the world and in the church. The Spirit's illumination of Scripture to reveal the Saviour is,

288

then, the vital prerequisite for any kind of Christian ministry. This new understanding of Jesus' person and work is something that Peter had not had before, even though he had spent many months in the company of Jesus as a disciple, and it is something that Peter needed to have before he could carry out the ministry which Jesus had ordained for him and his fellows (Matthew 28:19).

Our Lord, of course, had promised that the coming Paraclete would enlighten the disciples' minds concerning him: 'He will bring glory to me by taking from what is mine and making it known to you' (John 16:14). In fact, whenever the Holy Spirit comes in power and grace, he exalts our Lord Jesus Christ. We may assess every experience in the light of this principle: where the Holy Spirit is, Jesus Christ will be central. But what is particularly noteworthy is *the way* in which the Spirit glorifies Jesus. For here he grants to Peter an understanding of the Saviour *as he is presented in Scripture*. He reveals to Peter that it is in Jesus Christ that God has fulfilled what he promised and what the prophets foretold in Scripture; every aspect of the person and the work of the Son has been, is and ever will be in accordance with 'God's set purpose and foreknowledge' (2:23). We shall see this more clearly as we examine the titles 'Lord' and 'Christ' which Peter now uses with such depths of meaning.

God has made Jesus Lord

'Therefore let all Israel be assured of this: God has made this Jesus . . . Lord . . .' (2:36).

Peter knew this to some extent before Pentecost. His confession at Caesarea Philippi ('You are the Christ, the Son of the living God', Matthew 16:16) implied a recognition that Jesus was the Lord in whom the rule of God had come to earth (cf. Matthew 12:28). Moreover, Peter had witnessed his many mighty works; he had seen him die the death of the cross and rise again to become active in resurrection power; he had seen him ascend into heaven. Prior to Pentecost Peter's mind had, then, been wired with knowledge and was ready for the time when the power of the Spirit would illuminate it with a true understanding of Jesus Christ. And when the Spirit came, Peter realized that *everything fulfilled a divine purpose that had been foretold in the Scriptures.* Jesus did not just die on the cross and rise from the dead: he died and he rose to fulfil a foreordained plan and pattern. Nothing he did was accidental or haphazard; everything he did was a fulfilment of what had been planned by God and prophesied by his servants. This is the view of our Lord according to Scripture. In giving Peter this new understanding, the Holy Spirit enabled him to apprehend Jesus' uniqueness. In his sermons to the Jews in Jerusalem, Peter points to the depths out of which God raised his Son, and the heights to which he exalted him, each one being a fulfilment of what had been foretold in Scripture.

Raised from the depths

Peter reminds the gathered crowds of our Lord's humiliation: 'with the help of *wicked men* [they] *put him to death by nailing him to the cross*' (2:23).

1. Jesus was *crucified.* This word is so familiar that we perhaps miss the real significance of it. Jesus did not simply die: his enemies arranged for him the kind of death that, according to Scripture, was the most dishonourable imaginable, and belonged to the accursed of God. 'If a man guilty of a capital offence is put to death and his body is hung on a tree, you must not leave his body on the tree overnight. Be sure to bury him that same day, because anyone who is hung on a tree is under God's curse' (Deuteronomy 21:22,23). 'Christ redeemed us from the curse of the law by becoming a curse for us, for it is written: "Cursed is everyone who is hanged on a tree . . ."' (Galatians 3:13). There could be no more humiliating or shameful way to die (cf. Isaiah 53).

2. Jesus' death was a plain act of murder: he was *killed* by *wicked men.* This was not the state exercising capital punishment for a capital offence in accordance with Scripture. Pilate declared at least three times that Jesus was innocent (Luke 23:4; John 18:38; 19:4,6). He was saying to the Jews, in effect, 'Your accusations against this man do not stand. I find no crime in him. What, then, shall I do

with him?' The death of Jesus was not legally justified; it was tantamount to plain, black murder. Lawless men took the law into their own hands against the one who had fulfilled the law in its letter and in its spirit. They *murdered* the incarnate Lord.

3. But more than that: in order fully to plumb the depths out of which God raised his Son, let us look at what Peter says further on, quoting Psalm 16:10: 'He was not abandoned to the grave, nor did his body see decay' (2:31). This seems to imply that even though our Lord was not left in that dark spiritual world, he did in fact go there. This is a mystery, and we must be careful not to pretend otherwise. Our only clue to an understanding of it lies in Jesus' cry of dereliction from the cross, where he quotes Psalm 22:1: 'My God, my God, why have you forsaken me?' (Matthew 27:46). In other words, our Lord knew what it was to be forsaken of God because he bore the curse of our sin; in that experience of God-forsakenness, he entered into hell. He tasted death in all its horrors. Such were the depths to which he descended and from which God raised him up — the depths of crucifixion, murder and hell.

Exalted to the heights

Quoting Psalm 16:8, Peter says to the crowds: 'But God raised him from the dead, freeing him from the agony of death, because it was impossible for death to keep its hold on him. David said about him: "I saw the Lord always before me . . ."' (2:24,25). And further, alluding to Psalm 110, verse 1: 'God has raised this Jesus to life, and we all are witnesses of the fact. Exalted to the right hand of God, he has received from the Father the promised Holy Spirit and has poured out what you now see and hear' (2:32,33).

The murdered, accursed victim leaves behind him the dark prison-house of death. He shakes off its chains, rises on the third day (in accordance with Scripture, Hosea 6:2), and ultimately ascends to the highest place that heaven affords, to 'the right hand of God' (Psalm 110:1). God has made him Lord. Having been laid low by his enemies, he is now lifted high by God himself.

How did Peter know this? Wasn't this conjecture? Wasn't

it all in the realm of fancy and subjective thought? No, Peter knew. In the first place, he knew because Jesus had sent forth the Holy Spirit just as he had promised. He had assured his followers that he would send them 'another Paraclete' who would not simply be 'with them' but 'in them' as well (John 14:15–17). And because that promise was now obviously fulfilled at Pentecost, Peter was right in concluding that Jesus had arrived at the place of power where he could carry out such a promise.

Deity alone can command deity. This is something that we all need to learn. In prayer we may beg and yearn and crave, but there is one thing we cannot do — command the Deity. In our arrogance we sometimes appear to think that we can tell God what to do, but we cannot. Yet here is one, the Son of God, the Son of Mary, who says, 'I am going to die, I am going to rise again, I am going back home to my Father, and when I get there I am going to send forth the Holy Spirit, the third person of the Trinity, very God of very God!' 'When the day of Pentecost came, they were all together in one place' (2:1) *and he came!*

That was the experiential reason whereby Peter knew that Jesus was now ascended to the right hand of God, but it was not the only reason. For what really convinced Peter that Jesus was exalted as Lord was the insight gained from his new understanding of Scripture — the insight that Jesus was *appointed by God* to be exalted, just as he had been *appointed by God* to experience the depths of humiliation. Quoting from Psalm 110:1, Peter says, 'For David did not ascend to heaven and yet he said, "The Lord said to my Lord: Sit at my right hand until I make your enemies a footstool for your feet"' (2:34,35).

The clinching point for Peter was the fact that David had been inspired to write in this way about Jesus, which proves that Jesus was predestined by God to be exalted as Lord. His exaltation was no chance happening: God had purposed it, foretold it through his prophet in Scripture, then fulfilled it. What convinced Peter that God had made Jesus Lord was the work of the Spirit upon his mind, bringing into a single focus all the dimensions of meaning he had hitherto known — the experience of the coming of the Holy Spirit, the verbal promises of Jesus, the prophecies of Scripture — so that he was marvellously enabled to see the Saviour in true perspective. He now saw the Jesus of history as the Christ of the Scriptures. And that is the view of Jesus Christ that sends men out into the world to preach with conviction — the view that everything about him falls under the category of divine fulfilment.

God has made Jesus Christ

'Therefore let all Israel be assured of this: God has made this Jesus . . . Christ' (2:36).
We often refer to our Lord as 'Christ', meaning 'the Anointed One of God'. It appears from the context here in Acts 2, however, that Peter has in mind an even richer concept than that.

God made Jesus of Nazareth the Anointed One
Looking down the corridors of time, God from his throne viewed all the unborn ages of men, and from among them all he chose *one* to bear his special anointing. Prophets and priests and kings would also receive his anointing to perform their several roles, but this one person was to be uniquely appointed for a unique work. He was not simply to be anointed: he was to be 'the Anointed One of God'. That one was, of course, Jesus of Nazareth, Son of Mary, Son of God. In eternity, before he was born of the virgin, he was appointed by God to be Saviour.

What was predetermined by God in eternity eventually took place in time. Our Lord Jesus Christ was conceived of the Holy Spirit and born into the world. At the outset of his ministry that same Spirit came evidently to rest upon him, indicating his pleasure in him (Matthew 3:17) and signifying the sure provision of every spiritual need to fulfil his ministry of preaching and of teaching, of healing and of dying. When he eventually stood before men, he said, quoting from Isaiah 61:1,2: 'The Spirit of the Lord is upon me, because he has anointed me to preach good news to the poor. He has sent me to proclaim freedom for the prisoners and recovery of sight for the blind, to release the oppressed, to proclaim the year of the Lord's favour' (Luke 4:18,19).

Everything he did bore the mark of God's anointing. As he taught, worked miracles, preached, died on the cross, he did everything in the power of the Spirit, thus expressing God's saving grace and fulfilling God's saving purpose.

God made the Anointed One the Anointer as well

Here in Acts 2 is a complementary truth: God has made the Anointed One, Jesus, the Anointer of his body, the church. If the resurrection of Jesus from the dead and his exaltation to the right hand of God prove him to be the Anointed who was commissioned and enabled to accomplish redemption, what now takes place from his exalted position proves him to be the Anointer who shares the benefits of his finished work and his personal anointing with those he has redeemed. Peter says, 'Exalted to the right hand of God, he has received from the Father the promised Holy Spirit and has poured out what you now see and hear' (2:33). The Anointed One has anointed the whole community of the redeemed so that they may share in his ministry.

For when Jesus Christ ascended to the Father's throne, it was not simply the case that the Son of God was returning home. More than that, something happened in heaven at the exaltation of Jesus that had never happened before. When he ascended now on high and 'led captivity captive' (Psalm 68:18 AV), he ascended not simply as the Son of God, but also as the Son of Mary. He ascended as the incarnate Lord, the crucified Lamb of God, the High Priest of his people. He took our humanity with him, now glorified and dignified, and because he ascended to the throne as glorified man, he is now our representative at the right hand of God. He is now there as the Head of the church, the Shepherd of the sheep, the Mediator of the new covenant. This is not dry theology. Look at the difference it makes: he who died in our place on the cross, who was buried for us and rose for us, is now ascended for us! And God gives him the Holy Spirit. But our Lord cannot keep the gift exclusively for himself because he represents us and, in his representative capacity, he shares the gift with us, pouring the whole vial of precious ointment down upon the waiting church. That is what Pentecost is! We rightly admire that dear sinner woman pouring her alabaster jar of ointment upon the head of Jesus as he sat at table (Matthew 26:7), but here we have something incomparably more precious even than that: here is Jesus of Nazareth, our Lord and our Representative and our Substitute, pouring his 'alabaster jar of very expensive perfume' upon the whole church.

There is a symbolic picture of this in one of the psalms:

> How good and pleasant it is
>   when brothers live together in unity!
> It is like precious oil poured on the head,
>   running down on the beard,
> running down on Aaron's beard,
>   down upon the collar of his robes.
> It is as if the dew of Hermon
>   were falling on Mount Zion.
> For there the Lord bestows his blessing,
>   even life for evermore
>
>   (Psalm 133).

The anointing starts on the head and goes down to Aaron's beard and then to the collar of his robes, flowing all the way down. Jesus is the Head — the Head of the church, the King of the redeemed, my Saviour and yours. And having received the promise of the Spirit, not privately for himself alone as the Son of God, but in his official capacity as High Priest of his people and Head of the body, on the Day of Pentecost he pours forth that same benefit so that even the very least in his kingdom will share in it. As Peter says, from this day forth, 'The promise is for you and your children and for all who are far off — for all whom the Lord our God will call' (2:39).

The Anointed One is also the Anointer, arriving at the Father's right hand, receiving for us and pouring out upon us what God would give us to save our souls, to transform our lives and to sanctify us after his image. All this was foretold in the Scriptures and was foreordained by God; the Jesus of history was the Christ of the Scriptures. This new understanding of the Saviour was the Spirit's culminating work in Peter at Pentecost; it was the foundation for his whole future ministry as an apostle of Christ.

May we all see the Saviour in this same light! May our minds be illumined like Peter's, and like his may our souls be convinced, so that with a similar sense of glory and privilege we may go out into a dying world with a living Lord and Christ to declare and to show forth in our lives.

28.
The Holy Spirit and Peter's will

The fact that the Holy Spirit not only controlled Peter's tongue and personality and mind, but also marvellously re-energized his will, is clearly illustrated by a look at just one passage, Acts 3:1—10. Here we see that Peter is no longer a vacillating weakling; he has become a man of resolve who knows his Lord's will and is determined to do it, whatever the cost to himself.

Many of us have undoubtedly sometimes gone Peter's way and have been very weak-willed: we have known what was right, but have been unable to act on that knowledge. Ultimately the only answer to this kind of situation lies in the might and grace of the Holy Spirit working unhindered upon our wills, infusing them with his direction and his motivation. And he did such a work for Peter. In Acts 3:1—10 we witness Peter's maintenance of unity with his brother apostle, John, his perseverance in some measure of loyalty to the Jerusalem temple and his continuation of the ministry begun by his Lord Jesus Christ. To focus on Peter is not to imply that the Spirit did not do a similar work upon John's will and the wills of the other disciples. He did; these men could not otherwise have functioned together as a unified fellowship. But here we are looking particularly at the evidences of his work in the strong will of Simon Peter, whose history we are tracing.

Peter's maintenance of unity with John

> 'One day Peter and John were going up to the temple . . .' (Acts 3:1).

Some apparently simple statements have much more to
them than meets the eye. If the wills of Peter and John
had not been miraculously influenced by the Holy Spirit,
this statement could never have been written. Behind it
lies a whole unrecorded story of profound renewal and
transformation. Here were Peter and John going *together*
up to the temple, when, without this work of the Spirit
on their wills, Peter might have been going one way and
John another. Not only might their own relationship have
been strained to the point of rupture, they might very well
have become so antagonistic to each other that the whole
company of believers would have been split into two factions, one group marshalled behind Peter, the other behind
John. Two factors in particular might well have severed
the links of friendship and fellowship between these two
men.

Their different temperaments

Just as Peter was a man of strong emotion, impulsive action
and sudden decision, John was the exact opposite by this
time, it would appear: with one or two recorded exceptions,
the 'son of thunder' (Mark 3:17) has become as sanguine
as Peter was choleric. In the 'prologue' of his Gospel, for
example (John 1:1—18), we find John's personality vividly
demonstrated: he was profound and thoughtful; he delved
deeply into things; he expressed himself with warmth and
affection.

Yet, 'Peter and John were going up to the temple.' They
were united in soul and spirit. And this was indicative of the
might and the grace of the Holy Spirit alone. These two
men had worked together as fishermen and they had received
their Lord's calling and teaching together. But they knew
no such unity as this until the Holy Spirit came down and
welded them together with his indwelling, controlling
power — so much so that, even after the sound 'like the
blowing of a violent wind' (Acts 2:2) had ceased, and 'what
seemed to be tongues of fire' (2:3) had passed away, the
effect of the Spirit's ministry at Pentecost remained constant.
For Peter and John now not only had Christ outside of
them, sitting on the throne and interceding for them; they
also had Christ within them, by the Spirit, controlling their

wills and enabling them to maintain their 'unity of the Spirit through the bond of peace' (Ephesians 4:3). Peter's will, in particular, was strengthened so that temperamental differences were not allowed to disturb his unity with John. For where personality differences are great, unity between believers can be maintained *only by an act of will*; conversely, where wills are weak, this kind of unity is rarely found.

Their different vocational roles

Peter and John were appointed to very different vocational roles by our Lord and because of this, without the restraining, unifying work of the Spirit upon their wills, they might have become bitter opponents. They began life together and shared the same work as fishermen on the Sea of Galilee. They were neighbours and they were partners of sorts (cf. Luke 5:10), though we are not sure what this partnership actually entailed. Then Peter and John were called by our Lord at the same time to be his disciples (Matthew 4:18, 21; Luke 5:10) and along with James, the brother of John, they constituted an inner circle of disciples who were especially close to Jesus. But there were constant undertones of rivalry and competition even among these very privileged disciples as they followed our Lord during his life.

For instance, when it became apparent that Jesus was going to be King, the mother of John and James made a special approach to Jesus and asked him to appoint her sons to the top positions in the kingdom, one sitting at his right hand and the other at his left hand (Matthew 20:20,21). Whether or not this was with the connivance of her sons, we do not know; probably it was. In any case, our Lord did not grant the woman's request; instead, the power of the keys went to Peter! And there, grace apart, are all the ingredients for a deep-seated family and personal feud and for a long-standing grievance between the one man and the other. One can almost hear the mother's complaint: 'What, that loud fellow Peter made leader, and my James and my John turned down?' If this had aroused jealousy in John, it could have poisoned their own relationship, set their families at variance and even divided the disciples into two opposing camps.

Another incident which shows how sensitive things could be between Peter and John is one recorded by John himself at the end of his Gospel. Beside that charcoal fire by the Sea of Galilee, Peter had just confessed his love for Jesus and he had received the threefold commission from our Lord which reinstated him as his loyal follower. When Jesus then warned Peter that one day he would be bound and martyred for his loyalty, Peter immediately 'turned and saw that the disciple whom Jesus loved was following them. (This was the one who had leaned back against Jesus at the supper . . .) When Peter saw him, he asked, "Lord, what about him?" Jesus answered, "If I want him to remain alive until I return, what is that to you? You must follow me"' (John 21:20,22). Notice, Peter was less concerned about the seriousness of his own fate than with how it would compare with John's fate. There were indeed many latent possibilities of disruption, grievance and misunderstanding between these two men.

But now 'Peter and John were going up to the temple.' Arguing? Bickering? Turning their faces away, not wanting to see each other? No. They were now one in the Spirit, irrespective of differences in gifts or calling or personalities. By the power of the Spirit, they persevered in the maintenance of their God-given unity against all potentially divisive factors. The once very weak-willed Peter was as resolved as John to honour his Lord and the Spirit, so that he and John might labour together in the will of God.

Peter's perseverance in loyalty to the Jerusalem temple

'One day Peter and John were going up to the temple at the time of prayer — at three in the afternoon' (3:1).

The temple was successor to the tabernacle, or Tent of Meeting, which the Israelites built in the wilderness following their exodus from Egypt. It was at the Tent of Meeting that God met with his people; here he revealed himself to them and they worshipped him. And as God moved in the pillar of cloud, so did the people move and the tabernacle with them; they carried it on to the next pause in their wanderings and erected it again for worship (cf. Numbers 10:17,21). The temple which succeeded that Tent of Meeting was a permanent structure located in the heart of the city of Jerusalem, first built by King Solomon (1 Kings 6).

Our Lord Jesus Christ had considerable respect for the temple as an institution. He called it 'the house of God' (Matthew 12:4), 'a house of prayer for all nations' (Mark 11:17), and 'my Father's house' (John 2:16). He knew that its basic contents were sanctified by God (Matthew 23:17, 21) and, knowing that, showed a burning zeal for its cleansing when he saw that greed and avarice had led to its desecration. In this connection, in fact, our Lord did one of the most daring things ever done even by him: he single-handedly whipped the desecrators out of the temple (John 2:15). And he wept when he foresaw the temple's destruction, along with that of the rebellious city where it stood (Luke 19:41).

Apart from the ritual and sacrificial activity that went on in the Jerusalem temple, there were also certain set seasons of prayer. The Jewish day began at six o'clock in the morning and continued until six o'clock at night — a twelve-hour day. During that time there were three set seasons of prayer in the temple, the first at the third hour, the second at the sixth hour, the third at the ninth hour. In other words, Jewish worshippers met in the temple for the offering of prayer to God at 9 in the morning, 12 noon and 3 in the afternoon. Peter and John were on their way to the afternoon session, then, on the day in question here — it was 'three in the afternoon' (literally, 'the ninth hour') (3:1).

Now, the apostles' perseverance in respect for and attendance at the set services of the temple betokened very great grace. Not only did the temple epitomize opposition to their Lord throughout his entire public ministry; it was also the headquarters of the Sadducean party that had ultimately brought about his crucifixion. So Peter and John might well have turned their backs on the temple; impulse and human reasoning, at least, would certainly have seen such withdrawal as justified. But God had not yet completely withdrawn from the temple; how then could his saints legitimately do so? Therefore these two Spirit-filled men went up to the temple. Probably only by an enormous exercise of will-power did they make their way to those arid, formal rituals that constituted the hour of prayer. Probably only through resisting a natural inclination to do directly the opposite did they resolutely do the will of God. And only because their wills were now controlled by the Spirit of God did Peter and John have this grace to do his will rather than their own.

'The Spirit is present outside the temple'

How easy it would have been for Peter and John to argue, for example, that because the Holy Spirit had not come down upon the temple-goers in the exercise of their temple worship on the Day of Pentecost, but rather upon the 120 believers (1:15) who were meeting elsewhere, therefore God had no more use for the temple, and therefore there was no more need to attend its rituals and services. But, controlled as their wills were by the Holy Spirit, Peter and John did not try to make his presence outside the temple an excuse for not doing what the Lord required of them. To reason in this way would not only have been illogical; it would also have violated the divine plan for the temple. God had not yet said his last word to the temple-goers. His infinite mercy was such that he would still seek the ears and the hearts of those who had rejected his Son. In fact, he was planning to reach some of them that very afternoon through the presence of Peter and John in the temple at the set hour of prayer. He was going to gather his elect that very day, out of the heart of that spiritually desolate place.

We need to learn from this that God does not easily give men up to their sins, even when we would judge that they have gone beyond the possibility of redemption. We must be careful lest we arrogantly behave as if we were holier or more zealous than he is. To turn our backs on a divine institution such as the temple requires infinitely more justification than a mere argument provides. God himself must first make clear that such withdrawal is in accordance with his will.

'The Spirit is not present inside the temple'

Peter and John might have argued, from the other side, that there was no presence of the Spirit inside the temple; therefore they would not go there to pray. This charge would have been quite accurate at the time: dominated by a Sadducean influence that had scant respect either for the Scriptures or for the supernatural, the temple services could hardly be said to be under the blessing of the Spirit of Christ. The temple priests and worshippers appeared to be spiritually dead. Indeed, Peter and John could have argued that it would be spiritually defiling and physically dangerous to associate with that impenitent crowd of worshippers who, not all that long ago, had let the Son of God be crucified, if they had not actually demanded his death. Christ-honouring believers should surely stay away from this kind of company!

But such arguments against 'the establishment' can be more logical than spiritual, and we need to be very chary about using them. Had Peter and John reasoned in this way, it would, in fact, have been a great tragedy. Not only would a man who was lame from his mother's womb have missed divine healing, but his soul, along with those of the five thousand others who were gathered into the kingdom in the wake of his healing, might still be in darkness to this day. God is justified in forsaking men and institutions at any time; in this case, he certainly would have been justified in never uttering a word of mercy to Jerusalem again. But he desired otherwise. His heart still yearned to reach his people there. And while God still wants to reach an institution or a society, God's people must be careful not to withdraw from it. Heaven only knows how many souls are still in the power of evil today because some of us have withdrawn from places or people God still wanted to reach.

Peter and John did not try to argue against 'the establishment'. Thanks to the ministry of the Spirit upon their wills, they were enabled to do God's bidding rather than follow their own natural reasoning and inclination: they were together in doing what God required of them at that moment. The time would come (in A.D. 70) when God would turn his back upon the city of Jerusalem, the temple and the nation, but that time was not yet. Peter and John, therefore, could not legitimately turn their backs on the temple; in fact their presence in it that day was divinely ordained.

Peter's continuation of Christ's ministry

> *'In the name of Jesus Christ of Nazareth, walk'*
> *(Acts 3:6).*

Because Peter and John were determined to be loyal to their Lord and his Spirit, what emerges in the book of Acts is not simply a spiritual ministry, not simply a Christian ministry, but the continuation of the very ministry that Jesus himself began. This is how Luke opens the book of Acts: 'In my former book [the Gospel of Luke], Theophilus, I wrote about all that Jesus *began to do and to teach*' (Acts 1:1). What Jesus began to do and to teach, he continued to do through his apostles, by means of the Spirit's indwelling and the Word of the gospel. The unbroken continuity between what Jesus began and what now followed would not have been possible without steadfastness of purpose and strength of will on the apostles' part, enabled by the Spirit. In this Acts 3 context, Peter especially, in healing the paralytic man, manifests a continuity of the same compassion and daring and power that characterized Jesus' earthly ministry.

The same compassion

Near the Beautiful Gate of the temple, Peter and John come across a lame man, begging. He has been crippled from birth (3:2), and he is now over forty years of age (4:22). Having given up all hope of ever walking again, this man is resigned to trying to eke out some sort of living through begging. There he sits. And filled with compassion for him, Peter, through the power of the Spirit, speaks words to him that bring about his miraculous healing. This incident could very well belong to one of the Gospels which record our Lord's own acts of healing, for it perfectly exemplifies his own spirit of compassion. In fact it bears great similarities to two specific accounts of healing by Jesus himself. In Luke 5 we read of another paralytic who was brought into the presence of our Lord, carried by four friends. Jesus had compassion on him and healed him and saved him, saying, 'I tell you, get up, take your mat and go home' (Luke 5:24). That terse language resembles Peter's words to the beggar in this Acts 3 episode: 'In the name of Jesus Christ of Nazareth, walk' (3:6).

And in John 5 we read of another man, probably also a paralytic, one of the many 'blind, . . . lame, . . . paralysed' invalids (John 5:3) lying by the Pool of Bethesda, a man who had been ill for thirty-eight years. With the same swift understanding and terse speech that characterized the other healing, Jesus had compassion upon this man and made him well also.

And so here, just as the Saviour's heart went out to people in their suffering, so the hearts of Peter and John go out to this lame man. This compassion of our Lord continuing to be expressed in his people is beautiful to behold, but it is no automatic thing: it happens only when the wills of men, as well as their minds and hearts, are under the power of the Holy Spirit.

The same daring

We can never be loyal to our Lord without a measure of daring. We have to have God-given courage, for many things cannot be done without it. This miracle of healing takes place right outside the door of the temple! Peter and John call on the power of Jesus' name before the very eyes of those who had wanted him crucified and had blindly refused to accept the testimony of his own 'miraculous signs' (cf. John 2:11) when he was among them. That is daring in the extreme.

And it is exactly what Jesus did: he worked some of his mightiest miracles right in front of his bitterest foes. The miracle to which we have just referred in Luke 5, for instance, he performed in front of a whole gathering of scribes and Pharisees. These people who claimed to understand and interpret the law correctly had come from 'every village' of Galilee and Judea and from Jerusalem to scrutinize Jesus (Luke 5:17). And what he did was exactly what Peter and John do now: he healed the paralytic man by his own power, as a sign of his deity and messiahship. Again, Jesus performed the miracle to which we have just referred in John 5 beside the Pool of Bethesda, which was scarcely a stone's throw from the temple. Just as their Lord went into enemy territory in the power of the Spirit then, so do Peter and John go now.

The same power

Jesus was crucified, but his power is unabated. Jesus is ascended into heaven, but his power still prevails upon earth. Speaking to the beggar who waits with his hand outstretched, Peter says, in effect: 'Sorry to disappoint you, but I am not the type of man who has any silver or gold to spare. Just take a good look at us both, and you will see we're not rich!' Then, just as the man is going to withdraw his hand: '. . . *but what I have I give you. In the name of Jesus Christ of Nazareth, walk' (3:6).*

Here is the power of God. Pulled to his feet by Peter, this man who has never walked before now finds that his ankle-bones and his feet are strong, and he enters into the temple with Peter and John, full of the joy of redemption and of healing, 'walking and jumping, and praising God' (3:8). He gives God the glory, for the act of healing is so evidently supernatural and divine. The power of the Lord is still present in the world, through the Spirit, in his Spirit-filled apostles.

This continuity of Jesus' ministry challenges both his enemies and his friends. One thing in particular that we as his followers need to notice here is the power of the Holy Spirit to strengthen the human will. Only by an act of will, through the Spirit, are Peter and John able to maintain unity with each other in spite of many human differences. Only by an act of will, through the Spirit, are they enabled obediently to go up to the temple at the set hour of prayer. And only because they have been obedient in this way to their Lord's requirements, are they in the right place at the right time to channel his power of healing to the paralytic man.

It is so easy to lose heart and to come to terms with the flesh and the devil; it is so easy to settle for a kind of personal and church life that bears hardly any resemblance to that of our Lord and his apostles. Paul paints a vivid picture of our choice: 'So I say, live by the Spirit, and you will not gratify the desires of the sinful nature. For the sinful nature desires what is contrary to the Spirit, and the Spirit what is contrary to the sinful nature. They are in conflict with each other, so that you do not do what you want. The acts of the sinful nature are obvious: sexual immorality, impurity and debauchery; idolatry and witch-craft; hatred, discord, jealousy, fits of rage, selfish ambition, dissensions, factions and envy; drunkenness, orgies, and the like. I warn you, as I did before, that those who live like this will not inherit the kingdom of God. But the fruit of the Spirit is love, joy, peace, patience, kindness, good-ness, faithfulness, gentleness and self-control . . . Those who belong to Christ Jesus have crucified the sinful nature with its passions and desires' (Galatians 5:16, 17, 19—24).

We are called upon to be witnesses to the living Lord Jesus Christ, but we can be that only insofar as there is evident continuity between what he did and the way he did it, and what we do and the way we do it. There may have been certain gifts that were meant specifically for the apostolate, but it does not alter the principle. If the Spirit of Christ lives on in us, if the Word of Christ is given to us and we believe and proclaim that Word, then there should be some tokens of his presence with us and within us, just as in the case of Peter and John — something of his com-passion, something of his courage, and something of his Spirit's work.

Through the Spirit's power over our wills, we need to be steadfast in guarding the unity which he gave to his people, we need to prove our loyalty to every divine ordi-nance unless God releases us from our obligation to do so, and we need to be sure that we express in our lives some-thing of our Lord's life and grace and power. Let us pray that the Holy Spirit of God will strengthen our wills for these things.

Make me a captive, Lord,
And then I shall be free;
Force me to render up my sword,
And I shall conqueror be.
I sink in life's alarms
When by myself I stand;
Imprison me within thine arms,
And strong shall be my hand.

My heart is weak and poor
Until it master find;
It has no spring of action sure —
It varies with the wind.
It cannot freely move,
Till thou hast wrought its chain;
Enslave it with thy matchless love,
And deathless it shall reign.

My power is faint and low
Till I have learned to serve;
It wants the needed fire to glow,
It wants the breeze to nerve;
It cannot drive the world,
Until itself be driven;
Its flag can only be unfurled
When thou shalt breathe from heaven

My will is not my own
Till thou hast made it thine;
If it would reach a monarch's throne
It must its crown resign;
It only stands unbent,
Amid the clashing strife,
When on thy bosom it has leant,
And found in thee its life

George Matheson (1842—1906).

29.
The Holy Spirit and self-interest

It is generally true to say that when we see self-interest in other people, we consider it to be extremely obnoxious. Call it any name at all — plain, downright 'selfishness', or 'egoism', or 'self-centredness', or 'self-indulgence' — when it appears in others we easily see it for what it is, and we denounce it. But when it appears in ourselves, the strange thing is, not only do we often fail to see it for what it is, but in fact, this thing that we find to be so reprehensible in others, we may even find to be justifiable for us. Such is our nature.

Biblically considered, human self-interest reflects that grave condition of moral topsy-turvydom that entered our world with the Fall of man and the emergence of sin. In its perversity, self-interest readily turns a blind eye to the deserts of God and other people in order to focus on the interests of self alone. The self-centred person thinks chiefly of his own desires, his own will, his own image; God's will and God's glory are absolutely secondary (if they matter at all) and so is serving others. In greater or lesser measure, self-interest afflicts all the Adamic family; no human being is free of it. And so it appears everywhere, sometimes even in places where you would least expect to find it, not only in secular life but in the life of the church as well.

It is true that God often mitigates the effect of human self-interest. Concerned as he is for both the world and the church, he does restrain the sinfulness of mankind within certain limits, and he gives to mankind a certain grace that is common to everyone. Not, however, until this earth is finally purged of sin, not until that great day of which Peter writes, when all that now is shall be burned with fire, and 'a new heaven and a new earth' shall emerge as 'the home of righteousness' (2 Peter 3:13), not until Satan is finally bound and cast into the lake of fire (Revelation 20:10) — not until then will this deadly soul-worm finally be eradicated from human life.

In common with the rest of humanity, Peter knew something of this inbred tendency to self-interest. We have seen enough evidence of it in his life that it is sufficient now to refer to just one instance: in the very last incident recorded about Peter in the Gospels, we see him still reacting in a typically self-interested way. When Jesus warns him that there will come a time in his life when he will be bound and taken to a place where he would rather not go (a figurative allusion to Peter's ultimate martyrdom), Peter's instinctive reaction is to compare his fate with John's: 'Are you telling me that I've got to suffer? Well, what about John? Won't he have to suffer, too?' This is unabashed self-interest. Even after our Lord's resurrection and his reinstatement of Peter, self-interest still clouds Peter's attitude and thought.

But our concern now is to show how the grace of God overcame the self-interest in Peter's life. This is the good news and the message of the gospel! No matter how self-concerned Peter may have been at any given time, by the power of the Spirit he changed. Acts 3 and 4 form an expanded record of the consequences of the miracle of healing which Peter and John performed in Jesus' name and which we considered in the last chapter. Here we see in Peter a man whose frame of reference is no longer himself first and foremost — his own will and his own ambition being the motivating forces of his life. His frame of reference now is God first and foremost — God's will and God's glory are now the prime considerations of his life. Peter's new attitude is reflected in his refusal to accept any glory for himself (Acts 3:12,16) and in his obedient respect for God's authority above all other authority (Acts 4:8—12,19,20).

The glory Peter refused

The miracle performed by Peter and John on the crippled man by the Beautiful Gate of the temple was an event of extraordinary significance to those who witnessed it. It was wholly unexpected and humanly inexplicable.

> 'When all the people saw [the former cripple] walking and praising God, they recognized him as the same man who used to sit begging at the temple gate called Beautiful, and they were filled with wonder and amazement at what had happened to him' (Acts 3:9,10).

Day in and day out over the long years, this man had been carried by kindly friends to the temple gate, where he had become part and parcel of the landscape. He was known by everybody who regularly worshipped at the temple and who entered through this gate; they had seen him many a time, stretching out his hand and begging for money with which to eke out his existence as a cripple. The fact that he chose to be brought back again and again to the temple shows that the temple-goers were sympathetic towards him and gave him alms. But it would never have crossed their minds to try to bring healing to this man: he was a confirmed cripple, and that was how he would live out his life and die.

Then came Peter and John. They looked no different from the other temple-goers, except for their obvious poverty, but they did for this man what no other temple-goer could do — they healed him through the name of Jesus Christ of Nazareth. For Peter and John had something that the temple and the common Jewish people did not. They knew that Jesus was the Christ, the Messiah of the Scriptures. They knew that he had died for the sins of men, had risen again and was now given all authority in heaven and on earth (Matthew 28:18). They knew that he had commissioned them to go and make disciples of all nations (Matthew 28:19), waiting first in Jerusalem until they were given power from on high (Luke 24:49). And they knew that when the Holy Spirit had come down upon them at Pentecost, he had given them that power: many wonders and miraculous signs had already been done through the apostles (Acts 2:43). Knowing, therefore, that they had the resources of their Master at their command,

Peter and John gave the crippled man what they had —
healing. Peter said, 'In the name of Jesus Christ of Nazareth,
walk' (3:6). And the man did. And he went into the temple
with Peter and John, 'walking and jumping, and praising
God' (3:8) for his deliverance.

The opportunity for self-interest

Put yourself in Peter's shoes: you are responsible for bringing the grace of God to this man; you have said and done
everything that was said and done, as far as the human eye
can see. Surely, then, it is right and legitimate for you now
to accept the praise of men! Surely you should now enjoy
the gratitude of the healed man and the admiration of all
the temple-goers who see the change in him! Surely you
should now be right in the centre of the stage, in the lime-
light! After all, if you had not come this way, the man
would still be a cripple!

For Peter and John, here is an opportunity second to
none. If they let this incident be publicized, their lives
are made! They have healed a man who was crippled for
forty years. This healing is no fraud: there are many witnesses to its validity. Their fame is certain; they can have
easy access to every town in the land as long as they bring
their healing power with them. They have made a name
for themselves; popularity and a great following are virtually
guaranteed now.

How would you react? Such is natural, human self-interest
that most men would give almost anything for such a
moment of glory as this. Most men would leap at the chance
for such praise and honour by others.

The fidelity of Spirit-filled men

But how do Peter and John react? The facts of Scripture are
as startling as was the miracle of healing. For they actually
back away from the praise of men as if they are allergic to
it! Far from enjoying the crowd's adulation, they rebuke
the crowd for it and point away from themselves to the great
Healer whose power they have merely channelled. Nor is
their refusal to heed the praise of men due to any psychological aberration: time was when they would have loved to
be in the public eye, when self would have claimed that place
by right.

But now they are different. They have become spiritually sensitive to the prior claims of the one who is beyond and before them, and that is their God. They know that they have been just the frail human agents in this mighty act of healing; for them to take the credit would be to rob God of his exclusive due. With all the persuasive power at their command, then, they divert the admiring eyes of men from themselves to him who really worked the miracle. Their fidelity to God is as undoubted as their confession is clear. Listen to Peter, speaking for them both: 'Men of Israel, does this surprise you? Why do you stare at us as if by our own power or godliness *we* had made this man walk? The God of Abraham, Isaac and Jacob, the God of our fathers, has glorified his servant Jesus . . . By faith in the name of Jesus, this man whom you see and know was made strong. It is Jesus' name and the faith that comes through him that has given this complete healing to him, as you can all see' (3:12,13,16).

Such rejection of praise from men betokens a great work of the Spirit's power over self-interest in Peter and John. Such concern to give God the glory that belongs to him, and not to divert one single ray of it to oneself, reveals a rich spiritual maturity. Self lies crucified; God is really enthroned in the heart.

This is spoken of in various ways throughout the New Testament. This is what Paul has in mind, for instance, when he urges the Christians in Rome to consider themselves 'dead to sin and alive to God in Christ Jesus' (Romans 6:11). They are to be sensitive to the deserts of God and to what he requires in any given situation. This is what the catechism means when it asks, 'What is the chief end of man?' and answers, 'Man's chief end is to glorify God, and to enjoy him forever.' Man's chief end is so to order his life that 'in all things God may be praised through Jesus Christ' (1 Peter 4:11), as Peter himself later writes. And Paul shows how this applies to everything we do: 'So whether you eat or drink or whatever you do, do it all for the glory of God' (1 Corinthians 10:31).

We need to ask ourselves how far it can be said that the glory of God is the primary concern of our lives. For how many of us is it the chief goal of living, and not just one

among many goals? How far is it the thing for which we set
out into each new day — the thing for which we run our
businesses, teach our classes, do whatever our daily routine
entails? Life provides us with almost limitless opportunities
for glorifying God in one way or another, for 'magnifying'
him in the eyes of others. How dedicated are we to this
high calling? Or how often do we accept for ourselves what
belongs only to him? The Bible gives us ample room to
conclude that the cardinal sin in this world is to rob God
of his glory. Peter and John have much to teach us here,
through the Spirit.

The authority Peter respected

As we move into Acts 4, we meet another example of the
same God-glorifying attitude on the part of Peter and John;
here it takes the form of respect for God's authority, even
at risk of death. They refuse to obey any authority that
would prevent them from doing what God's glory requires
them to do — namely to witness by life and by word to the
resurrection of Jesus Christ.

The Sanhedrin and its requirement

As we saw earlier, a great commotion followed the
miraculous healing of the crippled man; temple-goers
gathered round in 'wonder and amazement' (3:10). The
miracle was so obviously genuine that it could not be denied.
How, though, could it be accounted for? Peter then proceeded to explain that it was a deed worked through the
name of Jesus — the Jesus whom the God of Abraham and
of Isaac and of Jacob had sent into the world as his Messiah,
but whom the Jews, on their part, had denied and killed.
God had raised him from the dead and now the living Lord's
name, 'by faith in the name of Jesus' (3:16) had made the
cripple well. Having been given this sign of Jesus' messiahship, therefore (Isaiah, for example, had prophesied that in
the messianic age 'the lame [would] leap like a deer', Isaiah
35:6), the Jews should repent of their killing of 'the author
of life' (3:15) and accept the salvation that God offered in
sending his servant 'to bless you by turning each of you

from your wicked ways' (3:26). We read that 'many who heard the message believed, and the number of men [alone] grew to about five thousand' (4:4).

When, however, 'the priests and the captain of the temple guard and the Sadducees' (4:1) discovered what was going on, and realized that Peter and John were publicly attributing this healing to the power of the risen Lord Jesus Christ, they were greatly disturbed because the apostles were teaching the people and proclaiming in Jesus the resurrection of the dead. They seized Peter and John and, because it was evening, put them in jail until the next day' (4:2,3). Next day, the Sanhedrin met to investigate the incident and to interrogate Peter and John (4:5—7).

Dominated by Sadducees, the Sanhedrin was the supreme court of Jewry — a most august assembly. As it was then constituted, it must have been the identical body that had demanded and later secured the death of Jesus. This fact in itself would be enough to arouse all kinds of fears in the hearts of Peter and John, but, further to that, the Sadducees were known for their stubborn antipathy to any belief in supernatural phenomena, such as the resurrection from the dead. It must have seemed to Peter and John that, humanly speaking, all the odds were against them in this interrogation.

Yet here they stood, next day, these two ordinary, uneducated men, accused before this high court. Already they had tasted something of the Sanhedrin's authority in their peremptory overnight imprisonment. Now they were required by 'Annas the high priest . . . Caiaphas, John, Alexander and the other men of the high priest's family' (4:6) to give an account of the miracle: 'By what power or what name did you do this?' (4:7.) The question was really a dare: would these men dare to repeat what they had said yesterday?

The apostles and their response

Neither cowed into silence nor frightened into a compromise, Peter and John accepted the challenge and boldly faced the august assembly.

> Then Peter, filled with the Holy Spirit, said to them: 'Rulers and elders of the people! If we

*are being called to account today for an act of
kindness shown to a cripple and are asked how he
was healed, then know this, you and everyone
else in Israel: It is by the name of Jesus Christ
of Nazareth, whom you crucified but whom God
raised from the dead, that this man stands before
you completely healed. He is "the stone you
builders rejected, which has become the capstone".
Salvation is found in no one else, for there is no
other name under heaven given to men by which
we must be saved' (4:8–12).*

Fearless of the Sanhedrin, despite its record of falsely
accusing and ultimately crucifying their Lord, despite its
obvious and ultimate power and despite the various forms
of punishment it could inflict upon Peter and John, these
men refused to deny what they had said the previous day.
'Filled with the Holy Spirit,' and thereby enabled to be
victorious over all considerations of self, they were loyal
to their risen Lord, obedient to their calling and faithful
to the truth.

'When they saw the courage of Peter and John,' the
Sanhedrin, strangely enough, 'were astonished' (4:13).
And seeing the healed man, 'there was nothing they could
say' (4:14). Realizing that they could not deny the fact
of the miracle, and made cautious by the crowd's positive
response to the preaching of Peter and John, the Sanhedrin
decided to let the men off with a warning: henceforth
they were 'not to speak or teach at all in the name of Jesus'
(4:18). Hear the instantaneous response of Peter and John:
*'Judge for yourselves whether it is right in God's sight to
obey you rather than God. For we cannot help speaking
about what we have seen and heard' (4:19,20).* The apostles
knew the stature of this court and they were not lacking in
respect for the Sanhedrin as such. But they were under
covenant to a greater authority — God's authority; therefore they could accept no rule which ran counter to his.
They must speak of what they had seen and heard.

What was at issue here was not a subjective experience
of any kind — a feeling of 'being led' which by definition
no one else can ever deny. What was at issue was a cluster

of verified facts, all of them resting on the one basic fact that God had raised Jesus the Messiah from the dead (3:15; 4:10). Peter and John were pledged, commissioned (1:8) witnesses to the truth of the resurrection of their Lord. They were also witnesses to the truth that God had raised Jesus to his right hand and had given him the Holy Spirit to share with his church, that the Holy Spirit had come in power at Pentecost and that the continuance of messianic blessings among men was evident in such manifestations as the healing of the cripple. And so, whether men liked it or not, and whether it meant life or death to themselves, Peter and John had to speak about what they had seen and heard and knew to be true.

And yet, how easy it would have been to act otherwise! Put yourself in Peter's shoes again. You have just spent a night in jail, and now the authorities have granted you your freedom on condition that you never again mention the name of this person whom you know to be risen from the dead. If you keep your mouth shut, your feet will remain free! How would you feel? Wouldn't you think of your comfortable home, the glories of liberty, the preciousness of being able to go about your business just as you please? Wouldn't there be a great temptation to self-interest — even to 'enlightened self-interest', as the phrase goes today? Wouldn't it be wise just to agree to be silent?

But Peter and John did not acquiesce. By the power of the Holy Spirit, they were victorious over self. Truth was more important to them than freedom and comfort. The necessity to witness to their Lord as God's promised Messiah would not even allow them to contemplate putting their own safety first. God's will and God's glory were what mattered now. He required their witness, therefore he must have it; he controlled their lives, therefore he could do what he liked with them. They were prepared to forego everything and to suffer anything in order to give God his due glory and to respect his absolute authority. What a remarkable change this exhibits, especially in Peter. In place of the old impetuous, unstable Simon there stood a new man of strong convictions, selfless courage and unflinching consistency.

How far is this true of us? How goes the battle against

self in our lives? Whose glory do we consider to be more important, our own or God's? Which authority, ultimately do we accept as final — human or divine? When last, at any cost to ourselves, did we seek God's glory over our own, or acknowledge his authority over every other? For it hardly matters what other experiences we may claim to have: they cannot be very significant if we rob God of glory, or if we have another authority in our lives that is greater than his.

May the same mighty Saviour who through his Spirit transformed Simon also pursue his gracious work in us. May we be able to say with Paul, 'I have been crucified with Christ and I no longer live, but Christ lives in me' (Galatians 2:20). And may we pray in the words of the hymn:

> O Jesus Christ, grow thou in me,
> And all things else recede!
> My heart be daily nearer thee,
> From sin be daily freed.
>
> Make this poor self grow less and less,
> Be thou my life and aim;
> Oh, make me daily, through thy grace,
> More worthy of thy name.
>
> Johann Caspar Lavater (1741—1801)
> trans. by Elizabeth Lee Smith (1817—1898)

30.
The Holy Spirit and prayer

Pentecost was a truly remarkable landmark in the life of the church: after Pentecost everything seems to change. However much the disciples may have matured along certain lines beforehand, for example, after Pentecost they seem to spring forward into fulness of life. Jesus had told them: 'You will receive power when the Holy Spirit comes on you' (Acts 1:8). The Greek word for 'power' here is *'dunamis'*, from which our English word 'dynamite' comes. It may be that this is the key to an understanding of the disciples' sudden leap into maturity; 'dynamite' perhaps is the word that properly describes the gift of God to his people in the sending of the Holy Spirit. For through the power they received at Pentecost, they were enabled to do many things they had never done before.

This is nowhere more evident than in the area of prayer. According to the Gospel records, the disciples learned much about prayer during Jesus' earthly ministry. They seem to have overheard their Master praying on certain occasions, and witnessed his entering into the presence of God with the total filial confidence of a child (Matthew 6:7–13). They received instruction from him as to the nature of true prayer (Matthew 6:5–15; Mark 11:20–25; Luke 11:1–13; 18:1–14). But they themselves are not recorded as having prayed much; indeed, the three disciples who were closest to Jesus were unable to stay awake to pray with him in Gethsemane (Matthew 26:40). We may conclude, therefore, that during our Lord's lifetime the prayer life of the disciples left much to be desired.

No sooner are we in the book of Acts, however, than we find these men to be on an altogether different level of spiritual life: time and time again it is reported that they pray. The only logical conclusion we can draw from this change is that one of the benefits of Pentecost is the transformation of our Lord's followers into men of prayer. Faced with evidently greater needs than ever, they are marvellously endowed with the capacity to ask and pray as Jesus had taught them. Through the Spirit's enabling power these men now know God as very real; and in their new-found awareness of his reality they are emboldened to approach him. Constantly they bring their burdens and their joys to him in prayer. To see what this transformation in their prayer life entails, let us look at the prayer which is recorded by Luke in Acts 4:23−30, noticing the concept of God that lies behind it, the content of the prayer itself and its consequences in the life of the Christian community and beyond. Although Peter does not feature here as an individual, he is certainly present as a participant (4:23). Thus we may safely assume that he shares the group's new understanding of prayer and that he experiences, as part of the group, the fresh downpouring of the Holy Spirit and the renewed sense of unity, charity and witnessing power that ensue.

The underlying concept of God

Prayer necessarily reflects our view of God: in fact it is the living out of what a person believes about him. The man who does not pray does not believe very much. No man believes more about God than he expresses in prayer. The Acts 4 prayer exemplifies these principles; it is a new expression of these early believers' enlarged conception of God.

'Sovereign Lord'

When Peter and John return to their friends after the Sanhedrin interrogation, and report that the chief priests and elders have warned them not to speak or teach again in the name of Jesus, all of the believers together lift up their voices to God and pray: *'Sovereign Lord, you made the heaven and the earth and the sea, and everything in them . . .' (4:24).*

This phrase 'Sovereign Lord' presupposes a concept of God which, unlike many, is anything but 'a compound of vagueness and nothing': it is the essence of precision and significance. 'Sovereign Lord' translates the single Greek word *'despotēs'* which means, first of all, 'one who has unlimited power', and secondly, 'one who has absolute rights of ownership'. These early believers are thinking of God as being absolutely unlimited in power: there is nothing you can ask him that he cannot do; there is no need in the life of his people that he cannot meet. In a word, he is omnipotent. And they are also thinking of God as having absolute proprietorship over the world and over his people: he owns everything; he has the right to everything; particularly, he has the right to use his people as he wills. In the phrase 'Sovereign Lord' Peter and his friends reveal that they view God as having all power and all rights.

And what is our concept of God? I wonder whether we have not suffered very much from the pagan and liberal tendencies of our day, with the result that our idea of God hardly corresponds to the true God at all. Our God does not bring us to our knees very often. And a God who does not bring his alleged people to their knees is no real God: he may be a fanciful toy or an image we have created in our own minds, but if he does not mightily and mercifully bring us down before him, he can hardly be the God of these people of the early church. No one can enter the heights of these early believers' prayer experience who does not come to prayer with the attitude that God is Sovereign Lord.

Petitionary prayer and intercessory prayer have as good as disappeared from many of our Protestant churches today. Many church people never ask God for anything *specific*. To many professing Christians, prayer is just saying nice things about the Deity. While these things may be true and scriptural and elevating in their way, it does not alter the fact that the people uttering them regard God more as an object of admiration than as a person of power. The fact that people do not ask God for specific things implies that basically they do not think of God as *capable* of dealing with these things: they do not recognize either his omnipotence or his right to be involved in all aspects of their

lives. They cannot honestly address God as 'Sovereign Lord!'
And you might as well pray to a lifeless god as pray to a
limited deity.

The Lord of history

Peter and John and their fellows are not trying to be theological or philosophical. But as they pray, their words reveal
their concept of God to be that of a God who reigns omnipotently, not only over the whole impersonal order of
created things, but also over all the affairs of human history
as well.

> '*"Sovereign Lord," they said, ". . . You spoke
> by the Holy Spirit through the mouth of your
> servant, our father David:*
> *'Why do the nations rage
> and the peoples plot in vain?*
> *The kings of the earth take their stand
> and the rulers gather together
> against the Lord and against his Anointed One.'*
> *Indeed Herod and Pontius Pilate met together
> with the Gentiles and the people of Israel in this
> city to conspire against your holy servant Jesus,
> whom you anointed. They did what your power
> and will had decided beforehand should happen"'*
> *(4:24–28).*

Peter and John and their fellows believe God to be the
God of history: he foreordained the events relating to the
life and death of Jesus, and he so controlled his enemies
that, although they did exactly what they pleased and
exactly what their sinful hearts plotted, yet they in fact
ultimately did what God himself had planned and had foretold in Old Testament prophecy. There is great mystery
here which no one can fathom. But we cannot close our
eyes to what we see time and again in human history: God
controls the movements of men without limiting their
freedom of action.

Sometimes God gives the devil enough rope to hang himself. In the context of the life and death of our Lord, in fact,
God gave the devil so much rope that there was enough of

it to hang both himself and everyone associated with him — Herod, Pontius Pilate, all of the Jews and the Gentiles alike who were united against Jesus (Luke 23:7—12) in order to get rid of him. For God had foreordained and foretold through his prophet David (Psalm 2:2) that this very thing should come to pass, and, without limiting their liberty or coercing any of his enemies to act against their will, yet he controlled all of them and made their evil actions serve his righteous ends. His enemies engineered Jesus' death in order to get rid of him; God, in turn, planned and used his death in order that he should rescue the perishing and redeem the lost. God gave his enemies enough freedom to defeat their own purposes. No wonder David writes, 'The One enthroned in heaven laughs; the Lord scoffs at them' (Psalm 2:4). Whatever comes to pass in human history is not, in the long run, what the Herods or the Pilates determine; what comes to pass is what is decreed by God!

This is the concept of God that underlies both this prayer in Acts 4 and the events that follow it (4:32—37). God is not only Lord of the entire creation; he is also the disposer of nations and of men. Having no doubts at all as to their Lord's sovereignty over all events of history, Peter and John and their fellow believers proceed to make confident petitions at his throne.

The content of the prayer

What do these believers ask of God in prayer? It is very challenging to see that, as far as the number of their words is concerned, they ask very little.

> *'Now, Lord, consider their threats and enable your servants to speak your word with great boldness. Stretch out your hand to heal and perform miraculous signs and wonders through the name of your holy servant Jesus' (4:29,30).*

It may well be that the more we believe about God, the less we need to say to him. Conversely, if we have doubts about him, we will go to great lengths to try to persuade him about this or that, and we will take great pains to try to explain all the intricacies of a situation to him. It is as if we were teaching a child at school: 'Now, Lord, do make sure you see this and understand that! And in case you haven't noticed this other thing, let me tell you . . .!' But when we tell God how to get on with his work like this we are really only exposing our own uncertainty about his omnipotence and his sovereignty. And when we are certain about these things, when our concept of God is truly that of 'Sovereign Lord', we do not need to say very much. The petitionary part of this prayer of Peter and his friends amounts to only forty-one words.

Before we look at what they pray for, let us see what they do not pray for. Here the context is important. Peter and John have been warned by the Sanhedrin not to speak or teach at all in the name of Jesus. In answer, the two apostles have affirmed that they must obey God rather than man, and must speak of what they have seen and heard in spite of the Sanhedrin's implied threats. What would *we* ask for in such a situation? Wouldn't many of us come to God and say, 'Look, Lord, these people are causing far too much trouble in the world! Please cut them down to size, or if possible obliterate them! Why should they be allowed to hurt your saints and stand in the way of your Prince Jesus? Why should they be allowed to threaten us when we are devoted to nothing but your honour and glory?' We might pray like that. But these believers do not. They do not ask for any such thing as the supernatural extermination or the ruthless destruction of their enemies. Indeed, what they do ask for sounds almost like an anticlimax.

'Lord, consider their threats'

There is a light touch about this first request. In the Greek, 'consider their threats' is an idiomatic way of asking God simply to keep his eye on things. Knowing their God's wisdom and grace and power, Peter and his friends trust his judgement in the situation and make no attempt to tell him what to do. Nothing could more eloquently express the genuineness of their faith than the brevity of this request. Genuine faith can very often manage with short petitions, even in the face of great danger. As servants of their

'Sovereign Lord', rather than presuming to ask for anything that would mitigate the physical or psychological consequences of discipleship, these people simply ask for their Master's continued oversight of events.

'Enable your servants to speak your word with great boldness'

The word translated 'servants' (*douloi*), actually means 'slaves' here. Seeing themselves as slaves at their Lord's disposal, Peter and John and their fellows ask no greater favour than the privilege of continuing to do his bidding through his emboldening of their hearts. In fact they are asking for strength to do the very thing that the Sanhedrin warned them not to do — 'to speak your [God's] word'. They are saying, in effect, 'Lord, give us the boldness to go on with the job which you have given us to do, not appeasing anyone or compromising your will.'

There are always two approaches to enemies. The one approach is worldly: it can mean shrinking back in fear, or it can mean riding roughshod over our enemies in our own strength. The other approach is spiritual: it means asking God to strengthen us 'with power through his Spirit in [our] inner being' (Ephesians 3:16), so that in the consciousness of his sufficiency we may go on to do his will in his way, irrespective of consequences. This is real victory, for 'the weapons of our warfare are not carnal, but mighty through God' (2 Corinthians 10:4 AV), and as such they embolden the weak to do the will of God, and that alone.

'Stretch out your hand to heal and perform miraculous signs and wonders through the name of your holy servant Jesus'

These servants of their 'Sovereign Lord' are prepared to be implicated in, and embarrassed by, any deed that God performs in the name of Jesus while they 'speak [his] word with great boldness'. Having asked that he should grant them courage to continue to do his will, they now ask that he should continue to do his will through them by magnifying the name of Jesus with healings and 'miraculous signs and wonders'. They are virtually asking to be put on the spot again and again by such miracles as the previous

day's healing of the cripple. If they go to the temple the next
day and meet another lame man, and if it is God's will, then
they are prepared to be caught in the consequences of whatever act he in his wisdom and sovereignty performs. Even
if it means another night in jail for them, or worse, what
matters is 'the name of your holy servant Jesus'. Far from
asking permission to be silent concerning Jesus' name, they
ask that it should be magnified at all costs, with themselves
expendable in the process.

What a prayer this is! I believe that if half a dozen of us
could honestly pray this kind of prayer together, it would
have incredible results. Never mind about us — on with
the King's business, regardless! This kind of prayer will
still move mountains, for it shows the utmost respect for
God and his Son and the gospel, and it is heedless of any
personal cost that obedience to the heavenly vision entails.

The consequences of the prayer

As is always his custom, in response to this prayer God
proved himself and honoured the faith of his people
(4:31—36). His answer had two parts: first, he gave to his
people a fresh infilling of his Spirit which, as they had asked,
inspired them with courage 'to speak [the] word with great
boldness'; secondly, he stretched forth his hand 'to heal'
and to perform 'miraculous signs and wonders', as they had
asked, through granting to the renewed believers themselves
striking outward manifestations of his divine power in the
sight of the unbelieving world.

The fresh infilling of the Spirit

> *'After they prayed, the place where they were
> meeting was shaken. And they were all filled with
> the Holy Spirit and spoke the word of God boldly'
> (4:31).*

No sound 'like the blowing of a violent wind' (2:2) nor
'what seemed to be tongues of fire' (2:3) came into the room
on this occasion. But God did remind his people that he was

the same sovereign Lord who had sent the Holy Spirit at Pentecost: this time the very walls of the place where they were praying began to shake. That was the outward sign of God's answer to his people's prayer for strength; the inward answer was a fresh infilling of his Spirit.

These men had been filled before, at Pentecost, but now they were filled again. Perhaps their capacity for welcoming the divine Guest had increased since then, so that now they could give him a more whole-hearted welcome. Or perhaps, on the other hand, they had lost power and needed to have it replenished. God's Spirit is always fresh and free, and those who learn to pray as these men learned to pray need never live on stale bread and wine. It looks, in fact, as if each new humbling of self and honouring of the Saviour can only result in a new inflow of the Spirit's grace and power. So God assures his loyal people that new demands made upon them cannot fail to meet with fresh supplies from him.

Outward manifestations

The Holy Spirit is never concerned merely with giving us 'kicks', or 'blessings', as we call them; to think this is to be selfish and limited in our Christian outlook. The Spirit's concern goes well beyond such ephemeral, personal experiences to matters of the permanent moral strengthening and beautifying of believers which, being seen by others, will result in the glorification of God. Three outward manifestations of the Spirit's infilling in Peter and John and their friends were a new unity, a new charity and a new credibility such as they had received at Pentecost, and such as are intended to be a continuing gift of God to his church throughout the ages.

1. *A new unity*
'All the believers were one in heart and mind' (4:32a).

Given fresh courage, the disciples apparently took to the streets again to do the very thing the Sanhedrin had warned them not to do — to preach and teach in the name of Jesus. We read that they 'spoke the word of God boldly' (4:31). Apparently, too, their teaching was fruitful in that there were those who believed (4:32). But over and above the miracle of converting these people from sin to Christ, the Holy Spirit worked the further miracle of imparting to the whole community of believers a deep sense of unity: through him, they were all 'one in heart and mind'. This is almost exactly what the Spirit had done at Pentecost, not only among the apostles themselves, but also among them and the new believers that then emerged (compare 2:42–45 with 4:32–35). Such unity was a continuing phenomenon. The unity of the church of Christ is not just something to be celebrated verbally every now and then; it is meant to be an integral, inherent characteristic of the church, as long as God is God and his Spirit is abroad.

Many Christians fail to appreciate the importance of unity. Speak to them about anything else — about some of the phenomena of the Spirit, for instance — and they are enthusiastic. But come down to brass tacks and mention that the fruit of the Spirit is Christian *unity*, then they become rather bored: 'The preacher is a bit jaded now; he's got nothing better to talk about!' But if the Spirit does not make us one with God and one with our brothers, then we had better make sure that no alien spirit is at work in us! Faith in Christ and the fulness of the Spirit necessarily bind us together into one holy, universal whole. Such unity is not externally imposed; it is inwardly discovered, then outwardly expressed.

2. A new charity

'No one claimed that any of his possessions was his own, but they shared everything they had' (4:32b).

This charity had also emerged after the coming of the Spirit at Pentecost (2:44,45). Being richly filled with the Spirit, these people were eager to share both their spiritual and their material benefits with each other. The Spirit of God has a real interest in this kind of sharing. Christians are to hold very loosely what they temporarily possess, and they are to be very sensitive to the needs of other Christians. The outward manifestation of the Spirit's infilling is never, 'This belongs to me and you can't have it,' but rather, 'If I have what you need, come and share it with me.'

Like the believers' new unity, this new spirit of charity was not imposed from outside. No church leaders and no state authorities stood with whips in their hands and told everyone to pool their resources. Nor did the needy ask for help. Rather, because the Spirit of God was in these believers' hearts, the constraint to share came from within. These men *wanted* to share; as they were 'one in heart and mind', so also were they one in what they possessed.

3. *A new credibility*
'With great power the apostles continued to testify to the resurrection of the Lord Jesus, and much grace was with them all' (4:33).

'Great power' and 'much grace', AV, 'great grace'! With 'great power' the apostles gave witness to the fact that Jesus Christ was risen from the dead. Of course, he was risen and he was working with them, by the Spirit — that was the power. But some people have much power and little grace: they can organize and push and boss folk around and get things done, or they can speak the truth very forcefully! The apostles, however, had 'much grace' in addition to their power. As we read on in the book of Acts, we find that the great grace that was manifest in their lives, by the Spirit, meant that what these people taught about the resurrection of the Lord Jesus Christ had *credibility*. Unbelievers were enabled to see that this was no human religion; nor was it the kind of dead religion that had been going on in the temple over the years: this was something new and alive and divine.

All this began with a very short but a very real prayer. Can we follow its pattern, beginning with the acknowledgement of God as Sovereign Lord — the God who has all power and all dominion over every thing and every creature and every person in his universe and throughout all history? Can we too see ourselves as his slaves, committed to doing only what he commands, available to him for whatever purposes he chooses? Then we shall also want to ask him to do this: not to bring comforts to us or exterminate our foes or take away our problems, but to give us such resources as we need to do anything he requires of us, irrespective of consequences.

In response, may the same Spirit of God come over the church again today! May he bring back his abundance of power and grace into the lives of his willing slaves so that, along with new unity and new charity, we shall receive credibility in communicating the life-changing message that is given us to declare in this unbelieving age.

31.
The Holy Spirit and discernment

'Now a man named Ananias, together with his wife Sapphira, also sold a piece of property. With his wife's full knowledge he kept back part of the money for himself, but brought the rest and put it at the apostles' feet. Then Peter said, "Ananias, how is it that Satan has so filled your heart that you have lied to the Holy Spirit and have kept for yourself some of the money you received for the land? . . . You have not lied to men but to God." When Ananias heard this, he fell down and died . . . About three hours later his wife came in, not knowing what had happened. Peter asked her, "Tell me, is this the price you and Ananias got for the land?" "Yes," she said, "that is the price." Peter said to her, "How could you agree to test the Spirit of the Lord?" . . . At that moment she fell down at his feet and died' (Acts 5:1—10).

Each new incident involving Peter in the book of Acts reveals a different facet of the change that our Lord Jesus Christ, through his Spirit, worked in Peter's life after Pentecost. In this rather terrifying episode we shall see how Peter was equipped by the Spirit with a supernatural ability to discern acts and attitudes that were not of God.

The gift of spiritual discernment is indispensable to the servants of God in any age, but it was especially essential to the apostles as the pioneer leaders of the early Christian church. If we remember that their task was to guide growing numbers of converts through all the moral and theological quicksands of the ancient world into the new ways of Jesus Christ, and that in the face of continual persecution by civil and religious authorities and vicious opposition from Satan, then we can understand how necessary it was for these leaders to be able to discern truth from falsehood, right from wrong, spiritual values from human values, what was of God from what was of man.

But where was such discernment to come from? It is remarkable that the Lord and Head of the church not only chose the most ordinary men to be his apostles, but among them he chose as leader the one who, naturally speaking, was probably the most obtuse and spiritually insensitive of them all — Simon Peter, a man who could be at one moment the mouthpiece of the Holy Spirit, and at the next moment the mouthpiece of Satan (Matthew 16:16,23). But divine omnipotence can afford to choose even a man like Peter to shepherd the flock through the most dangerous terrain, because divine omnipotence commands the necessary grace and gifts, irrespective of his natural endowments. And that is the miracle here: the very man among the Twelve who appeared to be least capable of seeing the true significance of anything was the man to whom God chose to give the rare and precious gift of discernment — the 'ability to distinguish between spirits'. Before turning to the grim episode before us, then, let us first take courage from this truth: God is able to communicate to the weakest and the neediest person whatever gift may be necessary in order to fulfil his destined ministry in the church or in the world.

An act of apparent Christian charity

The infant church was steadily moving towards its destiny despite every kind of opposition that Satan had engineered. The Pentecostal outpouring of the Spirit, the miraculous healing of the cripple and the prayer-empowered preaching of the apostles had drawn in thousands of converts who formed a unified, loving, witnessing community. There was bitter and consistent opposition, but so far, each attempt of the enemy to silence the witness of the church had not only failed, but had actually backfired.

Now, therefore, Satan decided to change his tactics.

Rather than continuing to confine his opposition to persecution of the church from the outside, he began to concentrate on trying to injure it from within. And he used in this
evil attempt a man and his wife, Ananias and Sapphira,
very devoted to what they believed, full of zeal and
ingenuity to act on what they believed, but at this stage
the dupes and agents of Satan.

The pattern they appeared to follow

When Ananias laid his gift of money at the apostles' feet
(5:2), he was imitating a very noble example that had
already been set. Something remarkable had taken place
both at Pentecost and after the Spirit's infilling of the
numerically enlarged church at the end of Acts 4. It was
what our Lord had referred to in anticipation when he
said, 'Whoever believes in me, as the Scripture has said,
streams of living water will flow from within him' (John
7:38).

What happened when the Spirit came was that 'streams
of living water' flowed from the hearts of the Spirit-filled
believers. One such river was a holy love: a river of joyous
affection and compassion and concern for their fellows
in need. Members of the early Christian community loved
one another dearly, and they would do anything for one
another. Contrary to usual human practice, they even dis-
claimed their exclusive rights to their own property, if
they owned any. And so we read at the end of Acts 2 that
after Pentecost, 'All the believers were together and had
everything in common. Selling their possessions and goods,
they gave to anyone, as he had need' (2:44,45).

Similarly we read at the end of Acts 4 that after the
second infilling of the Spirit, 'There were no needy persons
among them. For from time to time those who owned
lands or houses sold them, brought the money from the
sales and put it at the apostles' feet, and it was distributed
to anyone as he had need' (4:34,35).

One person whom Luke specifically cites (4:36,37) as
having sold property to provide help for others was a man
called Joseph, whom the apostles surnamed 'Barnabas'
('Son of encouragement') because he always encouraged
and comforted others. One expression of this was when

he sold a field and brought the entire proceeds to the apostles to distribute according to the needs of the community.

This was the example of holy love that Ananias and Sapphira were ostensibly following. Ananias alone, as head of the household, came to the apostles and sanctimoniously laid at their feet what he pretended were all the proceeds from the sale of a plot of land. To the undiscerning, this looked just like what the God-fearing Barnabas had done. And that was exactly the impression the couple wanted to make on the apostles and the community as a whole.

The principle they appeared to practise

To the casual onlooker, the sight of Ananias coming to the apostles with his bag of money and placing it unconditionally at their disposal seemed to express the purest and noblest kind of Spirit-inspired love. Humanly speaking, nothing can ever surpass this kind of thing: the sight of men publicly acknowledging their responsibility for one another by sharing their material treasures with their needy brothers is both impressive and sublime. It indicates that the effects of the Fall are being countered by the Spirit's renewing ministry.

We can well imagine what joy must have welled up in the hearts of the undiscerning community as they watched Ananias go through the same motions as Barnabas. How wonderful! Like Barnabas, Ananias and Sapphira were practising the principle: 'What is mine is yours'! Like Barnabas, they were disclaiming their rights to their own property in favour of the good of the community! Like Barnabas, they were willing to make great sacrifices for Christ and his church! Ananias and Sapphira were as godly as the godliest, as dedicated as the most dedicated. What wonderful people to have in the community!

An act of actual satanic hypocrisy

But things are not always what they appear to be. Judged solely in terms of its potential benefit to the needy, Ananias' and Sapphira's gift was, of course, as good as Barnabas' gift: it would indeed help to alleviate the sufferings of the poor. Judged in terms of the human heart, however, their gift was as perverted as Barnabas' was pure, as black as his was white. This man and his wife were actually acting a lie, and doing so out of sheer selfish ambition.

Pretending what was not true

In laying their money at the apostles' feet, Ananias was acting as if he and his wife were obedient to the Spirit and concerned for the saints, but both these implied claims were fraudulent. The inspiration of their deed was satanic, and the goal of their would-be generosity was selfish. Their apparent charity was merely a disguised move for self-aggrandizement. They were not parting with their money in order to provide for the needy, but rather, in order to ingratiate themselves with the leaders of what they assumed to be a gullible, undiscerning community. Ananias and Sapphira did not love their fellows: their contribution to the church merely represented the price they were willing to pay for the reputation of being as keen as the keenest. They were just actors playing a role, not Christians sharing their hearts' love at all.

And hypocrisy is no light matter. To pretend to God or to the people of God that we are something which we are not is sin of the deepest dye. Moreover, it amounts to playing with fire that will ignite the holiest wrath of God: Ananias and Sapphira both died the instant their black hearts were exposed! Let us fear God, and be what we seem to be.

Desiring what was not theirs

Not only did Ananias and Sapphira pretend to be what they were not; they also coveted what did not belong to them, and it was this craving that really motivated their deceitful act. First, they coveted the reputation of being filled with the Spirit; they wanted to be known as good Christians like Barnabas. For this would realize a second ambition — that of belonging to the inner circle of believers who led the Christian community; they yearned to be part of that élite group whose obvious powers of preaching and healing were earning enthusiastic public response. For if they could infiltrate the leadership of the church, Ananias and Sapphira could realize yet a third ambition — they could exercise influence there. It would, of course, be influence for Satan.

These two thus lied to God and his people because they coveted things that did not belong to them. They wanted reputation and honour and influence that could come only from God-given qualities which they absolutely lacked. The bold truth is that they were neither filled with the Spirit nor suited to spiritual leadership; their motives were neither God-like nor God-honouring, and their inspiration was alien.

Peter's gift of discernment

While the rest of the community was apparently impressed by Ananias' gift to the apostles and probably inclined to rate him as yet another 'Son of Encouragement', one person sensed something wrong. That was Peter. As he observed everyone else's enthusiasm, Peter must have felt abysmally lonely. He alone saw through the apparent spirituality of the act; he alone saw through the studied secrecy with which Ananias and Sapphira had conspired to deceive everybody; he alone perceived something clearly *alien*.

The absence of fidelity to the Holy Spirit

By means of the gift of spiritual discernment, Peter first sensed that, far from honouring the Spirit, as it appeared to do, this hypocritical act violently and seriously dishonoured him. Peter asked Ananias, 'Ananias, how is it that Satan has so filled your heart that you have lied to the Holy Spirit and have kept for yourself some of the money you received for the land? . . . You have not lied to men but to God' (5:3,4). In lying to Spirit-filled men, Ananias was lying to the Spirit of God himself. Moreover, in agreeing to perpetrate this fraud, he and Sapphira were agreeing 'to test the Spirit of the Lord' (5:9). These were Peter's charges. How jolted the onlookers must have been, and how disconcerted Ananias, and later Sapphira, to hear Peter proclaim the sordid truth about such an apparently holy act!

Such sensitivity as Peter's to the honouring or the dishonouring of the Spirit is a rare but essential gift in every church if it is to be saved from some of the more sinister attacks of Satan. It is something for which we ought regularly to pray, because, in its absence, evil can become entrenched in the holiest of circles. For it nearly gained entry into the circle of the apostles themselves, in the very wake of Pentecost!

The presence and activity of Satan

This must have been another shock. When everyone else assumed that Ananias' gift was another token of the out-flowing of the Spirit of God in generosity and kindness and charity, Peter said, 'It's not the Spirit of God at all! It's Satan!' Peter not only uncovered a condition of soul which failed to honour the Spirit; behind the camouflage of generosity towards the saints he also found and exposed the active presence of Satan himself!

What was Satan doing? He was so anxious to make inroads against the infant church at this time that he was pretending to be as generous as the saints in order to accomplish·that end; he was willing that his servants should appear to make the same sacrifices as the saints were making. It has always been one of Satan's foremost purposes to disrupt the work of the church, and this was particularly true with respect to the early church. If he could have silenced its unambiguous witness to the risen, crucified Lord, Satan could have brought the whole church movement to nothing. To gain that object-ive, then, he would gladly inspire one of his subjects to sell his possessions and give part of the proceeds to the church, thus appearing to be baptized in the Spirit, impress-ing the leaders of the community, and ultimately worming his way into a place of influence for his master.

And Satan has not changed. Let us be on our guard.

A counterfeit fulness

Look at the language Peter used: 'Ananias, how is it that Satan has so *filled your heart* . . .?' (5:3). At Pentecost the believers were filled with the Holy Spirit. But Ananias and Sapphira were filled with a satanic spirit. Each fulness was in opposition to the other, and the second was a counterfeit of the first.

Many major acts of God seem to be aped by Satan. What

Moses did by the power of God, for instance, the magicians of Egypt counterfeited by the power of Satan (Exodus 7:11 etc.). And when the holy Son of God became incarnate, all the demons of hell seemed to become incarnate: there was more demon possession in the first century, probably,[1] than in any subsequent century until this one. Similarly here, when the Holy Spirit came down at Pentecost to baptize his saints, so also the spirit of Satan made this sweep to baptize the agents of Gehenna with a power that would make them acceptable with the saints of God.

We need to learn from this that Satan can be as orthodox as the most loyal follower of Christ. He can be as generous as a Barnabas. He can appear to be as full of the Spirit as any true believer. And someone has to discern what he is doing, but where the gifts of the Spirit are not abroad, there is no one to do the discerning. This is one of many problems with so many churches today: one sometimes hears people speaking of the most Christ-dishonouring preachers and saying, 'Wasn't he good?' 'Wasn't he marvellous?' One hears the ostensible saints of God praising the plainly ungodly. And it is all because there is so little spirit of discernment, and so little real understanding of things. But God certainly gave this gift to Peter. By means of it, Peter was enabled to see in Ananias' and Sapphira's act an attempt by Satan to penetrate the ranks of the Spirit-filled and there to fulfil his own iniquitous purposes. Thus God has his man fully armed for the hour with the one gift necessary: discernment. And if it had not been for this one man and this one gift of God, the whole church might have been robbed of her witness to the resurrection of the Lord Jesus Christ.

What does this grim episode show us? It points, first, to the constant presence of God and his sufficiency to guard his people. It was he who gave Peter the gift of discernment. It was he who sent the swift visitation of death upon Ananias and then upon Sapphira. God quickly severed a malignant limb from the visible body of the church, thus preventing potential destruction of the whole community.

Just as Achan discovered that there is a sin unto death when he withheld treasure that rightly belonged to God, and thereby endangered the well-being of the people of

Israel at their entry into the promised land (Joshua 7), so also did Ananias and Sapphira suffer death when they kept back part of their gift to God, and thereby threatened to pollute the new Israel at its entry into the Canaan of Pentecostal blessings. And this points to a second truth: Satan's agents can never really go all the way with the children of God; they can only *appear* to go all the way. Ultimately they are incapable of honouring Christ as Lord.

And as for us, what goes on in our hearts? Are we really what we profess to be, or is there an absence of fidelity to the Spirit within us? What spirit generates our motives and our actions? In the last resort, we cannot assess that spirit in terms of generosity: the one real test is loyalty, or the lack of it, to Jesus Christ, the Lord and Head of the church. Could it be that any of us are active agents of Satan, even filled with a fulness of evil that can hypocritically masquerade as Christian? May God enable us to know ourselves, for an Ananias or Sapphira will surely die! Let us be sure that 'If anyone destroys God's temple, God will destroy him' (1 Corinthians 3:17).

God's Word to us is still what he said of old through Paul to the Corinthians: 'A man ought to examine himself . . . [for] if we judged ourselves, we would not come under judgement' (1 Corinthians 11:28,31).

There is a precious promise that all honest acknowledgement and forsaking of sin meets with God's full pardon and renewing grace: 'If we confess our sins, he is faithful and just and will forgive us our sins and purify us from all unrighteousness' (1 John 1:9).

May the Spirit of God who gave to Peter the gift of discernment that saved the early church from destruction also give to us a true perception of what really goes on in our hearts. And may he also give to those who lead in holy things the discernment they need to guide the people of God in the paths of his righteousness.

Reference

1.   For an article on 'The Occult Revival in Historical Perspective' by Richard Lovelace, see *Demon Possession*, edited by John Warwick Montgomery (Bethany Fellowship, Minneapolis, 1976), pp. 65 ff.

32.
The Holy Spirit and prejudice

In writing to the Corinthians, the apostle Paul insisted that 'If anyone is in Christ, he is a new creation' (2 Corinthians 5:17a). The whole of biblical revelation assures us that there are no exceptions to this rule: as surely as a person is rightly related to Christ, that person is born again and is a new creation. 'The old has gone, the new has come' (2 Corinthians 5:17b). In Simon Peter, we have been seeing how, through Christ, 'the old has gone' and 'a new creation' has come into being. Simon is transformed beyond recognition from the man he was by nature:. this roughest of human diamonds now glistens with grace and glory. Such is the power of God to make men anew.

Even so, as there will be in all of us, there are still some hangovers from his pre-Christian life in the heart of Peter; and in Acts 10 and the first part of Acts 11 God moves in to deal effectively with one such hangover: *prejudice*. This is an ugly word because it denotes an ugly phenomenon — in fact, one of the ugliest things in Satan's territory. The dictionary defines it as 'a judgement or opinion formed beforehand or without thoughtful examination of the pertinent facts, issues or arguments; especially an unfavourable, irrational opinion'. In prejudice, we decide the issue before we consider the facts. It is a pre-judgement based on a bias; and as such, it is a lie. That is why it is most unworthy of anyone who bears the name of Christ.

Prejudice can take many forms and have many different roots. It may arise, for instance, out of over-familiarity with a person or an institution: 'Only in his home town and in his own house is a prophet without honour' (Matthew 13:57). Why? Because everybody knows him. Remember what they said about Jesus: 'Isn't he the carpenter's son?

339

Don't we know his brothers and sisters? Don't we know all
about his pedigree and his upbringing? There can't be anything exceptional about him!' (cf. Matthew 13:55,56.) This
was prejudice. It had no necessary barb at that stage, but it
was an irrational and unjustifiable conclusion.

Prejudice may also arise out of social pride: 'Nazareth!
Can anything good come from there?' (John 1:46.) In
other words, Nazareth has never produced a prophet, so
Nazareth will certainly not now produce the Messiah! But
that assessment of the situation was entirely prejudiced:
it was made without due consideration of the Scriptures
of God or the facts of the case. It was not malicious, but
it was blind.

Then, again, prejudice can be the dagger-point for expressing hatred, jealousy, envy, anger and all the other
hideous things that Satan can produce in the heart of a
sinner. In this form it is irrational in its origins and destructive in its effects, sometimes terrifyingly so. Having
decided beforehand that no truth or goodness can possibly
exist in a person, race, social class, etc., this kind of prejudice
malevolently refuses to see truth and goodness where they
do, in fact, exist; and it blindly and furiously acts on the
premise that they are absent. Racial prejudice usually takes
this vicious form.

There are various graphic ways in which we may characterize prejudice: it looks through its telescope with a blind eye,
like Lord Nelson; 'it squints when it looks and lies when it
speaks,' to quote what is somewhere attributed to the
Duchess d'Abrantès; it infests the mind like a pestilential
presence, as someone else has expressed it less delicately:

> Prejudices are like rats and men's minds are like traps.
> Prejudice gets in easily, but rarely gets out again.

And Peter still has a rat in the trap of his mind. Although
he is indeed a new man, at this stage of his life he still
harbours a prejudice which is positively to be condemned
in the sight of God who, therefore, takes radical steps to
rid Peter of it.

Peter's lingering prejudice

Despite his profound understanding of Scripture, despite his divinely inspired confession of the Christ, despite his almost unrivalled knowledge of the God of Abraham and despite his experience of the Holy Spirit at Pentecost and afterwards — despite all this, Peter had a prejudice which was not only nauseating to God, but also injurious to his whole plan for the outreach of the church. Peter was meant to open the kingdom of God to the Gentiles just as he had opened it to the Jews at Pentecost, but he had a prejudice against the Gentiles. Before God's purpose for the Gentiles could be fulfilled through Peter, this prejudice of his had to be expunged; otherwise he would simply not be able to welcome and embrace men and women from every nation under heaven who came in penitence and faith to the feet of the Saviour.

National exclusiveness

To be fair, we have to point out that Peter inherited this anti-Gentile prejudice: he had been nursed and brought up on it, and it was still very much a part of the Jewish consciousness in his day.

The Old Testament shows that the Jewish nation owed both its origin and its continuance solely to the grace of God. In his grace he chose one unworthy man, Abram, when he was still a worshipper of idols; and out of his own heart's affection he decided to make a people of this man. He arranged that Isaac should be miraculously conceived. As the nation grew, he graciously delivered her from one danger after another, first in Egypt, then in the wilderness, then in Canaan. He constantly provided for her, both materially and spiritually, even sending a lawgiver to give the law, and prophets to interpret and apply it to the changing situations of Israel's history. And in his grace he kept his covenant with her, even when she forsook him. All this is clear from the biblical record.

But rather than seeing such divine grace as preparing her for a mission beyond herself to other nations of the world, the nation of Israel turned in upon herself, viewing herself as the end-goal, the objective of all God's deeds and purposes. Thus the whole movement turned sour and the people turned sulky: they came to pride themselves as the only nation favoured by God, and saw themselves as superior to all other nations. And so the Jew would gather his skirts about him as he walked on the street, in case he should touch a Gentile 'unclean dog'.

In fact there was such racial superiority present in Jewish minds that they regarded members of other nations as being less than human. There is evidence that they sometimes even went so far as to advocate refusal to help a Gentile woman at childbirth, however great the pain, because at best she would only bring forth another Gentile dog.[1] Such was the sheer prejudice, despite God's clear message to Abram right at the beginning that God was blessing him *in order that* the other nations of the earth should be blessed through him: 'I will make you into a great nation and I will bless you; I will make your name great, and *you will be a blessing* . . . and all peoples on earth will be blessed through you' (Genesis 12:2,3).

So Peter was heir to his nation's prejudice. Despite the prophecies of Scripture concerning the Messiah's mission to the Gentiles (cf. the latter part of Isaiah), despite our Lord's grace to such Gentiles as the Samaritan woman at Sychar's Well (John 4:7—42) and to the Syrophoenician woman (Mark 7:25—30), and despite the Spirit's blessing upon Samaritans (Acts 8:17) and the conversion of an Ethiopian court official (Acts 8:26—38), Peter's bias remained still firmly in line with this general Jewish exclusiveness. Two manifestations of his prejudice are recorded in Acts 10.

Manifestations of Peter's prejudice

1. First, Peter's classification of foods as 'clean' and 'unclean' (cf. Leviticus 11) revealed how typically Jewish his attitude still was. In the housetop vision, when *'Something like a large sheet'* containing *'all kinds of four-footed animals, as well as reptiles of the earth and birds of the air'* (10:11,12) appeared before him, and God commanded him to *'Get up . . . Kill and eat,'* Peter protested: *'Surely not, Lord! I have never eaten anything impure or unclean'* (10:14). Peter was still punctilious in observing the ceremonial food laws of the Jews.

But this punctiliousness was quite incompatible with Jesus' teaching. Our Lord had corrected, and trenchantly so, the legalistic assumption that what one eats can cause spiritual harm: '"Listen to me, everyone, and understand this. Nothing outside a man can make him 'unclean' by going into him. Rather, it is what comes out of a man that makes him 'unclean' . . . Don't you see that nothing that enters a man from the outside can make him 'unclean'? For it doesn't go into his heart but into his stomach, and then out of his body." (In saying this, Jesus declared all foods "clean".)' (Mark 7:14–19). Jesus firmly taught that those who break a ceremonial law and eat 'unclean' food are not thereby made morally or spiritually unclean, as the traditional Jewish outlook assumed. But Peter, in line with Jewish tradition and not with Jesus' teaching, was at this time still acting on the assumption that some foods were 'unclean'.

2. Secondly, Peter's first words to the gathered relatives and close friends of Cornelius at Caesarea revealed how narrow his attitude to other nations still was. Cornelius was a Roman — a Gentile, but a God-fearer: Scripture does not tell us when or how, but this pagan had come to respect and honour the God of the Jews (10:2). In response, God sent Peter to preach the gospel to Cornelius and his circle. What were Peter's first words of greeting to the gathering? *'You are well aware that it is against our law for a Jew to associate with a Gentile or visit him' (10:28).*

With all the gracelessness of prejudice, Peter was really saying, 'It is very difficult for a man who is a Jew to come to the house of a non-Jew like this, you know! It's not really the done thing because you are all unclean! But I've come, nevertheless.' Peter came carrying his prejudice in his soul. Though he came 'without raising any objection' (10:29) because of the compulsion of God upon him, it took nothing less than an evident divine intervention to persuade him, and he certainly brought with him his inherited Jewish sense of spiritual superiority. Thus there was an immense barrier of prejudice which had to be removed before Peter could be God's servant in evangelizing the Gentiles. Before he could welcome them into the Saviour's fold, he had to learn to love them; and before he could learn to love them, he had to be freed of his prejudice against them.

As for us, we may not see the significance of our prejudices any more easily than Peter saw the significance of his; we need to learn from his example that any form of exclusiveness both hinders the gospel and contradicts the Spirit of Christ. If a Christian congregation were to bar its doors to strangers, then there would be no point in preaching the gospel. For unless we as Christians have hearts of compassion and a welcoming grace and the knowledge that God is seeking the lost through us, we might just as well close up shop. So it was with Peter in his prejudiced state: what was the sense in his preaching in the name of Jesus, and then being unprepared to welcome the Gentiles into the fold?

God's liberating power

One of the most comforting and encouraging truths of the Bible is that God never begins a work that he does not finish. He never begins a work that it is not wise to finish, and what his wisdom sees as desirable, his power makes possible. He set his plan in motion at the creation of the world, and he will see it through to the end. The same is true of his dealings with his every child: he who began in each Christian a good work will continue it until the day of Christ, when it will be brought to completion (cf. Philippians 1:6). Although I would not have used his terminology, I agree with Francis Thompson's view of God as 'the hound of heaven' in the sense that God never gives up! Christians may rebel and sin and kick against the pricks and dishonour their Lord, but the hound of heaven will keep after them and, if necessary, he will bite their heels to get them to their knees: 'Because the Lord disciplines those whom he loves, and he punishes everyone he accepts as a son' (Hebrews 12:6).

So here with Peter in Acts 10: God pursues him. Having loved the world so much 'that he gave his one and only Son, that whoever believes in him shall not perish but have eternal life' (John 3:16), God will not now be frustrated by the prejudice of his servant, Peter. And having brought Peter so far along the difficult road of sanctification, God will not now readily let him go. He will get Peter into the centre of his purposes, and to do so he will convince Peter that his anti-Gentile prejudice is wrong. How does God do this? Through a carefully arranged sequence of various modes of persuasion: several divinely arranged coincidences prepare Peter to grasp a truth which God then gloriously confirms. God makes three moves to which Peter obediently responds.

A series of providential coincidences

God knows how to communicate with each of his children in a language that each will understand. What would be especially telling to someone of Peter's inherited understanding of God's ways would be exactly such a series of coincidences, or providences, as God now provides.

First of all, notice that when the vision of the animals in the sheet comes to Peter, he is at Joppa, lodging in the house of a tanner (9:43). A man like this, because he deals with dead bodies all the time, is, in the estimation of a Jew, perpetually unclean. The last kind of person a Jew would be expected to rub shoulders with was a tanner: according to Jewish custom, in fact, a tanner was required to build his house at least fifty cubits outside a city boundary because his work was unclean.

God's ways are remarkable. Just when he is about to do a whole series of things that will persuade Peter of the rightness of preaching the gospel to the Gentiles, God sees to it that Peter is already beginning to wrestle with one of his nation's most crippling prejudices through lodging with a tanner. God has his own ways of putting his children into the very situations where they can best hear his voice and understand his message.

Secondly, what happens is that two complementary visions occur. The first takes place at Caesarea, about thirty miles north of Joppa on the Mediterranean coast where Cornelius, a Roman centurion, is stationed with his battalion. He is a good man and a God-fearer, but a Gentile. As he prays to God at the ninth hour of the day, he has a vision (10:1–8) in which God, through an angel, says to him:

'Look here, Cornelius, you have been a God-fearing man for
a long time, and your prayers have now come before me.
I know that you have really been seeking after me, and
honouring every ray of light that you've had concerning me.
Now I am going to honour you: you shall bathe your soul
in the full light of the gospel. Send to Joppa and ask there
for a man named Simon Peter who is lodging with a tanner
by the seaside. Have him brought here, and he will tell you
how to leave the shadows and enter into the full light of the
knowledge of God.' Cornelius accordingly sends three men
to Joppa to find Peter.

Just as Cornelius' messengers are approaching the town
next day, Peter goes up onto the tanner's housetop to pray,
and it is divinely arranged that he becomes hungry. While
the people below are preparing a meal for him, Peter goes
on praying in the privacy of the rooftop. Suddenly he has a
vision (10:9–16) in which he sees something like a massive
sheet being let down by four corners from heaven and containing all kinds of reptiles and beasts and fishes. Then Peter
hears the voice of God: 'Peter, you are hungry, are you?
Well, just get up and kill and eat!' And, true to his old
nature, he impetuously responds: 'Not on your life, Lord!
Not me! You know my record, don't you? Never in my
life have I eaten anything that is unclean!' But God answers,
'Look, Peter, what I have cleansed, you must not call
unclean.' And three times the whole episode is repeated.
Three times, typically, Peter protests: 'Lord, what you are
asking me to do is wrong!' Three times God says in reply,
'Do not call anything impure that God has made clean.'

And thirdly, (10:17–21), just as the three men sent by
Cornelius are downstairs in front of Simon the tanner's
gate asking for Simon Peter, the Holy Spirit tells Peter that
three men are looking for him, and that he should go downstairs and accompany them without hesitation, for he, the
Spirit, has sent them. Peter accordingly goes down and
announces himself to the three men as the person they are
looking for, just as they are asking for him.

Now if you are not a Christian, you probably think that
these coincidences are too good to be true, but if you are
a Christian, you will be predisposed to believe them. This
is how our God acts: he sends unexpected symmetries into

life situations in order to alert his children to what he wants them to learn. Deliberately fitting one cog into the next cog and making the machinery of his sovereign grace work, God's hand is always in control. Peter recognizes this — he knows that there is nothing haphazard in the three coincidences. Thus God has engaged Peter's attention.

Peter's insight

God's next move in dealing with Peter's prejudice against the Gentiles takes place on an intellectual level: he gives to Peter a great perception of truth.

When Peter and six of his fellow believers from Joppa have travelled the day's journey to Caesarea, and Peter has received from Cornelius' own lips the account of his vision, the utter marvel of it dawns upon Peter and at the same time he suddenly sees the significance of his own vision. God's words of warning ('Do not call anything impure that God has made clean') suddenly make sense. And Peter opens his sermon to this group of gathered Gentiles with an expression of his new insight: *'I now realize how true it is that God does not show favouritism but accepts men from every nation who fear him and do what is right' (10:34,35).* In other words, Peter suddenly perceives the truth that God is no respecter of persons. This may be nothing new to us in the twentieth century; all of us have probably heard it since childhood. But to this prejudiced man it was a new and earth-shaking truth. And if· Peter had not grasped it, you and I as Gentiles might never have come to know the God of Abraham and Isaac and Jacob!

When Peter says, 'I now *realize* . . .' he is using a Greek word *'katalambanō'*. This word connotes a clear understanding of things, a vivid comprehension of truth. When Paul, writing to the Philippians about his own conversion, says that 'Christ Jesus took hold of' him (Philippians 3:12), he uses the same verb in the passive voice; it has connotations of being gripped or grasped or arrested. If you were a criminal and a policeman came up behind you and put his hand on your shoulder and said, 'Fellow, I've *got* you!' that would be the word. And so Peter is saying, 'I've got it! I suddenly see the point! All those coincidences, and all the things that God has told Cornelius and me in our visions add up: God is no respecter of persons! He cleanses men of *every* nation, and as a mark of their cleansing they fear God and work righteousness. Being cleansed of real impurity, which is sin, they are freed to render filial fear to God and justice towards their fellow man. This is not confined to Jews — it happens among people of every nation!' That is Peter's great new insight.

God's confirmation

God's third move in freeing Peter of his anti-Gentile prejudice takes the form of a confirmatory downpouring of the Spirit, as Peter acts on his new insight and preaches the gospel message to Cornelius and his friends and relatives.

What a wonderfully receptive congregation! Cornelius has already described their anticipation to Peter: *'Now we are all here in the presence of God to listen to everything the Lord has commanded you to tell us' (10:33)*. What a marvellous opportunity for Peter! For those whom God cleanses also embrace his Son as Saviour and Lord. And so Peter opens his heart and begins to tell out all the gospel story when, lo and behold, he is prevented from preaching his sermon right through to its conclusion: God interrupts him! To use his own words to the Jerusalem critics later on: *'As I began to speak, the Holy Spirit came on them [the Gentiles] as he had come on us at the beginning' (11:15)*. The Spirit of God comes down upon these Gentiles: this is, in fact, a Gentile Pentecost, the counterpart of the Jewish one. God is powerfully confirming Peter's insight that he is no respecter of persons. Just as he gave his all to the Jews who believed at Pentecost, so he is now giving his all to these Gentiles. They are no second-class citizens of his kingdom. In fact, his kingdom has *no* second-class citizens.

In retrospect we can see how fitting it was that Peter had taken six brethren with him from Joppa to Caesarea: the fact of the Spirit's coming upon the Gentiles was so critically important that it needed to be witnessed unequivocally; and in Jewish and Egyptian law, seven witnesses proved a case. Luke reports that when the Gentile Pentecost took place, the six men from Joppa, that is, *'the circumcised believers who had come with Peter were astonished that the gift of the Holy Spirit had been poured out even on* the Gentiles. *For they heard them speaking in tongues and praising God' (10:45,46).* The prejudices of these six men, like Peter's prejudice, were ground to powder!

Later, when word of the Gentile Pentecost reached the Jerusalem Church, and the circumcision party needed to be convinced that Peter had not done wrong to go 'into the house of uncircumcised men and [eat] with them' (11:3), Peter's witness, along with that of 'these six brothers' (11:12), was conclusive. What Peter said, and how it affected his critics, is described by Luke, as recorded in Acts: ' *"Then I remembered what the Lord had said, 'John baptized with water, but you will be baptized with the Holy Spirit.' So if God gave them the same gift as he gave us, who believed in the Lord Jesus Christ, who was I to think that I could oppose God!" When they [the critics] heard this, they had no further objections and praised God, saying: "So then, God has even granted the Gentiles repentance unto life"'* (11: 16—18). Exactly! God cleanses men in every nation by the atoning blood of his Son. Nothing else has power to make anyone clean, whether Jew or Gentile, and this is adequate for all. The lesson Peter heard on the roof of the tanner's house related immediately to food laws, but now Peter knew its wider implication and recognized how wrong he had been to brand any member of any nation as 'unclean'.

In his testimony to the Jerusalem Jews, Peter was also declaring victory over his old prejudice. He was saying, 'If God gave to the Gentiles the same gift (and not an inferior one) that he gave to us at Pentecost, how could I oppose God? I wasn't wrestling with flesh and blood, now; I knew that God was claiming the Gentiles as his own. I couldn't argue then, and I won't argue now. On the contrary, I'm on God's side! I'll move with him in all the ways of his providence and grace. God welcomes the Gentiles, and so shall I!' So much for Peter's prejudice — there was no trace of it left. And while it did try to reassert itself at a later date (cf. Galatians 2:11—16), it had no permanent success, for God had deftly and powerfully exposed its contaminating nature.

And how is God dealing with your prejudice and with mine? Have you any narrow views or baseless animosities or cherished biases in your heart? You will be a strange phenomenon if you haven't! Be sure of this: God can have no truck with the poison of prejudice, and, if you are a child of God, he will place you in such circumstances as will give you self-knowledge and an understanding of what is right in his sight. That will leave you with the challenge to yield to him in obedience. Often it is in the very process of obeying God that we discover the meaning of what he is trying to show us: it was through Peter's obedience in going to Caesarea that he learned the meaning of God's admonition to him on the rooftop in Joppa. And how impoverished the world would have been had Peter's prejudice not been expelled! Our gifts too, whatever they may be, may well be lost to successive generations of Christians and non-Christians alike if we continue to harbour prejudices. Let us, like Peter, yield to God and allow him to purge us of all old leaven, renewing a right spirit within us, so that, in the grace of God, we may be not only his servants, but his witnesses as well.

Reference
1.   W. Barclay, *The Acts of the Apostles* (St. Andrew Press, Edinburgh, 1953), pp. 83—84.

33.
How a Spirit-filled man reacts to extreme pressure

Peter is in a most challenging situation: imprisoned, he is looking straight into the face of death (Acts 12:1–11). In the wake of a campaign of persecution by Herod against the church in Jerusalem — a campaign which has already resulted in the murder of the apostle James — Peter has been arrested and put into prison under guard of four squads of soldiers. There is no possibility of escape. In terms of any realistic human assessment of the situation, the hour appears to have arrived when, as Jesus told Peter, ' " . . . you will stretch out your hands, and someone else will dress you and lead you where you do not want to go." Jesus said this to indicate the kind of death by which Peter would glorify God' (John 21:18,19).

Actually that time has not yet come for Peter — God still has work for him to do. But as far as he knows, he is actually facing death: it clearly seems as if he too is to be martyred as James had been. Now what does the Spirit of God do for a man in such a circumstance? What difference does it make to have the Spirit in your heart when death is at your door?

Like their Lord himself, the saints of God must suffer and must die. There is no such thing as ultimate avoidance of pain and death. Any doctrine of healing which suggests that anyone can be wholly exempt from these evils is misleading. While God certainly does at times break in with healing power upon our bodies and minds and spirits, the New Testament promises no such thing as absolute deliverance from pain and death until that day when 'the trumpet will sound, the dead will be raised imperishable, and we will be changed' (1 Corinthians 15:52). On that day we shall receive a body that will know neither pain nor sickness

nor death; but meantime all human beings, including the
saints, must suffer. It could even be argued, in fact, that
the saints of God must experience *more* sorrows, sufferings
and trials than those who are outside of Jesus Christ. If
you are a Christian, and are witnessing to your Lord, you
will have all kinds of difficulties, all kinds of dimensions
of distress, which the man of the world knows nothing
about. This is in accordance with our Lord's explicit
promise: 'I tell you the truth, . . . no one who has left home
or brothers or sisters . . . for me and the gospel will fail to
receive a hundred times as much in this present age . . . *and
with them, persecutions* . . .' (Mark 10:29,30).

And here is Peter, suffering persecution. He is in prison;
death seems inevitable; he is so hedged around by hostile
powers that, humanly speaking, he might well be tempted
to fall into a torment of despair or panic. But what actually
happens? Peter experiences exactly the kind of spiritual
triumph which Paul described when he asked, 'If God is
for us, who can be against us?' (Romans 8:31): *'We are
more than conquerors* through him who loved us. For I am
convinced that neither death, nor life, neither angels nor
demons, neither the present nor the future, nor any powers,
neither height nor depth, nor anything else in all creation,
will be able to separate us from the love of God that is in
Christ Jesus our Lord' (Romans 8:37—39). Although many
hostile powers are arrayed against Peter, he is more than
conqueror in this situation because God is for him. God's
greater power prevails.

The powers arrayed against Peter

Peter's human foes
The most obvious of these was Herod the king.

> 'It was about this time that King Herod arrested
> some who belonged to the church, intending to
> persecute them. He had James, the brother of
> John, put to death with the sword. When he saw
> that this pleased the Jews, he proceeded to seize
> Peter also. This happened during the Feast of

Unleavened Bread. After arresting him, he put him in prison, handing him over to be guarded by four squads of four soldiers each. Herod intended to bring him out for public trial after the Passover' (Acts 12:1—4).

This unscrupulous tyrant was Herod Agrippa I, a son of Aristobulus and a grandson of Herod the Great, an Edomite who had been brought up on the best that Greek culture could provide. But he was a pagan, and an unpleasant pagan at that: he was a man given to lust; he was dissolute; he cared neither for God nor for man. He was virtually his own god.

About the only consistent principle in Herod's life at this time was his determination to hold on to his Jewish domain, whatever the cost. Although there are some indications that he did see the superiority of the Jewish faith over all other faiths, it was primarily because of his overweening desire for power that Herod did everything he could to please the Jews. According to Josephus, he even went so far as to offer a daily sacrifice, and when the Roman Emperor Gaius wanted to have a statue of himself erected in the Jerusalem temple, it was Herod who dissuaded him — not because he really respected the temple, but because he wanted peace with the Jews at any price. His motivation was always utterly selfish. It was out of this same desire to please the Jews that Herod murdered the apostle James with a sword. Seeing how effective this was in pleasing them, he decided to go after another of the Christians whom the Jews disliked and dishonoured, namely Peter, the leader of the church. So Herod seized Peter and imprisoned him, intending to bring him out to the people after the days of Unleavened Bread.

In his shadow, however, we see another familiar foe — the Jewish community at large. If the Jews had not been so antagonistic to the church, Herod would not have been able to please them by persecuting its leaders. If they had not shown such evident pleasure at the murder of James, Herod would probably not have bothered with Peter. The Jewish community, therefore, constituted a second human adversary for Peter in his present situation.

Peter's psychologically harassing circumstances

Another kind of pressure exerted against Peter was mental oppression: his apparently hopeless situation in prison, combined as it was with painful memories of certain past experiences, was such that it could have broken him. James was slain, Peter was probably next on Herod's list and it was just about a year since Jesus had been crucified.

1. James was dead. Peter's association with James went back to their childhood: they appear to have grown up together, later becoming partners of some kind in the fishing business (Luke 5:10). They began to follow Jesus at about the same time, becoming two of the three most favoured disciples among the Twelve and being allowed to see and to hear many things that were denied to the others (on the Mount of Transfiguration, for example, and in the Garden of Gethsemane). James and Peter and John were always together. But now James was dead. The cruelty perpetrated on this beloved friend, as well as the shock and the grief of his death, would be deeply painful to Peter.

2. James' death constituted a threat to Peter. Here he was, now, completely at the mercy of Herod and his men, as James must have been when they murdered him. Peter was trapped. Death was at the door, coming for Peter next. And so dread was added to his grief.

3. If you have your sanity when you are in prison, you *think* more than you do outside prison walls; and if Peter was thinking at all, he would be vividly aware that it was at this time a year ago that his Lord's death took place. Peter was not in prison then: he had his freedom, and he was in the high priest's courtyard, but one taunt from a maid's lips had led to his threefold denial of Jesus. That could very well have a haunting effect upon him now, and add considerably to his remorse and dread.

Satan, the accuser

Behind the other two kinds of opposition, the arch-enemy of mankind, and of God's people especially, was at work. Infuriated as he must have been by the failure, thus far, of his evil purposes as they related to our Lord Jesus Christ, to the church in general and to the apostle Peter in particular, Satan was now pursuing a new strategy by playing upon Herod's self-interested determination to hold on to political power.

For Satan's failures to date had been numerous. First he had failed to hinder Peter from becoming an apostle: no matter what he incited Peter to do, no matter how he tempted him, the Lord Jesus Christ always lifted Peter up again, forgiving his sin and giving him fresh grace and sending him on his way rejoicing. Then Satan had failed to achieve his purposes in the death of Jesus. Oh yes, he had managed to find a disciple who would sell him for thirty pieces of silver; and he had other human agents who saw to it that Jesus was nailed to a cross and killed. But then God raised Jesus from the dead! The Lamb that was slain became the triumphant Lord! And Satan was frustrated again.

Then early in the history of the church, Satan had tried to poison the community by introducing hypocrites (Ananias and Sapphira) into the midst of the saints. But again he had failed. The church was marching forward in spite of all his efforts against it. So now Satan was trying another tactic: by playing upon the power-hunger of Herod, he was seeking to destroy Peter, the foundation-stone of the rapidly enlarging church of Jesus Christ.

These powers arrayed against the apostle Peter in prison made a formidable opposition. How did this Spirit-filled man approach the situation? What does the grace of God do for a person at a time like this?

The powers arrayed on Peter's behalf

Blessed are they who can say with Elisha of old when surrounded by enemy hordes: 'Don't be afraid . . . Those who are with us are more than those who are with them [the enemies]' (2 Kings 6:16). Elisha's servant felt sceptical. He asked Elisha, 'Where *are* these allies who are supposed to be with us? I see only enemies all around, and no means of escape!' But Elisha's eyes of faith could see beyond the range of human vision to 'the hills full of horses and chariots of fire all around Elisha' (2 Kings 6:17), as his servant was later given to see. God was indeed on the field.

Only those who have such vision of faith can find peace
when surrounded by foes and faced by death; and here in
Acts 12 we see that Peter finds exactly that peace. Despite
the pressures upon him and the apparent hopelessness of
his situation, and despite the fact that he is chained between
two soldiers who are right there in the cell alongside him,
Peter is lying there fast asleep! This is what the Holy Spirit
does for a Spirit-filled man under attack: he gives him the
sure confidence that whatever the morrow holds, God
holds him. He gives him peace in a total abandonment to
the will of God.

Peter is unafraid. Like Elisha, he knows that those who
are with him are greater than those who are with his enemies,
even if one of his enemies is death itself. If it be asked
what 'horses and chariots of fire' are arrayed on Peter's
behalf, we reply, 'A praying church, a ministering angel
and God himself.'

A praying church

*'So Peter was kept in prison, but the church was earnestly
praying to God for him' (12:5).*

This is far more important than we might at first think.
For a Spirit-filled man cannot do without the fellowship
of the church; and if he tries to, he will be the loser. The
Lord does not deal with Peter's plight simply on a direct,
personal basis here: instead, he makes his church a vehicle
of blessing. It is in answer to the church's prayers, in part,
that he brings victory: Peter is subsequently visited by an
angel and released from prison.

Though the concept of a praying church may be very
familiar to us, it was far from familiar to this early church.
As we saw in chapter 30, praying had assumed a new role
for these believers since Pentecost. The Old Testament had
stressed mankind's unworthiness to approach God directly
in prayer. The Holy of Holies, where God was said to dwell
among his ancient people Israel, was guarded on all sides
from approach by any human being except one: once a
year, on the Day of Atonement, the high priest was per-
mitted to enter through the thick blue curtains into the
shrine and into the presence of God. God was holy, men
were sinful, therefore men should keep their distance:

that was the general tenor of Old Testament religion. Prayers in Israel, therefore, were very formal, general and ritualistic. Those that we have in the book of Psalms are exceptions, expressing as they do the faith and the hope which only a minority possessed. As a rule, the Jew kept his distance from God; the better the Jew, the greater the distance he kept! The good man was the man who was most aware of God's transcendence and of his own corresponding unworthiness and creatureliness. He knew the fear of God, and had a strong sense of being separated from him.

With the coming of the Messiah, however, and especially with the completion of his work of atonement, the whole church entered upon a rich inheritance of direct access to God in prayer. When Jesus offered his own blood in his high-priestly sacrifice for his people, the veil of the temple was torn in two to symbolize the opening of 'the new and living way' (Hebrews 10:20) to God; and the church took advantage of this unrivalled privilege. With a rent veil in front of them and the Spirit of sonship within them, the Christians *had* to pray: now it was right and natural to draw near to God in prayer. And it still is one of the marks of the Christian that 'behold, he prayeth' (Acts 9:11 AV).

And so the early church finds it right and proper to carry its leader and brother, in his need, to God in prayer. Blessed is the man who belongs to a church like this, which knows the way to the throne of grace! If I were in secular employment and moving to a new city, I would look first of all for a church that, along with teaching the whole counsel of God, could and would pray for me. A church that cannot or does not pray for its members is no successor to the church here described in the book of Acts.

A ministering angel

To release his servant from prison, in addition to a praying church, God used a ministering angel: *'The night before Herod was to bring him to trial, Peter was sleeping between two soldiers, bound with two chains, and sentries stood guard at the entrance. Suddenly an angel of the Lord appeared and a light shone in the cell . . .' (12:6,7).*

In simplest terms, an angel is a messenger of God. Some of God's angels are very human: those who feed the hungry, for example, and give drink to the thirsty, welcome the stranger, clothe the naked, visit the sick and the imprisoned (Matthew 25:35,36) and 'orphans and widows in their distress' (James 1:27), are God's human angels. Some of God's angels, on the other hand, are of a non-human order: they can do things that human angels cannot do, such as unlocking prison doors and gates. They are God's special angels who can do anything he commands them, and who constantly wait to do his bidding anytime and anywhere. For God has at his command every kind of servant necessary to fulfil his will, and to save his people, whatever their circumstances may be. God is 'the Lord of hosts' (Psalm 24:10 AV): the sun and the stars are under his command; the wind and the rain, the seas and the skies all await his bidding; even the most perverse of men can occasionally be his unwitting servants; and when it pleases him, God can also call upon the more purely spiritual beings whom the Bible calls 'angels'.

And that is what he does now: he sends an angel to take Peter out of prison. The angel enters Peter's cell at night, wakens him, commands him to dress and to follow him. Then he leads Peter to freedom through the prison, past two guards and through the iron gate leading into the city (12:7–10).

A sovereign God

The last power mustered in Peter's defence is the most important of all: God himself. God's church and God's angel contribute nothing original to the situation: the most they can do is to bring the provisions of God to the place where Peter is. It is God himself who must act!

Here we see God as all-sufficient: he can supply all things that his people can ever possibly need. He has the keys to all prison locks (12:7); he can give deep sleep to the soldiers lying on either side of Peter, and indeed to his own servant engaged in doing his work (12:6); he can snap off Peter's chains (12:7); he can open the iron gate and let the prisoner out into the city (12:10); and he can summon any agency he needs to bring his resources where they are needed. Best of all, he himself can come alongside the angel and right inside Peter's heart, to give him peace on a night like this.

And, completely trusting such a sovereign Lord, firm in the assurance that 'horses and chariots of fire' are gathered round him, Peter is sound asleep: the angel even has to strike him on the side in order to waken him! (12:7.) Peter is unmoved at the prospect of death: he knows that God has already delivered him from prison twice since Pentecost (cf. Acts 4:21; 5:19,20), and if it is his will, he will do so again. Even at such a time, the Spirit in Peter's heart enables him to have *no will but God's will*. That is the key to his strength; and that is a foretaste of heaven for anyone, anywhere, whatever his situation.

'"You are Simon son of John? You will be called Cephas" (which, when translated, is Peter) [i.e. "rock"]' (John 1:42). Long ago, Jesus had promised to make a new man of Simon—a man of rock, of stability, of firm character. And now here is the man of rock, sleeping between two soldiers on the night before what could be his death. Here he is, unwilling to recant or to withdraw or to do anything at all to come to terms with his Lord's enemies, but willing for whatever God wills, no matter what that is. This is the man of rock whom the Saviour has brought into being: he who a year before was tripped into sin by the taunt of a maid now lies unmoved by the prospect of death. In fact, he is sleeping like a baby.

Perhaps we are not physically imprisoned as Peter was, yet we may be enmeshed in circumstances that are very trying. Do we belong to a praying church where we can be loved and surrounded and prayed for? Do we ourselves pray for others? Can we do anything to encourage more of our churches to be praying fellowships that nurse their every member from the cradle to the grave? God still has his angels, and though some of them are very human, others are not human at all: they can meet us wherever we are, no matter what the situation. And whether he sends his servants from the church or his angels from his own immediate presence, it is God himself who must come to break our chains and open the gate and lead us on and out.

And he will do this, if our wills are his, as Peter's was. May the Lord bring us to that place of rest and peace and abandonment to himself where we have no will but his will; may he grant us all to be strengthened 'with power

through his Spirit in [our] inner being' (Ephesians 3:16).
And may he himself dwell in our hearts, so that we '. . . being
rooted and established in love, may have power, together
with all the saints, to grasp how wide and long and high and
deep is the love of Christ and to know this love that sur-
passes knowledge — that [we] may be filled to the measure
of all the fulness of God' (Ephesians 3:17—19).

34.
How a Spirit-filled man reacts to valid criticism

'When Peter came to Antioch, I opposed him to his face, because he was in the wrong. Before certain men came from James, he used to eat with the Gentiles. But when they arrived, he began to draw back and separate himself from the Gentiles because he was afraid of those who belonged to the circumcision group. The other Jews joined him in his hypocrisy, so that by their hypocrisy even Barnabas was led astray. When I saw that they were not acting in line with the truth of the gospel, I said to Peter in front of them all, "You are a Jew, yet you live like a Gentile and not like a Jew. How is it, then, that you force Gentiles to follow Jewish customs?"' (Galatians 2:11–14).

The human writers of Scripture might very well have been tempted to write 'The End' after the Acts 12 episode of our last chapter. Peter's remarkable abandonment to the will of God, and God's miraculous intervention to release him from prison, together might, indeed, be taken to form the crowning point of Peter's long pilgrimage into Christian maturity. Peter could be regarded as having 'arrived' now. What could any additional biographical information really add to this picture of the apostle's full development?

But the divine author of Scripture, the Holy Spirit, knew better; and he wanted one more biographical sketch of Peter put on record, even though (or indeed *because*) it is one in which Peter does not appear in a very bright light. Here in Galatians 2 we see Peter, the foundation-stone of the church, God's chosen apostle to the Jews, the

Spirit-filled man who in Acts 12 had been unafraid of the very jaws of death — here we see Peter, in a moment of weakness, cowed by fear of a little pressure group from within the church. When members of the circumcision party come down from Jerusalem to Antioch to see that Peter toes the line, Peter allows himself to be bullied into acting as if he subscribes to their Judaistic views. In other words, this great man acts hypocritically.

At first sight this final glimpse of Peter may seem disappointing when viewed over against the many accounts in the book of Acts which have shown him to be a man full of the grace and the gifts of the Holy Spirit. Indeed, the incident may seem virtually unbelievable when compared with Peter's maturity in the Acts 12 episode. But the hard truth of the matter is this: the Galatians 2 incident is eminently realistic. It faces us with the continuing human frailty of Peter, and by doing so, it completes the whole account of the pilgrimage from Simon to Peter much in the way a postscript completes a letter: it qualifies, and it may even say something more important than everything that has gone before.

For one thing, the divine author of Scripture is showing us here that it is a delusion ever to think that anyone, even the great apostle Peter, finally, here in this life, 'arrives' as a Christian, in the sense of being morally infallible or without sin: 'If we claim to be without sin, we deceive ourselves and the truth is not in us' (1 John 1:8). Since the Fall, sin has been the ineradicable tendency of all human life, including the life of the most mature of Christians, and it is most powerful exactly when we are most unmindful of its existence. In humility, we need always to bear in mind our sinful nature. Peter himself still admonishes us in these words: 'Humble yourselves, therefore, under God's mighty hand . . . *Be self-controlled and alert.* Your enemy the devil prowls around like a roaring lion looking for someone to devour. Resist him, standing firm in the faith, because you know that your brothers throughout the world are undergoing the same kind of sufferings' (1 Peter 5:6—9).

Galatians 2:11—14 shows us that the keystone to Peter's spiritual maturity was not infallibility; rather, it was humility.

Peter's lapse into folly

Peter's initial stance

'Before certain men came from James, he used to eat with the Gentiles' (2:12).

Paul tells us there that, while visiting Antioch (the chief city of Syria), Peter at first enjoyed table fellowship with both Gentile and Jewish Christians there; he joined them at the Lord's table and he enjoyed hospitality in their homes. This was the natural and necessary thing to do — necessary because Peter had been taught very clearly that the ancient Jewish dietary laws were no longer binding, and that 'God does not show favouritism but accepts men from every nation who fear him and do what is right' (Acts 10:34,35). There are no second-class citizens in God's kingdom; colour, nationality, differences of background — all mean nothing in the church of Jesus Christ. He whom God cleanses is clean, and Peter knew this. His first days among the Antiochan Christians were, therefore, days of unrestricted Christian fellowship and joy. The chief apostle to the Jews mingled with Jewish and Gentile believers alike, eating at their tables and joining with them at the Lord's table, to the enrichment of all concerned. All were one in Christ.

Peter's ensuing change

'But when they arrived, he began to draw back and separate himself from the Gentiles because he was afraid of those who belonged to the circumcision group' (2:12).

Peter's change of stance coincided with the arrival from Jerusalem of a group who claimed, at least, to have some special connection with James, the brother of our Lord. The text is uncertain at this point: we do not know whether these people meant to say that James had sent them, or even that he had given them authority to do what they were doing. But apparently they did emphasize the fact that they had come from James, who was the leader of the Jerusalem Church.

The reference to Peter as 'afraid of those who belonged to the circumcision group' lets us know clearly, however, exactly what these people stood for. Being ultra-conservative in matters of theology, they continued to give to

circumcision a value and a significance that was a veritable
denial of the gospel. Thus they would consider it preposter-
ous for Peter to have table fellowship with uncircumcised
Gentiles. And whatever the reason, Peter became ensnared:
his old fear of human derision, perhaps, or his old anti-
Gentile prejudice, or both, got the better of him, and he
withdrew from fellowship with the Gentile Christians.

Of course, Peter's change of stance did not mean that
he ceased to believe that a repentant sinner is saved by
faith alone in Christ alone. But it did mean that he now
acted as if he no longer believed like that. The whole thrust
of the passage is that he became hypocritical in his
behaviour: he *acted as if* he believed that a circumcised man
had something to commend him that an uncircumcised man
had not; he *acted as if* he believed that the circumcised
constituted an élite group in the church, whereas the uncircumcised were second-grade believers with whom one
could not have fellowship. And in acting as if he believed
these false ideas, which detracted from both the glory and
the sufficiency of the Lord Jesus Christ, the great apostle
Peter, even at this advanced stage of his life and career,
behaved in such a way as to cast a cloud over the gospel.
His withdrawal from the physically uncircumcised Christians
with whom he had earlier enjoyed true fellowship was a
very grave offence. True, the tense of the verbs does suggest
that he withdrew gradually rather than abruptly, but he
withdrew!

Peter's behaviour was not only wrong; it was also harmful,
both potentially and actually. Think of the pain and the
heartsoreness it would cause to those Gentile believers:
they had repented of their sins, they owned Christ as their
treasure and their Saviour, they had been gathered into
the church at Antioch as part of the fellowship — yet an
apostle of Jesus Christ who had been closely associated with
them now withdrew and would not eat with them any longer.
And think, too, what terrible disharmony it would cause in
the local church — it would instantly create division among
Jewish and Gentile believers.

Moreover, we see that Peter's behaviour drove a wedge,
albeit temporarily, between two of the best friends in the
New Testament, Paul and Barnabas. Paul immediately saw

through Peter's behaviour and refused to tolerate it, but Barnabas either did not see so clearly or was less courageous. In any case, he was 'led astray by their hypocrisy' (that of Peter and the other Jews) (2:13). Thus a rift was created between the great apostle Paul and one of his best friends in the work of the Lord.

And then, Peter's behaviour virtually pushed the young church to the edge of a precipice, so that the church as we know it might never have come into being. For had Peter's hypocrisy not been corrected and the effects of it righted, the church as a whole could have been forever divided into two camps — Jewish and Gentile; thus her witness to the total sufficiency of Jesus Christ as Saviour could have been forever muted.

Paul's example of fidelity

At this strategic hour in its history, the church was saved from disaster by the insight and the intervention of one man — Paul. It would be interesting to examine different periods of history in order to see how often this kind of thing has taken place — how often God has had his one man to save the situation. Luther, for instance, stood alone for a long time. John Calvin stood alone. John Knox in Scotland stood alone. In most countries in the world some of the greatest things have been accomplished by one man standing alone, with God.

So it was with Paul here. His great fidelity, first to Jesus Christ, then to the gospel and to the church at large, left him with no alternative but to challenge the madness of his fellow apostle, Peter; and he had to do it alone, for along with Peter, all 'the other Jews joined him in his hypocrisy' (2:13). Enabled by his razor-sharp mind to perceive the significance of what was going on, and inspired by his almost unrivalled love for his Lord, Paul courageously stood up to Peter and 'opposed him to his face' (2:11).

Paul's challenge
'I said to Peter in front of them all, "You are a Jew, yet you live like a Gentile and not like a Jew. How is it, then,

that you force the Gentiles to follow Jewish customs?"'
(2:14.)

This challenge was directly related to principle and to principle only. It did not arise out of any petty personality clash, for instance. The fact that Paul could see the principle clearly, and Peter could not, was not due to their being temperamentally different: it was due to the fact that Paul was being obedient to God's revealed will and Peter, at that point, was not. Nor did Paul's challenge mean that he was out for a fight. He respected Peter deeply, having already acknowledged him to be one of the pillars of the Jerusalem Church (2:9). But principle came before persons with Paul; and principle also came before peace. Any silent acquiescence in Peter's behaviour was, therefore, absolutely out of the question.

Notice how Paul went about dealing with Peter. For one thing, he approached him directly ('I opposed him to his face' — 2:11): he did not talk behind Peter's back; nor did he take the matter to the local church without having discussed it with Peter first. Moreover, Paul did all this publicly, 'in front of them all' (2:14), that is, in the presence of the rest of the Jews, apparently, who were influenced by Peter's change of stance and 'joined him in his hypocrisy' (2:13). Peter had caused a scandal. He and the other Jewish believers had treated Gentile believers as second-class citizens. This was far too serious a matter to be treated quietly in a corner; if the rift were to be healed, it would have to be healed in the open, and Paul could see that.

Paul's specific charge

Paul was not content simply to register a protest; he was not simply concerned to ease his own conscience. Seeing clearly, as he did, that Peter's withdrawal from fellowship with the Gentile Christians could lead to permanent division in the church, and aiming, therefore, at a complete reversal of this action that had wronged the saints and dishonoured the gospel of Christ, Paul engaged in radical spiritual surgery: he got right down to the source of the trouble and isolated it so that Peter might see the error of his ways and repent. Paul's specific charge was twofold.

1. He charged Peter and all who joined him with

'hypocrisy': *'The other Jews joined him in his hypocrisy, so that by their hypocrisy even Barnabas was led astray' (2:13).* Vincent's comment is illuminating: 'Their act was hypocrisy because it was a concealment of their own liberal convictions, and an open profession of still adhering to the narrow Pharisaic view.'[1]

Peter did not really believe that circumcision was necessary for Christian fellowship: he knew that it was not necessary for salvation, and therefore it could not be necessary for fellowship. For if Peter had really believed in his heart of hearts that circumcision was a necessary prerequisite for real membership in the church of Christ, he would not have been a Christian. A Christian is a person who says,

> Nothing in my hand I bring,
> Simply to thy cross I cling.

A Christian does not bring his circumcision and put it down in the balances and try to claim: 'Here is my little bit of merit! I'm circumcised!' No. Nothing is necessary for salvation, or for fellowship, except Christ — Jesus Christ dying for us on the cross and then living in us by the Holy Spirit. Peter would never have claimed that, whereas only Christ is needed for salvation, both Christ and circumcision are needed for fellowship. He did not believe that, but he *acted as if* he did. Thus he was guilty of hypocrisy. And when we consciously behave in a manner that belies what we really believe, we are acting hypocritically.

Let us ask ourselves, do we ever act hypocritically like this? Do we, who so earnestly contend for the gospel as embodied in Christ and Christ alone, ever act as if we believed something else besides participation in Christ were necessary for Christian fellowship? Do we ever act as if we believed that unless a man is baptized in a certain way, we can't have real fellowship with him? Or as if we believed that unless a man has been confirmed by a bishop in a consecrated building, we can't have fellowship with him? Or — whisper it softly — do we ever behave as if we believed that unless a man speaks in tongues, we can't have fellowship with him — not *real* fellowship?

For if we do this, then we are in grave error, for this is

the old Galatian heresy dressed up! This heresy is found whenever we consider anything (a ritual, an experience, etc.) to be greater than Christ, or to supplement Christ, or to be an additional prerequisite for full Christian fellowship. This not only takes away from Christ and his gospel, deeply dishonouring both; it also taints us with the sin of hypocrisy, for although we profess to believe in salvation by faith in Christ alone, our behaviour belies our belief.

2. Paul enlarged upon his basic charge of hypocrisy by pointing out that Peter and the rest of the Jews were not 'acting in line with the truth of the gospel' (2:14). The Greek verb is *'orthopodeō'* — 'to step rightly': the idea is that once you embrace Christ and his gospel, a straight and narrow path immediately opens up at your feet. It is not the way of the world; it is the way of Jesus Christ who is 'the Way'. Either you walk straight in line with this path, or you turn your feet and veer off the path, going either to the left or the right. And Paul was charging Peter and the rest of the Jews with failing to walk in a straight line: by veering off to the right, they were moving off the course demanded by the gospel. No believer can do this and yet maintain real fellowship with God and his people: either he goes straight to the end of the road, or he goes off the road. And so Paul showed that Peter's hypocrisy entailed disobedience. This was a valid criticism: Peter had indeed lapsed into attitudes and behaviour that were absolutely unworthy of his Lord.

For us, this may make depressing reading. That Peter, so full of the grace and the gifts of the Holy Spirit as he was, should now, at this point in his ministry and his pilgrimage do *this kind of thing*, is, to say the least, a great let-down! Couldn't we have just overlooked this unfortunate incident in his life? Doesn't it actually call in question everything else we have learned about his spiritual maturity? The answer to both questions is *'No.'* To begin with, if we had ignored this incident, we would have falsified Scripture. Further, we would have missed out on two absolutely invaluable insights into the nature of true spiritual maturity.

First, the Galatians 2 incident shows us that spiritual maturity is not to be equated with moral infallibility. No person is wholly sinless or faultless. A man may be very mature spiritually, as Peter was, and yet still be capable of going off on a tangent that is hurtful and harmful and even potentially destructive to himself and to other people. But the episode yields a second, and positive, insight into spiritual maturity; out of the whole dismal episode one thing emerges which not only redeems Peter, but also gives us the key to what *is* the essential characteristic of the maturity which, as Christians, we all desire. This is humility: the capacity to be honest with oneself, with God, and with one's fellow men. And we see it in Peter's reaction to this valid criticism of his behaviour. Far from undermining all that we have learned about Peter's spiritual gifts and graces, this incident, in its ultimate outcome, actually enhances and completes and adds the qualifying colour to everything that has gone before.

The key to real spiritual maturity

The saving grace of immeasurable worth which emerges to redeem this otherwise shattering incident is the sheer honesty with which Peter faced Paul's criticism and responded to it. Imagine how humiliated Peter must have been to be challenged publicly by this more junior apostle. Remember Peter's natural temperament: how grievously tempted he must have been to leap to his own defence — to bark, and even to bite, in response to Paul. But he did not. Instead, he squarely and objectively faced up to Paul's criticism, and he realigned his paths according to God's Word. A man who can do that can be trusted and followed anywhere, at any time, under any circumstances. Such honesty is the mark of real maturity. For there is no one who never makes a mistake. Therefore, the most precious thing in the world is the humility that enables a man, when shown his mistake, to be honest enough to recognize it, to put it right and to go on in the light of truth and righteousness.

We all know how very difficult it is to be honest with ourselves, especially when a more clear-sighted Christian points out the error of our ways, and has to do so publicly for the glory of God. We all know how proud our human nature is; we know how it can urge us to close our ears and

minds and hearts to valid criticism. This can be just as true
of Christians as of those outside of Christ. There are men
and women in the church of Jesus Christ who show unending
zeal in serving their Lord, but they can never be shown
their faults. And if you try to do so, they will make mince-
meat of you! This is their fatal flaw: they consider themselves to be beyond criticism; they cannot be wrong. Such
blind arrogance is not only evil, it is also very dangerous.
Sooner or later it always leads to psychological or spiritual
illness.

But, thanks to the grace of God, Peter gained an
exemplary victory over this natural human tendency to reject
valid criticism. Even though he had risen so high as an apostle
of Jesus Christ and as leader of the church, he had not
become arrogant: he accepted Paul's criticism and set his
feet straight on the path of righteousness again.

The fault acknowledged

Although the Galatians 2 passage does not specifically say
so, subsequent history shows that Peter saw the hypocrisy
of his withdrawal from the Gentile Christians. It must have
been painful for him to admit that he was wrong, especially
in the light of his renown as leader. But it is clear that at the
Council of Jerusalem (Acts 15:6–35), if not before, Peter
reaffirmed Christ as the sole ground of both salvation and
fellowship. These were his words, probably referring to the
Gentile Pentecost at Cornelius' home in Caesarea (Acts 10):
'Brothers, you know that some time ago God made a choice
among you that the Gentiles might hear from my lips the
message of the gospel and believe. God, who knows the
heart, showed that he accepted them by giving the Holy
Spirit to them, just as he did to us. He made no distinction
between us and them, for he purified their hearts by faith.
Now then, why do you try to test God by putting on the
necks of the disciples a yoke that neither we nor our fathers
have been able to bear? No! We believe it is through the grace
of our Lord Jesus that we are saved, just as they are' (Acts
15:7–11).

Peter had the honesty to acknowledge (however tacitly)
that he had been wrong to withdraw from fellowship with
the Gentile believers. Without such unqualified honesty, no

one can grow in grace or in the knowledge of God; armed with such honesty, the very least can attain to the highest pinnacle of God's will for him. Are you honest with yourself and with God? Do you terribly resent having to face the truth about yourself, even when it *is* truth? If so, your spiritual life may be strangled at that point. Pray for Peter's kind of humility that will acknowledge whatever faults and sins God sees fit to expose to your view.

The folly forsaken

It is evident that Peter not only admitted that he had been wrong in his attitude to the Gentile Christians at Antioch; he also renounced the behaviour which had been so damaging to the fellowship there. His humility enabled him to grow in grace and in fellowship with all believers, whatever their background; and later, in his First Epistle, he laid heavy emphasis on both individual and corporate Christian growth. Christians were not only to *grow up* as individuals: 'Therefore, rid yourselves of all malice and all deceit, hypocrisy, envy, and slander of every kind. Like newborn babies, crave pure spiritual milk, so that by it you may grow up in your salvation' (1 Peter 2:1,2); they were also to *grow into* the fellowship of the church: 'You also, like living stones, are being built into a spiritual house to be a holy priesthood, offering spiritual sacrifices acceptable to God through Jesus Christ . . . you are a chosen people, a royal priesthood, a holy nation, a people belonging to God, that you may declare the praises of him who called you out of darkness into his wonderful light' (1 Peter 2:5,9).

Notice how Peter here viewed the whole believing community, of both Gentile and Jewish background, as the fulfilment in the Christian era of two of the most precious of Old Testament institutions — the temple and the Israel of God. Peter's history and his writings alike bear witness, then, that he retraced his way into the centre of God's good will after his lapse at Antioch.

The fellowship with Paul restored

Perhaps this is the most wonderful thing of all: we learn from the rest of the New Testament that, far from bearing a grudge against Paul for exposing his folly and causing

him public embarrassment, Peter spoke of him in the highest
and warmest terms. The language of 2 Peter 3:14—18
includes an affectionate reference to Paul; it also contains a
warning to its readers about the dangers of losing their
stability by being 'carried away by the error of lawless men'
(these being set over against Paul). One wonders whether
Peter had the Antioch episode in mind when he wrote this!
The context is the coming again of our Lord Jesus Christ:
'So then, dear friends, since you are looking forward to
this, make every effort to be found spotless, blameless and
at peace with him. Bear in mind that our Lord's patience
means salvation, just as *our dear brother Paul* also wrote
you with the wisdom that God gave him. He writes the
same way in all his letters, speaking in them of these matters.
His letters contain some things that are hard to understand,
which ignorant and unstable people distort, as they do the
other Scriptures, to their own destruction. Therefore, dear
friends, since you already know this, be on your guard so
that you may not be *carried away by the error of lawless
men* and fall from your secure position. But grow in the
grace and knowledge of our Lord and Saviour Jesus Christ'
(2 Peter 3:14—18).

Here Peter refers to Paul as someone whom he profoundly
respects, who is ahead of Peter in the understanding of
certain truths. This means that fellowship has in no way
been broken. The man whom Paul criticized and exposed
in public has had the grace to listen to what Paul was telling
him, to acknowledge the truth of it, to turn away from his
evil and to see how really indebted he is to the man who
dared to stand up and say, 'Peter, you're a great man, but
you're wrong!'

This all serves to show us that the man who is rocklike in
his convictions about Christ and the gospel must not be so
rocklike that he cannot change his mind when he is wrong.
We need to have rocklike assurance about the certainties
of divine revelation, just as Peter did that night in his prison
cell (Acts 12), but we dare have no rocklike assurance about
our own reliability, no matter how far along the road to
Christian maturity we may think we are. We are all fallible.
We need the humility constantly to remember that. And we
need the honesty of the humble man who can see when he

has done something wrong, can turn from it, can acknowledge it to be sinful if that is required, and can humbly return into fellowship even with those who have been the instruments of God's chastisement in his life.

It is this humble honesty that is the key to spiritual maturity, for without it we cannot be obedient to our Lord. And what is the purpose of our growth as Christians? What is the goal of our sanctification? Not infallibility: 'There is *only One* who is good' (Matthew 19:17). Peter knew our goal. He came to know it through all the vicissitudes of circumstance and temperament that marked his pilgrimage from Simon to Peter. And he wrote about it as part of his very first word to the readers of his First Epistle where, in the letter's salutation, he noted that they were, as we all are, 'chosen according to the foreknowledge of God the Father, by the sanctifying work of the Spirit, for obedience to Jesus Christ and sprinkling by his blood' (1 Peter 1:2).

The goal of our sanctification is 'obedience to Jesus Christ'. And it is only in and through this obedience that we can enter into the reality of God's covenant with us, through his Son: 'If anyone loves me, he will obey my teaching. My Father will love him, and we will come to him and make our home with him' (John 14:23).

May God, through his Spirit, make these great things real in our lives, as he did in Peter's, to the honour and the glory of his name. Amen.

Reference
1. M. R. Vincent, *Word Studies in the New Testament,* Vol. IV (Eerdmans, 1975), p. 102.

Other books from
EVANGELICAL PRESS

THE CLOUD AND THE SILVER LINING

Ezekiel, the Christian and the Power of God

Denis Lane

The world was a frightening place - turmoil in international affairs, particularly in the Middle East; armies of refugees; fear and violence a common experience in the streets; corruption within the establishment and a self-satisfied church that echoed the world's latest humanistic theories. This was the land of Judah at the time of Ezekiel, but is it not also a description of the present day?

Denis Lane shows that the message Ezekiel proclaimed is the message we need to hear today. God has not abdicated his throne. He is still the ruler of all creation. God broke into the threatening cloud that surrounded Ezekiel, bringing a renewed vision and a clear message of hope and power - a message that could not be more relevant to our own age.

A MAN AND HIS GOD

The Christian and the life of faith

Denis Lane

'If only I had more faith!' is a cry from the heart of many Christians. There are times of disillusionment, times when faith seems beyond our grasp, time when faith has not come up to our expectations.

Too often Christians impart to faith a magical quality that it was never meant to have. It is not a wand to wave over life in order that problems and difficulties may disappear.

True faith is a living link with God that affects every area of our life. Such faith is clearly exemplified in the life of Abraham. Here we see what the true relationship should be between 'A Man and his God'.

'I thoroughly enjoyed and profited from "A Man and his God" . . . This book cannot but be read with profit.'
Grace Magazine

'The message of the book is vital - it aims to clarify the average Christian's concept of faith and stimulate new confidence in the eternal God.'
Christian Herald